W9-CBJ-597

JAZZ

ON COMPACT DISC

A CRITICAL GUIDE TO THE BEST RECORDINGS

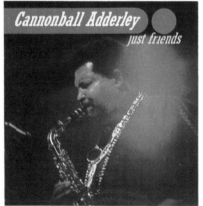

Cannonball Adderley
just friends

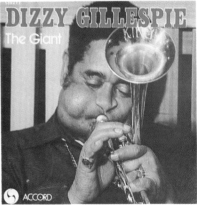

DIZZY GILLESPIE
The Giant

ACCORD

JAZZ
ON COMPACT DISC
A CRITICAL GUIDE TO THE BEST RECORDINGS

STEVE HARRIS

a Salamander book

Published by Salamander Books Limited
LONDON • NEW YORK

A SALAMANDER BOOK

Produced by Red Herring Publishing Ltd
for an on behalf of Salamander Books

Published by Salamander Books Ltd,
52 Bedford Row,
London WC1R 4LR,
United Kingdom

© Salamander Books Ltd 1987

ISBN 0-86101-332-8

Distributed in the UK by
Hodder & Stoughton Services,
P.O. Box 6,
Mill Road,
Dunton Green,
Sevenoaks,
Kent TN3 2XX.

All correspondence concerning the content of this volume should
be addressed to Salamander Books Ltd.

CREDITS

Editor:
Peter Herring

Designer:
Philip Gorton

Photography:
David Redfern Photography, London

Filmset:
Poole Typesetting Ltd, England

Colour and monochrome reproduction:
Rodney Howe Ltd, England

Printed in Italy:
Sagdos SpA, Milan

ACKNOWLEDGMENTS

Our thanks go to two major London
Compact Disc stockists for their considerable
and patient assistance in the preparation of
this book.
    Covent Garden Records of 84 Charing
Cross Road WC2 (an address as famous for
its literary associations as well as its musical
ones!) was one of the first retailers to go CD-
only and now offers a 6,000-title strong
demonstration stock. There is also a
comprehensive secondhand selection, and a
mail order service. Covent Garden also stock
a range of high-quality CD hardware.
    No less notable an address is No. 1
Piccadilly, home of **Tower Records** – 'the
biggest record store in the universe'. Tower
stocks an impressive range of CDs to suit all
musical tastes. Although relatively new to
Britain, Tower Records has, of course, been
long-established across the Atlantic, with
stores throughout the United States.

CONTENTS

THE AUTHOR

Steve Harris, who is editor of *Hi-Fi News & Record Review*, has been writing in the field of music and sound reproduction for around ten years. He was born in London, and read English at the University of Nottingham, after which he returned to London and worked as a journalist on a number of magazines while pursuing his musical interests as a record reviewer. He has been an avid collector of jazz records since his schooldays, and has followed the growth of the Compact Disc catalogue with an informed and critical ear.

HI-FI EQUIPMENT

Equipment used for evaluation in the preparation of this book included the following: Philips CD-150 and CD-360 Compact Disc Players; Technics SL-XP7 portable Compact Disc player; Audio Research, QED and Rotel amplifiers; Celestion and KEF loudspeakers; Sennheiser headphones.

BIBLIOGRAPHY

The author would like to acknowledge his indebtedness to the following, which have provided an invaluable reference:
Whitney Balliett. The Sound Of Surprise (Jazz Book Club)
Mike Leadbitter, Neil Slaven. Blues Records 1943-66 (Oak)
Ian Carr. Miles Davis (Quartet)
Brian Case, Stan Britt, Chrissie Murray. The Illustrated Encyclopedia of Jazz (Salamander)
Ray Charles, David Ritz. Brother Ray (Macdonald & Janes)
John Chilton. Who's Who of Jazz (Macmillan)
James Lincoln Collier. The Making of Jazz (Macmillan)
Stanley Dance. The World Of Duke Ellington (Macmillan)
Peter Gammond. Duke Ellington (Apollo)
Peter Gammond (ed). The Decca Book Of Jazz (Muller)
Dave Gelly. Lester Young (Apollo)
Dizzy Gillespie. To Be Or Not To Bop (WH Allen)
Joe Goldberg. Jazz Masters of the 50s (Da Capo Press)
Max Harrison, Charles Fox and Eric Thacker. The Essential Jazz Records Vol 1 (Mansell)
Derek Jewell. Duke: A Portrait Of Duke Ellington (Elm Tree Books)
Barry McRae. The Jazz Handbook (Longman)
Alun Morgan. Count Basie (Hippocrene/ Apollo Books)
Nat Shapiro, Nat Hentoff. Hear me Talkin' To Ya (Dover)
A B Spellman. Black Music: Four Lives (Schocken)
Brian Priestley. John Coltrane (Apollo)
Ross Russell. Bird Lives (Quartet)

INTRODUCING COMPACT DISC

Like popular music generally, jazz could not exist without recording; from the 1920s on, musicians could and did learn from records and the radio, and it was through these media that jazz became part of our culture. As with every previous technical advance, Compact Disc, the first domestic application of digital electronics in audio, will have its effect on the way the music is marketed, the way music is listened to and, ultimately, the way music is played.

Convenience of use really comes top of the list of Compact Disc benefits, particularly now that remote control is becoming the norm rather than a luxury. It is luxury indeed to be able to start the disc, find the tracks you want, whizz through those you do not and repeat tracks or short passages at will, without moving from the armchair, and it is this aspect of Compact Disc which makes it hard to go back to vinyl. CD also overcomes the disadvantages of 'completist' reissues which present several alternate takes of the same number, since tracks can be skipped or, if your player has 'Favourite Track Selection' even programmed out completely as desired; this allows you to have the best of both worlds, and you can have the alternate takes for reference or occasional comparison even if you don't

As this diagram shows, laser light is focused onto the disc's surface. The varying signals reflected back are converted into digital code by a photodiode, via a prism.

want to listen to them all the time.

Up to 75 minutes of music can be fitted on to a Compact Disc, and there are many collections and compilations which nearly reach this limit. It is possible to fit the entire contents of two LPs on to one CD, provided they are shortish ones, and this is quite often done. (Examples range from Louis Armstrong's *The Silver Collection* to some repackaged Grover Washington, Jr.) However, record companies usually prefer the CD package to be the same as the LP, which obviously keeps things simple and avoids extra royalty costs, even if it does sometimes result in apparently poor value for money. Many people will baulk at paying CD prices for just over 30 minutes of music and sometimes the 'original artwork' CD issues of 1950s albums seem like an

Theoretical illustrations of the digital audio encoding of the original musical waveform, and its subsequent decoding from CD into an exactly similar analogue signal for hi-fi reproduction.

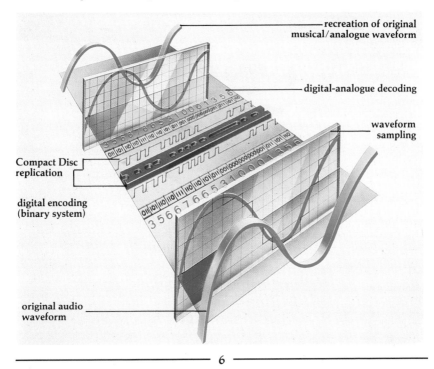

recreation of original musical/analogue waveform

digital-analogue decoding

waveform sampling

Compact Disc replication

digital encoding (binary system)

original audio waveform

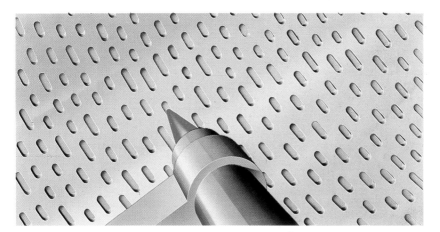

As the laser scans the alternating 'pits' and 'flats' of the disc surface, the beam will switch between being scattered and reflected back along its original path.

expensive luxury compared with the special-price two album sets offered on vinyl. A solution to this, where the material exists, is to put additional tunes or alternate takes on to the Compact Disc issue, while leaving the packaging otherwise the same as the LP. This can keep everybody happy, as playing time is extended without significant extra cost, and the CD purchaser gets something that was not available before.

At first sight, jazz might seem to have little to gain from the better sound quality promised by Compact Disc. Unlike rock, it is not music that depends on the sheer visceral impact of high volume levels, piercing treble attack and heavy bass; unlike classical music, it does not routinely demand a wide dynamic range, nor for the most part is its emotional impact so likely to be undermined

by the clicks and pops of surface noise during quiet passages. The fact that so much of the material we are interested in was recorded long ago might even lead on to the argument that jazz does not need good sound quality in order to communicate its message, and there is a grain of truth in this. To take an extreme example, there are available on LP some 1940s live recordings of Charlie Parker where the balance and overall sound is so poor that you can hardly hear the rhythm section; yet Parker's alto solo, which implies its own rhythmic universe, is still intelligible, coherent and worthwhile. But such arguments should not draw attention away from the fact that if properly treated, earlier recordings will sound far better than some might think possible; and jazz from every period does deserve the best possible sound quality, and it does benefit from the convenience and durability of the new system.

We have already come a long way since the earliest days of Compact Disc, when it was actually suggested or even assumed in some quarters that there would be no point in using this wonderful new medium for recordings made with old-fashioned analogue tape recorders, and that only master recordings from the latest digital

Cross-section through the lens photodiode/prism/laser system, which is the key to CD technology. The laser, at the base of the component, is a miniature diode type and of course totally safe.

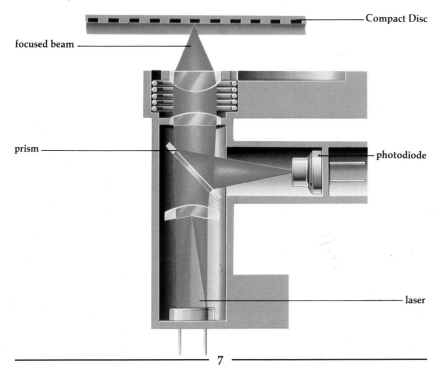

focused beam

Compact Disc

prism

photodiode

laser

studio equipment were worth using. If such attitudes had prevailed, this book would not have been written, since the only jazz available on Compact Disc would have been the few items described as 'DDD', recorded since about 1980 by a relatively small number of studios.

Fortunately, sanity prevailed, when record companies discovered what jazz listeners (not to mention some enlightened hi-fi enthusiasts) had known all along; that a very great number of the recordings made in the 1950s were superb examples of studio engineering, and that apart from a trivial amount of tape hiss they had no serious audible faults at all. When properly transferred for Compact Disc, these recordings simply sound better than ever.

Many vinyl LP reissues, particularly those put out during the 1970s, were done very badly, suffering not only from poor engineering in the transfer and cutting, but also from the effects of poor vinyl material, poor pressing and deterioration due to cheap packaging. Compared with these, Compact Disc can offer a striking sound improvement, and usually prove that there was nothing much wrong with the original master recordings. Bass frequencies are much more cleanly reproduced, allowing the true character of the bass drum and double bass to come through, and there may be greater clarity throughout the frequency range, reducing the 'veiled' or thick quality which so often mars vinyl reissues. On the other hand, the process of digital remastering for Compact Disc has sometimes failed to deliver intact those last subtleties of tonal character, along with a sense of space, ease and naturalness, which are to be had from the best vinyl records on good equipment.

It is safe to say that, although detailed comparisons between equivalent vinyl and CD issues are really becoming a waste of time, the absolute superiority of the digital transfer should not be automatically assumed.

Once pre-stereo material had started to appear on Compact Disc, it was not very long before pre-LP recordings began to appear in the digital medium, although those who are interested in jazz before the bebop era will still find very few titles on general distribution. Compact Disc really should

have the effect of forcibly raising the standard of 78 transfers, which on low-budget projects (for example, those which fall into the 'nostalgia' category rather than jazz) are often abysmal. It is very distressing to pick up a new LP reissue of some cherished material, only to find that the sound quality is worse than a previous reissue; it is still to be hoped that the inescapable clarity of Compact Disc will eventually prevent attempts to get away with thick, muddy sounding and crudely filtered transfers, though in truth there are some like this to be found.

Until recently, the major record companies, short of pressing capacity and aware from their market profiles that the kind of people who had rushed out and bought a CD were unlikely to be lovers of traditional jazz, had little time for the relatively specialised field of historic reissues, preferring to devote their resources to volume-selling material instead. Things may change for the better now, as the CD player population increases and it is no longer difficult to get short runs of discs pressed quickly and cheaply, but in the meantime, some significant historic releases have appeared from small companies. Most spectacular of all has been the series of 'Jazz Classics' released by the BBC following its tie-up with the Australian broadcaster, Robert Parker. Using his own equipment (including a Sony PCM-F1 digital recorder) to transfer and process the sound from private collectors' 78 rpm discs, Parker has been able to offer some of the greatest recordings of, for example, Louis Armstrong, Jelly Roll Morton and Bessie Smith. Helped by the fact that this material is out of copyright, he has assembled worthwhile collections and added informative notes. This is more than the major record companies, who have issued and reissued the material in the past, are doing.

From a purist point of view, it is perhaps unfortunate that Robert Parker's transfer and processing techniques do not aim simply at getting the best possible reproduction of what was originally recorded, in mono, in

Loading discs into the metalliser to receive their aluminium coating at Nimbus' plant.

the grooves of the 78. Instead, Parker's stated intention has been to create 'a clean stereo-impression' of how the artist would have sounded in live performance. To counteract the supposedly undesirable deadness of the studio acoustic, much reverberation is added, and to create the two 'stereo' channels, the mono signal is differently-equalised for 'left' and 'right'; listen to either of the two channels separately, and you will hear that the balance of bass, middle and treble frequencies is completely different. The effect of the two different-sounding channels is, at best, to fool the ear into thinking it is hearing something like a stereo recording, and it has to be said that there actually are points in Parker's recordings where instruments appear to be coming from different points.

Spread thus between the two speakers, the smooth, glossy sound achieved by Robert Parker is free of 78 surface noise and is also free of the boxy, thick quality generally associated with 78 discs, and has won him many thousands of devoted listeners in his Australian broadcast series, which has been repeated by the BBC; and the record and CD

The transparent, but 'pressed' CD is taken from injection moulding by a robot arm.

PRT's recording studio near London's Marble Arch has been the venue for many memorable jazz sessions, over the years.

issues have been very successful.

Taking the long term view, it would hardly be a satisfactory state of affairs if the fragile masterpieces of the 1920s were to end up being preserved only in this hyped-up form; adding 'effects' to old recordings is gilding the lily, and such additive processing applied to a tape made by playing a 78 is surely a waste of effort which could be better spent making sure that the best possible signal was coming off the disc as it was played.

Failure to do this is a failure to recognise that the intrinsic quality of a 78rpm recording chain could in fact be very good, and to carry out more than the minimum possible amount of processing afterwards is to trample ignorantly on the effects of the engineers who originally made the recordings.

There are few examples of relatively 'purist' transfers of pre-war material in this book, but one disc worth mentioning here is the DRG *Coleman Hawkins and Benny Carter* featuring Django Reinhardt (and included in his entry), a CD which for some reason does have a somewhat hard and

bright sound but shows just how much energy and attack, depth and detail was really being captured. Here, it must be said, the compilers were not working from inevitably worn 78 copies, but usually had the immeasurable advantage of being able to use the original metal parts, from which a brand-new vinyl 78 disc could be pressed. Needless to say, these are not always available.

After its final victory over the rival cylinder, which had struggled on into the 1920s, the 78rpm disc lasted until the advent of the long-playing microgroove record in the late 1940s. Made from hard-wearing vinyl material, the 33rpm LP has about 240 grooves per inch of radius compared with about 100 on a 78 disc, and gave an enormous increase in uninterrupted playing time, from the five minutes possible with a 12in 78 (only three on a 10in) to at least twenty minutes per side. By the early 1950s, studios were recording on magnetic tape, which unlike directly-recorded disc masters allowed additional instruments, voices or effects to be added afterwards.

Come the 1970s, the development of the transistor had brought much cheaper,

Currently top of the Marantz range of Compact Disc players is the CD94. Among other attributes, it employs the 16-bit, 4-times oversampling technique.

miniaturised electronics, and studios were equipped with multi-track recording which allowed almost any amount of re-recording, editing or mixing to get the final sound right. This kind of set-up did not do much for jazz groups, but often produced a sound that was tiring and artificial to listen to.

A closely-miked double bass, for example, would lose the resonances of the body which gave the sound character. Multi-tracking tended to detract from the impression of a group playing together, making the musicians sound as if they were playing in separate compartments, which in some cases is exactly what they were doing.

The introduction of digital tape recording could not make bad recording practices sound better, and probably the sheer quantity of microphones and electronics being used goes a long way to explaining the unsatisfactory nature of some digital

Recording has captured many of the immortal jazz performers for posterity – Billie Holiday is one.

recordings. There are exceptions to all this, though, as some gifted producers and engineers have learned how to use the digital equipment effectively. Dave Grusin's GRP recordings, it seems, have never aimed at the sound of a natural acoustic but instead produce a consistently impressive and polished, if clinical and artificial, sound-picture, utterly appropriate to the style of music GRP is associated with; the German company ECM continues to produce beautifully clean yet less hard-edged recordings that often make use of 'artificial' techniques such as multi-tracking, but create depth, space and proportion, stereo soundstages which are the landscape of some imaginary world rather than an attempted representation of an actual stage.

Ultimately, the merit of a disc's recorded sound quality can be almost as much a matter of taste as the music itself. Many people will prefer the big, widely, spread glamorous reverberant sound of the 'stereo spectacular' recordings so prevalent in the years when stereo was first being promoted; but it would be difficult to claim that this kind of sound is more 'natural' or 'accurate' than the opposite approach, even if subjectively preferred to the dry, often claustrophobically-close-miked quality of many 1970s recordings. The most appealing sounds of the 1950s seem to have come from Rudy van Gelder's studio, but even here the 'natural' quality is probably, like, the classic Decca classical recordings of the 1960s a case of the engineer's 'art that conceals art', rather than a cast-iron correctness of approach. Nonetheless, Compact Disc tends to highlight such differences.

When this project started, there were in fact precious few jazz Compact Discs. Major artists still went completely unrepresented and it would have been impossible to build a serious jazz library on CD. But this situation has now changed dramatically, although it has to be said that the existence of a disc in the catalogues does not guarantee its availability! As we finalised the selection of discs for this book, we could see that the choice was growing ever wider, until it can now be said that jazz is well represented in the new medium. This book is intended as a guide to what, for any jazz-inclined listener, really are the essential discs.

ABBREVIATIONS
Standard abbreviations have been used for instruments etc:
(cnt) cornet
(tp) trumpet
(flug) flugelhorn
(tb) trombone
(cl) clarinet
(b cl) bass clarinet
(fl) flute
(a fl) alto flute
(ss) soprano sax
(as) alto sax
(ts) tenor sax
(bars) baritone sax
(tu) tuba
(fr h) french horn
(p) piano
(el p) electric piano
(org) organ
(synth) synthesizer
(key) keyboards
(vib) vibraphone
(g) guitar
(vb) vibraphone
(bj) banjo
(b) bass
(el b) electric bass
(d) drums
(perc) percussion
(voc) vocal
(arr) arranger
(cond) conductor

NOTES ON THE REVIEWS
All the Compact Discs discussed in these pages have been evaluated for both technical and artistic merit, and in addition to the review comments, a basic assessment of each has been given by a 'star rating' system. Stars have been awarded for both performance and recording. Three stars indicate a disc of outstanding merit; two stars a disc that is still very good; and one star a disc that is generally acceptable. In many cases the number of stars awarded for the recording will not be same as for the performance: a three-star performance can clearly outweigh the disadvantage of a one-star recording. The final sound quality obtained from a disc is influenced by many factors (some of which are discussed in the introduction) and an attempt has been made to describe the peculiarities of sound quality in the reviews.

Inevitably, additions have been made to the CD catalogue since this book was compiled, and although we have tried to be as up-to-date as possible – often mentioning or recommending newly-released discs which simply arrived too late for inclusion as full reviews – many excellent performances previously unobtainable have now been transferred to CD. Among notable developments have been further Blue Note and Fantasy reissues and the 'Compact Jazz' series from (German) Polydor, drawing on Verve, Mercury, MPS and Polydor material to provide attractive single-artist collections of artists ranging from Erroll Garner to Sarah Vaughan. In general terms, the rather skeletal list of worthwhile jazz issues that was current a year or so ago has now filled out to much healthier proportions. It is safe to say, though, that the selection here will remain close to representing the core of the jazz repertoire on Compact Disc.

Abbreviations used for instruments are the standard ones and should not cause confusion. Full details of personnel and recording dates have been given wherever possible (in quite a few cases, we have given details which are omitted from the CD packaging); the exceptions to this are certain recordings taken from broadcasts or other 'obscure' sources, where the personnel remains unknown; and vocal recordings where a list of the members of several complete orchestras would have been just too unwieldy, and ultimately not very useful. Recordings can be assumed to have been made in the United States unless otherwise mentioned; the month and year of recording is given unless this is uncertain.

In common with some record labels, we have adopted the international standard coding to describe the mastering process employed for Compact Disc issues. **DDD** therefore indicates that the recording has been produced entirely digitally, with digital recording and digital mastering. **ADD** refers to an analogue recording which has been digitally remastered in its transfer to Compact Disc, while **AAD** refers to an analogue recording processed through analogue transfer equipment before the making of the Compact Disc master. However, it should be noted that in the case of most jazz reissues, the original master will be used to make the transfer without the intervention of additional mixing anyway. Remixing is the exception rather than the rule.

ONE HUNDRED BEST RECORDINGS

Listed here is a selection of 100 Compact Discs, chosen from the many reviewed in these pages. Most are those which have been given a three star rating ($\star \star \star$) for performance and good or at least adequate rating for performance too. This selection is a personal choice and of course cannot be said to include every important artist in the field, and not all the music will appeal to all ears, but taken in conjunction with the reviews this listing can offer a basic starting point in building a library.

Cannonball Adderley: In San Francisco/ Fantasy VDJ1530
Cannonball Adderley: Spontaneous Combustion/RCA ZD70816
Cannonball Adderley and Bill Evans: Know What I Mean? VDJ1518
Louis Armstrong: Great Original Performances/BBC CD 597

Louis Armstrong (And Ella Fitzgerald): Porgy And Bess/Verve 825 373
Count Basie: Basie Big Band/Pablo J33J 20048
Count Basie: The Atomic Mr Basie/Vogue VG561 600008
Count Basie: Kansas City Seven/MCA MCAD5656
George Benson: The Silver Collection/Verve 823 450
Sidney Bechet: Platinum For Sidney Bechet/ Vogue VG651 600026
Art Blakey And The Jazz Messengers: For Minors Only/Affinity CD CHARLY 23
Art Blakey: And The All-Star Messengers/ Baysound R32J 1004
Art Blakey And The Jazz Messengers: Album Of The Year/Spotlight CD CDSPG155
Clifford Brown (and Max Roach): In Concert/Vogue VG651 600032
Clifford Brown (and Max Roach): Study In Brown/EmArcy 814 646
Clifford Brown (and Max Roach): At Basin Street/EmArcy 814 648
Dave Brubeck: Time Out/CBS CD62068
Gary Burton: Chick Corea And Gary Burton In Concert/ECM 821 415
Gary Burton: Real Life Hits/ECM 825 235
Benny Carter: Further Definitions/MCA MCAD-5651
John Coltrane: Soultrane/Prestige VDJ1502
John Coltrane: And The Jazz Giants/Prestige FCD-60-014
John Coltrane: A Love Supreme/MCA MCAD5660
Chick Corea And Gary Burton: In Concert/ ECM 821 415
Chick Corea: Trio Music Live In Europe/ ECM 827 769
Miles Davis: Cookin' With The Miles Davies Quintet/Prestige VDJ1512
Miles Davis: Kind Of Blue/CBS CDCBS

62066
Miles Davis: Sketches Of Spain/CBS CD62327
Duke Ellington: Jazz Cocktail/ASV AJA 5024R
Duke Ellington (with Johnny Hodges): Side By Side/Verve 821 578
Duke Ellington: In The 60s/RCA PD89565
Bill Evans: Everybody Digs Bill Evans: Fantasy VDJ 1527
Bill Evans: Trio 64/Verve 815 057
Bill Evans: Quiet Now/Affinity CD CHARLY 25
Gil Evans (Kenny Burrell): Guitar Forms/ Verve 825 576
Ella Fitzgerald: The Cole Porter Songbook Vol 1/Verve 821 989
Ella Fitzgerald (and Louis Armstrong): Porgy And Bess/Verve 827 475
Ella Fitzgerald (and Count Basie): On The Sunny Side Of The Street/Verve 821 576
Ella Fitzgerald: The Songbooks/Verve 823 445
Stan Getz And Oscar Peterson: The Silver Collection/Verve 827 826
Stan Getz And Joao Gilberto: Getz/ Gilberto/Verve 810 048
Dizzy Gillespie: Dee Gee Days/RCA ZD70517
Dexter Gordon: Go!/Blue Note CDP 7 46094
Dexter Gordon: Our Man In Paris/Blue Note CDP 7 46394
Coleman Hawkins: Coleman Hawkins Encounters Ben Webster/Verve 823 120

Billie Holiday: Fine And Mellow 1939 And 1944/Commodore 8.24055
Billie Holiday: The Legend Of Bille Holiday/ MCA DBH TV1
Billie Holiday: The Billie Holiday Songbook/Verve 823 246
Abdullah Ibrahim (Dollar Brand): Water From An Ancient Well/Black Hawk Bellaphon BKH 50207
Milt Jackson: From Opus De Jazz To Jazz Skyline/RCA ZD70815
Milt Jackson: Milt Jackson Plus Count Basie Plus The Big Band Vol 2/Pablo J33J 20054
Keith Jarrett: The Koln Concert/ECM 810 067
Keith Jarrett: Standards Live/ECM 827 827

Quincy Jones: Birth Of A Band/EmArcy 822
469
Roland Kirk: We Free Kings/EmArcy 826
455
B B King: The Best Of B. B. King Vol 2/Ace
CDCH199
Wynton Marsalis: An American Hero/
Kingdom CD GATE 7018
Wynton Marsalis: Black Codes/CBS Sony
32DP 276
Wynton Marsalis: J Mood/Columbia CK
40308
Pat Metheny : As Falls Wichita, So Falls
Winchita Falls/ECM 821 416
Charles Mingus: The Black Saint And The
Sinner Lady/MCA MCAD-5649
Charles Mingus: Mingus Revisited/EmArcy
826 498
Modern Jazz Quartet:Echoes/Pablo 1311 241
Thelonious Monk: Thelonious Alone In San
Francisco/Riverside VDJ-1549
Thelonious Monk: Thelonious Monk With
John Coltrane/Riverside VDJ-1510

Thelonious Monk: Brilliant Corners/
Riverside VDJ-1526
Wes Montgomery: Full House/Riverside
VDJ-1508
Wes Montgomery: Round Midnight/Affinity
CD CHARLY 13
Jelly Roll Morton/Great Original
Performances/BBC CD 604
Gerry Mulligan: The Silver Collection
(Gerry Mulligan Meets The Saxophonists)/
Verve 827 436
Gerry Mulligan: Night LIghts/Mercury 818
271

Gerry Mulligan: Soft LIghts And Sweet
Music/Concord CCD-4300
Charlie Parker: Bird/The Savoy Recordings/
RCA ZD70737
Charlie Parker: Bird and Diz/Verve 831 133
Charlie Parker: Now's The Time/Verve 825
671
Joe Pass: Virtuoso/Pablo 3112-15
Art Pepper: Art Pepper Meets The Rhythm
Section/Contemporary VDJ-1556

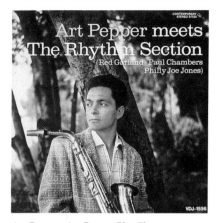

Art Pepper: Art Pepper Plus Eleven/
Contemporary VDJ-1578
Art Pepper (Milcho Leviev Quartet): Blues
For The Fisherman/Mole CD MOLE 1
PLUS
Oscar Peterson: A Jazz Portrait Of Frank
Sinatra/Verve 825 769
Oscar Peterson (with Milt Jackson): Very
Tall/Verve 827 821
Oscar Peterson: We Get Requests/Verve
810047
Oscar Peterson Big Six: At The Montreux
Jazz Festival 1975/Pablo J33J 20050
Bud Powell: The Scene Changes/Blue Note
CDP 7 46529
Django Reinhardt (original recordings) Pathé
EMI 746 5012
Buddy Rich: Lionel Hampton Presents
Buddy Rich/Kingdom CD GATE 7011
Max Roach: In The Light/Soul Note SN-
1053CD
Max Roach (featuring Anthony Braxton:
Birth And Rebirth/Black Saint BSR 0024
CD
Sonny Rollins: Sonny Rollins Plus Four/
Prestige VDJ-1524

Sonny Rollins: Saxophone Colossus/Prestige
VDJ-1501
Sonny Rollins: Way Out West/
Contemporary CA/802/98.600
Archie Shepp: On Green Dolphin Street/
Denon 38C38 7262
Jimmy Smith: The Cat/Verve 810 046
Sonny Stitt: Pow! Roulette ECD 59049
Sarah Vaughan: Sarah Vaughan/EmArcy
814 641
Sarah Vaughan/ The Rodgers And Hart
Songbook/EmArcy 824 864
Sarah Vaughan: Sarah Vaughan And Billy
Eckstine Sing The Irving Berlin Songbook/
EmArcy 824 864
Dinah Washington: Dinah Jams/EmArcy
814 639
Ben Webster: Ben Webster Meets Oscar
Peterson/Verve 829 167
Lester Young: The Savoy Recordings/RCA
ZD70819

CANNONBALL ADDERLEY
(b. Tampa, Florida, 15 September 1928; d. 8 August, 1975)

Julian 'Cannonball' Adderley was a fast, fluent and light-toned player whose conception was based firmly on that of Charlie Parker augmented with his own formidable harmonic understanding. The nickname, a corruption of 'cannibal', came from his healthy appetite. At high school he learned trumpet first, then studied at Tallahassee college and in 1948 became band director at Dillard High School, Fort Lauderdale, Florida. During a visit to New York in 1955, he sat in with Oscar Pettiford, and this led to his first record date (June 26, 1955), with brother Nat on trumpet, in a septet led by Kenny Clarke, for Savoy. The brothers formed their own group in January 1956, but met with little success. 'The best weeks were when the band didn't work,' said Cannonball later. 'Then at least we broke even.'

In October 1957, Cannonball joined Miles Davis' new group, and appeared on *Milestones* (1958) and *Kind of Blue* (1959), providing a melodic foil for the relentless John Coltrane. After nearly two years with Miles, he left to form his own group again, with brother Nat and pianist Bobby Timmons, whose hit tune *'This Here'* put the band firmly in the 'soul' groove and helped make it an instant success. Adderley, a far subtler musician than many of the 'soul' players, was untroubled by accusations that he had 'sold out'. He continued to produce happy, unpretentious music, before his premature death, of a stroke, in 1975; Cannonball Adderley had done much to broaden the jazz audience.

SPONTANEOUS COMBUSTION
Bohemia After Dark/Chasm/Willow Weep For Me/Hear Me Talkin' To Ya/With Apologies To Oscar/We'll Be Together Again/Spontaneous Combustion/Still Talkin' To Ya/A Little Taste/Caribbean Cutie
1–5 Donald Byrd (tp), Nat Adderley (cnt), Cannonball Adderley (as), Jerome Richardson (ts, fl), Horace Silver (p), Paul Chambers (b), Kenny Clarke (d), June 1955; 6 Nat Adderley (cnt), Hank Jones (p), Chambers (b), Clarke (d), July 1955; 7–10 Nat Adderley (cnt), Cannonball Adderley (as), Jones (p), Chambers (b), Clarke (d), July 1955.
Savoy ZD70816
AAD Running time: 69.46
Performance: ★ ★ ★   **Recording:** ★ ★

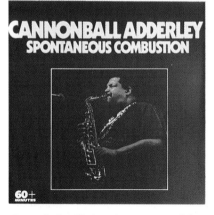

Cannonball Adderley's first ever record date was as a member of a septet assembled by Kenny Clarke, which produced the first five tracks here. The uptempo opener, in an ambiguous minor key, reveals the early 'soul' influence of Horace Silver, and the young Paul Chambers teams well with the peerless Clarke to provide a relaxed and fluid swing.

While *Willow Weep For Me* is a bluesy ballad vehicle for Cannonball, *Hear Me Talkin To Ya* is a brash soul blues, full of Silver's down-home crushed notes and gospel inflections. Launched from a boppish variation on *Georgia Brown*, *With Apologies To Oscar* is a high-speed workout with rather unfinished solos from Byrd and Nat Adderley, redeemed by a couple of 'chase' choruses in which the soloists take eight bars at a time. From a separate session comes *We'll Be Together Again*, a lyrical feature for Nat, recorded with lots of echo.

Cannonball was in more commanding form on the brothers' own July record date, which is self-evidently the work of a much more cohesive group, and here he shows the combination of technical mastery, inventiveness and relentless swing that eventually brought him well-deserved fame; it is this session which really deserves the stars. Van Gelder's mono recording adds a lot of reverberance to the horns and brings out the resonance of Chambers' bass, to give a pleasantly spacious and open quality.

JUST FRIENDS
Ease It/Just Friends/I Got Rhythm/Julie Ann/Awful Mean/There Is No Greater Love
1-3 Freddie Hubbard (tp), Julian Cannonball Adderley (as), Wynton Kelly (p), Paul Chambers (b), Jimmy Cobb (d); 4, 5 Hubbard (tp), Adderley (as), Kelly (p), Chambers (b), Philly Joe Jones (d); 6 as 4, but Hubbard out; February 1959.
Affinity CD CHARLY 58
AAD Running time: 39.38
Performance: ★ ★   **Recording:** ★ ★

These tracks, recorded under Paul Chambers' leadership on the Vee Jay label, have formerly been released under the album title *Ease It*. With an almost cavernous recorded acoustic, there is an immediately striking 'live' quality to the sound, which by modern standards is rather boomy and artificial, and on the first of the two sessions (with Cobb) makes the leader's bass rather recessed and woolly; but the overall sonic character of the recording clearly matches the drive and spontenaity of the performance. There is a happy sort of urgency in the air from the very first moments of *Ease It*, a be-bop blues launched in unison by Adderley and Hubbard (with mute). Hubbard, still only twenty years old but already a mature soloist, takes the first chorus on the fast *Just Friends*; while Adderley works out on the chords in a manner that momentarily resembles Art Pepper's *Straight Life*, then gets nearer the sound of Parker in the exhilarating *I Got Rhythm*. Hubbard picks up neatly from Adderley and keeps up the pressure. The pretty waltz *Julie Ann* is an effective feature for Chambers, with a quite Brown-like Hubbard solo and a typically lithe contribution from Adderley. One of the most gripping tracks is *Awful Mean*, the dark, Miles-like mid-tempo blues sparked by the presence of Philly Joe Jones; Chambers 'walks' with authority, supports Adderley's agile tempo doubling, then takes a bowed solo. Perhaps the star of the set is Kelly, who gets plenty of chances to stretch out in the idiom that suits him best, straight-ahead blowing; here none of the blowing goes on too long, and this disc leaves you wanting more.

THE CANNONBALL ADDERLEY QUINTET IN SAN FRANCISCO
This Here/Spontaneous Combustion/Hi-Fly/You Got It!/Bohemia After Dark
Nat Adderley (cnt), Julian 'Cannonball' Adderley (as), Bobby Timmons (p), Sam Jones (b), Louis Hayes (d), October 1959
Riverside VDJ-1530
AAD Running time: 48.24
Performance: ★ ★ ★   Recording: ★ ★

In the 1960s, the soul-jazz idiom pioneered by groups like Adderley's became the raw material of countless film and TV themes, but the original *This Here*, written by pianist Bobby Timmons in 3/4 time, still comes up fresh and infectiously joyful. Timmons also shines on *Spontaneous Combustion*, a tune dating back to the earlier, commercially unsuccessful group the Adderleys led in 1955-6, though here, as elsewhere, Nat sounds just too completely Miles-influenced.

In the fast, minor-key *Hi-Fly*, the band gets into a tremendous groove, and the excitement is maintained with the hard-bop classic *Bohemia After Dark*. Cannonball

blows effortless inventions over a superbly cooking rhythm section. (This was omitted from Milestone's double-album vinyl reissue *Coast To Coast*). Hayes' superb cymbal work, and his Blakeyesque breaks and bombs, are well captured on this exhilaratingly live recording, as is Jones' fat-toned bass, and really (as on the LP releases) the only major sonic blemish is the noticeable distortion on Timmons' piano, which seems to 'crunch' in loud passages, this presumably due to The Jazz Workshop's house PA system.

KNOW WHAT I MEAN
Waltz For Debbie/Goodbye/ Who Cares/ Venice/Toy/Elsa/Nancy
Julian 'Cannonball' Adderley (as), Bill Evans (p), Percy Heath (b), Connie Kay (d), January-March 1961
Riverside VDJ-1518
AAD Running time:
Performance: ★ ★   Recording: ★ ★ ★

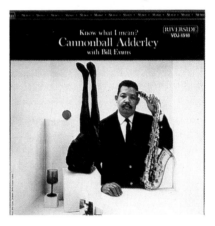

Though Evans too had worked with Miles, there could hardly be a greater contrast between the music of this group and the exciting recordings Adderley made with other sometime members of Davis rhythm sections; yet Heath and Kay really do swing, while at the same time bringing the polish and discretion so characteristic of their work with the MJQ. They seem to have fitted in perfectly with what Evans and Adderley set out to do here. Evans is in stunning form throughout, starting from his beautifully harmonised opening 3/4 theme in his own *Waltz For Debbie* (the group's rapport shows clearly in the switch to 4/4). Evans lends support of matchless sublety to an impasssioned Adderley on *Goodbye,* and in the final track, a most seductive ballad, contributes amazing, glistening chords behind a sweet-sounding, almost Hodges-like Adderley. *On Who Cares?*, which after a bright, neat and clean ensemble opening, builds up to a fast but not furious tempo, his light-fingered single line solo complements that of the dextrous alto player to perfection. Adderley's sheer lightfooted delicacy of phrasing comes through on *Elsa*, an intimate little waltz, and particularly on *Venice* (a John Lewis tune) where he plays the theme 'straight' with a lovely, pure tone. The collection (actually assembled from three recording dates) offers moments of real tenderness, flashes of unforced exuberance and enjoyable listening throughout. Despite a just-noticeable tape hiss, the recording quality is exemplary.

LOUIS ARMSTRONG
(b. New Orleans, 4 July 1900; d. New York City, 6 July 1971)

For many, Louis Armstrong epitomises the pleasures of jazz.

Still, for many people, the very symbol of jazz, Louis Armstrong was the first great jazz soloist and the inspiration for countless musicians on every instrument – not to mention vocalists.

Armstrong's childhood is still the subject of speculation (some sources suggest that he was really born in 1898). In 1913, after letting off a pistol in the street, he was sent to the Coloured Waifs' home, where he spent about eighteen months and played various instruments before settling on the cornet. In his later teens he worked at various labouring jobs; in 1918 he played his first gigs on the Streckfus company's riverboats with Fate Marable's band, and the next year worked with Marable on the boats sailing from St Louis and deputised for Joe 'King' Oliver, who had moved north to Chicago.

In 1922, Oliver sent for Armstrong to join his new Creole Jazz band, which began recording in April 1923; Armstrong played second cornet. In January 1924 he married Oliver's pianist, Lil Hardin; later

GREAT ORIGINAL PERFORMANCES
Wild Man Blues/Snake Rag/Muskrat Ramble/Melancholy Blues/Willie The Weeper/Ory's Creole Trombone/Struttin' With Some Barbecue/Hotter Than That/Symphonic Raps/West End Blues/Muggles/Save It, Pretty Mama/St James Infirmary/Knockin' A Jug/St Louis Blues/Lonesome Road.
1, 4, 5 Louis Armstrong (tp), John Thomas (tb), Johnny Dodds (cl), Lil Armstrong (p), Johnny St Cyr (bj), Peter Briggs (tu), Baby Dodds (d), May 1927; 2 King Oliver, Louis Armstrong (cnt), Honore Dutrey (tb), Johnny Dodds (cl), Lil Hardin (p), Bud Scott (bj), Baby Dodds (d), June 1923; 3 Louis Armstrong (tp), Ory (tb), Johnny Dodds (cl), Lil Armstrong (p), Johnny St Cyr (bj), December 1927; 6 as 3, September 1927; 7 as 3, December 1927; 8 as 3, add Lonnie Johnson (g), December 1927; 9 Louis Armstrong, Homer Hobson (tp), Fred Robinson (tb), Bert Curry, Crawford Wethington (as), Jimmy Strong (ts), Earl Hines (p), Mancy Cara (bj), Briggs (tu),

Zutty Singleton (d), July 1928; 10, 11 Louis Armstrong (tp, voc), Robinson (tb), Jimmy Strong (cl), Hines (p), Cara (bj), Singleton (d), December 1928; 12 Louis Armstrong (tp, voc), Robinson (tb), Don Redman (cl, as, arr), Hines (p), Dave Wilborn (bj), Singleton (d), December 1928; 13 as 10, add Redman (cl, arr), December 1928; 14 Louis Armstrong (tp), Jack Teagarden (tb), Happy Caldwell (ts), Joe Sullivan (p), Eddie Lang (g), Kaiser Marshall (d), March 1929; 15 Louis Armstrong (tp, voc), Otis Johnson, Henry 'Red' Allen (tp), J C Higginbottom (tb), Albert Nicholas (cl), Charlie Holmes (as), Teddy Hill (ts), Luis Russell (p), Will Johnson (g), Pops Foster (b), Paul Barbarin (d), December 1929; 16 Louis Armstrong, Zilner Randolph (tp), Preston Jackson (tb), Lester Boone, George James, Albert Washington (reeds), Charlie Alexander (p), Mike McKendrick (bj), John 'Joe' Lindsey (b), Tubby Hall (d), November 1931.
BBC Records BBC CD 597
ADD Running time: 50.42
Performance: ★ ★ ★   Recording: ★

that year he left Oliver to join the Fletcher Henderson orchestra in New York, returning after a year to join the band Lil had formed.

While in New York he had recorded with blues singers (including Bessie Smith) as well as with Henderson's band, but November 1925 saw his first recordings as a leader, and the classic series of Hot Five and Hot Seven records followed. With these, Armstrong discarded the established New Orleans ensemble style exemplified by Oliver's band, his musicians instead providing a framework for solos of unparalleled technical command and expressive emotional power. Legend has it that Armstrong invented the art of 'scat' singing when he had to improvise after dropping the lyric sheet while recording *Heebie Jeebies* (1926), and his vocal style and natural showmanship was soon as widely imitated as his playing. By 1928 he had switched permanently from cornet to the more brilliant-toned and penetrating trumpet.

In the years that followed Armstrong's success enabled him to front larger bands, including Luis Russell's, with the popular songs of the day as material. If the bands themselves were sometimes plodding compared with the earlier small groups, they did provide a setting for Armstrong's unique and memorable vocals on *After You've Gone, When You're Smiling, I'm Confessin' That I Love You* and many others. A tour of Europe in 1933-4 was followed by a lay-off due to lip trouble, but in October 1935, Louis was again fronting Russell's band, which he effectively led until the 1940s. Significant among many film appearances were 'Cabin In The Sky' (1942) and 'New Orleans' (1946), which coincided with a revival of interest in earlier jazz; in 1947, Armstrong launched his All-Stars, a smaller, ostensibly New Orleans style group, which soon became a formidable line-up including Barney Bigard, Earl Hines and Jack Teagarden.

Though there were many personnel changes, the All-Stars went from strength to strength during the 1950s, touring all over the world including the Eastern block countries of Europe as well as Africa. The All-Stars performance provides a memorable segment of the film 'Jazz On A Summer's Day', made at the 1958 Newport Festival. By the 1960s, Armstrong was a jazz institution, but in the last few years of his life he delighted a whole new audience with his hit vocal recordings of *Hello Dolly* and, later, *What A Wonderful World*. These may be musically insignificant compared with the triumphs of the 1920s, but are still imbued with the humour, indomitable spirit and sheer human warmth which lives on in all Armstrong's recorded work.

This collection of sixteen Armstrong titles covers what EMI's LP reissue series used to accurately describe as *His Greatest Years*, the period of the Hot Five and Hot Seven recordings, also looking forward to the era of Armstrong's use of bigger bands with the comedy-recitative number *Lonesome Road* from 1931.

Snake Rag, one of the great 1923 recordings of King Oliver's perfectly-balanced New Orleans band, is the earliest here; the disc would be in chronological order if *Wild Man Blues* had not been pulled out as the opener. This is the May Hot Seven version, not as intense a performance as the classic one Armstrong had recorded the previous month for another company under the nominal leadership of Johnny Dodds (as the Red Onion Jazz Babies, when they also did *Melancholy Blues*); here Armstrong fluffs during a break and Dodds, generally the most perfect foil for Armstrong, is not particularly inspired.

The remaining Hot Fives (*Struttin' With Some Barbecue, Hotter Than That, West*

End Blues) and Hot Seven (*Willie The Weeper*) are of course all classics, as is *St James Infirmary* from the similarly-constituted Savoy Ballroom Five. (This is one of the tracks on which compiler Robert Parker has deduced from the apparent key signature that the 78rpm issue's speed was in fact wrong, and so the music is slower here than on previous issues). It would have been nice to have had more of these performances, such as *Potato Head Blues, Tight Like That,* or even *Alligator Crawl* which, along with the Armstrong/Hines duet *Weatherbird,* had already been chosen for inclusion in the sampler *New Orleans* (BBC CD588).

On the other hand no-one can complain about what is here from the fascinatingly busy section work of *Symphonic Raps* to *Knocking A Jug* (Armstrong's first recording with white musicians) and the lavish 1929 treatment of *St Louis Blues,* in which Armstrong's contribution more than makes up for the distinctly lumbering nature of the orchestra.

In terms of sound quality, this reissue offers perhaps the most extreme examples of compiler Robert Parker's so-called 'Digital Stereo' processing technique; while the sound is 'sanitised' for modern ears, and is very impressively noise-free, the musical impact has suffered in the process. The effect of equalisation and excessive reverberation seems to have been to make Armstrong's trumpet sound like Eddie Calvert's, his vocals artificial-sounding and sometimes even less intelligible than they were before; the fake two channel processing is the cause of annoying phasiness and coloration on a good-quality system, and a quick flick of the balance control, to hear the two channels separately in turn, will reveal the trick that is being played on the ear here.

Robert Parker's collection gives us a lot of music here, but his sound processing embellishments only go to prove that you cannot get something for nothing and unfortunately disqualify this currently essential disc as a true archive.

THE SILVER COLLECTION

Top Hat, White Tie And Tails /Have You Met Miss Jones/I Only Have Eyes For You/ Stormy Weather/Home/East Of The Sun (And West Of The Moon)/You're Blasé/ Body And Soul/When Your Lover Has Gone/You're The Top/Nobody Knows The Trouble I've Seen/We'll Be Together Again/ I've Got The World On A String/Do Nothin' Till You Hear From Me/I Gotta Right To Sing The Blues.
Louis Armstrong (voc, tp), with orchestra arr and cond by Russ Garcia, August 1957.
Verve 823 445
AAD Running time: 63.33
Performance: ★ ★   Recording: ★ ★

Louis Armstrong's recordings for the Verve label may not all have been artistic triumphs, but they did include *Porgy And Bess* with Ella Fitzgerald *(qv)*, and they did present him against a variety of backgrounds quite different to the now rather worn-out formula provided by his own All Stars. The fifteen numbers here were originally issued as two separate LPs in 1958 and 1959.

Here, the programme consists of tuneful standards, the beat judiciously swung by a smooth-sounding rhythm section. The usual routine consists of once or twice through singing, then a trumpet chorus; exceptions are *East Of The Sun* and *Body And Soul,* which both start with a trumpet solo, and which, coincidentally perhaps, prove to be among the more affecting numbers here.

Armstrong, as expected, sounds relaxed throughout, but he is arguably at his best in a number like *Nobody Knows The Trouble I've Seen,* this being almost tempo-less with ethereal but subdued strings and the addition

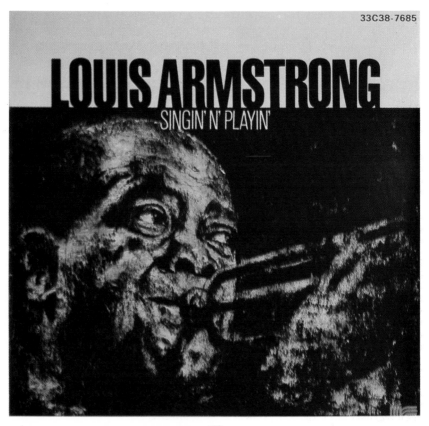

of tastefully down-home guitar chords, and with an opportunity for a straightforward trumpet solo. This set more or less manages to avoid the danger of the mushy, mid-tempo sing-a-long groove that a series of standards can easily fall into; there are one or two tunes that sound as if they were merely grist to Armstrong's mill, but spirited performances like I've Got The World On A String and I Gotta Right To Sing The Blues (with brass rather than strings) make up for this, while both the (stereo) recording and its transfer to CD are excellent.

THE SILVER COLLECTION: LOUIS ARMSTRONG MEETS OSCAR PETERSON

That Old Feeling/Let's Fall In Love/I'll Never Be The Same/Blues In The Night/How Long Has This Been Going On/I Was Doing All Right/What's New/Moon Song/Just One Of Those Things/There's No You/You Go To My Head/Sweet Lorraine/I Get A Kick Out Of You/Makin' Whoopee/Willow Weep For Me/Let's Do It (Let's Fall In Love).
1-12 Louis Armstrong (voc, tp), Oscar Peterson (p), Herb Ellis (g), Ray Brown (b), Louis Bellson (d), October 1957; 13-16, as 1-12, July 1957.
Verve 825 713
AAD Running time: 70.49
Performance: ★ ★   Recording: ★ ★ ★

This disc contains the dozen tracks of the original Louis Armstrong Meets Oscar Peterson release, while the last four tracks, adding twenty minutes or so to the running time, are Louis' solo singing tracks from the original Ella And Louis Again sessions (the duets are all to be found on the Ella And Louis Again CD, 825 374).

It would be hard to imagine a more completely competent, versatile and obliging accompanist than Peterson, yet it has to be said that the collaboration with Armstrong was not among the most successful of Peterson's many encounters with other solo stars. On the slowest ballads things tend to fall apart; in the latter stages of Blues In The Night, for example, Armstrong is positively wallowing, as if looking for support; he flounders on the definitely unbuskable verse of How Long Has This Been Going On, and does not really get to grips with What's New.

Better is There's No You, a much more solid and effective performance, and so is You Go To My Head, where Armstrong plays the melody first, straight-forwardly, before attacking the lyrics. Faster numbers, like It Was Just One Of Those Things seem

more promising, but here Louis just does not achieve the relaxed swing which, when present, makes his singing seem so natural; instead, a sense of strain gives the impression that he has been forced to sing in the wrong key, while Bellson's tick-tock beat lacks subtlety or swing. Here even Armstrong's matchless professionalism does not quite see him through. More successful than any of these is one of the oldest standards here, Sweet Lorraine, where Armstrong, as you would expect, finally seems completely at home.

The last four numbers, taken from the session with Ella, are rather different, with a vastly better feeling about the music, a nicer recorded balance despite (or because of) a return to mono, and a sense that the session has been better prepared. They include a well-rehearsed if rather careful-sounding I Get A Kick Out Of You; an attractive, blues-laden Willow Weep For Me, with a firm trumpet solo; a long, slow-and-steady Let's Do It. Though in terms of quantity, this issue gives almost the most Armstrong possible, in terms of quality it too often falls below the great star's usual standard.

SINGING' 'N' PLAYING

Hello Dolly/Mack The Knife/Muskrat Ramble/Blueberry Hill/That's My Desire/Ole Miss/When It's Sleepy Time Down South/A Kiss To Build a Dream On/St James Infirmary/Indiana
Louis Armstrong (tp, voc) with: 1, 2, Trummy Young (tb), Edmond Hall (cl), Billy Kyle (p), Dale Jones (b), Barette Deems (d); 3-10 Tyree Glenn (tb, voc), Joe Murray (cl), Marty Napoleon (p), Danny Barcelona (d) Probably mid 1960s, Europe.
Denon 33C38-7685
AAD Running time: 38.20
Performance: ★   Recording: ★ ★

As is so often the case with Denon's LRC recordings, dates and locations remain irritatingly obscure, but in any case these come from a period when Armstrong had long been spending vastly more time singing than playing. Even without the enormous popularity of his vocal style, he could not have been blamed for this; the trumpet is the most physically demanding of instruments, and as well as his recurring lip problems and bronchitis, Louis had by this time already suffered a serious heart attack. Yet singing his 1963 hit, Hello Dolly, he has the audience clapping along in no time. Mack the Knife and Blueberry Hill inevitably follow, along with the sentimental That's My Desire and Kiss To Build A Dream On.

The band members show faultless musicianship and are perfectly attuned to Louis' role as showman; once or twice Danny Barcelona sounds disquietingly like a circus drummer punctuating an acrobatic turn. In Muskrat Ramble and the appealing Indiana, Armstrong does take the lead in a rousing ensemble, but his sound is distinctly shaky.

Listening to St James Infirmary, we should reflect that Louis had first recorded that number nearly forty years earlier and, rather than criticising his later performances, should perhaps wonder at the fact that, after the magnificent achievements of his earlier years, he still felt the need or obligation to go on the road at all.

GATO BARBIERI
(b. Rosario, Argentina, 28 November 1934)

Though influenced by an uncle who played tenor sax, Leandro 'Gato' Barbieri started out on the clarinet-like *requinto;* his real interest in the saxophone began when he heard a Charlie Parker record at the age of 12. He rapidly became an avid collector of jazz records and his playing developed accordingly, but even as a teenager, his musical tendencies were in opposition to the nationalistic view of the regime, which required all musicians to include music of Argentinian origin in their repertoire.

In 1962, he left for Europe, ending up in Rome, where he met American musicians Jim Hall and Ted Curson; but it was his encounter with trumpeter Don Cherry in Paris which led to his violent-sounding contributions to 'free' jazz on Cherry's two Blue Note albums, *Complete Communion* and *Symphony For Improvisers.* Further recordings saw Barbieri collaborating with Steve Lacy and Dollar Brand, but a return to Argentina in 1970 also signalled a re-assertion of Latin influences; free jazz elements blended with Latin rhythms in *The Third World* and other albums. Barbieri composed the soundtrack of the 1972 film 'Last Tango In Paris', and subsequent recordings have tended towards a Latin/rock fusion, which most critics see as lacking both the intensity and the direction of his promising earlier work.

HAMBA KHALE
The Aloe And The Wild Rose/Hamba Khale/To Elsa/81st Street
Gato Barbieri (ts), Dollar Brand (p, cello), Milan, March 1968.
Affinity CD CHARLY 79
AAD Running time: 32.22
Performance: ★ ★   Recording: ★

This meeting on neutral ground represents an almost historic collaboration between two musicians who had assimilated jazz literally from opposite directions.

Brand opens *The Aloe And The Rose* with soft, diminished-like chords, against which Barbieri makes a sharply-dramatic and eerie-sounding entry. Brand switches to cello behind Barbieri's improvisation, but returns to the piano (with impressionist arpeggios) as Barbieri builds to a climax with fervent power, using the characteristic controlled screech of his overblown ultra-high register.

The brief *Hamba Khale* has the stately, hymn-like character familiar in many of Brand's compositions, and Barbieri plays the theme, unornamented, to bittersweet effect. Brand combines the influence of Thelonious Monk with repeated treble figures like those of the boogie pianists in the effective solo *To Elsa;* Barbieri returns to start *81st Street* alone, cadenza-style, his playing vibrant and

full of ideas, although these are not developed at length but instead are punctuated with flights into the false upper register, as Brand introduces his rounded, rhythmic piano below, adding a tambourine at the same time.

For some listeners, this will be a demonstration of Barbieri's expressive power; others will find that his extraordinary sounds set their teeth on edge. For those not in the latter category, this will prove a short but satisfying disc, recorded simply and well.

APASIONADO
Latin Lovers/Que Pasa/Last Tango In Paris/Terra Me Sienta/Angel/Tiempo Buono/Habanera
Gato Barbieri (ts), Bill Washer, Joe Caro (g), Eddie Martinez (key), Frank Ferrucci (synth), Gary King (b), Chris Parker (d), Minu Cinelu (perc), Pino Daniele (voc 4, g 6), January 1983.
Polydor 815 585
AAD Running time: 41.14
Performance: ★   Recording: ★ ★

With a lazy, easy-listening feel, this album perhaps typifies the diluted blandness of Barbieri's tango/rock/disco blend. But *Latin Lovers* is an attractive enough tune, and features a solid chorus/echo-effect guitar solo from Washer. *Que Pasa* has funkier overtones, busy with electronic keyboards and Weather Report-like tinkles from the percussionist, but Barbieri's theme is undistinguished, as he breathes what seems like a fragment of *I Only Have Eyes For You,* and later holds long notes over a pedal point only enlivened by a fast chuffing beat.

Daniele's vocal on *Terra Me Siente,* first scatting with Barbieri's line and then displaying the influence of Stevie Wonder, makes this an appealing track, and his semi-flamenco guitar solo on *Tiempo Buono* is also attractive. The theme from *Last Tango In Paris,* written more than ten years earlier, remains the best-structured item on the album, which does suggest a certain lack of progress.

COUNT BASIE
(b. Red Bank, New Jersey, 21 August 1904; d. Hollywood, Florida, 26 April 1984)

In the 1930s, the media crowned Benny Goodman as 'King of Swing'. But if anyone really deserved the title, it was William 'Count' Basie. In the succeeding decades he continued to produce vital and inspiring music, and few artists have reached out to delight such a wide audience, while never losing the heartfelt respect of the jazz world.

The young Basie learned piano from 'Fats' Waller in New York. While touring with a vaudeville show in 1927 he was stranded in Kansas City, and there joined Walter Page's Blue Devils, which included vocalist Jimmy Rushing, trumpeter Oran 'Hot Lips' Page and Eddie Durham as trombonist, guitarist and arranger. They were later to become the nucleus of Basie's own band. All soon moved to the more successful Bennie Moten band, although that foundered soon after Moten's death in 1935.

With altoist Buster Smith and other Moten men, Basie formed the nine-piece Barons of Rhythm (it was around this time that he adopted the nickname 'Count'). Basie's broadcasts from the Reno Club reached the ears of John Hammond, who brought the band to New York in 1936. The band cut its first Decca sides in January 1937, its star soloists now including trumpeter Buck Clayton and Texas-born tenor player Herschel Evans as well as Lester Young. On 7 July 1937, Decca recorded Basie's classic and widely-imitated *One O'Clock Jump*, with its string of near-perfect solos over building riffs.

The departure of Young in 1940 signalled the end of a first great epoch in Basie's recording career. Through the war years Basie recorded for Columbia, but postwar conditions killed off most of the big swing bands. Basie was forced to disband in February 1950, and for a while led an octet which included Clark Terry and Buddy de Franco. But he soon re-formed and by mid-1952 the new band was recording for Norman Granz's Clef label. Singer Joe Williams was sneered at by some critics, but in 1955 he gave Basie a huge hit with *Every Day I Have The Blues* and made the band a bigger draw than ever before. The instrumental *April In Paris*, with Basie's laconic 'one more time' tag ending, became an institution.

Moving to Roulette Records (now reissued on Vogue) in 1957, and back on Verve from 1962, Basie made several successful albums with arrangements from Neal Hefti and Quincy Jones. In the 1960s he recorded with Frank Sinatra, Tony Bennett, Sammy Davis and Ella Fitzgerald, while efforts like *Basie's Beatle Bag* exploited current popular material. Unusually adventurous was *Afrique* (1970, RCA), with evocative scores by Oliver Nelson. From 1973 on, a string of small-group albums on Granz's Pablo label gave Basie more solo space than he had ever allowed himself with the band.

Basie suffered a heart attack in September 1976, and from 1980 had to use a motorised wheelchair to come on stage, but he continued to tour almost to the end. Few can have been so loved.

COUNT BASIE:BASIE BIG BAND
Front Burner/Freckle Face/Orange Sherbet/
Soft As Velvet/The Heat's On/Midnight
Freight/ Give'M Time/The Wind Machine/
Tall Cotton.
Pete Minger, Frank Szabo, Dave Stahl,
Bobby Mitchell, Sonny Cohn (tp), Al Grey,
Curtis Fuller, Bill Hughes, Mel Wanzo (tb),
Danny Turner (as, fl), Bobby Plater (as),
Eric Dixon (ts, fl), Jimmy Forrest (ts),
Charlie Fowlkes (bars), Count Basie (p),
Freddie Green (g), John Duke (b), Butch
Miles (d), August 1975.
Pablo J33J 20048
AAD Running time: 43.54
Performance: ★ ★ ★
Recording: ★ ★ ★

Lifted by the crisp drumming of Butch Miles, and thriving on the compositions and arrangements of Sam Nestico, the Basie band of the mid-1970s reached a new peak of smooth precision and apparently effortless swing. This album is of course far better recorded than Denon's live *Basie In Europe*, which comes from the same period. Opening the set is a typically understated Basie blues, introduced by bassist John Duke, simple but effective piano building through solos from flute (Dixon) and tenor (Forrest) to a full band climax.

Set against a countermelody from trombones and saxes. Nestico's favourite trumpet-and-flute sound is heard on *Freckle Face*. Ex-Lionel Hampton altoist Bobby Plater, sounding more gentle than Hodges, floats beautifully on his feature *Soft as Velvet*. At full speed, the band is outstanding in *The Heat's On*, Miles driving superbly, and Jimmy Forrest blowing a stirring, shouting solo; the final chorus includes Basie's trademark 'plink . . . plink, plink' ending, all you really hear of him in this track. On numbers like the very slow, blues-saturated *Midnight Freight*, a feature for a plunger-wielding Al Grey, the band gets into a deep and satisfying groove. This disc, well recorded and full of variety, is simply excellent value.

BASIE IN EUROPE
Hittin' Twelve/Freckle Face/Things Ain't What They Used To Be/Whirly-Bird/The More I See You/Orange Sherbet/Way Out Basie/Basie!/Jumpin' At The Woodside
Sonny Cohn, Bobby Mitchell, Lyn Biviano, Waymon Reed (tp), Mel Wanzo, Bill Hughes, Al Grey, Dennis Wilson (tb), Bobby Plater, Danny Turner (as), Jimmy Forrest, Eric Dixon (ts), Charles Fowlkes (bars) Count Basie (p), Freddie Green (g), John Duke (b), Butch Miles (d). Munich and South of France, early 1970s.
Denon 33C38-7481
AAD Running time: 39.05
Performance: ★ ★   Recording: ★

During the 1970s, Basie made a long series of small-group recordings for Norman Granz's Pablo label, but continued to tour with his big band, captured on this disc during European travels. The material cannot be dated precisely and even the personnel is only presumptive. Nobody, apparently, even remembered then what it was that Clark Terry sat in on *Basie!* (a fast and furious descendant of *Lester Leaps In*) but his dextrously slippery, wryly humorous solo is

instantly recognisable. A rather brash run through of *Whirly-Bird* represents Neal Hefti's contribution to the Basie book, while Sam Nestico's *Orange Sherbet* recalls the earlier hit *Shiny Stockings*.

The recorded balance is often poor: Duke's bass frequently thudding and even becoming distorted, Miles' drums sometimes far too loud, soloists going off mic and sections sounding thin. But these failings hardly diminish the live impact of the band heard playing for a real audience, and the tremendous warmth and excitement of the Basie sound.

COUNT BASIE AND THE KANSAS CITY SEVEN
Oh, Lady Be Good/Secrets/I Want A Little Girl/Shoe Shine Boy/Count's Place/Senator Whitehead/Tally-Ho, Mr Basie/What'ch Talkin'?
1, 3-5, 7 Thad Jones (tp), Frank Foster (ts), Eric Dixon (ts, fl, cl), Count Basie (p, org), Freddie Green (g), Ed Jones (b), Sonny Payne (d); 2, 6, 8 Frank Wess (fl) replaces Foster, March 1962
MCA/Impulse MCAD-5656 JVC-457
AAD Running time: 36.26
Performance: ★ ★   Recording: ★ ★ ★

Basie's famous pre-war small-group recordings provided the title and some of the material for these 1962 sessions; the sympathetic producer was Bob Thiele, who, as a young and enthusiastic independent record producer, had himself recorded some memorable small-group sessions of Lester Young and others in the 1940's.

But despite the familiarity of the themes, it is probably just as well to forget about the 'original' versions. From the opening bars of *Lady Be Good*, it is obvious that Kansas City was a long time ago. But, stating the theme over a beautifully flowing rhythm section, Basie's piano still has magic, and it is nice to hear him over an unhurried 64 bars.

Dixon eases (Don Byas-like) into a strong, warm-sounding tenor solo, followed by a lithe and agile Thad Jones and a mellifluous Foster on tenor. Jones provides the 'cry-baby' muted sound on the slow, evocative *I Want A Little Girl*, which as the liner notes point out, sounds like a thoroughly-rehearsed performance though it was in fact quickly routined in the studio; while Dixon provides a clarinet solo of Ellingtonian richness, Basie plays organ, producing a beautiful sound although, to British ears, he veers at one point towards a seaside quality. The uptempo *Shoe Shine Boy*, though launched by a jaunty Basie piano introduction, bears even less resemblance to its pre-war antecedent, but this particular cut turns out to be a fine performance anyway.

Of the remaining titles, all of which were actually 'head' originals put together for the session, *Secrets* and *Senator Whitehead* are bright and witty tunes by Frank Wess, with himself and Dixon on flutes; *Count's Place* and *Tally-Ho* are a mid-tempo 'head' arrangements building riffs on the blues and *I Got Rhythm* respectively, while *What'Cha Talkin'* is a cunningly altered blues by Thad Jones.

Recording quality is excellent (as it turns out to be on most Impulse reissues), with an open clarity and freshness to all the instruments, flutes well captured, a tactile quality to drums and a limpid intimacy to the piano sound.

Ignoring the historical associations, and remembering instead that this was 1962, it is a very worthwhile disc.

THE ATOMIC MR BASIE
The Kid From Red Bank/Duet/After Supper/Flight of The Foo Birds/Double-O/Teddy The Toad/Whirly Bird/Midnite Blue/Splanky/Fantail/Li'l Darlin'
Wendell Culley, Snooky Young, Joe Newman (tp), Henry Coker, Al Grey, Benny Powell (tb), Marshall Royal (as), Frank Wess (as, ts), Eddie 'Lockjaw' Davis, Frank Foster (ts), Charlie Fowlkes (b), Count Basie (p), Freddie Green (g), Eddie Jones (b), Sonny Payne (d), October 1957.
Vogue VG651 600008
AAD Running time: 39.22
Performance: ★ ★ ★
Recording: ★ ★

Vogue have reproduced the mushroom-cloud front cover of the original album, but have not used the back, on which the title appeared; so the CD is simply called *Count Basie*. With 'Lockjaw' Davis as the main soloist, this famous set of Neal Hefti arrangements shows off the precision and drive of the whole band, with writing that still sounds fresh, unhackneyed and thoroughly musical. With incredibly disciplined section playing, combined with the superb bounce of the rhythm section and the apparent spontaneity of Basie's piano, the band achieves a sense of balance, of controlled power. This disc shows that a big band could be exciting without resorting to the kind of stylistic excess that so often makes such music sound dated; in other words, it shows maturity. Sound quality is

'big' and spacious, with great attention to detail, a good example of an early-stereo attempt to capture the life and excitement of a big band, which it does effectively and enjoyably although the instruments seem to hang in a haze of reverberation rather than in a real acoustic.

Untypical, but setting the pace, is Basie's own opening feature, *The Kid From Red Bank*. His solo passages of Waller-style stride piano (with a touch of boogie) alternate with punchy riffs, somewhat in imitation of the 'head' arrangements of the band's early days, but here a little contrived by comparison. Basie's blues playing is heard to great advantage against a cunningly structured and superbly voiced Hefti background in *Midnite Blue*. Unimaginatively titled but beautifully played is *Duet*, featuring the muted trumpets of Jones and Newman. In *Flight Of The Foo Birds* Hefti provides a bright, modern setting with just a glance back at the traditional Basie textures; Wess soars in his alto solo, while Davis is at his most metallic and honking, as he is in *Double O*, but the gentler sound of Frank Foster illuminates the classic *Splanky*. Though 'Lockjaw' predominates as a soloist, this is a disc of varied moods, from the great flagwaver *Whirly Bird* to the whimsical trombones and muted trumpets of *Teddy The Toad*; and the best is saved until last, in the shape of *Li'l Darlin'*, a truly classic performance which, for many people, still epitomises Hefti's contribution to the Basie story.

THE BEST OF BASIE
Jumping At The Woodside/Blue And Sentimental/Red Bank Boogie/Shorty George/ Rock-a-bye Basie/Every Tub/Swinging The Blues/Sent For You Yesterday/Boogie Woogie/Jive At Five/Texas Shuffle/Tickle Toe/Doggin' Around/Dickie's Dream/Topsy/Lester Leaps In/Out The Window/Broadway
1-7, 11-17 Sonny Cohn, Snooky Young, Thad Jones, Joe Newman (tp), Al Grey, Henry Coker, Benny Powell (tb), Marshall Royal (as, cl), Frank Wess (as, ts, fl), Frank Foster, Billy Mitchell (ts), Charlie Fowlkes (bars), Count Basie (p), Freddie Green (g), Ed Jones (b), Sonny Payne (d), Joe Williams (voc); 8,9,18 Gus Johnson (d) replaces Payne; 10 Jimmy Nottingham (tp), Seldon Powell (ts), Payne (d), replace Thad Jones, Foster, Johnson, June-July 1960.
Roulette VG651 600040
AAD Running time: 59.02
Performance: ★ ★   **Recording:** ★ ★

Like Ellington's, Basie's recordings of the 1950's and 1960's often resorted to more or less systematically recreating to the hits of earlier decades. Ellington could still field musicians who had been with him in the late 1920's, whereas Basie's great soloists of the 1930's were all gone; though Basie's righthand (or should it be lefthand) man, Freddie Green, remained in the rhythm section. This continuity is well exploited in *The Best Of Basie*, which consists entirely of re-recordings of earlier material. Since the talent and musicianship of this band was second-to-none, the results are good at least where the impact depends on the band as a whole (*Jive At Five*, *Texas Shuffle*); less successful are numbers like *Every Tub* or

Doggin' Around, hurried versions of the original arrangements, where the absence of the old great soloists rapidly becomes the dominant factor. Frank Foster's approximations to the great Lester Young solos, competent as they are, can do little more than awaken or re-awaken the desire to hear the originals. Joe Williams, of course, doesn't attempt to sound like Jimmy. Rushing but is his usual self on *Sent For You Yesterday* and *Boogie Woogie*. Such is the dedication and sheer dynamism in the band that it seems unfair to make too much of the fact that these tracks do sound like what they are, re-makes, and that they ultimately lack the force and life of the originals; this is still an hour of very well-played and enjoyable music.

COUNT BASIE: KANSAS CITY 7
Jaylock/Exactly Like You/I'll Always Be In Love With You/If I Could Be With You One Hour Tonight/Honi Coles/Blues For Norman.
Freddie Hubbard (tp, flug), J. J. Johnson (tb), Eddie 'Lockjaw' Davis (ts), Count Basie (p), Joe Pass (g), John Heard (b), Jake Hanna (d), April 1980.
Pablo J33J 20007
AAD Running time: 44.40
Performance: ★ Recording: ★ ★ ★

Under the name Basie had first used with a select group of sidemen from the late 1930s band, and had revived in the 1960s, this is in many ways a typical Pablo session from the great leader's late years. Johnson and Davis had played many such dates (both were on the first *Basie Jam* album, a rather more spirited gathering from 1973), and the opening slow blues builds to quite effective climaxes in both trombone and tenor solos. Hubbard is a less familiar figure in this context, but as it turns out he contributes the most exciting moments on the album.

Basie is heard little on *Exactly Like You*, played at a fast tempo which at first makes Heard and Hanna sound as if they are merely ticking off the bars, rather than really swinging. But things get going with a crackling solo from Hubbard, and then, after some slick but not very memorable playing from Pass, the three hornmen play three progressively wilder choruses of fours before taking it out. *I'll Always Be* offers a particularly warm and melodic Hubbard solo on flugelhorn, but *One Hour* seems lacklustre. Basie solos, but in a spare and lag-along fashion that makes him sound almost as if he is merely accompanying an imaginary solo from somebody else.

In the end, neither the fireworks from Hubbard nor some superb playing from Johnson can quite save this from being a rather run-of-the-mill album, though a well recorded one.

COUNT BASIE AND HIS ORCHESTRA: 88 BASIE STREET
Bluesville/88 Basie Street/Contractor's Blues/The Blues Machine/Katy/Sunday At The Savoy.
1, 2, 4, 5 Bob Summers, Sonny Cohn, Frank Szabo (tp, flug), Dale Carley, Jim Crawford (tp), Booty Wood, Grover Mitchell, Dennis Wilson, Bill Hughes (tb), Eric Dixon, Eric Schneider (ts, fl), Danny Turner, Christopher Woods (as, fl), John Williams (bars), Count Basie (p), Cleveland Eaton (b), Dennis Mackrel (d), Sam Nestico (arr, cond), May 1983; 3, 6 Summers (tp), Woods (as), Kenny Hing (ts), Basie (p), Joe Pass (g), Eaton (b), Mackrel (d), May 1983.
Pablo 3112-42
AAD Running time: 41.24
Performance: ★ ★ Recording: ★ ★ ★

In addition to the big band tracks, Norman Granz used this date (actually two sessions) to produce two small-group cuts, with Joe Pass as a prominent guest star. On the mid-tempo *Contractor's Blues* he could be said to be too prominent, since after providing the introduction, Basie's piano almost disappears behind the guitar-augmented rhythm section. Pass and the hornmen all offer well-turned solos. The other small-group number, the final track in the programme, is another blues, this time at a lugubriously slow tempo which seems to inspire no-one, although Pass runs through the 'low-down' clichés with virtuosity; again, Basie stays in the background until near the end, when he wakes things up with a burst of barrelhouse tremolandi.

If the small group tracks are hardly special (at least by Basie's standards), the big band is excellent, playing with fire and panache, punch and precision; Sam Nestico deserves all credit for the elegant tunes and richly effective arrangements. Basie himself seems happier fronting his own superb organisation than he does when trying to create something out of nothing in the somewhat artificial atmosphere of a Norman Granz 'jam session'. The big band numbers here show that even in 1983, the Basie Orchestra was a force to be reckoned with. For anyone that appreciates Basie at all, these tracks at least will be sheer enjoyment.

SIDNEY BECHET
(b. New Orleans, Louisiana, 14 May 1897; d. Paris, France, 14 May 1959)

In the early 1920s Sidney Bechet was probably the most accomplished jazz soloist. He was forceful enough on clarinet, but his blistering soprano sax would dominate any group – except possibly one containing Louis Armstrong.

Bechet played with New Orleans bands in his teens, but left the city with a travelling show in 1914. He crossed the Atlantic in 1919 as the 'hot' soloist with Will Marion Cook's Southern Syncopated Orchestra, left the band in London, and visited Paris. Back in New York by the end of 1922, he played in touring shows and recorded with Louis Armstrong, but in late 1925 headed for Europe again with the celebrated Revue Negre, which featured singer Josephine Baker. He played in Russia during 1926, then worked in Germany and (with Noble Sissle) in France. Returning to New York in 1931, Bechet rejoined Sissle, then toured with Ellington, before forming the New Orleans Feetwarmers, with Tommy Ladnier on trumpet, in 1932.

In 1933, disillusioned, he left full-time music and opened a tailoring business, but was soon back with Sissle. In 1938, he took part in the 'New Orleans' record sessions supervised by French critic Hughes Panassié and intended as a reaction against 'swing'. Then, in 1939, Bechet had a hit with *Summertime* on the new Blue Note label. In 1940 came the Bechet-Spanier Big Four recordings (where the straight lead trumpet of Muggsy Spanier balances Bechet's clarinet perfectly) as well as more Victor sessions. The New Orleans revival of the mid 1940s saw Bechet recording with 'rediscovered' trumpeter Bunk Johnson, and helping his own young imitator, Bob Wilber.

Bechet settled permanently in France in 1951, but undertook concert tours to the USA (several times), Britain (1956) and South America (1957); he went on performing until silenced by cancer.

PLATINUM FOR SIDNEY BECHET
Petit Fleur/Promenade Aux Champs-
Elysees/Passport To Paradise/As-Tu Le
Cafard?/Marchand De Poissons/Si Tu Vois
Ma Mere/Ce Mossieu Qui Parle/Bechet
Creole Blues/Madame Becassine/Blues In
Paris/Moulin A Cafe/Sobbin' And Cryin'/
Les Oignons/Premier Bal/Egyptian Fantasy/
Temperamental/Buddy Bolden Story/Dans
les Rues D'Antibes
1, 5, 5, 18, Guy Longnon, Claude Rabanite
(tp), Bernard Zacharias (tb), Claude Luter
(cl), Sidney Bechet (ss), Christian Azzi (p),
Roland Bianchini (b), 'Moustache' Galepides
(d), Paris, January 1952; 2, 15 Pierre
Dervaux, Longnon (tp), Luter (cl), Bechet
(cl, ss), Azzi (p), Claude Philippe (tp, bj),
Bianchini (b), Galepides (d), Paris, May
1951; 3 Longnon (tp), Jean-Louis Durand
(tb), Andre Reweliotty (cl), Bechet (ss),
Eddie Bernard (p), Zozo d'Halluin (b),
Jacques David (d), Paris, June 1956; 4, 12
Dervaux, Gil Thibaut (tp), Benny Vasseur
(tb), Luter (cl), Bechet (ss), Yannick Singery
(p), Philippe (bj), Bianchini (b), Marcel
Blanche (d); 7, 8, 17, as 2 except Mowgli
Jospin (tb), replaces Longnon, Paris,
October 1949; 9, 11 as 1 except add Dervaux
(tp), Longnon, Rabanite out, Paris, October
1950; 13 Claude Gousset (tb, Bechet (ss),
Jean-Claude Pelletier (org), Alix Bret (b),
Kansas Fields (d), Paris, December 1958; 14
as 3 except Singery (p), Blanche (d), replace
Bernard, David, Paris, March 1957; 16 as 14
except Michel Pacout (d) replaces Blanche,
Paris, March 1954.
Vogue VG651 600026
AAD Running time: 58.03
Performance: ★ ★   Recording: ★

Most of these tracks, which span the last decade of Bechet's career, were recorded with Claude Luter's orchestra. Some date from 1949 and 1950, before he had moved to France permanently, and despite the boxy sound and noticeable surface noise, these are in some ways the most satisfying tracks. With the French rhythm section taking a purely accompanying role, the steady-paced *Blues In Paris* allows Bechet to stretch out over several powerfully-developed blues choruses without interruptions or distractions. *Buddy Bolden Story* opens with a discussion in French between Bechet and Luter (who askes Bechet if he had played with Bolden!), after which Bechet plays the tune elsewhere called *I Thought I Heard Buddy Bolden Say*; the rest of the Luter group has a rather clogging effect, a criticism which predictably applies to a number of other titles, although the ever-forceful Bechet overcomes such obstacles.

Also among the earlier material is *Madame Becassine*, with a good beat, some wonderful playing by Bechet and a tolerable comedy vocal by trombonist Zacharias and drummer 'Moustache'. Of the mid-1950s tracks, the blues *Sobbin' And Cryin'* from December 1954 is particularly outstanding, as are the Bechet solos which bring to life an otherwise plodding *As-Tu Le Cafard*. The 1952 live performance of Bechet's anthem *Petite Fleur* is a stirring one despite the incredibly nasal sound quality, and although not particularly helped by Pelletier's Milt Herth-era organ style, he is still in good form on *Les Oignons* from 1958. Not the best of Bechet, nor the best recorded, but good enough to rate as indispensible.

GEORGE BENSON
(b. Pittsburg, Pennsylvania, 22 March 1943)

Perhaps John Hammond was overstating the case when he said that, as a guitarist, George Benson had more to offer than Wes Montgomery, but Benson's star status as a popular entertainer should not prevent the appreciation of his jazz talent.

Benson won a local singing contest when he was five, and was even recorded as a boy singer in 1954. He was given his first guitar at seven by his stepfather, who also introduced him to Charlie Christian's records. In his teens, he played and sang in a rock and roll band, but (as he later said) hearing a jazz album by Nashville guitar wizard Hank Garland made him 'realise all the possibilities of the guitar'. Hearing Charlie Parker's records further inspired him to vocalise his guitar sound in horn-like solos, and he was now studying his instrument in earnest, seeking help from name guitarists as they passed through his home town.

His apprenticeship was really completed by a three-year stint with organist Brother Jack McDuff's quartet, which he joined in 1961; he formed his own group (using Lonnie Smith on organ) in 1965. He appeared on Miles Davis' *Miles In The Sky* and, also in 1968, worked on Jaki Byard's *With Strings* album, but a couple of years later began a commercially-successful series of orchestrally-backed recordings for producer Creed Taylor.

A move to Warner Bros made him a very big star in the late 1970s, when the album *Breezin'* sold over two million copies and its one vocal track, *The Masquerade*, became a single hit. Benson's 'scatting' in unison with guitar line quickly became a trademark. It is Benson's warm and attractive voice which has endeared him to a huge audience around the world, while his personality and good looks may soon bring him further success as an actor. But on the rare occasions when he is heard in a jazz context Benson invariably proves to a critical audience that he can still deliver the goods.

THE SILVER COLLECTION

Billie's Bounce/Low Down And Dirty/
Thunder Walk/Doobie, Doobie Blues/
What's New/I Remember Wes/Windmills of
Your Mind/Song For My Father/Carnival
Joys/Giblet Gravy/Walk On By/Sack o'
Woe/Groovin'
1-3, 5 George Benson (g), Herbie Hancock
(p), Ron Carter (b), Billy Cobham (d),
Johnny Pacheco (cga), February 1967; 4
Benson (g), unknown (p), Bob Cranshaw (b),
Jimmy Johnson (d), November 1968; 7 same
with orchestra added; 6 Arthur Clarke,
George Marge (ts, fl), Jack Jennings (vib),
Paul Griffin (p), Benson (g), Chuck Rainey
(el b), Leo Morris (d), strings arranged and
conducted by Horace Ott, November 1968.
8, 9 and Clark Terry (tp), Garnett Brown
(tb), November 1968; 10-12 Ernie Royal,
Snooky Young (tp), Jimmy Owens (tp, flug),
Alan Raph (b tb), Pepper Adams (bars),
Herbie Hancock (p), Benson, Eric Gale (g),
Bob Cranshaw (b), Billy Cobham (d), Eileen
Gilbert, Lois Winter, Albertine Robinson
(voc), arranged and conducted by Tom
McIntosh, February 1967; 13, 14 vocalists
out, February 1967.
Verve 823 450
AAD Running time: 62.41
Performance: ★ ★ ★ Recording: ★ ★ ★

Some of these Verve recordings echo the
guitar-plus-orchestra format which had
recently worked so well for Wes
Montgomery, though it has to be said that
neither *Walk On By* (complete with wordless
girl singers) or *Windmills* (overpowered by
orchestral effects) are not as successful as
some of Montgomery's in a similar vein.

On the other hand, some of the tracks are
small-group sides which reveal a
Montgomery influence (*Thunder Walk*, for
example, starts with a 'soul' backbeat but
then switches to the stop-time chords of
Montgomery's *Movin' Along*), but
demonstrate that the young Benson was
already a virtuoso soloist in his own right;
fast, inventive, controlled, yet drawing
powerfully on the blues. Hancock is
impressive throughout, while the unknown
pianist on the fourth track, which is an
effective down-home blues, provides a sort
of jazzily light-fingered impression of
Memphis Slim.

Less successful than these opening
numbers is the dated-sounding 'funky'
twelve-bar *Giblet Gravy*, which even
Benson's speed and inventiveness (he sounds
like a well-read Mel Brown here) cannot save
from banality. Like the ballads from

Benson's recordings with organist Brother
Jack McDuff a couple of years before,
What's New suffers from a slightly hurried
quality, but still contains some superb
playing.

From a later session comes the out-of-
tempo solo *I Remember Wes* and, though the
added strings take it to the verge of
schmaltz, this is a tender, beautiful and
moving tribute. And, like most of this set, it
brings out the best in George Benson,
another very great guitarist.

THE ELECTRIFYING GEORGE BENSON

Love For Sale/Li'l Darlin'/There Will Never
Be Another You/(I'm Afraid) The
Masquerade Is Over/All Blues/Oleo
George Benson (g), Mickey Tucker (p),
George Duvivier (b), Al Harewood (d), April
1973.
Affinity CD CHARLY 9
AAD Running time: 68.23
Performance: ★ ★ Recording: ★

An unusual and intriguing live recording,
this disc captures Benson with a straight jazz
quartet in a small New Jersey club. Tape hiss
is a minor drawback, while the relatively
poor quality of the piano (dull sounding,
slightly out of tune, with very suspect
dampers) and sometimes indifferent balance
are more serious ones. But the quality of the
performance largely overcomes such
problems, as indeed it would have done for
the audience hearing it live at the time.

Tucker kicks off *Love For Sale* with an
attention-getting Latin/funk beat, over
which Benson attempts to float the melody,
hampered by the sonics of the situation; but
the number gets into a solid groove once the
rhythm changes to an even 4/4. Tucker, who
turns out to be a fine all-rounder, draws on
the whole range of influences from Tatum to
Powell and follows Benson's solo
exuberantly; Benson returns with some of his
fastest arpeggios in double time, throws in
some bluesy licks, then lays back into some
sweet chords.

These constantly varied approaches are
typical of Benson's resourceful, energetic and
(of course) technically masterful playing on
this disc, which often finds him switching
effortlessly into octave runs, then to dazzling
single note passages, his solos clearly
structured . Happy and relaxed, the group
takes *Li'l Darlin'* at an appropriate slow and
easy tempo, demonstrating fine rapport;
Tucker's piano builds effectively, while
Duvivier solos interestingly. *There Will
Never Be Another You*, uptempo, starts
raggedly, but Benson audibly takes
command, using a full touch with reverb,
providing an excellent solo over what
becomes, in the excitement of the moment, a
too-loud piano.

After this Tucker provides excellent
accompaniment for *The Masquerade Is
Over*, here a successful vocal feature on
which the honey-voiced Benson steers firmly
past the piano's potentially upsetting
intonation problems. *All Blues* is strong and
effective, a very fast *Oleo* less so. Clearly a
one-off, this disc offers some very fine
playing by Benson in a setting which is
congenial, full of life and energy even though
it clearly lacks the clinical perfection of
studio recordings.

ART BLAKEY
(b. Pittsburgh, Pennsylvania, 11 October 1919)

Drummer Art Blakey has led his Jazz Messengers through thick and thin for more than thirty years. Even more remarkably, he still produces some of the most exciting music there is.

Like his father before him, Blakey went to work in the steel mills, but played piano in local clubs. He switched to drums when he found an exceptional young pianist for his band – Erroll Garner. He worked with Mary Lou Williams and Fletcher Henderson, before joining the newly-formed Billy Eckstine band in 1944. After the Eckstine band broke up, Blakey freelanced around New York, recording on the earliest Thelonious Monk sessions for Blue Note.

On these records Blakey's swishing cymbals and hi-hat are already unmistakeable, as is the way he relentlessly drives the band. At some point in the late 1940s, Blakey took a trip to Africa and spent several months in Nigeria and Ghana. 'For the first time,' he told Joe Goldberg 'I experienced something like brotherhood.' Around this time he acquired his Moslem name, Abdullah Ibn Buhaina.

In the next few years, Blakey played with the acknowledged greats

Although no longer the most technically accomplished of jazz drummers, Art Blakey – at the age of sixty-eight – remains one of the most exciting.

of modern jazz, including Parker, Navarro, Powell and Davis. By 1954 he was co-leading a quintet with pianist Horace Silver, and in 1955, a Blue Note recording of Silver's tune *The Preacher* launched the Jazz Messengers (with Hank Mobley, Kenny Dorham and Doug Watkins). It also effectively launched the 'soul' reaction, using a strong gospel element to make jazz simpler, more infectiously swinging and more accessible. When the attempt to run the group as a co-operative proved unsuccessful, Blakey re-formed and kept the Jazz Messengers name.

Over the next few years, a host of rising stars passed through the ranks, setting a pattern which Blakey maintains to this day. Blakey's sax players have included Benny Golson, Jackie McLean, Johnny Griffin and Wayne Shorter, while the line of distinguished trumpeters runs from Lee Morgan, Freddie Hubbard and Donald Byrd through to Wynton Marsalis and Terence Blanchard. The Messengers may have changed, but the message remains much the same, and it comes over as strongly as ever.

ART BLAKEY AND THE ALL STAR MESSENGERS
Moanin'/City Bound/Blues March/Night In Tunisia/I Remember Clifford/Briellsamba
Freddie Hubbard (tp, flug), Curtis Fuller (tb), Benny Golson (ts), Cedar Walton (p), Buster Williams (b), Art Blakey (d), April 1982.
Baysound R32J 1004
AAD Running time: 49.01
Performance: ★ ★ ★　Recording: ★ ★

This Japanese release documents a 1982 reunion of distinguished Messengers, and from the opening bars the group projects a kind of tension and excitement which further justifies the 'All Star' tag. All give excellent performances: pianist Cedar Walton is absolutely rock-solid on *Moanin'* and *Blues March*, trumpeter Hubbard is dazzling on *Night In Tunisia* and moving on *I Remember Clifford*, while Benny Golson is succinctly effective on his own tune *City Bound*. In fact, Golson's *Briellsamba* is a sweet Latin theme which sounds entirely untypical of the recent Blakey line-ups, but again features outstanding solo work by Hubbard, with sympathetic comping by Walton.

Recording quality is fine, the sound faultlessly clean, 'dynamic' and impressive, if by the same token rather overpowering and lacking in space compared with the records of earlier decades. But this is a minor criticism of the disc as a whole, since the music it has to offer is excellent.

BUSTER WILLIAMS　BENNY GOLSON　CEDAR WALTON　ART BLAKEY　CURTIS FULLER　FREDDIE HUBBARD

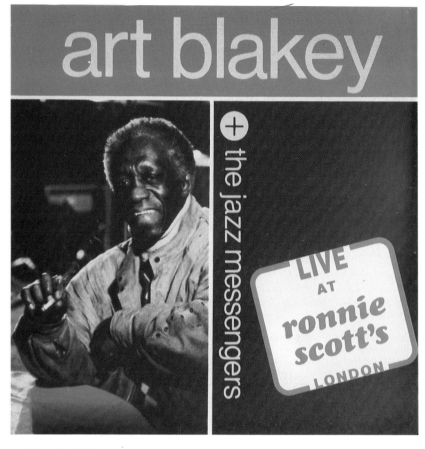

ALBUM OF THE YEAR
Oh, By The Way/Duck Soup/Cheryl/Ms
B.C./In Case You Missed It/Little Man/
Witch Hunt/Soulful Mr Timmons
1, 2 Terence Blanchard (tp), Donald
Harrison (as), Bill Pierce (ts), Johnny O'Neal
(p), Charles Fambrough (b), Art Blakey (d),
1982; 3–8 Wynton Marsalis (tp), Robert
Watson (as), Pierce (ts), James Williams (p),
Fambrough (b), Blakey (d), 1981.
Timeless CDSJP 155
ADD Running time: 55.02
Performance: ★ ★ ★   **Recording:** ★ ★

This disc features two vintage editions of
The Jazz Messengers, showcasing the young
Wynton Marsalis as well as his talented
successor in the Blakey ranks, Terence
Blanchard. The 1981 session kicks off at
speed with the bop blues line *Cheryl*, and
Marsalis really shines here and on the very
fast *Ms B.C.*. The final cut is pianist
Williams' tribute to Bobby Timmons, with a
warm early-1960s feeling and a superb, big-
toned solo from Marsalis. All the sax players
produce exciting solos, with particularly
strong contributions from the fluent Pierce.

NIGHT IN TUNISIA
A Night In Tunisia/Moanin'/Blues March
Valery Ponomarev (tp), Robert Watson (as),
David Schnitter (ts), James Williams (p),
Dennis Irwin (b), Art Blakey (d), February
1979.
Philips 800 0064-2
DDD Running time: 34.28
Performance: ★   **Recording:** ★

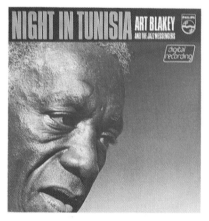

Recorded in Japanese Victor's Tokyo studio,
this was one of the first jazz Compact Discs
to appear, and for a long time seemed to be
the only one of Blakey. The three long tracks
capture the intensity that Blakey can create
as he drives his soloists, but hardly represent
the Messengers at their best. The drum
sound is impressively conveyed, but the

sound overall is hard and tiring to listen to. This disc, once a CD yardstick, is included here only as a reminder that both Blakey's band and digital recording technology have shown improvements since 1979.

LIVE AT RONNIE SCOTT'S

On The Ginza/I Want To Talk About You/ Two Of A Kind/Dr Jekyll
Terence Blanchard (tp), Donald Harrison (as), Jean Toussaint (ts), Mulgrew Miller (p), Lonnie Plaxico (b), Art Blakey (d), 1985.
Wadham/Hendring WHCD001
AAD Running time: 52.16
Performance: ★ ★ Recording: ★ ★

Four long tracks make up this memento of one of Blakey's visits to the famous London jazz club. Starting with Wayne Shorter's *On The Ginza*, the pace is fast and furious, a wild Donald Harrison making the meticulous Blanchard sound almost introspective. Harrison features strongly on the next tune, starting as a ballad and building in the Blakey manner, then on the third Toussaint gets a chance, his gruff, adenoidal sound a little reminiscent of the shouting Eddie Chamblee. Blanchard's solo here flings out some brilliant phrases without really building to a climax, but he makes up for this on the intense *Dr Jekyll*. Recording quality clearly reflects the venue, and while Murray's piano sounds a little jangly Plaxico's close-miked bass is often flatulent. For all that, this disc is a pretty accurate portrayal of a typical night with Blakey.

ART BLAKEY AND THE JAZZ MESSENGERS/MAX ROACH QUINTET: PERCUSSION DISCUSSION

Scotch Blues/Flight to Jordan/ Transfiguration/Exhibit A/Gershwin Medley; Rhapsody In Blue; Summertime; Someone To Watch Over Me; The Man I Love/Crackle Hut/Speculate/That Ole Devil Love/Audio Blues/C.M./Four-X
1–5 Bill Hardman (tp), Jackie McLean (as), Sam Dockery (p) Spanky De Brest (b), Art Blakey (d), spring 1957; 6–11 Kenny Dorham (tp), Hank Mobley (ts), Ramsey Lewis (p), George Morrow (b), Max Roach (d), January 1958.
Vogue 600091
AAD Running time: 66.34
Performance: ★ ★ Recording: ★

Misleadingly, this title embraces two unrelated sessions. Blakey's set reflects his live repertoire of the time, with much fine playing by McLean and the youthful

Hardman. The opener's bagpipes-imitation gimmick (recalling Benny Goodman's *Riffin' The Scotch*) and the strange, distant and watery sound quality of other tracks could be two good enough reasons why the tracks remained unissued until 1965, but Blakey's sardonic spoken intro to the Gershwin medley is as historic a curiosity as the medley itself.

The Roach set provides plenty of solo space for the brilliant Kenny Dorham, while a youthful Ramsey Lewis shows a mastery of the soul idiom, though remaining audibly cautious rather than over-stretching his technique. Roach himself, consistent and crisp as ever, suffers from the muffled and substandard recording quality.

FOR MINORS ONLY

For Minors Only/Right Down Front/Deo-X/ Sweet Sakeena/For Miles and Miles/Krafty/ Late Spring/Tippin
3 Bill Hardman (tp), Johnny Griffin (ts), Sam Dockery (p), Spanky de Brest (b), Art Blakey (d), October 1957; 1, 2, 4–7 Junior Mance (p) replaces Dockery, October 1957; 8, 9 Donald Byrd (tp), John Coltrane (ts), Walter Bishop (p), Spanky de Brest (b), Art Blakey (d) December 1957.
Affinity CD CHARLY 23
AAD Running time: 51.52
Performance: ★ ★ ★ Recording: ★ ★

There are helpings of basic soul jazz here, especially on the gospel changes of *Right Down Front*, but there are other recipes too. The title track is sweet and cool, with a complex, muted theme; *For Miles and Miles* resembles Davis' own subtle, pre-cool line, *Milestones*; *Deo X*, on which Griffin really 'cooks' and the young Hardman proves to be an adept though slightly mechanical Clifford Brown disciple, is strictly hard bop. The same goes for the loping *Sweet Sakeena*, with its fast-fingered solo from Bishop.

Though the October line-ups offered variety and excitement, the last two tracks here, from December 1957, reveal a transformation. Coltrane, who appeared on many 'blowing albums' around this time, seems to bring solidity, purpose and intensity to the music, his tenor sounding clean and joyful; Byrd, who was also recording prolifically at this period, shows Gillespie's influence as well as Brown's in his structured, controlled and dynamically shaded solos. And throughout, Bethlehem's clear if slightly pinched studio sound captures Blakey's drums well and helps make this a relaxed and warmly enjoyable disc.

CARLA BLEY
(b. Oakland, California, 11 May 1938)

An accomplished keyboard player, Carla Bley's lasting influence has nonetheless been as a composer, organiser and leader rather than as an instrumentalist.

Her reputation as a composer was enhanced when her 'dark opera without words', *A Genuine Tong Funeral* was lavishly recorded by Gary Burton (with Larry Coryell and Gato Barbieri, Steve Lacy and others). Her large-scale jazz opera *Escalator Over The Hill* took more than three years to complete, and was recorded by JCOA as a three-record set. In the early 1970's, Bley and Mike Mantler opened their own label and studio under the banner Watt Works, and recorded a number of other artists (Gato Barbieri, Paul Motian, Don Cherry, Jack Bruce). Her own writing projects have included '3/4', a work for piano and orchestra first performed by Keith Jarrett. Since the late 1970's, she has led her own ten-piece band, and worked with Charlie Haden's Liberation Music Orchestra. Today she is respected as a leader who has succeeded in controlling the production and marketing of her own music; this in itself is no mean achievement.

LIVE
Blunt Object/The Lord Is Listenin' To Ya,
Hallelujah/Time And Us/Still In The Room/
Real Life Hits/Song Sung Long
Michael Mantler (tp), Steve Slagle (as, ss),
Tony Dagradi (ts), Gary Valente (tb),
Vincent Chancey (fr, h), Earl McIntyre
(tuba, b, tb), Carla Bley (p 3, org,
glockenspiel), Arturo O'Farrill (p, org 3),
Steve Swallow (b), D Sharp (d), August
1981.
ECM WATT/12 815 730
AAD Running time: 41.41
Performance: ★ ★   Recording: ★ ★ ★

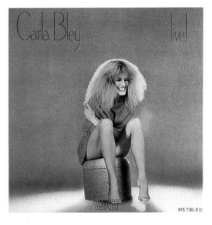

Here Carla Bley's 10-piece band is heard in a live recording, taken from three nights at The Great American Musical Hall, San Francisco. After an introduction using a mysterious diminished figure from piano and guitar, *Blunt Object* is a full-tilt opener; it struts menacingly on seventh chords, a funky backbeat and urgent horn riffs, changing tonality upwards to build tension in the manner of a Hitchcock soundtrack. Virile solos come from Slagle and McIntyre (on an almost growling bass trombone). *The Lord Is Listenin' To Ya, Hallelujah* is a complete change of pace, slow and 'sanctified', a virtuoso (but slightly sardonic) trombone feature for Valente, while suitably churchy organ from Bley develops into a nice solo section. Through the dreamy *Time And Us*, a more urgent Afro-funk *Still In The Room*, with an effective solo by Swallow, to the angular *Real Life Hits* and a

final, funky *Song Sung Long*, The band is always tight and punchy in ensemble. The soloists here are able to whip up more excitement than is to be had from some of Bley's gentler studio work. Sound quality is excellent, the horns captured cleanly and well, the rhythm section un-muddied.

CARLA BLEY: NIGHT-GLO
Pretend You're In Love/Night-Glo/Rut/
Crazy With You/Wildlife: Horns; Pause
Without Claws; Sex With Birds.
Randy Brecker (tp, flug), Tom Malone (tb),
David Taylor (b tb), Paul McCandless
(oboe, fr h, ss, ts, bars, b cl), John Clark (fr
h), Carla Bley (org, synth), Larry Willis (p,
el p),Hiram Bullock (g), Steve Swallow (el
b), Victor Lewis (d), Manolo Badrena (perc),
June-August 1985.
ECM WATT/16 827 640
AAD Running time: 36.42
Performance: ★ ★   Recording: ★ ★

Despite the number of musicians involved, and the often intricate arrangements, this seldom sounds like a large group; on the early tracks, the horns are mainly used to fill out a comfortable cushion of sound for guitar and keyboards to lean on. The title tune contrasts a disco-like backbeat with long-held chords and subtle riffing by the brass; an energetic Randy Brecker solos over call-and-response figures from the other horns. *Rut* opens with ominous-sounding organ chords and chunking rhythm guitar, then has the tune entering, somehow, from the most unexpected direction. The final track, *Wildlife*, is a work of some depth which grows in stature with repeated listening. Bley's flowing organ sound takes the lead over busy rhythm parts in *Horns*, before a soaring rock guitar solo from Bullock. Later sections offer some sensitive writing for the brass and effective use of the oboe as a solo voice.

Though some parts of the album appear as bland, warm and repetitive if instantly accessible music for relaxation, there are compensations. Recording quality is fine, though even in CD form it seems to lack the absolute crystal clarity expected from ECM, but perhaps only because of the number of parts which made up this beautifully-crafted whole.

ABDULLAH IBRAHIM (DOLLAR BRAND)
(b. Cape Town, South Africa, 1934)

South African musician Abdullah Ibrahim, formerly known as Dollar Brand.

Blending influences of American jazz and even colonially-imported hymns into his own heritage of African music, South African born Dollar Brand has become an internationally-popular pianist, composer and leader. He took the name Abdullah Ibrahim on his conversion to Islam in 1968.

Christened Adolf Johannes Brand, 'Dollar' came of Bazuto parentage; as a child, his early interest in music was encouraged by his grandmother, who played piano in her local church, and the harmonic influence of European hymns remains a strong one in his work. Later, in his teens, he joined a vocal group called The Streamline Brothers, played piano with the Tuxedo Slickers and by 1959 was working with Willie Max. In 1961 he formed his own group, The Jazz Epistles, which also included Hugh Masakela and Kippy Moeketsi, but in January the following year he finally made his escape from South Africa; with his wife, singer Sathima Bea Benjamin, he settled in Switzerland and began a long residency at the Cafe Africana in Zurich. In 1963 he was invited to the Antibes and Palermo jazz festivals, and was also heard by Duke Ellington, passing through on a European tour; he arranged for the pianist to record his first album in Paris. Two years later, in 1965, Ellington persuaded Brand to travel to the USA, where he played with Elvin Jones during 1966.

After a short visit to South Africa in 1968, Ibrahim travelled extensively but during the early 1970s made his home first in Swaziland and then in Cape Town and Johannesburg. His recordings have been extremely varied, and they include piano solos and collaborations with other musicians, notably an album with tenor saxophonist Gato Barbieri, as well as the most recent records made with his own group Ekaya.

Apart from Ellington, whom he once described as 'my musical father', Ibrahim's most obvious American influence was the late Thelonious Monk; there is no doubt that his powerful, uncompromising yet accessible music will continue to flourish, and continue as a very positive force.

THE PILGRIM

The Pilgrim/Ntsikana's B..l/Msunduza/
Namhanje/Saud/Moniebah (The Pilgrim
Abdullah Ibrahim (p, fl, voc)), Johnny
Dyani (b, voc). 1–3, 6, 1973; 4, 5, 1979.
Enja 2048-06
AAD Running time: 55.50
Performance: ★ ★ ★   Recording: ★ ★ ★

The tracks here are compiled from *Good
News From Africa* and *Echoes From Africa*,
two albums made in Ludwigsburg,
Germany, for the Enja label in 1973 and
1979. Here, as the album titles imply,
Ibrahim and Dyani work with traditional
musical materials, and Ibrahim is heard
singing, and playing a sometimes strongly
vocalised flute as well as the piano.

However, *The Pilgrim* opens with a
plangent, gentle piano theme, Ibrahim
rippling and breaking up its smooth surface
with stabbing dissonances and flurrying
runs. *Namhanje* centres on a hypnotic,
endlessly-repeated rolling piano figure, while
Saud, dedicated to McCoy Tyner, develops
from a gently lyrical opening to a powerful
and eerie climax. Finally, *Moniebah* returns
to the opening theme. Recording quality is
superb, tactile, brilliant and spacious, and
this Japanese disc is most definitely worth
seeking out.

DUKE'S MEMORIES

Star Crossed Lovers/Water Edge/Virgin
Jungle/Way Way Back/The Wedding/Black
and Brown Cherries/For Coltrane/In A
Sentimental Mood/Angelica; Purple Gazelle
Carlos Ward (ts, ss, fl), Abdullah Ibrahim
(p), Rachim Ausur Sahu (b), Andrej Strobert
(d), Stuttgart, July 1981.
String 233853
AAD Running time: 42.46
Performance: ★ ★   Recording: ★

Five of the nine tunes here are Ellington's,
and the dues-paying intention of the album is
clear from the first Duke-like piano
introduction; nonetheless, *Star Crossed
Lovers* contains a piano solo almost
completely in the style of Monk, Ibrahim
being perhaps the only man who could do
such a thing successfully. *Virgin Jungle* has a
snappy, bouncing beat, while Ward's
soprano sax sound leaps with insistent
agility; he produces a ringing, bluesy solo on
Way Way Back. Tracks 4-9 are from a live
concert, the first of these being a particularly
strong and atmospheric version of Ibrahim's
The Wedding (the theme appeared earlier, in
piano solo form on the Denon CD, *Anthem*

For The New Nations), with a thunderous
rolling piano beat from Ibrahim changes the
pace for a typically stately theme, *Black and
Brown Cherries*. A more uncharacteristically
decorative, almost Corea-like piano style
emerges from *In A Sentimental Mood*.
Recording quality is rather too lush
(overpoweringly so at times, for instance in
the opening track's echoing flute solo), as if
the studio tracks have had reverberant
effects added to match the live ones; the live
sound, on the other hand, is marred by the
fuzzy, treble-dominated 'electric' piano
sound. This may be a drawback, but the
music is very good.

WATER FROM AN ANCIENT WELL

Mandella/Song for Sathima/Manenberg
Revisited/Tuang Guru/Water From An
Ancient Well/The Wedding/Sameeda
Carlos Ward (alto fl), Dick Griffin (tb),
Ricky Ford (ts), Charles Davis (bars),
Abdulla Ibrahim (p), David Williams (b),
Ben Riley (d), October 1985
Black Hawk/Bellaphon BKH 50207
ADD Running time: 46.44
Performance: ★ ★ ★   Recording: ★ ★ ★

A second album from Abdullah Ibrahim's
group Ekaya (meaning 'home'), this fully
demonstrates the rich tone-colours of the
individual players and hence of the ensemble
as a whole. This is outstanding in a majestic
treatment of *The Wedding*, while Ibrahim's
great theme *Manenberg* appears here,
Revisited by the horns of Ekaya; they play
Basil Coetzee' original tenor sax solo in
unison, together sounding as fresh and
vibrant as a single, extemporising voice, over
a solid but bubbly bass pattern. *Mandella* is
a celebratory rather than a sombre
dedication, a tuneful, loose limbed dance;
featured solo instruments are the warm,
gusty baritone of Charles Davis and the full,
mellow and almost fruity trombone of Dick
Griffin. *Song For Sathima*, slow and
thoughtful has a quietly melancholy piano
introduction, followed by a beautiful theme
statement from Ford, who plays over full-
bodied chords from the other horns, then
Davis contributes a fine baritone solo.
Sameeda strikes deeper into the same vein,
with the pianist staying in the background to
make way for the sonorous yet agile
harmony of the horns. Sound quality, as you
would expect from Van Gelder's studio, is
fine if with just a hint of hardness, the
balance and ambience (actually quite dry),
clearly appropriate and helpful to the very
strong and appealing music on this disc.

ANTHONY BRAXTON
(b. Chicago, Illinois, 6 June 1945)

Multi-instrumentalist and composer Anthony Braxton arrived towards the end of the 'free' jazz revolution, and his varied work since the late 1960s has drawn on elements ranging from earlier jazz forms to 'straight' European music.

Braxton's strongest early interest was in classical music, and his first jazz influences included the light-toned saxophonists Paul Desmond, Lee Konitz and Warne Marsh as well as Miles Davis. During a period of military service which took him to Korea, he gained experience playing in the army band. In 1966, back in Chicago, the young *avant garde* saxophonist Roscoe Mitchell introduced Braxton to Chicago's Association For The Advancement Of Creative Musicians, where he was soon spending most of his time; he cut his debut album *Three Compositions Of New Jazz* in 1968, but during this period often made ends meet by playing chess for money.

In 1970, Braxton and Chick Corea formed Circle, with Dave Holland on bass and Barry Altschul on drums; the group was recorded on the *Paris Concert* album but broke up in 1971. Braxton was now becoming part of the European free music scene, and acquiring instruments at the extremes of the reed spectrum, from the gigantic contrabass clarinet to the tiny sopranino saxophone. Before returning to the US in 1974, he recorded *In The Tradition* with a trio led by pianist Tete Montoliu and played duo dates with guitarist Derek Bailey, but in the next few years he wrote works for chamber orchestra and larger forces and, in 1978, toured Europe with his own orchestra. He was now increasingly involved with electronic music. Into the 1980s, he continued to compose works for orchestra and to perform with his own quartet.

One of the prime movers in the 'free jazz' movement, Chicago-born Anthony Braxton has mastered a wide range of instruments.

IN THE TRADITION
Marshmallow/Goodbye Pork Pie Hat/Just
Friends/Ornithology/Lush Life/Trane's
Blue.
Anthony Braxton (as, contrabass cl), Tete
Montoliu (p), Neils-Henning Orsted
Pedersen (b), Al 'Tootie' Heath (d), Paris,
May 1974.
Steeplechase 32JD-84
AAD Running time: 47.43
Performance: ★ ★   Recording: ★ ★ ★

Substituting for Dexter Gordon who was
unable to make the date because of illness,
Anthony Braxton completed this European/
American quartet with radically different but
fascinating results. With no rehearsal time
allowed for, the tunes had to be familiar
vehicles anyway. With Pedersen's bass, in
unison, sounding quite high by comparison,
Braxton plays the melody of *Ornithology* as
low as possible on his contrabass clarinet, so
low in fact that the fundamentals are
inaudible and it is difficult to hear the pitch
of the notes; all that really seems to be there
is a deep, resonant buzz, sounding like some
grotesque bullfrog.
  Abetted by Pedersen's arco groans,
Braxton opens *Goodbye Porkpie Hat* with
some seagull-like squeaks above in contrast
with foghorn-like blasts from the depths.
Aside from these spectacular contributions,
he offers a light, firm and almost woody alto
sound on *Lush Life*, a chunky approach to
the theme (with the adept Montoliu playing
a harmony part) on *Trane's Blues*, and
sounds like a tougher Desmond on *Just
Friends*. On the uptempo opener (the
Cherokee-like tune named for its composer,
Warne Marsh), all play hard, Heath driving
the group effectively on to playing that has

no trace of flabbiness, and Montoliu's solo,
particularly, is outstanding.
  Braxton's alto playing may seem
superficially anarchic but in fact, like most
of his work, reveals the operation of an
organising mind. Sound quality is fairly
close and intimate yet with some natural
space around the instruments.

SIX COMPOSITIONS (QUARTET) 1984
Composition No 114 (+108A)/Composition
No 110C/Composition No 115/Composition
No 110A (+108B)/Composition No 110D/
Composition No 116
Anthony Braxton (as, ss, C-melody s, cl, fl),
Marilyn Crispell (fl), John Lindberg (b),
Gerry Hemingway (perc), September 1984.
Black Saint BSR 0086 CD
AAD Running time: 36.17
Performance: ★ ★   Recording: ★ ★ ★

In the 1970s Braxton had started giving
formulae as the titles of his albums, and by
1981 his numbered compositions had
reached 50; the six compositions here are
presented with a note on 'Pulse Track
Structures', some explanatory diagrams, and
reference to the full examination of the pieces
in 'Composition Notes Book E', though the
composer says he can give no date when that
might become available! With all this in
mind it is hardly surprising if these Braxton
compositions are far from accessible to the
newcomer. *Composition No 114 (+108A)* is
based on the repeated scale of C major,
running up and down again over two
octaves with rhythmic emphasis, Braxton
being the first member of the group to 'jump
off' (the phrase he uses in the notes) this
ladder-like basis for improvisation.

ANTHONY BRAXTON
SIX COMPOSITIONS (QUARTET)1984

CLIFFORD BROWN
(b. Wilmington, Delaware 30 October 1930; d. Pennsylvania, 26 June 1956)

A mere three years separated Clifford Brown's first Blue Note recordings from the issue of that label's *Memorial* album, yet his recorded legacy reveals him as one of the greatest of all trumpeters.

After college, where he majored in mathematics Brown gigged around Philadelphia, and was encouraged by Fats Navarro and Dizzy Gillespie, but a 1950 car accident put him out of action for nearly a year. In 1951, he deputised in Charlie Parker's group for a week, then formed his own band, but it was with R&B singer Chris Powell that he made his first recordings (for Okeh, now on the CBS album *The Beginning And The End*) in 1952.

There were no more records until June 1953, when he appeared on three dates: his first quintet recordings (with Lou Donaldson, on Blue Note); a session with Tadd Dameron's nine-piece band (Prestige); and one with J. J. Johnson's sextet (Blue Note again). The same summer brought his only Blue Note date as leader (including *Cherokee*), after which Brown sailed for Europe with Lionel Hampton's band. Along with other Hampton men, he made recordings (against the leader's strict orders) in Paris and Stockholm, and these had brought Brown some fame by the time he appeared with Art Blakey and Horace Silver at Birdland in February 1954 (recorded as *A Night At Birdland*, Blue Note).

A month later, he joined the quintet of Max Roach, who soon gave the young trumpeter the status of co-leader; the group's music was a final flowering of what had been called be-bop, and also echoed the dictum of Tadd Dameron: 'It has to swing, sure, but it has to be beautiful'. The quintet was broken up by the tragic deaths of Brown, pianist Richie Powell and Powell's wife Nancy, in a car crash in the small hours of June 26, 1956. Many musicians since have echoed the heartfelt tribute paid by Benny Golson with his beautiful and moving composition, *I Remember Clifford*.

STUDY IN BROWN
Cherokee/Jacqui/Swingin'/Land's End/George's Dilemma/Sandu/Gerkin for Oerkin/If I Love Again/Take The 'A' Train
Clifford Brown(tp), Harold Land (ts), Richie Powell(p), George Morrow (b), Max Roach (d), August 1955.
EmArcy 814 646
AAD Running time: 40.00
Performance: ★ ★ ★   Recording: ★ ★ ★

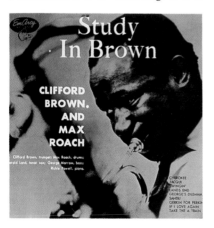

These nine tracks come from the middle of the quintet's short but incredibly fruitful period with Mercury/EmArcy Records. Here, *Cherokee* is a perfected, virtuoso showpiece for Brown, who is so effortlessly in command that the breakneck speed no longer sounds fast. Powell's tune *Jacqui* is a cheerful, witty composition which exemplifies the group's ability to bring lighter, cooler, West Coast influences (Land remained a West Coast resident) to the music, while numbers like the high speed workout *Swingin'* (on the chords of *I Never Knew*) or the mid-tempo blues *Sandu* sprang more directly from the bebop roots. Roach provides a supple 'Afro-Cuban' framework for *George's Dilemma*, a tune most conveniently described as a gentler *Night In Tunisia*, while the saxophonist's *Land's End* is an outstanding example of the Brown-Roach group's ability to produce truly memorable, melodic originals. Though it is apparently an odd number out, *Take The 'A' Train* is far more than a filler, with excellent solos all round. As usual with Mercury (unfortunately not with many other companies) the fine original sound has been preserved rather than tampered with through the years. Compared with a good stereo master, these 'dry' studio recordings can sound a little 'small' and perhaps lacking in obvious dynamic punch, but the sound (like the music) remains smooth, clear and profoundly satisfying.

MORE STUDY IN BROWN
I'll Remember April/Junior's Arrival/Flossie Lou/Mildama/Jor-Du/These Foolish Things/Land's End/The Blues Walk
Clifford Brown (tp), Harold Land (ts), Richie Powell (p), George Morrow (b), Max Roach (d), August 1955
EmArcy 814 637
AAD Running time: 42.40
Performance: ★ ★ ★   Recording: ★ ★ ★

All the numbers here are to be found on EmArcy's comprehensive Brown-Roach reissue in the late 1970's (The EmArcy Jazz Series), and some are on *Study In Brown* and *At Basin Street*, but the eight performances on *More Study In Brown* are all alternative takes which remained unreleased until this compilation was made. The differences between takes are, at least with hindsight, fairly unimportant, and so this remains a valid and valuable disc. In any case, only three tunes are actually duplicated on current CDs (not counting the live *Jor-Du* from *In Concert*).

It remains only to bemoan the fact that some of the great Brown-Roach performances (*Joyspring, Daahoud, Delilah*) remain unissued in Compact Disc. This cannot be for long.

AT BASIN STREET
What Is This Thing Called Love/Love Is A Many Splendored Thing/I'll Remember April/Powell's Prances/Time/The Scene Is Clean/Gertrude's Bounce
Clifford Brown (tp), Sonny Rollins (ts), Richie Powell (p), George Morrow (b), Max Roach (d), 1956.
EmArcy 814 648
AAD Running time: 40.18
Performance: ★ ★ ★   Recording: ★ ★ ★

By this time, the Brown-Roach quintet had reached its final form, with Sonny Rollins adding a new intensity in the saxophone department, and the gifted pianist Richie Powell doing the arrangements. In some ways this disc gives the best of both worlds; it has the clean sound of studio recording, but the music has the urgent, here-and-now quality of a live performance when things have clicked. The group sizzles from the opener; Brown simply takes flight in his solo, which serves as a reminder of just how far ahead he was, and how far behind were his first generation of imitators. The subsequent exchange of fours with Sonny Rollins is superb.

Apart from the waltzing introduction to *Love Is A Many Splendored Thing*, the first four numbers keep up an almost unvaried fast and furious tempo, but Powell's *Time* (written with the sad wait of the prisoner in mind) is a beautiful, slow tune harmonised by Brown and Rollins. *The Scene Is Clean* makes a joyful use of the Tadd Dameron tune, which provides a mid-tempo vehicle for an excellent Rollins solo. Despite the superb rapport within the group and fine solos from Powell and Roach himself,

Brown's role is central throughout, and he is in absolutely commanding form, his effortless speed and flow of ideas apparently unlimited.

From this late recording, it is difficult not to conclude that Brown was getting better and better in the last year of his short career. Fortunately for us, EmArcy have done a fine job in preserving these sessions.

BIG BAND
Quick Step/Bum's Rush/Chez Moi/No Start No End/All Weird/Brown Skins/Deltitnu/Keeping up With Jonesy
1,2 Clifford Brown, Art Farmer, Walter Williams (tp), Quincy Jones (tp, arr), Jimmy Cleveland, Al Hayse, Benny Vasseur (tb), Gigi Gryce, Anthony Ortega (as), Clifford Solomon, Andre Dabonneville (ts), William Boucaya (bars), Henri Renaud (p), Pierre Michelot (b), Jean-Louis Viale (d), Paris October 1953; 3, 4, 5 Brown, Farmer, Jones, Fernand Verstraete, Fred Gerard (tp), Hayse, Cleveland, Bill Tamper (tb), Gryce, Ortega (as), Solomon, Henri Bernard (ts), Renaud (p), Michelot (b), Alan Dawson (d), Paris, September 1953; 6, 8 Brown (tp), Cleveland (tb). Gryce (as), Solomon (ts), Boucaya (bars), Renaud (p), Jimmy Gourley (g), Marcel Dutrieux (b), Viale (d); 7 Brown (tp), Cleveland (tb), Gryce, Ortega (as), Solomon (ts), Boucaya (bars), Quincy Jones (p), Jimmy Gourley (g), Marcel Dutrieux (b), Viale (d), Paris, October 1953.
Vogue VG 651 600025
AAD Running time: 47.52
Performance: ★ ★   Recording: ★

On tour in Europe in the autumn of 1953, Brown, fellow trumpeter Quincy Jones and altoist Gigi Gryce, along with most of the other members of Lionel Hampton's orchestra, formed their own big band with a French rhythm section for the series of recordings documented here. Arrangements were by Gryce and Jones, while the horns were also augmented by Frenchmen Vasseur, Dabonneville and Boucaya. As to recording quality, although the soloists are 'brought in' quite effectively, there is some noticeable distortion (*Chez Moi*) and the sound of the band has the slightly distant, indistinct and watery quality that seems to be characteristic of French studios (or perhaps, mainly, of Vogue's atrocious fake stereo). Where the writing uses the contrasting attack and colour of brass and reeds, the reeds suffer wooliness while the brass seems merely loud. Much of the playing is excellent, as in for example *Keeping Up With Jonesy*, where Brown trades phrases with Art Farmer, both using mutes and Jimmy Cleveland is excellent on *Chez Moi* and *No Start No End*; Gryce sometimes sounds too studious a Parker imitator (this is an unfair criticism to make of any young altoist's 1953 recordings, of course). *Brown Skins* here is a fairly well disguised *Cherokee*; Brown is rhapsodic in the out-of-tempo 'verse', then solos confidently and easily over a supple and punchy Gryce arrangement. These recordings are among those which helped bring Clifford Brown's name to the jazz public, but the disc must be described as interesting rather than essential; some would say less so than the small group recordings *Clifford Brown With Gigi Gryce* (Vogue VG51 600020) which seemed to be unavailable at the time of writing.

IN CONCERT
Jor-Du/I Can't Get Started/I Get A Kick Out Of You/Parisian Thoroughfare/All God's Chillun Got Rhythm/Tenderly/Sunset Eyes/Clifford's Axe
1-4 Clifford Brown (tp), Harrold Land (ts), Richie Powell (p), George Morrow (b), Max Roach (d); 5-8 Brown (tp), Teddy Edwards (ts), Carl Perkins (p), George Bledsoe (b), Roach (d), 1954
Vogue VG651 600032
AAD Running time: 50.51
Performance: ★ ★ ★   Recording: ★

This familiar reissue offers recordings from two West Coast concerts under the Gene Norman Presents' banner. Between the first and second dates (actually presented here, though not on the original pair of 10in LPs, in reversed chronological order), all three sidemen in the co-led Roach-Brown quintet had changed, but such was the strength of the principals that the different styles of pianists, saxophonists and bassists cause little discontinuity. The appealingly busy, thick toned tenor of Edwards does make a pleasant contrast to the more reticent approach of Land, though. Brown is in magnificent form, from his first solo on the opener *Jor-Du*, the pretty, minor-key tune by Duke Jordan; with clarity and purity of tone, his endless melodic ideas flow effortlessly over the rhythm so smoothly laid down by Roach. Brown's first ballad feature *I Can't Get Started* is a masterpiece of control and taste; with such a performance, the sonic blemish of a resonant ringing from the microphone has to be tolerated. *Tenderly* (where there is no such quibble) simply makes this an essential recording. The standard is maintained throughout the rest of

the set, which ranges from the fascinating and perfectly executed *Parisian Thoroughfare*, evoking street bustle, car horns and all, to the waltz-to-4/4-transitions of the uptempo *I Get A Kick Out Of You*, to Brown's straight forward blowing on *Clifford's Axe* (fast, on *Lover Come Back To Me* chords, with many Parker quotations). It is a pity that the fake stereo of the LP reissue has been retained, but this can hardly be much of a deterrent.

CLIFFORD BROWN WITH STRINGS
Yesterdays/Laura/What's New/Blue Moon/Can't Help Lovin' Dat Man/Embraceable You/Willow Weep For Me/Memories Of You/Smoke Gets In Your Eyes/Portrait Of Jenny
Clifford Brown (tp), Richie Powell (p), Barry Galbraith (g), George Morrow (b), Max Roach (d), with orchestra arr and cond by Neal Hefti, January 1955.
EmArcy 814 642
AAD Running time: 40.44
Performance: ★ ★ ★   Recording: ★ ★ ★

Most of the current Clifford Brown Discs offer jazz originals and standards to the virtual exclusion of slow ballad features; *Clifford Brown With Strings* remedies this apparent neglect. In all ten selections here, Brown explores a well-known song against the cunningly-wrought orchestral backgrounds provided by Neal Hefti, the rhythm section usually faded down to near inaudibility. Hefti's arrangements are always appropriate, though often syrupy. Brown had to tread the thin line between the banality of playing the tune absolutely straight, and, on the other hand, of losing the support of the inflexible strings if he improvised too freely. In this he succeeded, and the fact that it took him many takes to do so on some numbers proves only how difficult the task and how dedicated the trumpeter. The whole album is a monument to his good taste as well as to his fantastic ear, flawless technique and beauty of tone. Some numbers do work better than others; *Willow Weep For Me* is a natural candidate for an interpretation that is fairly loose and bluesy in a genteel way; *What's New*, *Memories Of You* and a lovely *Portrait Of Jenny* are more successful than a near-turgid *Laura*, an almost trite *Can't Help Lovin' Dat Man*, and a somewhat lumbering *Smoke Gets In Your Eyes*. Sound quality and balance is good, and though the orchestra sometimes sounds a little boxed-in, this record defies condemnations of its *genre*.

DAVE BRUBECK
(b. Concord, California, 20 December 1920)

Some of Dave Brubeck's time-signature experiments have purported to embrace non-western musical forms, but it was really the heavy infusion of European classical music which helped win him such enormous success in the early 1950s. With altoist Paul Desmond, he epitomised the characteristics of 'West Coast' jazz; the music was clever and 'cool', made accessible and at the same time intellectually acceptable to its white audience by its classical borrowings.

Brubeck was a thoroughly-trained pianist who studied composition under Darius Milhaud at Mills College, Oakland. Though his first serious jazz group was an octet, by 1951 he had settled on the quartet format, featuring Desmond, and the group soon became extremely popular on the 'college circuit'; among his recordings for the Fantasy label (which he helped to found), the most successful was *The Oberlin Concert* in 1954. Soon after this, he signed for Columbia Records and his first Columbia LP, *Jazz Goes To College*, became easily the biggest-selling jazz album released up to that time. With the arrival of the outstanding drummer Joe Morello in 1956, the quartet went from strength to strength, but by 1959 Morello was being accused of dominating the group from the drums. Perhaps this was not surprising in view of Brubeck's increasing preoccupation with rhythm.

Desmond, who had recorded occasionally with other musicians but had spent the greater part of his musical life with the Brubeck quartet, left in 1967. After this, Brubeck worked with Gerry Mulligan, a partnership which produced *Blues Roots* and *Last Set At Newport*; but in the 1970s Brubeck re-emerged with a new group featuring (variously), his sons Darius and Chris Brubeck, and reflecting the rock/fusion trends of the time while continuing to use earlier material in updated form. The electronic sounds pleased neither Brubeck's older fans nor the critics, most of whom had never liked him anyway; but saxophonist Joe Bergonzi and, recently, clarinettist Bill Smith brought a lighter touch to complement Brubeck's still-powerful piano.

TIME OUT
Blue Rondo A La Turk/Strange Meadow Lark/Take Five/Three To Get Ready/Kathy's Waltz/Everybody's Jumpin'/Pick Up Sticks
Paul Desmond (as), Dave Brubeck (p), Gene Wright (b), Joe Morello (d); 4-6 June 1959, 2, 3 July 1959; 1, 7 August 1959.
CBS CDCBS 62068
AAD Running time: 38.49
Performance: ★ ★ ★　　Recording: ★ ★ ★

After the enduring *Take Five*, a top ten single hit in 1962 and now a standard, the most familiar tune here is *Blue Rondo A La Turk*, where the hammering theme in 9/8 alternates with a cool blues; neither the flawlessness of the transitions nor the fact that the piece is (as Steve Race's liner note points out) 'in classical *rondo* form' prevent it from sounding contrived and even irritating today. *Strange Meadow Lark*, though, is a delight, with Brubeck refraining from the use of massive chords as he expounds an evocative, wistful theme resembling the verse of *Stardust*; Desmond's contribution is rhythmically free, lyrical and beautifully structured. *Three To Get Ready* is a simple and familiar tune, but after the theme statement comes the rhythmic catch, as it starts alternating two bars of 3/4 with two bars of 4/4; *Kathy's Waltz* starts in 4/4 before becoming a pretty jazz waltz in the hands of Desmond, until Brubeck introduces a strong cross-rhythm. *Everybody's Jumpin'* is not the good-time tune that the title might seem to imply, but is a neat, 'cool' exploration on a simple idea.

In the 6/4 *Pick Up Sticks*, Brubeck builds up through a jaggedly-effective single-note solo before finally breaking out in heavy block-chord style. 'Though Desmond's work is excellent, *Time Out* offers none of the happy 'contrapuntal'sound which had brought the quartet its earlier fame, but the reverberant recording helps Desmond and Morello to shine. This remains an attractive, even essential album, but now that the strange time signatures are no longer a novelty, the content and pseudo-academic approach seems as old fashioned now as it in fact was when the album was first released.

THE QUARTET
Castillian Drums/Three To Get Ready/St
Louis Blues/Forty Days/Summer Song/
Someday My Prince Will Come/
Brandenburg Gate/In Your Own Sweet Way
1–6 Paul Desmond (as), Dave Brubeck (p),
Gene Wright (b), Joe Morello (d); 7, 8 add
Darius Brubeck (synth). Dates unknown.
Denon 33C38-7681
AAD Running time: 54.37
Performance: ★ ★   Recording: ★

This disc does provide some ammunition for
the once-prevalent argument that altoist Paul
Desmond was artistically restricted by
remaining with Brubeck so long. The
vaunted piano-alto interplay appears on the
light-stepping jazz waltz *Three To Get
Ready*, which also provides the first of
several attractive Desmond solos. But in
most of the numbers here, the heavily-
percussive piano of Brubeck eventually
dominates, and his unvarying attack on the
keys becomes monotonous after a while. On
the second waltz, *Someday My Prince Will
Come*, Desmond's airy solo follows a
particularly clanging introduction by
Brubeck, who returns with restraint, only to
build up to brutal pitch as he hammers out a
four-over-three cross rhythm.

While the first six tracks are
straightforward live recordings of the classic
Brubeck quartet, the other two remain
obscure, offering unidentified samples of the
later modernised group which Brubeck
created by bringing in one or more of his
sons. Those who care for the 'old' Brubeck
will appreciate *In Your Own Sweet Way*,
with clarinet presumed to be by Desmond.

As with many of the Denon recordings
licensed from LRC, the liner note
information is scanty, doubtful and self-
contradictory. Recording quality is fair, with
some hiss and distortion.

DAVE BRUBECK: CONCORD ON A SUMMER NIGHT
Benjamin/Koto Song/Black and Blue/Softly,
William, Softly/Take Five.
Bill Smith (cl), Dave Brubeck (p), Chris
Brubeck (el b, b, tb), Randy Jones (d),
August 1982.
Concord CCD 4198
AAD Running time: 39.44
Performance: ★ ★   Recording: ★ ★

A warm and happy atmosphere surrounds
this recording, live in the open air at the 1982
Concord Jazz Festival. A free-swinging Jones
and the younger Brubeck, on bass, kick off

the bright and bouncy tune *Benjamin*; Smith
starts his solo in the lower register, then
explores the changes as Dave Brubeck chops
the chords behind him. Brubeck's own solo,
surprisingly, seems to have moments of
stiffness, but he changes gear effectively for
the reflective *Koto Song*, and it is here that
the glow of the summer night seems almost
tangible.

Here, using his brittle sound, with skilful
pedalling and quasi-oriental scales, Brubeck
evokes the Japanese instrument of the title,
while Smith adds an ethereal clarinet played
with multiple echo effects. Fats Waller's
Black and Blue is usually remembered for
Louis Armstrong's early recording; here it is
a half-sentimental, half-whimsical feature for
Chris Brubeck's bass trombone. He is then
heard providing a sort of flatulent
counterpoint as Brubeck senior takes over
with a crashingly bravura piano solo. Smith
features the echoing clarinet again on *Softly*,
then, finally, the long version of *Take Five*
proves to be a good one, and rounds out a
set that will please all Brubeck fans.

Recording quality is enjoyably 'live' and if
not absolutely stunning in high-fidelity
terms, it captures the life and drive of the
music to good effect.

REFLECTIONS
Reflections Of You/A Misty Morning/I'd
Walk A Country Mile/My One Bad Habit/
Blues For Newport/We Will All Remember
Paul/Michael, My Second Son/Blue Lake
Tahoe
Bill Smith (cl), Dave Brubeck (p), Chris
Brubeck (el b, tb), Randy Jones (d),
December 1985.
Concord CCD 4299
AAD Running time: 43.58
Performance: ★ ★   Recording: ★ ★ ★

As Brubeck explains in the liner note, the
title is meant to refer to reflections in the
sense of thoughts as much as in the physical
meaning, and the numbers (all Brubeck
compositions) all have personal associations.
The most poignant are *We Will All
Remember Paul* (for Paul Desmond, who
died in 1977), an obliquely romantic theme
played with surpassing delicacy, and
Michael My Second Son, which combines a
wistful strain with something of the
jauntiness of carefree childhood. Equally
evocative is *Blue Lake Tahoe*, a pretty waltz
with the piano suggesting gently-lapping
ripples, while Brubeck maintains a light
touch in *A Misty Morning*.

Clarinettist Bill Smith makes sensitive
contributions to all of these, though it could
be wished that he would give up using the
echo device that he still switches on from
time to time. *Reflections Of You* works well
as an opener, Brubeck's full-sounding chords
in the out-of-tempo intro giving way
suddenly to a fast swing, with an agile and
well-constructed solo from Smith, after
which the pianist offers a chord solo in his
percussive style. Here Chris Brubeck plays a
fast, slippery but dead-toned electric bass,
but his broad trombone playing is featured
in the ballad *My One Bad Habit*. Recording
quality is impeccably clean; and this
relatively recent disc shows that the re-
established partnership of Brubeck and
Smith has continued to be a creative and
interesting one.

GARY BURTON
(b. Anderson, Indiana, January 1943)

It seems to be generally agreed that vibraphonist Gary Burton has produced his best work in the company of other strong musical characters, but there is no doubt that he is a true virtuoso.

As a teenager, Burton developed his vibraphone technique to astonishing levels, increasing his speed and adding harmonic capabilities by using two mallets in each hand. He had just reached his twenties when he worked briefly with George Shearing, and (from 1964 to 1966) with Stan Getz. He formed his own quartet, with guitarist Larry Coryell, in 1967; this group turned out to be primarily rock influenced and was successful only until the 'psychedelic' era faded at the turn of the decade. But Burton's career entered a new and positive phase when he joined the ECM label. He recorded duo albums with both Keith Jarrett and Chick Corea, and formed a new quartet (*The New Quartet* was also the title of its first, 1973, album) with Michael Goodrick on guitar, Abraham Laboriel on bass and Harry Blazer on drums; the group also recorded a less successful album with the NDR symphony orchestra in Hamburg. A further reunion with Corea, this time plus string quartet, produced *Lyric Suite For Sextet* in 1982. Burton also recorded with Eberhard Weber before teaming up with another star bassist, Steve Swallow, *Matchbook* was the first of his successful collaborations with guitarist Ralph Towner. In recent years, Burton's teaching post at Berklee has enabled him to recruit perform and record with outstanding students, notably altoist Jim Ogden and pianist Makoto Ozone.

CHICK COREA AND GARY BURTON IN CONCERT
Senor Mouse/Bud Powell/Crystal Silence/ Tweak/Falling Grace/Mirror, Mirror/Song To Gayle/Endless Trouble, Endless Pleasure
Chick Corea (p), Gary Burton (vib), Zurich, Switzerland, October 1979.
ECM 821 415
AAD Running time: 61.23
Performance: ★ ★ ★   Recording: ★ ★ ★

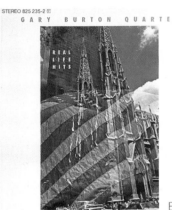

STEREO 825 235-2
GARY BURTON QUARTET
REAL LIFE HITS

ECM

One of the earliest of Burton's 'virtuoso duo' partnerships was that with Corea, and the association was very successfully revived when they toured together at the end of the 1970s. ECM's exquisitely recorded *In Concert* was originally packaged as a double album. Six of the eight tunes are Corea's, and these include his *Bud Powell*, a musical tribute to the great and influential jazz pianist, the theme played here in deftly swinging unison by vibes and piano. *Crystal Silence* is a Corea classic, its 'spacey' mood opened out here by the glow of the vibes, while Corea, with astonishing virtuosity, adds magical shimmering effects. Rhythmic intricacy features again in Steve Swallow's *Endless Trouble, Endless Pleasure*; and though vibes and piano might seem to offer little in the way of tonal colour, Burton and Corea build up *pointilliste* sound pictures that soon become absorbing.

REAL LIFE HITS
Syndrome/The Beatles/Fleurette Africaine/ Ladies In Mercedes/Real Life Hits/I Need You Here/Ivanushka Durachok
Gary Burton (vib), Makoto Ozone (piano), Steve Swallow (el b), Mike Hyman (d), Ludwigsburg, Germany, November 1984
ECM 825 235
DDD Running time: 50.21

Performance: ★ ★ ★   Recording: ★ ★ ★

Burton's re-formed quartet featured three excellent musicians in Ozone, Swallow and Hyman; they seem to be urging him on from the opening bars of *Syndrome* (written by Carla Bley), in which Burton rapidly builds a dense texture over a frenetic pulse. Ozone's solos here and throughout this disc are agile, precise and structured, with a bright and ringing piano sound. *The Beatles* (composed by guitarist John Scofield), shifting subtly in and out of an ambiguous minor key, gently probes the harmonies Lennon and McCartney wrote on. It also provides solo space for the eclectic Swallow, whose *Ladies In Mercedes* float along prettily on a gentle Latin beat, with nice chording from Hyman behind Burton's virtuoso marimba solo. On *Real Life Hits* (by Carla Bley), Hyman sets up an undercurrent of patterning menace behind Burton's vibes, occasionally breaking out into angular solo figures; this hypnotic performance is followed by *Ivanushka Durachok*, a very fast minor-key semi-blues which allows Burton to shine in a lengthy solo over a straight four beat, a satisfying finale for a varied and occasionally brilliant set.

BENNY CARTER
(b. New York City, 8 August 1907)

One of the great bandleaders of the early 1930s, Benny Carter soon became one of the most sought-after arrangers. He played trumpet as well as the alto saxophone.

Starting on piano, the young Benny Carter saved up for a trumpet in order to emulate Bubber Miley, but soon traded this for a saxophone. In the 1920s he worked for Earl Hines, Horace Henderson, Charlie Johnson, Ellington and Fletcher Henderson, first forming his own band in 1928; in 1930 he was back with Fletcher Henderson, then worked briefly with Chick Webb and McKinney's Cotton Pickers before launching his own band again in 1932. He was now arranging for several bands, including (by 1934), Benny Goodman's. He left the US for Europe in 1935, working first in Willie Lewis's band in Paris, then as arranger (non-playing) with Henry Hall's orchestra in London. There were memorable recordings in London, Holland and Paris (with Django Reinhardt) before he returned to New York in 1938. He led bands of various sizes, moving to Los Angeles in 1945.

After this he spent more and more of his time as a composer and arranger for the Hollywood studios, and by the 1960s had produced many TV themes and continued to write major film scores. Touring again in recent years, Carter's wonderful musicianship and continued vitality have defined the art growing old gracefully.

FURTHER DEFINITIONS
Honeysuckle Rose/The Midnight Sun Will
Never Set/Crazy Rhythm/Blue Star/
Cottontail/Body And Soul/Cherry/Doozy.
Benny Carter, Phil Woods (as), Coleman
Hawkins, Charlie Rouse (ts), Dick Katz (p),
John Collins (g), Jimmy Garrison (b), Jo
Jones (d), November 1961.
MCA/Impulse MCAD-5651
AAD Running time: 33.55
Performance: ★ ★ ★   Recording: ★ ★

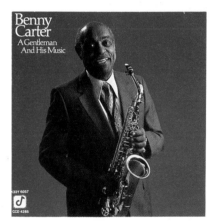

On this celebrated album, the presence of four saxophones allows us to hear some of Carter's intriguing writing as well as his distinctive solo work; there are also plenty of excellent solos from an expansive Hawkins.

Opening at a zippy tempo, the tight horn ensemble gives way to neatly-turned solos from Rouse and Woods before a heavier-toned, almost bleary-sounding Hawkins solo and a typically quick-thinking one from Carter. Hawkins is at his most luxuriant on the Quincy Jones ballad tune *The Midnight Sun Will Never Set*.

The horns open *Body And Soul*, with Carter's scoring of Hawkins' famous 1939 version, but Hawkins own solo here (following Woods, Rouse and Carter) still has great impact as he closes the number in commanding fashion. A mid-tempo blues wraps up this collection. The buoyant rhythm of Jo Jones and the solid (rather closely-recorded) Garrison helps all the soloists (though Katz is often weak) to give of their best.

A GENTLEMAN AND HIS MUSIC
Sometimes I'm Happy/A Kiss From You/
Blues For George/Things Ain't What They
Used To Be/Lover Man/Idaho.
Joe Wilder (tp, flug), Benny Carter (as),
Scott Hamilton (ts), Gene Harris (p), Ed
Bickrt (g), John Clayton (b), Jimmie Smith
(d), August 1985.
Concord CCD 4285
AAD Running time: 47.57
Performance: ★ ★   Recording: ★ ★ ★

On this thoroughly fresh and enjoyable recording, Benny Carter is surrounded by an eminently compatible group. In the happy-sounding, medium-paced opener, the horns state the theme in ensemble, with Hamilton recalling Lester Young as he takes the bridge, to launch a typically fluent thought-provoking solo by Carter, followed by a muted chorus from Wilder. Then Hamilton, Bickert and Harris in turn all relax into the easy groove.

The extemporised blues named in memory of George Duvivier is appropriately opened by Clayton's bass, playing a slow boogie; solos include a clean and fluid-lined one from Bickert and an emotive contribution from Wilder on flugelhorn. *Things Ain't What They Used To Be* is also a twelve-bar blues, of course, but it rocks along with a marching 'soul' backbeat, Hamilton offering a restrained sort of R&B shout, while Carter plays an amazingly potent, swinging and structured solo.

Closing the set is a fast, swinging *Idaho*, with Carter twinkling and deft as ever. It would be unnecessary to add that the great altoist celebrated his 78th birthday less than a week after this beautifully-recorded session, but for the fact that Benny Carter shows no sign of ageing here.

RAY CHARLES
(b. Albany, Georgia, 23 September 1930)

It was Ray Charles who first brought the undiluted expressionism of black singing to a white audience. He has made only a few 'jazz albums', but in a broad sense he can be considered a great jazz singer.

Born Ray Charles Robinson, he was brought up in Greenville, Florida. His sight failed gradually until, aged seven, he was sent to the St Augustine school for the blind, where he had piano and clarinet lessons. After school, he played with a hillbilly band in Tampa, then went to Seattle, where his piano/guitar/bass trio made some now-obscure recordings.

He moved to Los Angeles in 1950, then toured with blues singer Lowell Fulsom's band. Leaving Fulsom in late 1952, he recorded *It Should've Been Me* and *Don't You Know*, his first sides for Atlantic Records. In 1954, he started touring and recording with his own band, featuring tenor sax player David 'Fathead' Newman, and *I Got A Woman* became the first of a series of gospel-based hits. In 1957, the band sound was strengthened by the addition of a four-girl singing group, The Raelettes, and two years later, Charles realised a long-standing ambition by recording with strings for *The Genius Of Ray Charles*.

Offered a good royalty deal and continuing artistic freedom, Ray went to ABC records and had an immediate hit with *Georgia*. In 1961, he recorded *Genius + Soul = Jazz*, with members of the Basie orchestra, and an album of duets with jazz singer Betty Carter. But it was the 1962 album, *Modern Sounds in Country and Western Music* which gave him his biggest hit to date, *I Can't Stop Lovin' You*. Charles had finally broken through into the white pop market, and during the next decade he applied 'soul' to an ever-broadening spectrum of material, including Lennon-McCartney songs.

In 1977, his recorded distribution returned to Atlantic; since then Charles has continued to tour with his own big band and singers, and though recent album releases may have been somewhat mundane, he remains a truly electrifying performer.

THE LEGEND LIVES
Together Again/Yesterday/Born To Lose/ Your Cheatin' Heart/You Don't Know Me/ Eleanor Rigby/Take These Chains From My Heart/I Can't Stop Loving You/Georgia On My Mind/Crying Time/Hit The Road Jack/ What'd I Say/Ruby/Baby It's Cold Outside/ Makin' Whoopee/Busted/Let's Go Get Stoned/Here We Go Again.
Ray Charles and his orchestra: 1, 5, 12, 15 1965; 2, 18, 1967; 3, 8 1962; 4, 7, 16 1963; 6 1968; 9, 11 1960; 10, 17 1966; 13 1961; 14 add Betty Carter (voc), 1961.
Arcade ADEH CD 780
AAD Running time: 61.15
Performance: ★ ★ **Recording:** ★ ★ ★

Drawing on a dozen of Charles' post-Atlantic albums covering the fertile 1960-68 period, this compilation here goes for broad appeal by leaning heavily in a country/easy listening direction. Nevertheless, the set does include perhaps his greatest ever ballad performances, *Ruby*, and the still-breathtaking *Georgia*, along with the soulful *Hit The Road Jack*, still a pop classic with its dramatic 'story' duet, the message punched home by brilliant background vocals, incredible swing and tight, superbly-economical horn parts. Along with the compelling narrative of *Busted* and the irresistibly powerful slow beat of *Let's Go Get Stoned*, this 1960 chart success clearly represents just about the nearest thing on this disc to the unadorned excitement of Charles' earlier style.

What'd I Say is not the original hit recording, but comes from the 1965 *Live In Concert* album, as does *Makin' Whoopee*; also in the novelty category is *Baby It's Cold Outside*, sole representative of the 1961 album *Ray Charles and Betty Carter*, while the dated treatments of two Lennon-McCartney numbers (which also suffer from a peculiar tunnelly sound) are best ignored; but still standing out from the sticky mass of country and western schmaltz is the memorable *I Can't Stop Loving You*. It would be hard to say that this disc is poor value, but hardly any of the singer's excellent jazz-tinged 1960s material has been chosen.

STANLEY CLARKE
(b. Philadelphia, Pennsylvania, June 30, 1951)

By the end of the 1970s, the electric bass had ceased to be an unglamorous rhythm instrument. In the hands of the new generation of bass players, it had developed its own expressive voice, soulful, percussive and almost as fast as the guitar. If any one musician epitomised this change, it was Stanley Clarke.

As a boy, Clarke studied violin, and then 'cello. Into his teens, he grew too tall for this instrument and took up the double bass instead. Though he was also playing bass in local rhythm and blues bands, and was already listening keenly to the great jazz players from Charles Mingus to Paul Chambers to Scott LaFaro and Ron Carter, he continued his classical studies, majoring in bass at the All-Philadelphia Musical Academy.

Clarke first attracted attention when he played with Horace Silver while still only eighteen. Arriving in New York towards the end of 1970, he worked with Art Blakey, Stan Getz and Dexter Gordon, as well as appearing with some rather more *avant garde* musicians like Joe Henderson and Pharoah Saunders. He even worked with Gil Evans for a while, but in 1972 joined Chick Corea's band Return To Forever. It was in Return To Forever that Clarke's contribution to the art of the electric bass became apparent.

Clarke left in 1976 to begin a solo career. His work was now clearly categorised as rock, at the commercial-pop end of the fusion spectrum, and while his approach became grossly simplified in the interests of producing instantly-exciting dance music, his playing still contained passages of stunning virtuosity. Along with *Stanley Clarke, Journey To Love* and *School Days*, Clarke produced an unusually star-studded album in *I Wanna Play For You*, with guest appearances by Freddie Hubbard, Stan Getz, Tom Scott, George Duke, Airto Moreira and Jeff Beck.

Recently, Clarke has worked with fusion keyboard star George Duke in the Clarke/Duke project, and has continued to be in demand as a session bassist and producer; he has recorded with Aretha Franklin, Quincy Jones, Paul Simon, Paul McCartney and Santana, and produced artists ranging from Natalie Cole to Ramsey Lewis.

OLD FRIENDS

Hideaway/Overjoyed/My Love, Her Inspiration/Where Do We Go/The Boys Of Johnson Street/Old Friends/When It's Cold Outside/Listen To The Beat Of Your Heart/Basketball/I'm Here To Stay.
1 Stanley Clarke (el b, g, key etc), Gerry Brown (perc); 2 Stanley Clarke (el b, b, tenor el b), Stanley Jordan (g), Alan Pasqua (key), Brown (d, perc); 3 Clarke (tenor el b), George Howard (ss), Wayne Linsey, Pasqua (key), Alphonso Johnson (el b), Rayford Griffin (d, perc); 4 Gary Herbig (as), Paul Jackson Jr (g), Pat Leonard, Pasqua (key), Clarke (al b), June Kuramoto (kotos), Tristan Imboden (d), Angela Bofill (voc); 5 Clarke (tenor el b), Herbie Hancock, Pasqua (key), Stewart Copeland (d); 6 Dan Huff (g), David Sancious, Pasqua (key), Clarke (el b), Brown (d, perc); 7 Clarke (all instruments); 8 Clarke (tenor el b), Leonard, Pasqua (key), Jackson (g), Bernard Jackson (voc), Howard Hewitt, Josie James (backgroundvoc); 9 Clarke (tenor el b), George Howard (ts), Robert Brookins, Pasqua (key), Paul Jackson Jr (g), Griffin (d, perc); 10 Pasqua, Linsey (key), Clarke (el b), Larry Graham (el b, voc), John Robinson (d, perc), Hewett, James (background voc), 1986.
Epic CDEPC 26964
AAD Running time: 44.05
Performance: ★ ★   Recording: ★ ★ ★

As can be seen from the rather complex personnel listing, members of Clark's band do appear, but so do various other luminaries, notably Herbie Hancock, Larry Graham amd Stanley Jordan, and the presentation of the album indicates a change of direction compared with the disco-pop of albums like *Find Out*.

In more restrained mood, Clarke duets effectively with Jordan on the Stevie Wonder tune *Overjoyed*, producing a texture like a less acoustic-sounding Earl Klugh. After a solo from Clarke, Jordan's single-string entry sounds momentarily thin in tone, but soon dazzles with a typically fluid solo. Hancock's guest appearance is a melodic contribution to the almost introspective *Boys Of Johnson Street*. *My Love, Her Inspiration* jogs along encouragingly, if rather soporifically, with Clarke's pretty tenor-bass solo, after an opening duet with straight-toned soprano saxist Howard; his style offers an interesting contrast with the rugged metal-mouthpiece sound of tenorist Gary Herbig, behind and around Angela Bofill on the effective if rather too Sade-influenced vocal number *Where Do We Go*. Later tracks have Clarke getting into a funky groove, though Larry Graham's vocal feature *I'm Her To Stay* swings things back towards the middle ground. A very varied but ultimately bland album of unpretentious jazz/pop.

ORNETTE COLEMAN
(b. Fort Worth, Texas, 19 March 1930)

Overcoming more hostility from other musicians that even the early beboppers had faced, Ornette Coleman won through to become a prime mover in 'free' jazz at the end of the 1950s.

Coleman's first engagements were with R&B bands around his home town, but on leaving High School he joined a travelling variety show, from which he was fired in Natchez for allegedly trying to interest the other players in bebop.

There were many similar rejections, but by 1956 Coleman had met the young trumpeter Don Cherry, and was rehearsing with a group of musicians who shared his approach to improvisation. In 1958, Coleman tried to sell some of his tunes to Lester Koenig of Contemporary Records; Koenig recorded Coleman and Cherry on their first album *Something Else!!!*.

Through Percy Heath, Coleman caught the ear of John Lewis, who arranged for Coleman and Cherry to attend the Summer School at Lenox University with which he was connected. A follow-up album *Tomorrow Is The Question* led to a season at the Five Spot Cafe in New York and to a contract with Atlantic Records.

Though he could now get work, Coleman was disillusioned by the working conditions and fees that nightclub owners offered him, and after recording *Town Hall* in 1962 with his trio (David Izenzon on bass and Charles Moffett on drums) he dropped out of the music scene. By the time he returned, in 1965, he had become the major influence on a stratum of younger musicians, their ranks headed by Archie Shepp, Steve Lacy and Albert Ayler.

OF HUMAN FEELINGS
Sleep Talk/Jump Street/Him And Her/Air Ship/What Is The Name Of That Song?/Job Mob/Love Words/Times Square.
Ornette Coleman (as), Charlie Ellerbee, Bern Nix (g), Jamaaladeen Tacuma (el b), Ornette Denardo Coleman, Calvin Weston (d), April 1979.
Antilles J33JD-20002
DDD Running time: 36.36
Performance: ★ Recording: ★

Opened by Tacuma, who is quickly joined by the straightforward funky offbeat of the drummers and the busy rhythm chords of the guitars, *Sleep Talk* is actually a simple, haunting theme by Coleman. The performance settles into a steady rock over which Coleman's more frantic variations bring it to a climax. *Jump Street* uses a chant-like repeated figure over a fast backbeat, while *Him And Her* features a sinewy line from Tacuma, over a relentless beat that gives a Mingus-like illusion of steady acceleration.

Of Human Feelings is an uncompromising album which offers no conscious attempt at variety, and with a static mix (except that Coleman moves nearer and further from the mic), it makes no attempt at sonic sophistication, yet is a powerful collective performance that should be heard.

PAT METHENY AND ORNETTE COLEMAN: SONG X
Song X/Mob Job/Endangered Species/Video Games/Kathelin Gray/Trigonometry/Song X Duo/Long Time No See.
Ornette Coleman (as, vln2), Pat Metheny (g), Charlie Haden (b), Jack DeJohnette (d), Denardo Coleman (perc), December 1985.
Geffen 9 24096
AAD Running time: 48.45
Performance: ★ ★ Recording: ★ ★ ★

P A T   M E T H E N Y

O R N E T T E   C O L E M A N

X

C H A R L I E   H A D E N

J A C K   D E J O H N E T T E

D E N A R D O   C O L E M A N

This collaboration opens frenetically, with DeJohnette's superbly controlled pulse carrying Coleman's solo while Metheny adds a speringy sounding obbligato; Metheny's strand eventually emerges in its own right.

Bearing only a faint resemblance to Prime Time's *Job Mob*, the contrasting *Mob Job* is open and airy at first, Coleman and Metheny playing the theme in loose and echoey-sounding unison over a mobile bounce from the rhythm section; then, after a gutsily lyrical alto solo, Coleman picks up the violin and plays a squalling solo.

Endangered Species is a wasps' nest of repeated cries from guitar and sax, driven with furious accuracy by DeJohnette and Denardo Coleman. *Video Games* is a fast Coleman theme running up and down the instrument, again flinging out jagged fragments, then releasing into a solo over racing bass and drums, with interjections by Metheny, whose guitar and synth lines sounds like an ensemble of angry horns.

This is a significant recording, and as you might expect with Metheny's involvement, it is a technically excellent one.

JOHN COLTRANE

(b. Hamlet, North Carolina, 23 September 1926; d. New York, 17 July 1967)

One of the great innovators of jazz, John Coltrane is still revered by, and remains an influence on the horn players of today.

Coltrane's search for new approaches occupied almost every waking moment in the last ten years of his life. At one stage he took the concept of playing over chord changes to its logical conclusion, by trying to play every possible combination of notes against each chord before leaving it. Later, he became interested in applying Indian scales or ragas; finally, and perhaps paradoxically in view of his obsession with practice and technique, he became involved with the 'free' jazz of Ornette Coleman and others.

After early experience with a Navy band in 1945-47, he played with various R&B bands until joining Dizzy Gillespie in 1949. Then he played with Earl Bostic for a while, and in 1953 spent a few months with Johnny Hodges, but was playing R&B back in Philadelphia, where he was raised, when Miles Davis sent for him in the autumn of 1955. The quintet which Coltrane joined had the old standard line-up of trumpet, sax, piano, bass and drums, but Miles' choice of players ensured that it sounded like something new. Coltrane's tenor solos, notes spilling chaotically and a big, almost honking sound, offered the most dramatic contrast for Miles' trumpet.

Leaving Miles in late 1956, Coltrane went home, kicked his by-now debilitating drug habit, then spent the next summer with Thelonious Monk's quartet at the Five Spot Café. In September 1957 he recorded *Blue Train* for Blue Note, but a month later was back with Miles Davis. This time, he stayed until early 1960, when he left to form his own quartet. He enlisted McCoy Tyner on piano and Steve Davis on bass, but several drummers came and went in quick succession before Elvin Jones joined in October 1960. Bassist Davis was replaced by Reggie Workman, who stayed from May to December 1961, when Jimmy Garrison took his place.

Coltrane had discovered the soprano sax in 1959, and he now used it to full effect on *My Favourite Things*, which started something of a craze for the instrument. *A Love Supreme*, devotional in character and hypnotic in effect, is said to have sold about 250,000 copies, an enormous figure for a jazz album in the early 1960s.

He continued to experiment, often using two bass players, and eventually adding 'free jazz' horn players Pharoah Sanders and Archie Shepp, who appear on *Ascension* (1965). However, the quartet started to disintegrate under the strain: McCoy Tyner left in December 1965 and, with the arrival of free drummer Rashied Ali, Jones left in March 1966, saying 'The other drummer had a different sense of time from me, so it didn't sound any good.' Jimmy Garrison walked off during a Japanese tour.

These last developments, which were halted by Coltrane's untimely death from cancer of the liver, probably dismayed all but his most fanatical devotees. But unlike Coltrane, whose musical quest seemed to become a desperate race against time, we can continue to explore the complex legacy he left behind, and appreciate the breadth and depth of his influence.

JOHN COLTRANE: LUSH LIFE
Like Someone In Love/I Love You/Trane's Slow Blues/Lush Life/I Hear A Rhapsody.
1-3 John Coltrane (ts), Earl May (b), Art Taylor (d), August 1957; 4 Donald Byrd (tp), Coltrane (ts), Red Garland (p), Paul Chambers (b), Louis Hayes (d), January 1958; 5 Coltrane (ts), Garland (p), Chambers (b), Al Heath (d), May 1957.
Prestige VDJ 1544
AAD Running time: 36.29
Performance: ★ ★   Recording: ★ ★

Taken from three sessions, these numbers feature Coltrane in trio, quintet and quartet settings. The piano-less trio, with a prominently-recorded Earl May and a relatively subdued Art Taylor, allows Trane unlimited space and freedom from harmonic restrictions on the first three tunes. They are, respectively, a ballad performance of sustained intensity, Coltrane's solid, vibrato-less sound already becoming impregnably consistent from top to bottom of the horn; a slow to medium-paced rendition with a fascinating middle-eastern intro reminiscent of Gillespie; and a steady, measured blues, resembling those of the Davis group a year earlier, but May's rather deliberate walking style is no match for the supple swing of Chambers.

The contrast is brought home with the appearance of Chambers on the next track; *Lush Life* is the Billy Strayhorn tune, and in this carefully-routined and beautifully-played quintet reading, Coltrane's sound is a little softer, almost romantic. Garland's solo is a delight, Byrd's brash in tone and full of secondhand Brown-isms but still appealing.

Finally, with the quartet number *I Hear A Rhapsody*, at a medium bounce tempo, Coltrane stretches out comfortably while Chambers, Garland and drummer Al Heath start to cook behind him. A mixed bag, but quite well recorded and, musically, with seldom a dull moment.

KENNY BURRELL AND JOHN COLTRANE
Freight Trane/I Never Knew/Lyresto/Why Was I Born?/Big Paul
John Coltrane (ts), Tommy Flanagan (p), Kenny Burrell (g), Paul Chambers (b), Jimmy Cobb (d), March 1958.
Prestige VDJ-1533
AAD Running time: 39.33
Performance: ★ ★   Recording: ★ ★

Though hardly an obvious front-line team, Burrell and Coltrane were apparently good friends and the results from this typical Prestige 'blowing' date were quite good. On the atrociously-named opener, Trane blasts in, after a well-turned unison theme, with a probing, rhythmically-varied solo; Burrell follows, then Flanagan. Burrell sets up *I Never Knew* at a fairly easy tempo, but the rhythm section soon starts to cook again, and there are nice solos from Flanagan and Chambers. A catchy theme, *Lyresto* really swings, with Chambers' line supplying harmonic solidity as well as a springy rhythmic bounce. While the rhythm section lays out, Burrell accompanies Trane then plays a chord solo on *Why Was I Born?*; the last track is a medium blues.

If nothing extraordinary for Coltrane, this set is memorable enough for the contributions of the others. Recorded in mono by van Gelder, the sound is a little less clear and lively than on some similar dates, perhaps because of the need to balance guitar and tenor satisfactorily.

AFRICA
Dial Africa/Tanganyika Strut/Gold Coast/ Oomba/B.J.1/Anedac/Once In A While
1–4 Wilbur Harden (tp, flug), Curtis Fuller (tb), John Coltrane (ts), Tommy Flanagan (p), Al Jackson (b), Art Taylor (d), June 1958; 5–7 Howard Williams (p) replaces Flanagan, May 1958.
Savoy ZD70818
AAD Running time: 58.45
Performance: ★ ★ **Recording:** ★ ★ ★

Coltrane's contribution again provided reason enough for the repackaging of these two dates under the leadership of trumpeter/ flugelhornist Wilbur Harden. Despite the atmospheric tom-toms and striking theme, *Dial Africa* soon settles into a minor-key blues groove (with an exceptional solo from Flanagan), and the pattern is similar with the next two titles. *Oomba* turns more strongly to African roots, discarding Western thematic ideas completely. Coltrane flourishes here, but Fuller sounds rather at a loss.

After this, the essentially conventional blowing of the May date sounds ordinary. *B.J.1.* is almost a parody of a mid-tempo bop blues theme, while *Anedac* repeats the formula at a slightly more deliberate pace. But the last track is a truly outstanding ballad, with good performances by Harden and Fuller prefacing a ravishing Coltrane solo. Once again, superbly recorded by van Gelder (though Jackson's bass sounds a little flaccid) and perhaps better value than the *Countdown* set, this disc lacks the significance or impact of *Blue Train* or *Giant Steps* from the same period.

JOHN COLTRANE AND THE JAZZ GIANTS
Airegin/Mating Call/Monk's Mood/Trinkle, Tinkle/I Love You/Soft Lights And Sweet Music/Billie's Bounce/Lover/Russian Lullaby/Invitation
1 Miles Davis (tp), John Coltrane (ts), Red Garland (p), Paul Chambers (b), Philly Joe Jones (d), October 1956; 2 Coltrane (ts), Tadd Dameron (p), John Simmons (b), Jones (d), November 1956; 3 Coltrane (ts), Thelonius Monk (p), Wilbur Ware (b), April 1957; 4 add Shadow Wilson (d), probably July 1957; 5 Coltrane (ts), Earl May (b), Art Taylor (d), August 1957; 6 Coltrane (ts), Garland (p), Chambers (b), Taylor (d), August 1957; 7 Donald Byrd (tp), Coltrane (ts), Garland (p), George Joyner (b), Taylor (d), December 1957; 8 Chambers (b) and

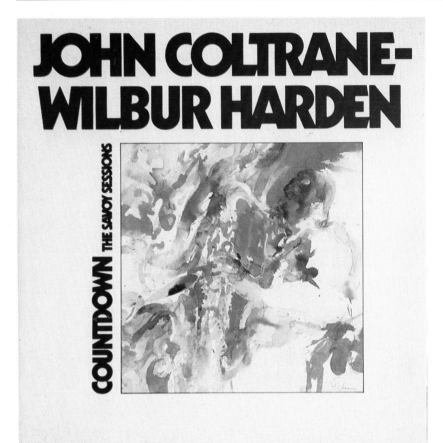

Louis Hayes (d) replace Joyner and Taylor, January 1958; 9 Byrd out, Taylor (d) replaces Hayes, February 1958; 10 Wilbur Harden (tp), Coltrane (ts), Garland (p), Chambers (b), Jimmy Cobb (d), July 1958
Prestige FCD-60-014
AAD Running time: 68.11
Performance: ★ ★ ★   Recording: ★ ★ ★

This set offers examples of Coltrane's work on the Prestige label, mostly as a featured sideman rather than as leader, in the years 1956 to 1958; rounding out the collection are two memorable tracks with Monk, originally recorded for Riverside. All the material has been issued on LP and much of it is now on CD, many tracks being duplicated in other selections reviewed here. But none of this stops the disc being exceptional value for money. Apart from his obvious technical mastery, Coltrane at this period was already a player of unmatched intensity whose sound simply commanded attention. Here he is revealed as bustling and explosive with Miles, lyrical with Monk, imperious with Garland; it is a collection which does show, in an appealingly chronological way, just what happened when Coltrane was teamed with the other musicians that Prestige call, without much exaggeration for once, the jazz giants.

SOULTRANE
Good Bait/I Want To Talk About You/You Say You Care/Theme For Ernie/Russian Lullaby
John Coltrane (ts), Red Garland (p), Paul Chambers (b), Art Taylor (d), February 1958
Prestige VDJ-1502
AAD Running time: 39.54
Performance: ★ ★ ★   Recording: ★ ★ ★

On the face of it, this is yet another casual Prestige blowing session with the then ubiquitous Coltrane; but this one is different, firstly in that it is Coltrane's session and he is the only horn present, and secondly in the unusual quality and empathy of the rhythm section. To hear Trane stating the theme of *Good Bait* is to appreciate his feeling for what had gone before, but to hear his solo (a long and comprehensive exploration of the theme's possibilities) is to witness a man looking ahead; the next track is a great ballad performance, lyrical yet absolutely unsentimental.

Red Garland is a perfect accompanist, though his glistening tone and gentle approach can make his solos seem like a downward change of gear after Coltrane's. Meanwhile, Taylor is exuberant, Chambers intensely swinging and always interesting. A fast *Russian Lullaby* (far removed indeed from the intentions of composer Irving Berlin) shows just what heights this group of exceptional musicians could reach. In short, this is happy, buoyant and unfettered Coltrane, captured appealingly with that warm van Gelder sound, and not to be missed.

COUNTDOWN/THE SAVOY SESSIONS
Wells Fargo (2 takes)/E.F.F.P.H./ Countdown (2 takes)/Rhodomagnetics (2 takes)/Snuffy/West 42nd Street
Wilbur Harden (flug), John Coltrane (ts), Tommy Flanagan (p), Doug Watkins (b), Louis Hayes (d), March 1958.
Savoy ZD70529
AAD Running time: 68.03
Performance: ★ ★   Recording: ★ ★ ★

Recorded under the leadership of Wilbur Harden, this was one of many 1958 dates on which Coltrane appeared as a dominant, hard-blowing sideman. The 'van Gelder sound' of the recording is appealing as always, the rhythm section is one of the very best, and as the shortest track turned out to be just over seven minutes long, there was plenty of unrestricted blowing. E.F.F.P.H. bubbles and boils over an Afro-Cuban beat, while Countdown is a very fast blues, superbly driven by Taylor; the medium-fast Snuffy is the ghost of a be-bop tune, while Harden's theme and solo for the last track, an attractive medium bounce, is straightforwardly 'cool' Miles. In the end, though, the only reason for this reissue (as the notes admit) is the presence of Coltrane. The alternate takes do offer differing solos, but they also mean that the content of the disc is somewhat less substantial than the playing time suggests.

LIVE IN STOCKHOLM 1963
Mr PC/Traneing In/Spiritual/I Want To Talk About You
John Coltrane (ss, ts), McCoy Tyner (p), Jimmy Garrison (b), Elvin Jones (d), Stockholm, October 1963.
Affinity CD CHARLY 33
AAD Running time: 41.46
Performance: ★ ★ ★   Recording: ★

For Coltrane, 1963 had already been an eventful and much-recorded year when he paid his third successive autumn visit to Scandinavia. This recording comes from a concert at the Konserthausen, Stockholm, where the Coltrane group plus Eric Dolphy had been recorded two years before (the results are on the Affinity album Coltraneology Vol 1). The quartet is heard here in a settled period after the work with

Dolphy, and before the arrival of the true 'free' players.
The four long numbers are all on familiar themes. Mr PC is named for Paul Chambers, who appeared on Coltrane's first recording of the tune on Giant Steps in 1959; Traneing In dates back to 1957; while Coltrane had first adopted Billy Eckstine's I Want To Talk About You in 1958 (it appears on Soultrane, also reviewed); Spiritual appeared, with Dolphy, on Live At The Village Vanguard (Impulse). The music is bursting with energy and there are excellent solos from Tyner — on Traneing In, his solo reaches a level where only Coltrane could have followed without bathos. Needless to say, he does so, with a magisterial entry which perhaps reflects something of the influence of Hodges. I Want To Talk About You is deeper, firmer and extended by a long and riveting candenza. Recording quality is a little distant and even fuzzy at times, but not sufficiently below par to lessen the impact of the music.

A LOVE SUPREME
Acknowledgement/Resolution/Pursuance/ Psalm
John Coltrane (ts), McCoy Tyner (p), Jimmy Garrison (b), Elvin Jones (d), September 1964
MCA Impulse MCAD-5660
AAD Running time: 33.09
Performance: ★ ★ ★   Recording: ★ ★

Not all of Coltrane's work on the Impulse label had pleased the critics; most of them had been able to welcome Giant Steps as an exciting exploration not too far beyond the familiar territory of hard bop, but were not equipped to accept the stark newness of Live At The Village Vanguard. With a A Love Supreme, Coltrane produced a work whose clear unity of purpose and dedicated execution swept aside such quibbles, and it remains a milestone. From the first section Acknowledgement, in which the words A Love Supreme are repeated, the music progresses through the stern Resolution to the quicksilver Pursuance, and finally to the majestic Psalm.
Apart from the benefit of not having to turn the record over (an important aid to appreciation here), the Compact Disc does full justice to the power and the delicacy of Jones' drums (particularly in Pursuance) and Garrison's bass. Although there is an occasional suspicion of added hardness, the remastering has brought out Coltrane's tenor in all its consistent strength and beauty.

CHICK COREA
(b. Chelsea, Massachusetts, 6 December, 1941)

Though at one time closely identified with a rather narrow commercial fusion of jazz and rock, Armando 'Chick' Corea is in fact a thoughtful keyboard virtuoso and composer who has brought a wide range of influences into his music.

Corea started on piano at the age of four, encouraged by his father, Armando senior, who played trumpet and bass; by his early teens Chick was playing in his father's bands in local clubs. At eighteen he went to Columbia University in Manhattan, but stayed only two months. He returned home to prepare for an audition at Juilliard, where he studied until, dissatisfied with formal training, he left to become a professional musician. He had been interested in Latin music since high school days and his first important gigs were with Mongo Santamaria (1962) and Willie Bobo.

Though he recorded with Stan Getz and Herbie Mann, it was Corea's rather fragmented period with Miles Davis that established him as one of the pioneers of jazz-rock. He appeared on the *Filles de Kilimanjaro* album in 1968, later replacing Herbie Hancock as a regular member of the Davis group and contributing (along with Keith Jarrett) to *In A Silent Way*, *Bitches' Brew* and *Big Fun*. Davis encouraged Corea to play electric keyboards all the time, apparently even stopping him from using an acoustic grand piano on gigs where one was available. Leaving Davis, Corea formed Circle in 1970, the other members being Anthony Braxton, Dave Holland on bass and Barry Altschul, drums. The group folded when Corea left in 1971. Then, with bassist Stanley Clarke, he formed the durable jazz-rock group Return to Forever, which featured Airto Moreira and Al DiMeola and despite changes of personnel, produced a string of consistently successful albums.

By the mid-1970s, Corea was also in great demand as a solo performer. He formed a piano duo with Herbie Hancock, and also

made some very successful concert appearances with vibraphonist Gary Burton. At the end of the decade he worked with saxophonist Michael Brecker, bassist Eddie Gomez and drummer Steve Gadd to produce the 1981 *Three Quartets* album, then formed the trio with Vitous and Haynes which is captured at length on *Trio Music*. More recent projects have included a recording featuring Steve Kajula on flute.

Corea's extensive body of work on the ECM label is being comprehensively reissued on Compact Disc, and the catalogue now includes the sampler *Works*, which must be recommended; the small number of titles reviewed below have been chosen to briefly represent the variety of music which this gifted and still prolific pianist/composer has already produced.

EARLY DAYS
The Brain/Converge/Waltz For Bill Evans/Sundance/Dave/Vamp/Jamala
Woody Shaw (tp), Hubert Laws (fl, pic), Bennie Maupin (ts), Chick Corea (p, el p), Horace Arnold, Jack De Johnette (d), Dave Holland (b), 1969
Denon 33C38 7969
AAD Running time: 67.24
Performance: ★ ★   Recording: ★ ★

Maupin, De Johnette, Holland and Corea himself all worked for Miles Davis during 1969, but though sometimes frenetic, the music produced on this session doesn't seem to be underlined by the sheer creative tension that Davis infused in the studio. While *The Brain* has a fast pulse to propel the Coltraneisms of Maupin, *Sundance* features a characteristically frenzied Corea attack on the piano keyboard.

On *Vamp*, Corea turns to the electric instrument, starting lyrically and building to a central section in which Shaw adds a slender Harmon-mute sound to the ensemble interplay of Laws and Maupin. *Coverage* is a superbly constructed nocturnal collage, starting with a threateningly repeated chirrup from Laws, Holland then adding a frog-like booming note to create the effect of a menacing night in some tropical cave. The recording is generally dry and a little hard in character, and, typically for the time, there is little attempt to use stereo to create space. The music itself can have a claustrophobic effect too, and in some aspects sounds derivative and dated. But much of it is very effective and in any case documents an important period in Corea's progress to fame.

CHICK COREA: PIANO IMPROVISATIONS Vol 2
After Noon Song/Song For Lee Lee/Song For Thad/Trinkle Tinkle/Masqualero/Preparation1/Preparation 2/Departure From Planet Earth/A New Place: Arrival/Scenery/Imps Walk/Rest.
Chick Corea (p), April 1971.
ECM 1020 829 190
AAD Running time: 40.12
Performance: ★ ★   Recording: ★ ★ ★

This acoustic solo work from Corea includes a couple of tunes written by others as well as the expected originals, which include the suite-like second half of the album. Corea's tribute to Monk (*Monk's Trinkle Tinkle*) is appropriate and cunningly executed, but has

a hurried quality which seems to have often been a hallmark of Corea's playing at this period, but never appeared in Monk's; the other non-original is an appealing reading of Wayne Shorter's dramatic *Masqualero*.

There is an abrupt change of direction as we come to *Preparation*, in which Corea invokes anxiety and tension with nerve shredding repetitions and discords; he makes the piano rumble portentously for *Departure*, pedal full on, hitting it inside and out as tension and speed increase to unbearable levels, and finally conveys the sensation of things rushing past as we leave planet Earth. *A New Place* completes this programmatic journey, with repetition now conveying brightness, expectation, hope and, at last, *Rest*. Excellent if rather close recording.

CHICK COREA: TRIO MUSIC, LIVE IN EUROPE
The Loop/I Hear A Rhapsody/Summer Night; Night and Day/Prelude No 2; Mock-up/Transformation/Hittin' It/Mirovisions.
Chick Corea (p), Miroslav Vitous (b), Roy Haynes (d), September 1984.
ECM 1310 827 769
AAD Running time: 62.00
Performance: ★ ★ ★   Recording: ★ ★ ★

Recorded at two German venues, this set effectively captures over an hour of music from a happy and extremely creative trio. Corea echoes the sound of Bill Evans on the opener, building from an introductory haze of chords to a free-sounding jazz waltz. He sparkles, too, on *Rhapsody*: after an expansive treatment of the theme, his solo revels in the twists and turns of this tune's changes. He is rhapsodic on an out-of-tempo

Summer Night, which first acquires a beat, then, after an interlude, metamorphoses quite naturally into an up-tempo and richly-chorded *Night and Day*.

The *Prelude No 2* belongs to the Russian composer Scriabin, and seems (from the sound) to mark a switch to the more cavernous of the two venues. Corea's piano sound here is lush and lucid, and the audience evidently held spellbound. From this, after some wandering, he segues into *Mock Up,* displaying his Spanish affinities with flurrying runs and a steadily building rhythmic intensity. *Transformation* is Vitous' arco tribute to the great cellist Pablo Casals while *Hittin' It* is an attractively melodic-sounding feature for the great Roy Haynes, the resourceful, distinctively fresh and vital sounding drummer whose work is often brash and forthright but never seems bombastic. His drums are very well recorded, as indeed are all three instruments in this clean sounding trio, and it is hard to fault this disc.

CHICK COREA: THE CHICK COREA ELEKTRIC BAND
City Gate/Rumble/Side Walk/Cool Weasel Boogie/Got A Match?/Elektric City/No Zone/King Cockroach/India Town/All Love/Silver Temple.
1, 8, 11 Chick Corea (key), Scott Henderson (g), John Pattitucci (el b), Dave Weckle (d, el d); 2 Corea (key), Weckle (d, el d, perc); 3 Corea (key), Carlos Rios (g), Weckle (d, el d); 4, 6 Corea (key), Rios (g), Pattitucci(b, el b), Weckle (d); 5, 7, 9, 10 Corea (key), Pattitucci (b, el b), Weckle (d), 1986.
GRP D9535
AAD Running time: 57.38
Performance: ★ ★   Recording: ★ ★

Track titles and visual presentation leave little room for doubt as to the intention of this set, Corea clearly ready with synth drums and ráp culture (in a rather self-conscious and polite form), to get back down to the street. Keyboards and electronics aside, there are good contributions from the two guitarists here; Rios soars excitingly, sometimes with shades of Carlos Santana, on the appallingly named *Cool Weasel Boogie,* a contrast to the high-energy hard rock sound of the equally dextrous Scott Henderson.

While Henderson solos (as on *King Cockroach*), Pattituci switches to Fender bass, but on several numbers he puts in a virtuoso performance on the upper registers of his Smith & Jackson six string bass. Among these, and in fact something of a standout track, is the incredibly fast and effervescent *Got A Match,* in which Corea explores the more electric areas of his generally more familiar Spanish-tinged territory with dazzling runs.

Corea wrests predictable sitar effects from the keyboards in the gentler *India Town,* though the gong and synth bass make a poor substitute for Indian percussion. Showing his virtuoso command of synthesizer options he goes for more orchestral sounds on the final *Silver Temple,* where a fragmented melody full of MOR changes and suspensions produces the strange effect of distant Muzak; the set reaches its final resting place, though it is not a strange one.

Recording quality is nothing if not dynamic, with the usual GRP clarity, if a certain hardness in the sound; though this may accord with the content, it reinforces the idea that not everyone will love this bright, intensely electric music.

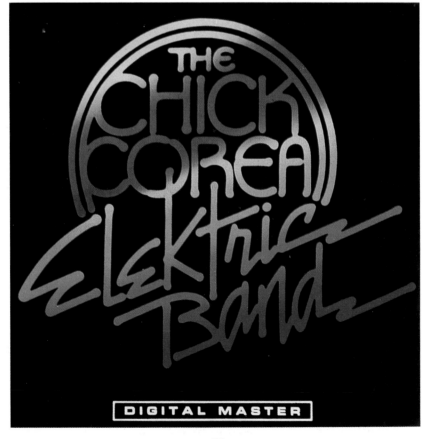

MILES DAVIS
(b. Alton, Illinois, 25 May 1926)

Recently, Miles Davis has yet again been transmuting the materials around him into the gold of his own music. It is a kind of alchemy that he has performed regularly, with fresh results every time, for forty years.

Miles Dewey Davis III was a year old when his family moved to East St Louis. His father, a successful dentist, gave him a trumpet on his thirteenth birthday, and while still at high school, he worked with Eddie Randall's Blue Devils. In 1944, he deputised for third trumpet Buddy Anderson when the Eckstine band (which included Charlie Parker and Dizzy Gillespie) played St Louis, and stayed with the band two weeks. After this encounter, he was determined to get to New York, and enrolled at Juilliard School of Music. He first recorded in May 1945, with vocalist Rubberlegs Williams, but vastly more

Ever seeking new directions for his music (sometimes not at all to the liking of jazz purists!), Miles Davis remains an exciting and unique performer, and an inspiration.

significant was his appearance on Parker's Savoy date, 26 November.

While Gillespie and Parker headed for the West Coast, Davis went back to East St Louis, then joined Benny Carter's band for a tour which took him to Los Angeles. Here he played and recorded (on Dial) in what was to become the classic Parker quintet; Miles' deliberately understated trumpet provided the perfect foil for Parker. Back in New York, Miles also played and contributed themes on Bird's 1947 Savoy sessions.

By 1948, Miles was enough of a 'name' to assemble the ambitious *Birth of the Cool* nonet, which recorded a dozen arrangements by Gil Evans and Gerry Mulligan for Capitol in 1949–50. Despite critical acclaim, the records did not sell, and from 1951 Davis was recording for a smaller company, Prestige, notably with Sonny Rollins. But it was in autumn 1955 that he put together his first first great quintet. With Miles' haunting muted trumpet, the explosive tenor of John Coltrane, forceful drums of Philly Joe Jones and delicate piano of Red Garland gave the group a new balance and power.

After the quintet's first album, Prestige agreed to release Miles provided he still recorded the four albums outstanding in his contract, and the resources of Columbia allowed him to develop bigger projects. *Miles Ahead*, recorded in May 1957 was the first of several collaborations in which Gil Evans directed a large ensemble to provide a concerto-like setting for Miles' trumpet and flugelhorn. Miles also went from strength to strength with his small group, which became a sextet through the addition of Cannonball Adderley, and in 1959 reached the serene new heights of *Kind of Blue*.

By 1960, Miles' success enabled him to record more or less when, and what, he wanted to, but as the decade wore on, CBS was becoming more interested in the exploding rock market. *Miles In The Sky* (1968), on which Herbie Hancock used an electric piano, marked another new beginning. Miles showed, as Ian Carr put it, that: 'jazz into rock will go', and keyboardists Hancock, Zawinul, Jarrett and Corea were all shaped by working with Davis. Today, he has a huge audience for both his current and earlier work, which is now at last adequately represented in the digital medium.

BAGS' GROOVE
Bags' Groove (two takes)/Airegin/Oleo/But Not For Me (take one)/Doxy/But Not For Me (take one)
1,2 Miles Davis (tp), Milt Jackson (vib), Thelonious Monk (p), Percy Heath (b), Kenny Clarke (d), December 1954; 3-7 Davis (tp), Sonny Rollins (ts), Horace Siver (p), Heath (b), Clarke (d), June 1954
Prestige VDJ-1531
AAD Running time: 46.17
Performance: ★ ★ ★   Recording: ★

The classic *Bags' Groove* is well conveyed on Compact Disc, especially the leader's spitting and crackling trumpet sound, echoing yet intimately captured. On a modern hi-fi system, the heavily reverberant recording, which had served to give the mono sound life and vitality, sounds a bit too obviously faked, but it still has immediacy and impact. It was at this tense Christmas Eve session that Davis insisted on Monk being silent during his solos and (especially on take two) the pianist's own solo is wonderfully, and it would seem pointedly, perverse. Jackson actually sounds almost cautious here in comparison with his more characteristically uninhibited work.

The rest of this set comes from another epochal Prestige date a few months earlier, on which Sonny Rollins not only played with Miles but also contributed three tunes, two at least of which have become jazz standards; so Rollins, clearly at an early peak, is relaxed, confident and tuneful, his tone big and warm. The sound on this session is a little dryer, clean and detailed, and in fact excellent for the year. If not absolutely an essential disc, this transitional Davis group does make for fascinating comparison with the quintet featuring Coltrane, which finally gelled in 1956.

BAGS GROOVE
MILES DAVIS
sonny rollins, milt jackson
thelonious monk, horace silver
percy heath, kenny clarke
PRESTIGE 7109

COOKIN'/WITH THE MILES DAVIS QUINTET/PRESTIGE 7094

VDJ-1512

MILES DAVIS: WALKIN'
Walkin'/Blue'n Boogie/Solar/You Don't
Know What Love Is/Love Me Or Leave Me.
1,2 Miles Davis (tp), J J Johnson (tb), Lucky
Thompson (ts), Horace Silver (p), Percy
Heath (b), Kenny Clarke (d), April 29 1954;
3-5 Davis (tp), Davey Schildkraut (as), Silver
(p), Heath (b), Clarke (d), April 1954.
Prestige VDJ 1541
AAD Running time: 37.55
Performance: ★ ★   Recording: ★ ★

The sextet session of April 29 did not turn
out as planned, but in *Walkin'* produced a
classic 'cool' blues. Apparently, Lucky
Thompson had written arrangements for the
date, but somehow the group just could not
make them work and they had to be
abandoned for familiar material. It does not
seem too fanciful to hear traces of the
resulting tensions in the music; Thompson,
often underrated, blows a smouldering,
compelling tenor both on *Walkin'* and on the
faster twelve-bar, Gillespie's *Blue'n'Boogie*.

These performances foreshadow Silver's
later groups, while the spare, introspective
but still swinging sound of *Solar*, from the
3 April quintet date, has the elements of the
later Davis style but in a less perfected
setting. The trumpeter does not completely
discard the original theme on the ballad *You
Don't Know What Love is*, but seems
reluctant to refer to it too obviously, while
Love Me Or Leave me still has the lingering
flavour of the be-bop era. Schildkraut offers
a well-finished and full-toned alto style
which nonetheless lacks the bite of Art
Pepper or the ear-catching idiosyncracy of
Paul Desmond, and so, at least by
comparison with Davis' most cohesive
group, this is an album of transitional music.

COOKIN'
My Funny Valentine/Blues By Five/Airegin/
Medley: Tune Up; When Lights Are Low
Miles Davis (tp), John Coltrane (ts), Red
Garland (p), Paul Chambers (b), Philly Joe
Jones (d), October 1956.
Prestige VDJ-1512
AAD Running time: 33.40
Performance: ★ ★ ★   Recording: ★ ★ ★

Two marathon sessions, on 11 May and
25 October 1956, produced enough material
for four Prestige albums, released over the
following three years. *Cookin'* was the first
of these, though the tracks came from the
second of the two sessions. Basically, the
quintet went into the studio and played its
repertoire as if on a club date. So
consistently excellent were the results that
there is little to be said about *Cookin'* that
does not equally apply to the other three
titles, all now available in this series.

The quintet had perfected its routines, was
working with an incredible degree of
rapport, especially in the rhythm section,
and provided Miles with the balance he had
been looking for: the turbulent Coltrane
offered the perfect foil for his own trumpet,
while the subtle Garland set the scene.
Despite the period tape hiss (never really
intrusive) these monaural recordings have
preserved the music admirably, and sound
excellent on silver disc; the only criticism of
any of the four CDs is that, collectively, they
represent poor value for money compared
with the long-current double-album vinyl
sets entitled *Miles Davis* (with the contents
of *Cookin'* and *Relaxin'*, originally Prestige
7094 and 7129) and *Working' and Steamin'*
(repackaging Prestige 7166 and 7200
respectively).

KIND OF BLUE

So What/Freddie Freeloader/Blue In Green/
All Blues/Flamenco Sketches
1 Miles Davis (tp), Julian 'Cannonball'
Adderley (as), John Coltrane(ts), Bill Evans
(p), Paul Chambers (b), Jimmy Cobb (d); 2
Wynton Kelly (p), replaces Evans; 3 as 1,
Adderley out, March 1959; 4, 5 as 1, April
1959.
CBS CDCBS 62066
AAD Running time: 45.12
Performance: ★ ★ ★
Recording: ★ ★ ★

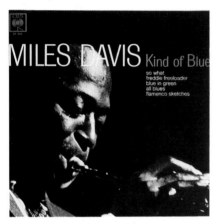

Miles Davis may not yet have had quite the
longest career in jazz, but no-one can come
close to matching the number of times he has
asserted and reasserted his influence and
supremacy. One such moment came with
Kind Of Blue in 1959. Evans had left some
months before the famous March 2 date, but
Davis wanted him for the session; and it was
Evans who set the mood for *So What*, a

much-copied theme which simply and
elegantly moves back and forth between two
tonalities. Kelly, who was the group's
regular pianist at the time, appears only to
apply his own unmistakeable combination of
crisply mobile, 'modern' harmonic sense,
blues feeling and swing to the superbly
economical 12-bar, *Freddie Freeloader*. *Blue
In Green*, which Benny Green's liner note
described as a 10-bar 'fragment of
melancholia' and the utterly remarkable *All
Blues* (often 'covered' but seldom
approached) are both classic archetypes.
Flamenco Sketches, with its pure, pearl-like
solo from Coltrane, a lyrical contribution
from Adderley and forward-looking piano
from Evans closes a complete, coherent and
enormously influential piece of work.
Fortunately, it sounds just as good on
Compact Disc.

SKETCHES OF SPAIN

Concierto de Aranjuez/Will O' The Wisp/
The Panpiper/Saeta/Solea
1 Miles Davis (tp, flug), Bernie Glow, Ernie
Royal, Louis Mucci, Taft Jordan (tp), Frank
Rehak, Dick Hixon (tb), John Barrows, Jim
Buffington, Earl Chapin (fr h),Jay McAllister
(tu), Albert Block, Eddie Caine, Harold
Feldman (woodwinds), Danny Bank (bcl),
Paul Chambers (b), Jimmy Cobb (d), Elvin
Jones (perc), Janet Putnam (harp), Gil Evans
(arr, cond), November 1959; 2-5 Johnny
Coles (tp), Joe Singer, Tony Miranda (fr h),
Bill Barber (tu), Romeo Penque
(woodwinds), Jack Knitzer (bassoon),
replace Mucci, Jordan, Barrows, Chapin,
McAllister and Caine, March 1960.
CBS CDCBS62327
AAD Running time: 41.37
Performance: ★ ★ ★ **Recording:** ★ ★ ★

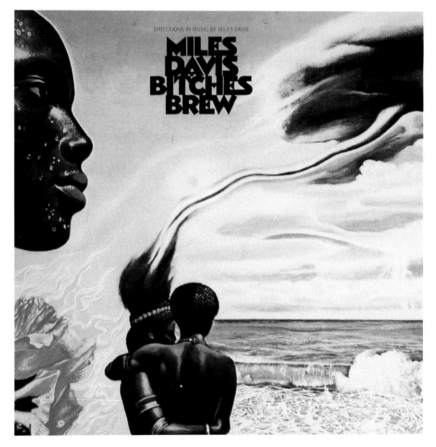

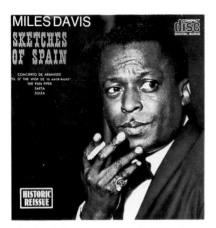

The third album project on which Davis worked with an orchestra arranged and conducted by Gil Evans, *Sketches Of Spain* in some ways represents the most impressive achievement of the three. Although their previous collaborations had sloughed off restrictive notions of what could and could not be done by a jazz soloist and orchestra, Davis and Evans were entering dramatically different territory here, and the result was another *tour de force*.

In the *Concierto de Aranjuez* of Rodrigo, Davis provides a perfect solo voice, while Evans' arrangement offers tonal colours which would be simply astounding if they were not also so natural; and as a conductor, the ever meticulous Evans extracts performances which are flawless yet full of life. The CD transfer is fine, though with perhaps just a slight thinning and loss of 'space', but whatever the medium, this disc certainly deserves the 'Historic Reissue' label it carries.

BITCHES BREW

Pharaoh's Dance/Bitches Brew/Spanish Key/John McLaughlin/Miles Runs The Voodoo Down/Sanctuary
1,3 Miles Davis (tp), Wayne Shorter (ss), Benny Maupin (bcl), Chick Corea, Joe Zawinul, Larry Young (el b), John McLaughlin (g), Dave Holland (b), Harvey Brooks (el b), Lenny White, Jack DeJohnette, Charles Alias (d), Jim Riley (perc); 2, 6 Young out; 4, 5 Zawinul out; August 1969.
CBS CDCBS 66236
AAD Running time: 93.59 (2 discs)
Performance: ★ ★   Recording: ★ ★

In February 1969, Miles had broken new ground with the recording of *In A Silent Way*, which had been the result of maximum spontaneity in the studio (Zawinul and McLaughlin both being last minute recruits) and a lot of editing. With that album the jazz trumpet star finally shot into the rock firmament; for *Bitches Brew*, he added more drums and percussion as well as more keyboards and the bass clarinet of Benny Maupin. Although there was still a lot of editing, the end result was a set of six long tracks in which the music, propelled by repetition, develops through hypersensitive interaction of the players. The sound is dense, often dark and menacing, with heavy, indistinctly overlaid bass notes and distorted electric keyboard sounds (there are still doubts about who actually played on which tracks) sometimes creating the dirty, gritty and grainy sound quality typical of multi-tracked rock records in the early 1970s. Maupin and McLaughlin often rise above the *melee*, but the leader's full, declamatory trumpet soars unhindered and effortlessly over the boiling ferment below.

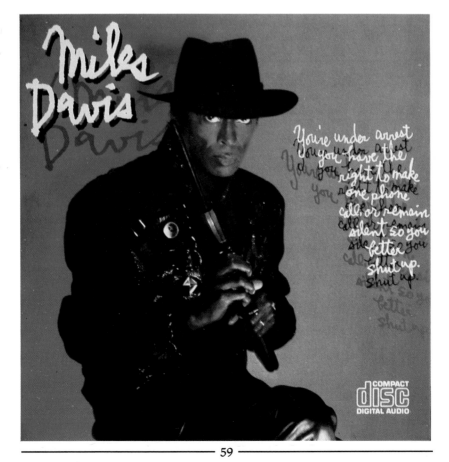

YOU'RE UNDER ARREST
One Phone Call; Street Scenes/Human
Nature/Intro;MD1; Something's On Your
Mind; MD2/Ms Morrisne/Katia Prelude/
Katia/Time After Time/You're Under
Arrest/Medley: JeanPierre; You're Under
Arrest; Then There Were None
1 Miles Davis (tp, voices); Bob Berg (ss),
Robert Irving III (synth), John Scofield (g),
Darryl Jones (b), Al Foster (d), Steve
Thornton (perc, voice), Sting (voice), Marek
Olko (voice), James Prindiville ('handcuffs');
2, 3 Davis (tp), Irving (synth), Jones (b),
Scofield (g), Vince Wilburn Jr (d), Thornton
(perc); 7 Davis (tp), Irving (synth), Scofield
(g), Darryl Jones (b), Al Foster (d), Steve
Thornton (d); 8 Davis (tp), Berg (ts), Irving
(synth), Jones (b), Foster (d), Thornton
(perc); 9 as 8 add Scofield (g), 1985
CBS CD26447
AAD Running time: 42.18
Performance ★ ★　Recording ε ε

Standing out as a new Miles anthem is the
relaxed, catchy melody of *Human Nature*, in
which the most distinctive trumpet sound in
jazz lands on a piece of quintessentially
popular material. But *You're Under Arrest*
has much else to offer, even apart from the
programmatic opening (street noises,
policeman's voices, the arrest). The classic
Miles sound is strongly melodic again in
Cyndi Lauper's *Time After Time*, floating
over plangent guitar chords on a near-
caribbean beat, like a warm, velvety-dark
summer night. For *Ms Morrisine*, Davis
adopts an open horn sound tailing off the
notes like a wilting, despairing member of
the Tijuana Brass. Then in the final medley
the 1980's are closing in on us again. It is
sonically superb too.

TUTU
Tutu/Tomaas-Portia/Splatch/Backyard
Ritual/Perfect Way/Don't Lose Your Mind/
Full Nelson
Miles Davis (tp), Marcus Miller (synth, b
etc), with: 1 Paulinho de Costa (perc); 2
Paulinho da Costa, Omar Hakim (perc),
Bernard Wright (synth); 4 Steve Reid (perc);
5 George Duke (key); 7 Bernard Wright
(synth); 7 Michael Urbaniak (el vln), 1986.
Warner Bros 925 490
AAD Running time: 42.24
Performance: ★ ★ ★　Recording: ★ ★ ★

There is no doubt that the year 1986 saw yet
another renaissance for Miles, who
celebrated his sixtieth birthday in April. The
Trumpeter ended his thirty year association
with Columbia when he signed with a new
record company, and *Tutu* was his first
album for Warner Bros. Most of the sounds
on the album were produced by multi-
instrumentalist and master of the synthesizer
Marcus Miller; on the title track, he creates
great monochrome caverns of sound for
Miles to stand in. Over an edgy street beat,
Miles' sound on *Tomaas* has all that
uniquely lone, distant but invulnerable
quality. George Duke is a prominent guest
on *Backyard Ritual*, which makes use of a
wistful fragment of a tune, assembled over
an irresistible beat.
　Some ears will continue to find the
electronic instruments lacking in colour and
timbre, but interest never flags, and Miles, as
always, maintains creative tension.
Production and recording are superb, though
this is a disc which challenges the abilities of
the replay system (it will sound muddy and
gritty and mediocre equipment), and more
important, it swings.

JACK DEJOHNETTE
(b. Chicago, Illinois, 9 August 1942)

DeJohnette began on the piano at the age of four, and kept up his classical studies for ten years. But early on he also started listening to jazz, largely through an uncle who was a top Chicago disc jockey and had an enormous record collection. In his middle teens, DeJohnette was already playing piano in cocktail bars, but by the early 1960s he had joined the free jazz movement known as AACM (Association for the Advancement of Creative Musicians), and became associated with Sun Ra, Joseph Jarman and others. He studied briefly at Wilson Junior College, but then, in 1966, decided to visit New York. Fortunately, sitting in at jam sessions immediately led to a job as drummer with John Patton, and he never used his return ticket.

A three-year stint with the popular group led by saxophonist Charles Lloyd set the seal on De Johnette's reputation, but perhaps his biggest career boost came from a period with Miles Davis, when he worked on *Bitches Brew*. He has worked with singers including Abbey Lincoln and Betty Carter, and with great jazz stars ranging from Stan Getz to Sonny Rollins to Freddie Hubbard; most recently, his work with his own Special Edition has continued to show how versatile, dynamic and fresh-sounding a drummer he can be.

SPECIAL EDITION
One For Eric/Zoot Suite/Central Park West/
India/Journey To The Twin Planet
Arthur Blythe (as), David Murray (ts, b cl),
Peter Warren (b, cello), Jack DeJohnette (d,
p, melodica), March 1979.
ECM 827 694
AAD Running time: 39.25
Performance: ★ ★ ★   Recording:

NEW DIRECTIONS IN EUROPE
Salsa For Eddie G/Where Or Wayne/Bayou
Fever/Multo Spiliagio
Lester Bowie (tp), John Abercrombie (g),
Eddie Gomez (b), Jack DeJohnette (d, p),
Switzerland, June 1979.
ECM 829 158
AAD Running time: 56.38
Performance ★ ★   Recording ★ ★ ★

With two important and powerful horn players in the group, this 'Special Edition' gives the impression of a much larger group than the quintet on the *New Directions* recording, and the music is certainly more compelling and intense; the ensemble sound is particularly arresting when Murray uses the bass clarinet, which he plays with an almost fearsome density of tone, masterful technique and deep feeling. Murray and Blythe combine to play astonishing unison passages, starting with the sharp, clean-cut asymmetry of *One For Eric*, then, in the main theme of *Zoot Suite*, offering what could be described as a virtuoso parody with a feverish riff-like be-bop/jump tune over an old-timey descending bass figure; Blythe and Murray leap off from this transmuted stylistic base into wilder explorations, again demonstrating the rapport which had begun when Murray joined Blythe and Bobby Bradford's Black Infinity Band a few years before.

In an atmospheric live recording (which is nonetheless a technically excellent one), DeJohnette's 'Special Edition' stretches out in a largely Latin-flavoured programme. After DeJohnette's typically shimmering intro, the bassist himself joins in to give heavyweight support to *Salsa for Eddie G*, which continues with Abercrombie (using his squeakier mandolin guitar on this track) and some delightfully loose Latino trumpet from Bowie. Solos from Gomez and DeJohnette resolve effortlessly back to a final statement of the catchy theme. More impressionistically, *Where Or Wayne* is buoyed up by whooshing cymbals and features Bowie in a different vein, making reference to the fragmented ballad style of middle-period Miles before the band falls into an understated yet tough and insistent urban groove. In a change of pace, Abercrombie shoots off urgent phrases over a doubled pulse from DeJohnette, then hands over to Gomez.

AL DI MEOLA
(b. Jersey City, New Jersey, 22 July 1954)

Bringing to his instrument the combination of superb technical ability and a comprehensive musical training, in the mid-1970s Al Di Meola reasserted the guitar's true power and versatility in the keyboard-dominated world of jazz-rock.

His father introduced him to Italian classical music, but the young Di Meola also drew early inspiration from the work of Tal Farlow, Kenny Burrell and others; he began his guitar studies at the age of eight, under Robert Aslanian. After school, he studied at Berklee music college for a short time, then worked in a quintet led by Barry Miles. He joined Chick Corea's Return To Forever in 1974, and appeared on the albums *Where Have I Known You Before?*, *No Mystery* and *Romantic Warrior*. Leaving to pursue a solo career in 1976, he developed his own personal synthesis of electrified instrumental jazz/rock, drawing heavily on Spanish (flamenco) and Latin music, which was heard to the full effect in the 1977 album *Elegant Gipsy*.

A couple of years later, he became a member of the all-star acoustic guitar trio which also included John McLaughlin and the great flamenco guitarist Paco de Lucia, which undertook very successful international tours and produced the big-selling albums *Friday Night In San Francisco* (1980) and *Passion, Grace And Fire*. Di Meola, of course, continues to work in an electric context too, and has recently made use of guitar synthesizers to expand his already formidable instrumental resources.

TOUR DE FORCE - LIVE
Elegant Gipsy Suite/Nena/Advantage/ Egyptian Danza/Race With The Devil On Spanish Highway/Cruisin'.
Al Di Meola (g), Jan Hammer, Victor Godsey (key), Anthony Jackson (b), Steve Gadd (d), Mingo Lewis (perc), February 1982.
CBS CDCBS 25121
AAD Running time: 39.16
Performance: ★ ★   Recording: ★ ★

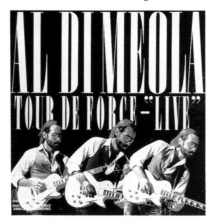

All the band members here had played on Di Meola's albums, but this was the first time they had appeared together on a concert stage. The set opens with the title suite from the *Elegant Gipsy* album, though sound is heavier as it gets into a gritty rock groove. *Nena* is a pretty tune, Di Meola's virtuoso guitar remaining controlled and tender over a straightforward, uppish samba beat, while *Egyptian Danza*, with its overtones of the belly-dance, is built over more challenging rhythms from Steve Gadd, a hectic first section giving way to a moderate loping beat, which accelerates to a frenzied climax. Again from *Elegant Gipsy*, the *Race With The*

Devil On A Spanish Highway is similarly fiercer than the studio track, though dynamic contrasts are reduced. Clearly, this was a very successful concert and well captured on disc, although the actual sound quality is unremittingly strident; how much this will detract depends on the replay system, and also, of course, on whether the driving, upbeat side of Di Meola is appreciated in such undiluted form.

PASSION GRACE AND FIRE
Aspan/Orient Blue/Chiquito/Sichia/David/ Passion, Grace And Fire
John McLaughlin, Al Di Meola, Paco de Lucia (g), London, September-October 1982.
Philips 811 334
AAD Running time: 31.53
Performance: ★ ★   Recording: ★ ★

Recorded in London, this Philips disc effectively provided a follow up to the hugely successful CBS live recording *Friday Night In San Francisco*. Here, the studio recording has been mixed and edited with care, the three guitarists disposed (as before) to left, centre and right in the stereo stage and, in sonic terms, there is little to complain of. Democratically, the three guitarists contribute two compositions each, but the exchange of influences between the Yorkshireman, the Italian-American and the Spaniard makes this almost irrelevant, except that here the forces of flamenco have almost driven out the last traces of jazz rock.

McLaughlin's *Aspan* kicks off with an idea of flamenco drama; Di Meola's *Orient Blue* starts lyrically and reflectively, and his Ovation offers a distinctive underpinning to the gut-strung flamenco/classic guitars of the other two; Di Meola's masterful solo is a tribute not only to his technique but also to the versatility of his instrument. The title track is Di Meola's evocation of the flamenco world, executed with power and gusto.

ERIC DOLPHY
(b. Los Angeles, 20 June 1928; d. Berlin, 29 June 1964)

Associated with Ornette Coleman, Charles Mingus, Max Roach, George Russell and above all John Coltrane, the multi-instrumentalist Eric Dolphy became an important figure in the 'new jazz' of the 1960's, before his premature death at thirty-six.

In his youth Dolphy mastered several woodwind instruments, but was also inspired, like most musicians of his generation, by Charlie Parker. After working in the bands of Gerald Wilson and Buddy Collette, he became a member of Chico Hamilton's group in 1958; moving to New York, he joined Charles Mingus in 1960. As well as alto sax and flute, he now played the bass clarinet, which he used notably in duets with Mingus and with another bassist, Richard Davis. In 1961 he played on Oliver Nelson's album *The Blues And The Abstract Truth*, which primarily featured his flute playing.

In the same year he began working with Coltrane, whom he had known personally since 1954, also writing the arrangements for *Africa Brass*, and (despite some opposition, notably from the critics, who attacked Coltrane's *Live At The Village Vanguard* album) the relationship continued with Dolphy joining the group on an informal basis. When the Coltrane group toured Europe, Dolphy stayed on, but returning to the US allowed him to work with Mingus again; among the recordings are a spring 1964 Town Hall concert, including an untitled blues which was given the title *So Long Eric* in tribute after his death. But it is Dolphy's own last album *Out To Lunch* which best ensures that he will be long remembered.

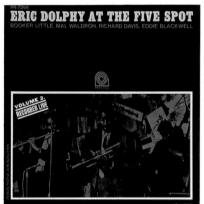

AT THE FIVE SPOT: VOLUME ONE
Fire Waltz/Bee Vamp/The Prophet
Booker Little (tp), Eric Dolphy (as, b cl), Mal Waldron (p), Richard Davis (b), Ed Blackwell (d), July 1961.
Prestige VDJ-1504
AAD Running time: 47.38
Performance: ★ ★   Recording: ★ ★ ★

With the superb Booker Little on trumpet, the strongly individualistic pianist Mal Waldron and with a fine rhythm section in Davis and Blackwell, Dolphy's 1961 quintet was a compatible if short-lived unit, which was recorded by Prestige during its engagement at the Five Spot Cafe in New York.

At the start, Dolphy and Little plunge straight into the theme, a contemporarily sour jazz waltz, then Dolphy's alto snakes bonelessly over the solid 3/4 beat. Little follows, with a strong solo that also gives unostentatious evidence of his commanding technique and subtle approach to more-or-less conventional jazz idioms, full of hints and feints such as a quote from *How High The Moon*. Waldron, who was perhaps having some understandable difficulty in overcoming the quite audible mediocrity of the Five Spot's Piano, is typically robust, with a dash of *I Loves You Porgy*.

After this, there is a feeling that the group has warmed up, but there is still a sense of struggle rather than of the kind of complicity with the audience which is usually a feature of 'pre-free' jazz.

AT THE FIVE SPOT:VOLUME TWO
Aggression/Like Someone In Love
Booker Little (tp), Eric Dolphy (b cl, fl), Mal Waldron (p), Richard Davis (b), Ed Blackwell (d), July 1961.
Prestige VDJ-1525
AAD Running time: 37.16
Performance: ★ ★   Recording: ★ ★ ★

In the second volume of 1961 material from the Five Spot, Dolphy's group plays just two numbers of album-side length; recording conditions and overall sound quality are unchanged. *Aggression* is fast and unrelenting, with a pounding solo from Waldron and long, unflagging drum solo from Blackwell. At this furious tempo, Booker Little demonstrates speed and authority, while Davis matches Blackwell in stamina and power.

Dolphy switches from bass clarinet to flute for *Like Someone In Love*, the 1940's ballad which Coltrane had adopted; here it gets an exhaustive treatment, first in out-of-tempo form, Dolphy adding a dissonant counterpoint to Booker Little's relatively pure-sounding and lyrical line, then moving into a mid tempo over which Dolphy plays fast, squirming figures, often in 16th notes; Little offers a warm-toned solo which still keeps the dissonant edge. After *Volume One*, this continuation album must be a secondary choice; and it has to be hoped that Dolphy's work (whether with Mingus, Nelson Coltrane or his own somewhat short-lived recording groups) will soon be more fully represented on Compact Disc.

DUKE ELLINGTON
(b. Washington DC, 29 April 1899; d. New York City, 24 May 1974)

The career of Edward Kennedy Ellington, as songwriter, arranger and musician, spanned no less than five decades: affectively remembered one of the undisputed jazz giants.

It would be impossible to summarise Duke's life and work in a few words, but the pianist Don Shirley must have echoed the feelings of many others who knew Ellington: 'He was not God, but he came very darn close to it!'

Miss Clinkscales, as he characterised his teacher, gave the young Edward Kennedy Ellington his first piano lessons in 1906. While still in high school he gigged at the Washington True Reformers Hall, then deputised as a pianist at the Poodle Dog Cafe, where he produced his first composition, *Soda Fountain Rag*. He continued to study harmony, worked in the bands of Elmer Snowden and others, and with drummer Sonny Greer, trumpeter Artie Whetsol and saxophonist Otto Hardwick (all to be long-serving band members) and made a first and unsuccessful attempt to get work in New York. Rejoining Snowden, he eventually took over the band (known as The Washingtonians) from him in 1924; with Joe Trent, he wrote the *Chocolate Kiddies* revue, then toured New England from 1925–27. He worked in various New York clubs before opening at the legendary Cotton Club on December 4, 1927, where he stayed (with breaks for tours and theatre dates) until 1931. The band was seen to good effect in the 1930 film *Check and Double Check*. Growl trumpeter Bubber Miley, who along with Joe 'Tricky Sam' Nanton produced the 'jungle' sound of the first classic Ellington recordings, left in 1929, but was replaced by the spectacular Cootie Williams.

By now a whole generation of great soloists were entering the band; Harry Carney and Barney Bigard (who joined in 1927), Johnny

Hodges (1928), Juan Tizol (1929), Lawrence Brown (1932). In that year Ivie Anderson first sang *It Don't Mean A Thing If It Ain't Got That Swing*, and Ellington also wrote *Sophisticated Lady*. After a first European tour (including London) in 1933, the band continued to tour the US, and Ellington composed prolifically, producing for example *Solitude* (1934) and *Caravan* (with Juan Tizol, 1936). But it was at the end of the 1930s, after the addition of revolutionary bassist Jimmy Blanton, and the arrival of the brilliant composer and arranger Billy Strayhorn, that the band entered perhaps its greatest period. Soloists now included trumpeter/violinist Ray Nance (who replaced Williams in 1940) and tenorist Ben Webster (from 1940–43), while Hodges, Tizol and Carney were at the height of their powers. January 1943 saw the premiere of the first major Ellington suite, *Black, Brown and Beige*, at the first of an annual series of Carnegie Hall concerts, which also introduced subsequent longer works.

Personnel changes were frequent through the 1940s but it was not until 1951, when times were so hard for big bands that most had already folded, that Hodges, Brown and Greer all left the band. The arrival of Clark Terry, Willie Cook, Britt Woodman and, particularly, Louie Bellson, had a strong impact in modernising the band's sound, but it had slipped out of fashion and was in decline. In 1956, though, Ellington started a triumphant comeback at the Newport Jazz Festival (where tenorist Paul Gonsalves played twenty-seven choruses on *Diminuendo and Crescendo in Blue*), appeared on the cover of 'Time' and produced major new works including *Such Sweet Thunder*. In the next decade, the orchestra went from strength to strength, touring the world. Ellington received numerous honours, though he was deeply hurt by the Pulitzer committee's decision not to give him a special award in 1965. In the same year, he gave the first of his concerts of sacred music, which eventually became his major preoccupation.

Despite the deaths of Strayhorn, in 1967, and Hodges, in 1970, and his own failing health, Ellington continued to work as hard as ever, and in 1972 the band undertook a long tour of the Far East. Soon after this, he learned that he was dying of lung cancer. In 1973, tired but indomitable, he premiered the Third Sacred Concert in London's Westminster Abbey, and also gave a Royal Command Performance at the London Palladium. By a sad coincidence, when the end came in May 1974, Paul Gonsalves and trombonist Tyree Glenn both died during the same week. Harry Carney, a mainstay of the band for 45 years, outlived Ellington by less than six months.

During his life, Ellington wrote and recorded so much that the current CD repertoire has barely scratched the surface. There must be plenty to look forward to in future reissue programmes.

JAZZ COCKTAIL
Stevedore Stomp/Creole Love Call/It Don't Mean A Thing (If It Ain't Got That Swing)/ Hot And Bothered/Rose Room/Old Man Blues/Jungle Nights In Harlem/Tiger Rag/ Sweet Jazz Of Mine/Mood Indigo/Sing You Sinners/Limehouse Blues/Double Check Stomp/Swing Low/Jazz Cocktail/Creole Rhapsody
4 Bubber Miley, Arthur Whetsol (tp), Joe Nanton (tb), Johnny Hodges (cl, as, ss), Barney Bigard (cl, ts), Harry Carney (cl, as, bars), Duke Ellington (p), Lonnie Johnson (g), Fred Guy (bj), Wellman Braud (b), Sonny Greer (d), Baby Cox (voc), October 1928; 8 as 4, add Freddy Jenkins (tp), Otto Hardwick (as, bars), Johnson, Cox out, January 1929; 1 as 8, Cootie Williams (tp)

replaces Miley, Hardwick out, March 1929; 11 Whetsol, Jenkins, Williams (tp), Nanton (tb), Juan Tizol (valve tb), Hodges (cl, as, ss), Carney (cl, as, bars), Bigard (cl, ts), Guy (bj), Braud (b), Greer (d), Irving Mills (voc), March 1930; 13 as 11, Jenkins, Mills out, April 1930; 7 as 11, Mills out, June 1930; 6 as 7, October 1930; 10 as 7, December 1930; 16 as 7, January 1931; 12 as 7, June 1931; 2, 3, 5 as 7, Add Lawrence Brown (tb), Ivie Anderson (voc 3), February 1932; 15 as 2, Add Benny Carter (arr), Anderson out, September 1932; 14 as 15, Carter out, September 1932.
ASV CD AJA 5024R
AAD Running time: 55.45
Performance: ★ ★ ★
Recording: ★ ★

Though it just misses the earliest Ellington masterpieces, *East St Louis Toodle-oo, Black And Tan Fantasy*, this collection offers good coverage of the period 1928-32. As can be seen from the personnel details, the tracks are not in chronological order, but have instead been mixed up to give a varied and entertaining programme. (Listing the personnel in track order would have proved impossibly cumbersome here.)

The *Creole Love Call* here is not the great recording of 1927, and *Mood Indigo* is not quite the same as the October 1930 recording; but *It Don't Mean A Thing* (with the great Ivie Anderson, who had just joined the band), and a dozen others, make up for this. *Hot And Bothered*, taken at breakneck speed features the alluring vocal growl of Baby Cox, trading scat phrases with the growl trumpet of Bubber Miley, then a great solo from Barney Bigard and a fine one from guest guitarist Lonnie Johnson. *Jungle Nights In Harlem* epitomises what the Ellington band meant in the world at that time; fast, in a minor key, the growling horns and rumbling sax riffs produce an intensely doomy atmosphere, and there is an incredible scale-running solo from Bigard. *Old Man Blues* is energetic but cannot quite match the swing of the contemporary Fletcher Henderson band; but both *Jazz Cocktail* (written and arranged by Benny Carter) and Ellington's own *Swing Low*, from the autumn of 1932, seem to look forward to the arranged perfection of the great black bands in the mid 1930s.

Sound quality is good, as the stereo reprocessing has not, apparently, been accompanied by too much other trickery, although there is some added reverb. This collection is a thoughtful and thoroughly enjoyable one, which is excellent value; and as long as there is no other early-to-middle Ellington on CD, it is essential.

THE 1953 PASADENA CONCERT
The Tattooed Bride/Diminuendo In Blue; Crescendo In Blue/The Hawk Talks/ Monologue/St Louis Blues/VIP's Boogie; Jam With Sam/Without A Song/Do Nothing Till You Hear From Me/Street Blues/ Perdido/Ellington Medley
Ray Nance (tp, voc 5), Willie Cook, Clark Terry, William 'Cat' Anderson (tp), Britt Woodman, Quentin Jackson, Juan Tizol (tb), Jimmy Hamilton (cl, ts) Russell Procope (cl, ss), Rick Henderson (as), Paul Gonsalves (ts), Harry Carney (cl, bars), Duke Ellington (p), Wendell Marshall (b), Butch Ballard (d), Jimmy Grissom (voc 7-9), Oscar Pettiford ('cello 10), March 1953.
Vogue VG651 600105
AAD Running time: 56.14
Performance: ★ ★   Recording: ★ ★

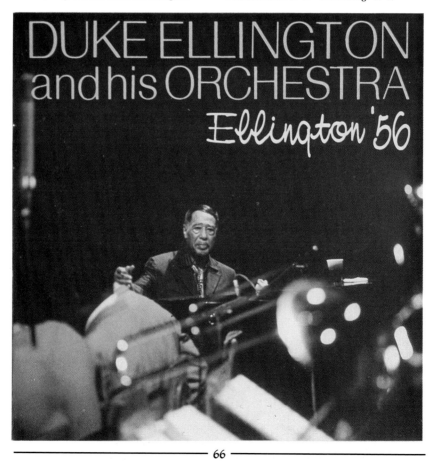

VOGUE

Perhaps the early 1950s were not the greatest Ellington period; but though temporarily without Johnny Hodges, the band does include the great Willie Cook on trumpet, alongside Nance, Terry and Anderson, and the fine trombonist Britt Woodman (who is featured on the long opener), as well as Quentin Jackson, who now took the plunger role. By this time Louis Bellson had left, his legacy being the *The Hawk Talks* and a more modern rhythm section sound. Gonsalves was already a crowd-pleaser, and whips up the excitement on *Diminuendo*, the number which three years later would mark the saxophonist's finest hour at Newport.

Monologue, a droll little parable narrated urbanely by Ellington over beautifully-played clarinets arranged and led by Hamilton, is exquisitely done, but not something you want to listen to repeatedly; the same goes, perhaps, for Nance's bustling, raucous vocal on an up-tempo *St Louis Blues* and to a lesser degree for the light-voiced Jimmy Grissom's vocal features (*Without A Song*, *Do Nothing*, and *Street Blues*), although the last of these is a shouting blues with the band really rocking in almost pure R&B style; Grissom ends it with a reference to Willie Mabon's hit *I Don't Know*. *VIP's Boogie*; *Jam With Sam* is an uptempo 'introduce the band' number, starting with excellent Carney and ending (predictably) on an Anderson high note. Oscar Pettiford's guest appearance on 'cello (*Perdido*) is remarkable. The band produces good music as well as good entertainment, and the recording is pleasantly light, superficially clean but slightly distant.

ELLINGTON '56
East St Louis Toodle-oo/Creole Love Call/Stompy Jones/The Jeep Is Jumpin'/Jack The Bear/In A Mellow Tone/Ko-Ko/Midriff/Stomp, Look and Listen/Unbooted Character/Lonesome Lullaby/Upper Manhattan Medical Group/Cottontail/Daydream/Deep Purple/Indian Summer/Laura/Blues
William 'Cat' Anderson, Willie Cook, Clark Terry (tp), Ray Nance (tp, vln), Britt Woodman, Quentin Jackson (tb), Jimmy Hamilton, Russell Procope (cl, as), Johnny Hodges (as), Paul Gonsalves (ts),Harry Carney (bars), Duke Ellington (p), Jimmy Woode (b), Sam Woodyard (d), February 1956.
Affinity CD CHARLY 20
AAD Running time: 64.02
Performance: ★ ★   Recording: ★ ★ ★

Ellington always had to face audience demand for his old hits, and in February 1956 he recorded a whole bunch of them for two albums *Historically Speaking* and *Duke Ellington Presents*. The contents of both, less some vocal numbers and non-Ellington tunes, are included in this reissue. The recording quality represents mono 'hi-fi' studio sound at its best – clean, glossy, detailed, and managing a good sense of depth, space and dynamics. *East St Louis Toodle-oo* is taken at such a slow pace it sounds as if the musicians are playing under water, but the classic ensemble of *Creole Love Call*, beautifully recorded, is simply stunning. We move rapidly from the 1920s to the 1940s with *Jack The Bear*, Hodges' feature *The Jeep Is Jumpin'* and a slightly less successful *Cottontail*.

New material for these sessions included Strayhorn's swinging *Upper Manhattan Medical Group* along with the quaintly appealing *Lonesome Lullaby*, and the programme is filled out effectively enough by three non-Ellington standards (Hodges is perfection on *Indian Summer*) and a blues.

As it turned out, 1956 was the year of Ellington's comeback, the beginning of the world fame he so richly deserved. This essential disc shows just how good the band was at that time.

WITH JOHNNY HODGES: SIDE BY SIDE
Stompy Jones/Squeeze Me/Big Shoe/Going Up/Just A Memory/Let's Fall In Love/Ruint/Bend One/You Need To Rock
1, 2, 4 Harry 'Sweets' Edison (tp), Johnny Hodges (as), Les Spann (g, fl), Duke Ellington (p), Al Hall (b), Jo Jones (d), February 1959; 3, 5-9 Roy Eldridge (tp), Lawrence Brown (tb), Hodges (as), Ben Webster (ts), Billy Strayhorn (p), Wendell Marshall (b), Jo Jones (d), August 1958.
Verve 821 578
AAD Running time: 46.10
Performance: ★ ★ ★   Recording: ★ ★ ★

SIDE BY SIDE

DUKE ELLINGTON and JOHNNY HODGES
plus others

Ellington only appears on three of the nine tracks here. The justification for inclusion is, firstly, that for some reason the earlier Ellington/Hodges recording of *Back To Back* had not appeared on CD at the time of writing; and secondly, that the other six tracks feature Ellington's musical *alter ego*, Billy Strayhorn (who is heard mainly comping unobtrusively) as well as possibly the single most important voice of the Ellington band, Johnny Hodges, and its greatest tenor player Ben Webster (who plays beautifully on *Just A Memory*, for example). Equally important, from a purely musical point of view, is the presence of Jo Jones, probably the greatest drummer of the swing idiom. Les Spann plays a pretty guitar solo on *Stompy Jones*, and a perhaps less appropriate flute on *Going Up*. Nonetheless, unlike some of Norman Granz's 'all star' sessions, this one works because all the musicians really do speak the same language. Roy Eldridge blows a typically uninhibited solo on *Big Shoe*, while Lawrence Brown's wonderfully smooth and rich sound features melodically in *Let's Fall In Love*. Hodges, still displaying a touch of the early Bechet influence, is at his skirling best on the mid-tempo *Big Shoe* and *Bend One*. Ellington introduces *Squeeze Me* with some flaring chords, then plays the tune in his own brash, yet economical and accurate piano style. Recording quality is excellent on this early stereo disc (the instruments beautifully spread); musically, it may not be essential, but it is supremely likeable.

DUKE ELLINGTON MEETS COLEMAN HAWKINS

Limbo Jazz/Mood Indigo/Ray Charles' Place/Wanderlust/You Dirty Dog/Self Portrait (Of The Bean)/The Jeep Is Jumpin'/The Ricitic
Ray Nance (cnt, vln), Lawrence Brown (tb), Johnny Hodges (as), Coleman Hawkins (ts), Harry Carney (bars), Duke Ellington (p), Aaron Bell (b), Sam Woodyard (d), August 1962.
MCA Impulse MCAD 5650
AAD Running time: 39.12
Performance: ★ ★ ★   Recording: ★ ★ ★

Although *Limbo Jazz* provides a light, Latin-tinged warm-up, the solid *Mood Indigo* is undoubtedly the centrepiece of this collection, with Hawkins on tenor taking the clarinet theme and playing a solo that reveals the subtlest nooks and crannies of that familiar melody. After a jaunty 12-bar *Ray Charles' Place*, knocked up quickly for the session and hustled along by Woodyard's shuffle beat, the horns ease into the rich theme of *Wanderlust*, a classic Ellington slow blues (and one-time signature tune for BBC radio's Jazz Record Requests') over the slow rock of Bell's walking bass, short solos by Hodges, Nance (on cornet), Carney and Brown build up to two loose but full-bodied choruses by Hawkins.

Though written for Hawkins by Ellington and Strayhorn. *Self Portrait* is a solo feature in which the subject for once alludes clearly to the rhapsodic ballad art of his earlier

years. The *Jeep* here is entirely typical of the most swinging kind of Ellington small group, with the addition of a blustering Hawkins solo. Finally *The Ricitic*, spelt without 'k's because of its Latin flavour, and featuring Nance on violin, closes the set as informally as it opened. Superbly recorded by van Gelder, this disc represents an intriguing late revival in Hawkins' playing.

DUKE ELLINGTON AND HIS ORCHESTRA FEATURING PAUL GONSALVES

C-Jam Blues/Take the 'A' Train/Happy-Go-Lucky Local/Jam With Sam/Caravan/Just A Sittin' And A Rockin'/Paris Blues/Ready, Go
Ray Burrowes, William 'Cat' Anderson, Bill Berry, Ray Nance (tp), Lawrence Brown, Leon Cox, Chuck Connors (tb), Jimmy Hamilton (cl, ts), Russell Procope, Johnny Hodges (as), Paul Gonsalves (ts), Harry Carney (bars), Duke Ellington (p), Aaron Bell (b), Sam Woodyard (d), May 1962
Fantasy CA/802/98.547
AAD Running time: 38.52
Performance: ★ ★   Recording: ★ ★ ★

An untypical Ellington session, this set really does feature Gonsalves above all else; this time *Jam With Sam* introduces only one soloist. While the numbers seem to represent a particular side of Ellington's composition, they conspire to show off several sides of Gonsalves. On *'A' Train*, for example, the tempo halves then doubles again, with the tenor player running the gamut from the lyrical to the frenetic. The next track, one of the greatest of all 'train blues', builds up to speed wonderfully here, and provides the ideal blowing vehicle for a truly wailing Gonsalves, while the band is sheer delight. On *Caravan*, Gonsalves proves, unexpectedly perhaps, that he can create an atmosphere of middle-eastern mystery with the best.

If this particular date was set up in the hope that Gonsalves might relive the glory of his twenty-seven choruses on *Diminuendo And Crescendo In Blue* at the 1956 Newport Festival, it only partially succeeds; history does not repeat itself. But as a showcase for one of the most exciting and intelligent sax players of his generation, and a worthy successor to Ben Webster, it succeeds admirably.

Recording quality on this reissue is fine, with a big, open stereo image and smooth clear sound projecting the music effortlessly and always enjoyably.

S.R.O.

Take The A Train/Medley: I Got It Bad And That Ain't Good; Things Ain't What They Used To Be/West Indian Pancake/Medley: Black And Tan Fantasy; Creole Love Call; The Mooche/Soul Call/El Gato/Open House/Rockin' In Rhythm/Jam With Sam/Adlib On Nippon/C Jam Blues/The Hawk Talks

1-7 William 'Cat' Anderson, Roy Burrowes, Cootie Williams, Ray Nance (tp), Lawrence Brown, Chuck Connors, Buster Cooper (tb), Jimmy Hamilton, Russell Procope (cl), Johnny Hodges (as), Paul Gonsalves (ts), Harry Carney (bars), Duke Ellington (p), Aaron Bell (b), Sam Woodyard (d); 8-10 Herbie Jones, Nat Woodard and John Lamb replace Burrowes, Nance and Bell; 11, Anderson, Nance, Willie Cook, Clark Terry (tp), Britt Woodman, John Sanders (tb), Procope, Hamilton (cl), Hodges (as), Gonsalves (ts), Carney (bars), Jimmy Woode (b), Woodyard (d); 12, add Quentin Jackson (tb). Europe, late 1960s.
Denon 33C38-7680
AAD Running time: 65.35
Performance: ★ ★   Recording: ★

IN THE SIXTIES

Take The 'A' Train/I Got It Bad And That Ain't Good/Perdido/Mood Indigo/Black And Tan Fantasy/The Twitch/Solitude/Do Nothing Till You Hear From Me/The Mooche/Sophisticated Lady/Creole Love Call/Rain Check/Daydream/Rock Skippin' At The Blue Note/All Day Long/After All/Snibor/U.M.M.G.

1, 2, 5, 6, 9, 10, Cootie Williams, William 'Cat' Anderson, Mercer Ellington, Herbic Jones (tp), Lawrence Brown, Buster Cooper, Chuck Connors (tb), Russell Procope, Jimmy Hamilton (cl), Johnny Hodges (as), Paul Gonsalves (ts), Harry Carney (bars), Duke Ellington (p), John Lamb (b), Sam Woodyard (d); 7, 8, Wilbur 'Bud' Brisbois replaces Williams; 3, 4, 12, 14-17, Aaron Bell and Steve Little replace Lamb and Woodyard; 18, add Clark Terry (flug); 13, Terry out, Jeff Castleman and Sam Woodyard replace Bell and Little. May 1966-November 1967.
RCA PD89565
AAD Running time: 69.10
Performance: ★ ★ ★
Recording: ★ ★

Here, history is dealt with mainly in the two medleys. The first one is Hodges' feature, an average (for him) *I Got It Bad* followed by a rather singalong *Things Ain't What They Used To Be*. It is hard to know how serious Ellington was being when he announced a title like *West Indian Pancake*, but it provides a good blowing vehicle for Gonsalves. The second medley is yet another reminder of the way Ellington's always-requested 1920s numbers stay fresh. After some absolutely evil clarinet from Procope, the growl playing of Brown and Williams brings the house down. Then, up-to-date with a bang, Gonsalves blows again (quoting from *Be-bop*) on the flag-waving *Soul Call*. Anderson's high-note feature *El Gato* is a marching, stop-time mock-Mexican minor-key lament.

The last four tracks are from a different concert. *Jam With Sam* is an unmemorable and incomplete introducing-the-band routine, but Ellington starts *Ad Lib Nippon* (he had toured Japan in May 1966) with an intriguing and atmospheric piano-bass duet before the whole band enters. The recording is fairly well balanced, but not very open, detailed or dynamic, and there is noticeable distortion, presumably due to the house PA. This can hardly claim to be essential Ellington, but then, it is still Ellington, and that in itself is almost enough.

Despite the title, few of the numbers here were new in 1966, but many represented newly definitive recordings. Ellington, at the piano, launches *Take The 'A' Train* with one chorus in 6/8, then another in 4/4, and so absorbing is this intro that you forget, until you hear its magnificent entry, that his real instrument is the band.

On the other hand, of course, the band was still made up of great soloists, who are featured in turn on a series of familiar titles. Hodges' *I Got It Bad* is simply perfect, and *Perdido* has a fine solo by Carney, who is not heard enough on many Ellington LPs. But Carney comes to the fore as usual on *Black and Tan Fantasy*, a number dating back to the year he joined the band, 1927. In this version, Cootie's growl trumpet breaks sound a bit overdone, probably because of fairly heavy reverberation. In fact, the studio sound is glossy and 'big', a little over-glamorised for today's equipment and taste.

The Twitch has more flawless Hodges (someone once asked him why he never played a wrong note, to which he replied: 'Why should I?'), Brown and Williams. It would be pointless to compare any of the performances here with those of the band as it was in 1928 or 1941, which no Ellington enthusiast could be without. But nobody, anywhere, should be without this amazingly well-filled disc.

BILL EVANS

(b. Plainfield, New Jersey, 16 August 1929; d. 15 September 1980)

Although he was brilliantly gifted pianist, Bill Evans never paraded his technique purely for the sake of it, and has left a legacy of outstanding trio recordings.

A pianist of impeccable technical ability, Bill Evans' well-schooled but utterly individual approach brought the beginnings of a new freedom to the piano, and influenced a whole generation of keyboard players in the 1960s.

Studying piano, violin and flute, at sixteen Evans had a band with his brother, but moved south to take a degree at Southeastern Louisiana College. Here he met guitarist Mundell Lowe, who later brought him to the attention of Riverside Records. In the early 1950s he worked with commercial bands including that of Jerry Wald, but in New York joined clarinettist Tony Scott and made his first recordings while in Scott's group. Riverside released Evans' first album under his own name in 1957, but he first attracted real attention when he joined

Miles Davis in February 1958, staying for a fruitful if exhausting eight months. Evans clearly contributed much to Miles' conception at the time, and the experience seems to have driven the last trace of hesitancy from his playing. In fact, his best-known recorded work with Miles came some months after he had officially left the group, on *Kind of Blue* in March 1959, and by this time he had already recorded the solo *Peace Piece* and further trio performances for Riverside with ex-Davis sidemen Philly Joe and Sam Jones.

Later in 1959 Evans formed a trio with the innovative bassist Scott La Faro and drummer Paul Motian. After La Faro was killed in a car crash in 1961, Evans' search for a compatible bassist brought him Chuck Israels, Gary Peacock and finally Eddie Gomez, while Motian was succeeded first by Shelly Manne, then by Jack de Johnette. Signing for Verve in 1962, Evans recorded *Conversations With Myself* (1963), in which he played three pianos by over-dubbing; a 1967 follow-up, *Further Conversations*, had two piano tracks. A late recording, *The Paris Concert* (Elektra Musician), made a year before his premature death at fifty-one, shows how much Evans still had to give to music.

BILL EVANS: TRIO 64
Little Lulu/A Sleeping Bee/Always/Santa Claus Is Coming To Town/I'll See You Again/For Heaven's Sake/Dancing In The Dark/Everything Happens To Me
Bill Evans (p), Gary Peacock (b), Paul Motian (d), December 1963.
Verve 815 057-2
AAD Running time: 35.26
Performance: ★ ★ ★   Recording: ★ ★ ★

Slickly produced by Creed Taylor, this Verve album tends to emphasise a jauntier side of Evans' pianism, with Motian's drums recorded a little more prominently than on the Riverside sessions. But we still hear that characteristic deliberate hesitancy on the opening of *A Sleepin Bee*, which became one of Evans' favourite standard vehicles. The Noel Coward song *I'll See You Again* gets a whimsical jazz-waltz treatment, and Evans toys deviously with the time in his mid-tempo *Dancing In The Dark*. Evans' ballad fancy takes flight effectively on the final track, with Motian and Peacock in restrained support. Recorded quality is perhaps brasher and brighter than earlier Evans recordings, but little the worse for that.

EVERYBODY DIGS BILL EVANS
Minority/Young And Foolish/Lucky To Be
Me/Night And Day/Epilogue/Tenderly/
Peace Piece/What Is There To Say
Bill Evans (p), Sam Jones (b), Philly Joe
Jones (d), December 1958.
Riverside VDJ-1517
AAD Running time: 43.08
Performance: ★ ★　Recording: ★ ★ (★)

The pianist had just left Miles Davis when
these Riverside recordings were made, and
Philly Joe's superbly urgent drumming
propels a sharply incisive Evans on the
Miles-flavoured *Minority* and *Oleo*. Not all
are trio tracks, and in fact some of the most
attractive music is contained in Evans' solos;
the lyrical *Peace Piece* develops at length
over the simplest of motifs, sustained by that
unequalled delicacy of touch and pedal
work. The wistful ballad *Lucky To Be Me*
and the two short *Epilogue* fragments are
equally appealing, and Evans' piano sound
does not lose its limpid beauty when the trio
comes in on the ultra-slow *What Is There To
Say*. In terms of running time, this straight-
reissue Compact Disc (with the original
sleeve artwork) is less good value than the
old Milestone 'twofer' *Peace Piece And
Other Pieces*; but with a bright, fairly close-
sounding piano and big, atmospheric drum
sound, this essential phase of Evans'
recording career is well presented here.

QUIET NOW
Very Airy/Sleeping Bee/Quiet Now/Turn
Out The Stars/Autumn Leaves/Nardis
Bill Evans (p), Eddie Gomez (b), Marty
Morell (d), 1969.
Affinity CD CHARLY 25
AAD Running time: 30.30
Performance: ★ ★ ★　Recording: ★ ★

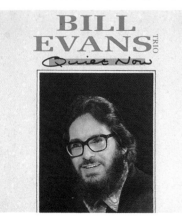

The departure of Paul Motian changed the
balance of the Evans trio; the relatively
inexperienced Marty Morell, who joined in
1968, played a very subdued role, but this
seems to have suited Evans' music well
enough. Eddie Gomez, who had joined
Evans in 1966, proved to be the ideal bassist,
sympathetic and warm-toned in
accompaniment, and with his awesome and
effortless technique, he was outstanding
(never merely flashy or over-prolix) as a
soloist.

So this set is the work of a trio which had
developed a high level of rapport, allowing
Evans to create extended structures, as in the
centrepiece *Quiet Now*, which has an
ethereal, yearning theme, with echoes of
Long Ago and Far Away. Building from this,
Evans offers variations against incredibly
lush left hand harmonies, then goes into
some characteristically deceptive sorcery
with the time, then emerges into a superb
'locked hands' passage.

After such a performance, there is a
danger that *Turn Out The Stars* might seem
merely sentimental, but of course it isn't.
Despite the short playing time and the
slightly hissy recording, this disc offers an
admirably coherent memento of Evans' work
of the period, which grows deeper with each
listening.

QUINTESSENCE
Sweet Dulcinea/Martina/Second Time
Around/A Child Is Born/Bass Face
Harold Land (ts), Bill Evans (p), Kenny
Burrell (g), Ray Brown (b), Philly Joe Jones
(d), May 1976.
Fantasy FCD-611-9529
AAD Running time: 35.55
Performance: ★ ★　Recording: ★ ★

Superb musicianship is apparent from the
opener, Land and Burrell stating Kenny
Wheeler's sweet-and-sour theme in restrained
unison. In solo terms, Burrell is outstanding
on the dreamlike *A Child Is Born*, which also
has a lovely floating solo from Land.
Particularly noticeable on this track is the
rather closer recording of Brown, giving a
'modern' sound, heavy on clacking string
noises and light on fundamentals. In fact the
sound generally is close, tight and dry, with
Evans and Land both sounding a little thin.
Bass Face starts with a lazy soul-blues feel,
Land offering Coltrane-like flurries over
funky chording by Burrell and a rock-steady
Brown. Evans follows, then the pulse
doubles for an effective blues solo by Burrell,
after which all take fours with Jones. This is

a pleasant enough disc, but it has to be said that it is not really the quintessential Evans suggested by the title.

CONVERSATIONS WITH MYSELF
Round Midnight/How About You/ Spartacus: Love Theme/Blue Monk/Stella By Starlight/Hey There/N.Y.C.'s No Lark/ Just You, Just Me/Bemsha Swing/A Sleeping Bee
Bill Evans (p), January and February 1963.
Verve 821 984-2
AAD Running time: 44.00
Performance: ★ ★   Recording: ★ ★

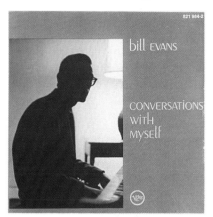

With these 1963 sessions, Evans used an unusual technique to achieve something of a group feeling from the piano; having laid down the one piano track, he added second and third pianos by overdubbing to produce, as he said 'more the quality of a "trio" than a solo effort'. The results are sometimes just too confusing (*Hey There*); sometimes have an interesting helter-skelter quality (*Just You, Just Me*); sometimes have an effectively dramatic and doomy quality (*N.Y.C.'s No Lark*); and sometimes, as on the last two tracks, the rhythmic convolutions really do strike new sparks from the tunes. Not everything worked, and this is not the best introduction to Evans' music, but it demands to be taken seriously.

EXPLORATIONS
Israel/Haunted Heart/Beautiful Love/Elsa/ Nardis/How Deep Is The Ocean?/I Wish I Knew/Sweet And Lovely
Bill Evans (p), Scott LaFaro (b), Paul Motian (d), February 1961.
Riverside VDJ-1527
AAD Running time: 39.55
Performance: ★ ★ ★   Recording: ★ ★ ★

This Riverside date captured the first great trio assembled by Evans after his period with the Miles Davis group, a trio whose perfect balance and sense of ease was never quite recaptured by Evans' later accompanists. Bassist LaFaro, who was killed in a car accident later in 1961 still aged only twenty-five, had developed an unusually melodic approach and enhanced his speed by lowering the action of his instrument. Though the resultant sound was relatively 'soft' (on recorded evidence), it still had authority and LaFaro took a pivotal role in the trio. He and Evans display breathtaking rapport, reaching inspired heights over the solid, supple pulse laid down by Motian. Riverside's original recording is sympathetic if slightly cloudy in quality, Evans' piano tactile, Motian's drums often miraculously delicate and LaFaro not over-recorded but firmly present. Essential.

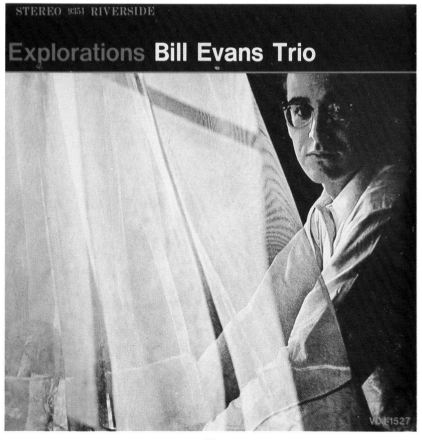

GIL EVANS
(b. Toronto, Canada, 13 May 1912)

One of the innovators of jazz orchestration, Gil Evans, surprisingly, had little formal training. 'I never did have any what you'd call proper lessons,' he told Raymond Horricks. 'I just had to work things out by myself.'

Born Ernest Gilmore Green (he later took the surname of his stepfather), Evans moved with his Australian-born parents to Spokane, Washington and then to Stockton, California. He wrote for and co-led his first professional band in 1933, then led a band at Balboa Beach from 1936 until 1939, remaining as arranger when vocalist Skinnay Ennis took over leadership. In 1941 he moved to New York and became arranger for the Claude Thornhill band. Thornhill's own unorthodox voicings became, as Evans put it, 'part of my own timbre box.'

In the Thornhill band, Evans had met Gerry Mulligan, and their discussions with Miles Davis led to the formation of the nonet which played the Royal Roost in 1948 and went on to produce the *Birth of the Cool* recordings in 1949 and 1950. Evans then worked mainly in the pop field until 1957, when he worked with Davis again, arranging and

One of the great jazz arrangers, Canadian Gil Evans is still perhaps best remembered for his timeless collaborations with Miles Davis, Porgy and Bess *and* Sketches of Spain.

directing the orchestra on the triumphant *Miles Ahead* album. After this, Prestige recorded Evans' own album *Gil Evans Plus Ten*, and apart from the further successful collaborations with Miles, he recorded *Out of the Cool* (Impulse) and other albums including one with Cannonball Adderley.

In the 1960s, Evans arranged Astrud Gilberto's *Look To The Rainbow* album, and played some festivals, but work in the jazz field again become sporadic. A planned collaboration with Jimi Hendrix was prevented by the guitarist's death, though Evans recorded the tunes anyway. (It is interesting to note that Miles Davis had also become friendly with Hendrix.) *Svengali*, 1973, was a turning point, with Evans' first use of electric piano, David Horovitz on synthesizers, and much more 'free' playing from trumpeter Marvin 'Hannibal' Peterson and tenorist Billy Harper. Today, Evans' orchestra allows maximum freedom of expression for its members, including synthesizer wizard Peter Levin. Its often self-effacing leader, among whose recent projects was the *Absolute Beginners* film score, remains one of the most respected writers in jazz.

KENNY BURRELL: GUITAR FORMS
(arranged and conducted by Gil Evans)
Downstairs/Lotus Land/Terrace Theme/
Prelude No 2 (excerpt)/Moon And Sand/
Loie/Greensleeves/Last Night When We
Were Young/Breadwinner
1, 3, 9 Kenny Burrell (g), Roger Kellaway
(p), Joe Benjamin (b), Grady Tate (d), Willie
Rodriguez (cga); 4 Burrell (g); 2, 5–8 Burrell
(g), Johnny Coles or Louis Mucci (tp), Jimmy
Cleveland, Jimmy Knepper (tb), Andy
Fitzgerald (fl, Eng horn), Richie Kamuca (ts,
oboe), Lee Konitz (as), Steve Lacy (ss), Bob
Tricario (ts, fl, bassoon), Ray Alonge or
Julius Watkins (fr h), John Barber (tuba),
Ron Carter (b) Elvin Jones and Charlie
Persip (d), Gil Evans (cond, arr), December
1964 and April 1965.
Verve 825 576-2
AAD Running time: 38.31
Performance: ★ ★ ★　Recording: ★ ★ ★

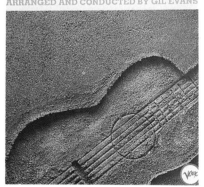

825 576-2
KENNY BURRELL/GUITAR FORMS
ARRANGED AND CONDUCTED BY GIL EVANS

With this project, Kenny Burrell set out to demonstrate the sheer scope of his instrument, and he is heard in a wide variety of settings, provided by Evans and his orchestra, or (on three numbers) a small jazz group. In order, the tracks present: traditional blues (Burrell sounding like a polite and cultured Lightnin' Hopkins); flamenco (of a gentle sort, with brooding background by Evans); modern blues; classical solo; bossa nova; Spanish or Latin ballad (Evans using woodwinds and horns);

folk; modern ballad; and finally, Latin-influenced modern jazz. On the orchestral tracks, Evans'subtle and usually melancholy tone colours enfold Burrell's richly-recorded Spanish guitar, which will surprise those who know only Burrell's bluesy combo recordings. Uncategorisable, this disc is an intriguing demonstration of Burrell's versatility and unfailing good taste.

PRIESTESS
Priestess/Short Visit/Lunar Eclipse/Orange
Was The Colour Of Her Dress Then Silk
Blue
Lew Soloff (tp, piccolo tp), Ernie Royal,
Marvin 'Hannibal' Peterson (tp), James
Knepper (tb), John Clark (fr h), Howard
Johnson, Robert Stewart (tuba), David
Sanborn, Arthur Blythe (as), George Adams
(ts), Pete Levin (synth, clav), Gil Evans (p),
Keith Loving (g), Steve Neil (b), Susan Evans
(d), May 1977
Antilles J33D 20001
AAD Running time: 41.11
Performance: ★ ★ ★　Recording: ★ ★ ★

One long piece (the title track) and three short selections make up this well-structured set. *The Priestess* begins with a slow, deep, wah-ing synth line, which soon gives on to a stirring rhythm; over this we hear stately horn figures, voiced with the almost unmistakeable Evans subtlety, so that they sometimes cease to sound like brass at all. A

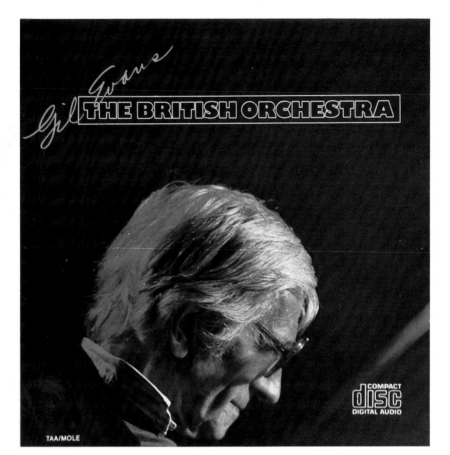

mannered solo by Sanborn is followed by an excellent one from Blythe, who takes things up to another level; on this plateau arrives an expansive Soloff. Sanborn features again, with Junior Walker overtones, in the loping jazz-waltz-based *Short Visit*, which actually lasts some twelve minutes. After the busily atmospheric *Lunar Eclipse*, Evans is heard on piano in the final track, affectionately introducing a full-bodied reading of the Mingus tune, part whimsical, part bittersweet, with very fine and muscular playing from Adams. Possibly the CD transfer has introduced just a very slight treble hardness, but on the most complex passages the recorded sound is still clean, full of detail, spacious and inviting.

THE BRITISH ORCHESTRA
Hotel Me/Friday The 13th/London/Little Wing
Guy Barker, Miles Evans, Henry Lowther (tp), Malcolm Griffiths (tb), Rick Taylor (tb, b, tb), Chris Hunter (as, ss, fl), Stan Sulzmann (ts, ss, fl), Don Weller (ts, ss), John Surman (bars, ss, b, cl, synth), Ray Russell (g), Gil Evans (el, p, p), John Taylor (key), Mo Foster (el b), Bradford, England, March 1983.
Mole Jazz CD MOLE 8
AAD Running time: 47.46
Performance: ★   Recording: ★ ★

Though accustomed to leading his own orchestra, Gil Evans has (as Barry McRae puts it) 'never been averse to organising bands, on site'. This is what happens when, to the greatest excitement of the British jazz scene, Gil Evans visited the UK in 1983 and assembled a British orchestra; the personnel reads like a *Who's Who* of Progressive UK

musicians at that time. The undertaking was made possible by Arts Council funding. On the recording made at the St George Hall, Bradford are four long numbers, the main soloists being tenorist Stan Sulzmann, well known baritone sax player John Surman and guitarist Ray Russell. *Hotel Me* opens with the rock-style guitar of Russell, while the band moves into a loping, slumping beat; the horn ensemble has a bleary texture, sharpened by the gutsy sound of Sulzmann's tenor, and the fulminating bottom end and searing upper-register cries of Surman. Surman launches Monk's *Friday The 13th*, the orchestra entering to flesh out the descending minor-key chord sequence; Malcolm Griffiths solos with alternate rhythmically-tied and 'free' phrases, his tone bright and strident. *London*, a commissioned work, starts with spacey, abstract sounds; a pulse develops, with almost fanfare-style brass; Russell enters with a guitar style that is Hendrix out of ECM as the chords from the brass become more static, like sounds hanging in the clouds. Russell of course features again on the Hendrix number *Little Wing*. Considering the momentous nature of the occasion, many listeners may be disappointed by this disc; solos are fragmentary and without structure while the ensemble work (inevitably perhaps, given the nature of the performance) is loose, rhythmically defocused and not without intonation problems. Evans' legendary ability to conjure magic tone colours from brass instruments is hardly in evidence. A cynical listener will be reminded that this event and recording could not have taken place without the charitable patronage of the Arts council; on the other hand, fans of British jazz will find this disc fascinating.

ART FARMER
(b. Council Bluffs, Iowa, 21 August 1928)

Many trumpeters have doubled on flugelhorn, but Art Farmer, with his careful good taste almost concealing a matchless technical command, has perhaps done most to exploit the smooth and accessible sound of the instrument in a variety of settings.

Farmer's early experience included jobs in the bands of Horace Henderson and Benny Carter, after which he joined Lionel Hampton. A sample of Farmer's work with the Gerry Mulligan quartet of 1958 appears in the film *Jazz On A Summer's Day*, but by 1959 he had left to co-found the Art Farmer-Benny Golson Jazztet. Farmer moved to Vienna in the late 1960s but returned to the US in 1975; in recent years he has been a successful recording artist, and though a purveyor of mood music, has continued to record in a jazz format. A 1982 Festival reunion with Golson led to the re-emergence of The Jazztet.

MIRAGE
Barbados/Passos/My Kinda Love/Mirage/
Cherokee Sketches/Smiling Billy
Art Farmer (tp, flug), Clifford Jordan (ts),
Fred Hersch (p), Ray Drummond (b), Akira
Tana (d), Milan, September 1982.
Soul Note SN1046 CD
AAD Running time: 41.43
Performance: ★ ★   Recording: ★ ★

Away from his recently familiar orchestral settings, Farmer is heard here leading a tight quintet which moves straight ahead over familiar ground. On the theme of *Barbados*, the two horns are exquisite, and the switch from Caribbean to straight 4/4 is well handled; but later in this set, as for example in the ultra-fast *Cherokee Sketches* (on *Cherokee* chords), the rhythm section begins to sound busy, managing a metronomic precision rather than a true swing. Pianist Fred Hersch shows plenty of speed here, but on the Latin-flavoured *Passos* he is plodding. Sound quality is good, though apparently rather close-miked; more 'air' might have made this disc sound more relaxed.

MAIDEN VOYAGE
Nica's Dream/Ruby My Dear/Blue Bossa/
Goodbye Pork Pie Hat/Blue In Green
Art Farmer (flug), Masahiko Satoh (p, el p),
Ron Carter (b), Jack DeJohnette (d), David
Nadia (vln, concertmaster), Charles Libove,
Barry Finclair, Jan Mullen, Elena Barere,
John Pintavalle, Richard Sortomme, Lewis
Eley, Masako Yanagita, Regis Landioro
(vln), Emanuel Vardi, Al Brown (viola),
Charles McCracken, Jonathan Abramowitz
(cello), John Beal (b), April 1983.
Denon 38C38-7071
AAD Running time: 43.38
Performance: ★   Recording: ★ ★

Set against the tasteful, if sometimes monochromatic backdrop of a large string orchestra, Art Farmer's beautiful flugelhorn sound is heard to advantage. With a 'magical', romanticised introduction, Monk's *Ruby My Dear* is sentimental, while Miles' *Blue In Green* becomes a rather pedestrian sort of vehicle for some interesting but somehow unrelated string writing. The intelligence and subtlety of Farmer's playing only just saves these tracks from condemnation as pure schmalz; without the strings, he uses a mute to produce a mournfully effective theme statement on Mingus' *Goodbye Pork Pie Hat*, while Kenny Dorham's *Blue Bossa*, with the softest bossa beat, is a classic of the middle-of-the-road genre.

AMBROSIA
The Windmills Of Your Mind/Once Upon A
Summertime/Watch What Happens/What
Are You Doing The Rest Of Your Life/You
Must Believe In Spring/The Years Of My
Youth/The Summer Knows/I Will Wait For
You
Art Farmer (flug), Hank Jones (p), Eddie
Gomez (b), Jimmy Cobb (d), Takashi Katoh
(vln, concertmaster), Masao Kawabata,
Hiromichi Hara, Kunihiro Kohno, Chizuko
Tsunda, Takashi Fukumori, Etsuo Ejiri,
Kaori Koyamatsu, Hiroshi Ikeda, Setsuka
Ryu (vln), Hiroshi Watanabe, Shunichi
Hirayama (viola), Hiroto Kawamura, Yoh
Kigochi (cello), Toshio Katayama (b),
Tokyo, October/November 1983.
Denon 38C38 7091
DDD Running time: 43.19
Performance: ★   Recording: ★ ★

This collection of Michel Legrand compositions does deliver the sweetness promised by the title, with rich, syrupy strings. Though dramatic sound quality cannot conceal the fundamental banality of *The Windmills Of Your Mind*, there are better moments to come; Hank Jones, inaudible much of the time, is heard to good effect in *The Years Of My Youth* and *I Will Wait For You*. Gomez, rather close-miked, opens *What Are You Doing The Rest Of Your Life* to introduce a muted theme from Farmer (recorded with ridiculous amounts of echo). But despite the superior talents of The Great Jazz Trio (Jones, Gomez and Cobb), and the excellent string writing, in the end this disc lacks the smooth and easy gloss which is the trademark of so many similarly-conceived A&M recordings.

ELLA FITZGERALD
(b. Newport News, Virginia, 25 April 1918)

Best known for her near-definitive recordings of the great popular standards, Ella Fitzgerald continues to delight both jazz fans and the broader audience.

As a teenager, her 'amateur night' appearance at the Apollo Theatre led first to a professional debut with Tiny Bradshaw's band, then to a job with Chick Webb's band at the Savoy. Her earliest recording was *Love and Kisses* in 1935, but she had her first hit in 1938 with the reworked nursery rhyme, *A-Tisket, A-Tasket*. After Webb's death in 1939, Ella led the band until it finally broke up in 1941.

She toured for a while with a vocal group called The Four Keys, then worked as a single. In the late 1940s she sang with be-bop players and developed her well-known 'scat' style to suit. She first worked with Norman Granz in 1946, when she began touring with JATP, but was still recording for Decca. She cut some superb performances in the late 1940s with pianist Ellis Larkins, but her recording career really blossomed when she signed for Verve in 1956 and recorded *The Cole Porter Songbook*, the first of a long and successful series.

Other Verve recordings teamed Ella with Louis Armstrong, Duke Ellington, Count Basie, Ben Webster and Stan Getz, and though still thought of as a jazz singer she became a leading figure in the entertainment world. But Norman Granz's return to the record business (with the Pablo label) led to a long series of 1970s recordings with smaller star jazz units, and she has since toured extensively with a group led by pianist Tommy Flanagan.

THE COLE PORTER SONGBOOK:
VOLUME 1
All Through The Night/Anything Goes/
Miss Otis Regrets/Too Darn Hot/In The Still
Of The Night/I Get A Kick Out Of You/Do
I Love You/Always True To You In My
Fashion/Let's Do It/Just One Of Those
Things/Ev'ry Time We Say Goodbye/All Of
You/Begin The Beguine/Get Out Of Town/I
Am In Love/From This Moment On
Ella Fitzgerald (voc), orchestra arranged and
conducted by Buddy Bregman, February
1956.
Verve 821 989
AAD Running time: 54.07
Performance: ★ ★ ★   **Recording:** ★ ★ ★

VOLUME ONE

ELLA FITZGERALD
THE
COLE PORTER
SONGBOOK
Ella's brilliant performance of 16 of Porter's greatest songs.

So many of these songs are now indelibly associated with Ella Fitzgerald that it seems almost unbelievable that she went on to bring much the same level of interpretative inspiration to the work of half a dozen other great American songwriters. The best known performance from this set is of *Ev'ry Time We Say Goodbye*, a song made popular by this recording, but Ella's versions must have done nearly as much for many of the other songs here. On every number, she demonstrates the subtle art of not just staying close to the melody, but getting inside it, but at the same time keeping at least some of that freedom of expression which is conventionally supposed to identify the jazz singer.

Bregman's orchestra provides swinging backgrounds for numbers like *From This Moment On, Just One Of Those Things* and *Begin The Beguine*, a jazz feel for *All Of You* and that inspired rhumba for *In The Still Of The Night*; but he offers equally effective small-group backing where appropriate. A discreet piano is the perfect complement to the definitive reading of *Miss Otis Regrets*; a soft guitar lends intimacy to *I Get A Kick Out Of You*. Among the least familiar of the Porter compositions here is the striking *Get Out Of Town*, which receives a deep, sombre and absolutely compelling treatment from Ella.

Sound quality, in mono, was always excellent and has transferred well to Compact Disc, as has *Volume 2* (Verve 821 990); this completes the Cole Porter story with another, equally attractive, selection of 16 songs, including *Night And Day, What Is This Thing Called Love, I Love Paris, Love For Sale, I've Got You Under My Skin* and other favourites.

ELLA AND LOUIS
Can't We Be Friends/Isn't This A Lovely Day/Moonlight In Vermont/They Can't Take That Away From Me/Under A Blanket Of Blue/Tenderly/A Foggy Day/Stars Fell On Alabama/Cheek To Cheek/The Nearness Of You/April In Paris
Louis Armstrong (tp, voc), Ella Fitzgerald (voc), Oscar Peterson (p), Herb Ellis (g), Ray Brown (b), Buddy Rich (d), August 1956.
Verve 825 373
AAD Running time: 54.20
Performance: ★ ★   Recording: ★ ★ ★

The verse to *Isn't It A Lovely Day* is as perfect an example of Ella Fitzgerald's art as any, and the subsequent unashamedly hammy vocal chorus from Armstrong is a real contrast; what is remarkable is the way Ella's chorus follows so beautifully, with delicate trumpet obbligato behind it from Armstrong, who joins her in a final duet. Louis takes the verse and the first chorus of *A Foggy Day* (the disc is worth having just to have the pleasure of hearing him sing 'the British museum had lost its charm'), Ella enters with a more decorative version, then, after a spirited trumpet solo, Louis joins in her final chorus with his customary 'yeahs'.

Armstrong engagingly talks his way out of *The Nearness Of You* and *April In Paris*, in each case following absolutely flawless, breathtaking performances from Ella; he opens *Stars Fell On Alabama* on trumpet, and there is something about this chorus that fleetingly recalls his earlier instrumental

greatness. But that is not really what this collection is about; Armstrong may not contribute instrumental virtuosity to this disc, but offers his inherent musical warmth, almost self-mocking as he refuses to take things too seriously. The follow-up album *Ella and Louis Again* (Verve 825 374) includes such duets as *A Fine Romance, I Won't Dance* and *Let's Call The Whole Thing Off*.

THE SONGBOOKS
Oh, Lady Be Good/Nice Work If You Can Get It/Fascinating Rhythm/All The Things You Are/Yesterdays/Can't Help Lovin' Dat Man/Come Rain Or Come Shine/It's Only A Paper Moon/Over The Rainbow/Laura/Skylark/This Time The Dreams On Me/Puttin' On The Ritz/Alexander's Ragtime Band/Cheek To Cheek/My Funny Valentine/Have You Met Miss Jones/The Lady Is A Tramp/Manhattan
1-3 Ella Fitzgerald (voc), with orchestra arranged and conducted by Nelson Riddle, January/March 1959; 4-6 Fitzgerald (voc) with orchestra arranged and conducted by Nelson Riddle, January 1963; 7-9 Fitzgerald (voc) with orchestra arranged and conducted by Billy May, August 1960/January 1961; 10-12 Fitzgerald (voc) with orchestra arranged and conducted by Nelson Riddle, October 1964; 13-15 Fitzgerald (voc) with orchestra arranged and conducted by Buddy Bregman, August 1956.
Verve 823 445
AAD Running time: 65.12
Performance: ★ ★ ★   Recording: ★ ★

With the exception of Cole Porter and Duke Ellington, all Ella Fitzgerald's 'Songbooks' are sampled here. In order, there are three songs each from Gershwin, Kern, Arlen, Mercer and Berlin, then four from Rodgers. These last are actually the earliest recordings, and though the liner note mentions that all selections are stereo, the description seems pretty doubtful in this case. But only *Have You Met Miss Jones* ('Sir Jones' here) fails to make the grade musically, a minor lapse when you have a lovely *Funny Valentine*, a joyful, swinging *Lady Is A Tramp* and, of course, *Manhattan*. Similarly, with the Irving Berlin group, Ella seems to be working hard to breath life into a dated *Puttin' On The Ritz*, while in *Alexander's Ragtime Band* the novelty is a switch from Dixie (Ella affects a circus-barker voice which doesn't suit her) to modern jazz ('. . . hear that Swanny River played in cool time'), but all is forgiven when we hear *Cheek To Cheek*.

Nelson Riddle was not afraid to set slow tempos for *Lady Be Good* or *Can't Help Lovin' Dat Man*, where Ella's verse is particularly brilliant, or a relatively fast one for *All The Things You Are*. Excellent as the others are (Billy May, for example, making brilliant use of strings and a 1940s-style sax section on *Over The Rainbow*), Riddle emerges as the most subtle, imaginative and supportive arranger.

Sound quality is mostly fine, although there are moments when the balance on Ella's voice seems slightly odd. This could be partly the effect of putting together tracks from sessions cut years apart; and whatever quibbles there might be over this, the disc needs no further justification.

PORGY AND BESS

Overture (medley): Summertime; I Got
Plenty O'Nuttin; Bess You Is My Woman
Now; It Ain't Necessarily So; I Wants To
Stay Here/Summertime/I Wants To Stay
Here/My Man's Gone Now/I Got Plenty
O'Nuttin/Buzzard Song/Bess You Is My
Woman Now/It Ain't Necessarily So/What
You Want Wid Bess/A Woman Is A
Sometime Thing/Oh, Doctor Jesus/Medley:
Here Come De Honey Man; Crab Man; Oh
Dey's So Fresh And Fine - Strawberry
Woman/There's A Boat Dat's Leavin' Soon
For New York/Bess, Oh Where's My Bess?/
Oh Lawd, I'm On My Way
Ella Fitzgerald (voc), Louis Armstrong (voc,
tp), orchestra conducted by Russel Garcia,
1958.
Verve 827 475
AAD Running time: 66.14
Performance: ★ ★ ★
Recording: ★ ★ ★

ELLA AND BASIE: ON THE SUNNY SIDE OF THE STREET

Honeysuckle Rose/'Deed I Do/Into Each Life
Some Rain Must Fall/Them There Eyes/
Dream A Little Dream Of Me/Tea For Two/
Satin Doll/I'm Beginning To See The Light/
Shiny Stockings/My Last Affair/Ain't
Misbehaving/Sunny Side Of The Street
1-3, 6-12 Joe Newman, Al Aarons, Sonny
Cohn, Don Rader, Flip Ricard (tp), Henry
Coker, Grover Mitchell, Benny Powell,
Urbie Green (tb), Marshall Royal (as, cl),
Frank Wess (as, ts, fl), Eric Dixon (ts, fl),
Franc Foster (ts), Charlie Fowlkes (bars),
Count Basie (p), Freddie Green (g), Buddy
Catlett (b), Sonny Payne (d), Quincy Jones
(arr); 4, 5 Newman (tp), Urbie Green (tb),
Basie (p), Freddie Green (g), Catlett (b),
Payne (d), July 1963.
Verve 821 576
AAD Running time: 42.11
Performance: ★ ★ ★   **Recording:** ★ ★ ★

Though the two stars had already recorded
Ella and Louis and *Ella and Louis Again*, this
third collaboration was on a rather different
scale. The recording did not attempt to give
the whole opera, but to present all the best
known numbers to the best possible
advantage. As it stands, the programme runs
for over an hour.

Ella Fitzgerald was to sing all the female
parts, Louis Armstrong all the male; in the
end, most of the numbers were shared if not
actually sung as duets, while Ella sang *The
Buzzard Song*, which had originally been
intended for Porgy, was dropped from the
first production, then gained some
popularity of its own. Armstrong is effective
in *A Woman Is A Sometime Thing*,
appropriately relaxed in *I Got Plenty
O'Nuttin* and *There's A Boat That's Leavin'
Soon For New York* (taking rather a broad
view of these tunes, not to mention the
lyrics), warm on *Bess You Is My Woman
Now* and, above all, moving in *Bess, Oh
Where's My Bess*. He plays some very fine
solos too, notably the fierce and blues-laden
chorus in *It Ain't Necessarily So*, and in
Summertime, on which Ella offers a
definitive performance. She is incomparable,
particularly, on *I Want To Stay Here* and
My Man's Gone Now, but she provides
many other delights too, sounding almost
girlish on *Plenty Of Nuttin*, for example, and
majestically feminine on *Bess, You Is My
Woman Now* ('Porgy, I's your woman now
. . .'). Throughout, the orchestra is fine, the
recording excellent, the transfer to CD well
done, and this disc deserves its success.

With a rather reactionary tone entering his
liner note ('it's refreshing that this kind of an
album has been recorded today in the welter
of nonsense that unfortunately has found a
wide acceptance'), producer Norman Granz
makes it quite clear that the aim was to
swing. *Ella and Basie* certainly succeeded in
this; the combination of Ella's voice, Basie's
band and Quincy Jones' arrangements
proved just about as refreshing as Granz
could have wished, and effectively
revitalised the material.

The choice of songs includes not only the
two most familiar of all Ellington tunes,
Satin Doll and *I'm Beginning To See The
Light*, but one of the Basie band's catchiest
(written by Frank Foster), *Shiny Stockings*;
the coy lyric was added by Ella, who fits in
like a guest soloist. The two Fats Waller
standards come up fresh here, probably
partly because they are seldom sung any
more, partly because of the quality of the
arrangement and perfect choice of tempo,
Honeysuckle Rose is fast and foot-tapping
with just Basie and the rhythm section, until
the band comes punching in after the bridge,
swinging out at the end with Sonny Payne's
vigorous backbeat, while *Ain't Misbehaving*
is charming at a slighter slower pace than
expected. Quincy Jones attempts to update
The Inkspots' *In to Each Life Some Rain
Must Fall* with a near-R&B treatment, and
(more successfully) freshen up that most
hackneyed standard, Jimmy McHugh's *The
Sunny Side Of The Street* by swinging it
with a sort of streamlined train rhythm, for
an uplifting finale.

JAN GARBAREK
(b. Mysen, Norway, 4 March 1947)

Though there have been many gifted European jazz musicians, hardly any have been acknowledged as innovative contributors to the development of jazz itself. But in the last few years, the Norwegian tenor and soprano saxophonist Jan Garbarek has emerged as a truly individual voice.

Garbarek took up the saxophone at fourteen; his first inspiration came from hearing John Coltrane's *Countdown* on the radio. Within a year, he was leading a Coltrane-influenced quartet, with which he entered the non-traditional section of the 1962 Norwegian Amateur Jazz Championship. Three years later, he met George Russell at the Molde Jazz Festival and became interested in Russell's 'Lydian Chromatic' concept, later recording as soloist on several of Russell's works.

In the early 1970s, Garbarek became a key artist on the ECM label, appearing on several albums with Keith Jarrett and subsequently recording with Ralph Towner, Egberto Gismonti and Charlie Haden, while his own group usually included the distinctive bassist Eberhard Weber. His saxophone style often reflects the influence of Coltrane but is also characterised by his own very personal sound: a stark, hard-edged quality in the upper registers, an instantly identifiable *cri de coeur*.

WAYFARER
Gesture/Wayfarer/Gentle/Pendulum/Spor/Singsong.
Jan Garbarek (ts, ss), Bill Frisell (g), Eberhard Weber (b), Michael DiPasqua (d, perc), Oslo, March 1983.
ECM 811 968
AAD Running time: 46.30
Performance: ★ ★   Recording: ★ ★

Jan Garbarek Group
Wayfarer
ECM

With this 1983 album, Garbarek demonstrated his quartet's ability to produce intense drama and changing moods without the use of big orchestral forces or synthesisers. Frisell uses the heaviest sounds of his lower strings to create the atmosphere of menace in the title track, while using watery (tremolo) chord effects to surround Garbarek's blaring lead. Then DiPasqua sets up a pulse with an Elvin Jones-style barrage, while Garbarek wails and overblows with Trane-like chord effects.

After the soft respite of *Gentle*, *Pendulum* picks up from a slow opening to a measured beat, then alternates between an explicitly-stated uptempo and cooled-down sections where the pulse, though suppressed, is still felt below. Then Frisell bursts out, keeping his guitar constantly on the edge of feedback, allowing it to release wild and distorted cries when it goes over. *Singsong* starts with a tune that is a sort of sad theatre-music parody, then flings this aside with another searing solo from Frisell. It is a well structured set, and as usual with ECM, recording quality is hard to fault.

IT'S OK TO LISTEN TO THE GRAY VOICE
White Noise Of Forgetfulness/The Crossing Place/One Day In March I Go Down To The Sea And Listen/Mission: To Be Where I Am/It's OK To Listen To The Island That Is A Mirage/It's OK To Listen To The Gray Voice/I'm The Knife Thrower's Partner.
Jan Garbarek (ts, ss), David Torn (g, g synth, DX7 synth), Eberhard Weber (b),Michael DiPasqua (d, perc), Oslo, December 1984.
ECM 825 406
AAD Running time: 43.08
Performance: ★ ★   Recording: ★ ★ ★

Recorded less than a year after *The Wayfarer*, this album features David Torn, playing guitar synthesiser and Yamaha DX7 as well as guitar, replacing Frisell. The change contributes to a very different ensemble character: where Frisell sounded tough, his guitar thunderous or screaming, Torn is sweeter-toned, melodic, sparing of effects. He does go for Frisell's rippling, wavering chord sound on *Mission*, and can produce a heavy rock sound with the best, but usually prefers to add eerie, echoing notes in the distance. All the titles on the disc are taken from the poems of Tomas Transtromer; the set has a quiet unity of concept, helped sonically by a very spacious soundstage. Garbarek's familiar keening sound is heard (with a second soprano overdubbed) on the half-comic, half-tragic fifty-four seconds of *I'm The Knife Thrower's Partner*, a provocative coda to the whole; elsewhere, he is lyrical, even rhapsodic, on tenor. This disc may yet appeal to those who have hitherto found Garbarek too much of an acquired taste.

STAN GETZ
(b. Philadelphia, Pennsylvania, 2 February 1927)

Stan Getz – one of the great stylists of the tenor saxophone.

Most successful and distinctive of a group of white Lester Young-influenced tenor players, Getz developed a clear, almost translucent sound that is always instantly recognisable. He remains in essence a swing player whose melodic approach makes his music accessible and his popularity enduring.

When Getz left school at fifteen to join Dick Rodgers' orchestra, he was brought back by the authorities, but at sixteen he was playing with Jack Teagarden, and a year later with Stan Kenton. Briefly with Jimmy Dorsey and Benny Goodman, he soon moved to California, where he led a trio, then joined Gene Roland's four-tenor band. From this group, in September 1947, Woody Herman took Getz, Zoot Sims and Herbie Steward, along with a tune by Jimmy Guiffre whose title became a tag for all these players, *Four Brothers*. Getz left Herman to form his own quartet in 1949. In 1953, he successfully added the warm sound of valve trombonist Bob Brookmeyer to the group.

Record dates in the 1950s included guest appearances with Lionel Hampton, Dizzy Gillespie and J. J. Johnson, but on a 1958 JATP tour, Getz decided to stay in Copenhagen. He returned to the USA in 1961, and shortly afterwards recorded *Focus* with a string quartet playing music by Eddy Sauter. He then went on to spectacular success with the *bossa nova* albums recorded first with Charlie Byrd and subsequently with Joao Gilberto and Luiz Bonfa; these recordings helped launch the craze for Brazilian rhythms which soon spread throughout popular music.

In the mid 1960s, Getz led a quartet which included Gary Burton on vibes, with bassist Steve Swallow and drummer Roy Haynes, but at the end of the decade returned to Europe. In 1971 he was recorded at Ronnie Scott's Club, London, for the double album *Dynasty*, and also worked with the Kenny Clarke/Francy Boland big band. Though he has never really been a major innovator, Stan Getz has kept abreast of the times even since the bossa days, recording with Chick Corea on *Captain Marvel*, for example. His Verve recordings now are well represented on Compact Disc.

STAN GETZ WITH THE OSCAR PETERSON TRIO: THE SILVER COLLECTION

I Want To Be Happy/Pennies From Heaven/ Ballad Medley: Bewitched, Bothered and Bewildered; I Don't Know Why I Just Do; How Long Has This Been Going On?; I Can't Get Started; Polka Dots And Moonbeams/ I'm Glad There Is You/Tour's End/I Was Doing All Right/Bronx Blues/Three Little Words/Detour Ahead/Sunday/Blues For Henry
Stan Getz (ts), Oscar Peterson (p), Herb Ellis (g), Ray Brown (b), October 1957
Verve 827 826-2
AAD Running time: 62.48
Performance: ★ ★ ★   Recording: ★ ★ ★

This session, presented for the first time in its entirety, is not perfect all the way through, but much of it is very nearly so. Less than satisfying is the ballad medley, in which the players (in the order Getz, Ellis, Peterson, Brown, Getz) each take a single solo chorus; *I'm Glad*, which follows, is a much better Getz ballad. On *Tour's End* (over *Georgia Brown* chords) he really blows the cobwebs away, with some agile stop-time breaks; and these provide the only section, apart from the two *Blues* which are in any case the least

successful tracks, where the absence of a drummer is actually noticeable.

I Was Doing All Right, at an easy mid tempo, is outstanding, while *Detour Ahead* is another small masterpiece, Getz's tone as smooth and rich as caramel. At a boppish tempo, *Three Little Words* (where he takes breaks again) shows just what a master Getz had become, especially when buoyed up by the matchless swing of the trio.

WITH EUROPEAN FRIENDS

All God's Children Got Rhythm/Broadway/ Lady Bird/Dear Old Stockholm/East Of The Sun/They All Fall In Love/Theme For Manuel/Our Kind of Sabi
Stan Getz (ts) with: 1, 2, 5, 6, Martial Solal (p), Pierre Michelot (b), Kenny Clarke (d); 3, 4, Rene Urtreger (p), Jimmy Gourley (g), Clarke (d); 7, 8, Rene Thomas (g), Eddie Louiss (org), Bernard Lubat (d). France, 1958–9.
Denon 33C387679
AAD Running time: 50.45
Performance: ★ ★ ★   Recording: ★

These recordings date from a period when Getz was at the height of his powers, just a few years before the Brazilian-influenced recordings which were to bring him

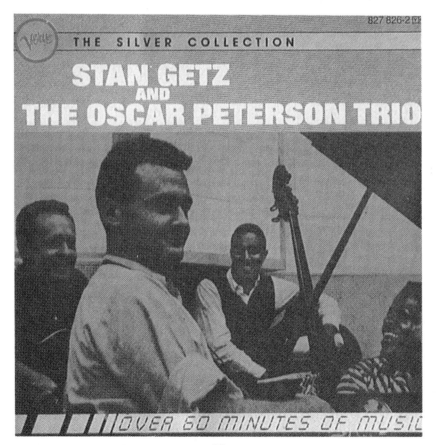

unprecedented fame. The inimitable Kenny Clarke, who had been living in Paris since 1955, lifts the group and gives it a loose and open feel. Getz's playing shows unusual freedom and obvious enjoyment as well as his usual airy grace and melodic dexterity. Solal offers a crisp and well-turned solo on *East Of The Sun*, while Gourley contributes strongly on *Lady Bird*. On the ballad feature *They All Fall In Love* (which bears a strong resemblance to *Ghost Of A Chance*), Getz is supreme, shading his sound from the muscular to the tender, from lyric cries to cool poise. The two organ tracks seem exploratory in approach, though *Our Kind of Sabi* is a kind of proto-samba with funky overtones, which after some wandering, manages to reach an effective climax.

Though Getz himself is captured effectively, the recording balance is not good. The drums are too loud, the bass poor, and though there seem to be some anomalous differences between channels; this is effectively a mono recording. Musically, though, of all the many recordings made by American soloists with European sidemen, this is one of the most interesting.

STAN GETZ AND CHET BAKER: LINE FOR LYONS
Just Friends/Stella By Starlight/Airegin/My Funny Valentine/Milestones/Dear Old Stockholm/Line For Lyons
Chet Baker (tp, voc 1, 4), Stan Getz (ts), Jim McNeeley (p), George Mraz (b), Victor Lewis (d), Stockholm 1983.
Vogue VG651 600034
AAD Running time: 51.03
Performance: ★ ★ Recording: ★ ★ ★

Recorded at a very happy-sounding Swedish gig, Getz and Baker complement each other perfectly. *Just Friends* comes over very well with Baker's appealing vocal delivery, his sheer charm and intuitive taste overcoming an almost complete absence of voice or technique; though his *Funny Valentine* vocal, slow, heavily mannered and with suspect intonation, will probably not improve with repeated listening.

Baker's warm, soft-edged trumpet sound is supple in the relaxed but precise ensembles of *Milestones*, where he also proffers a predictably Miles Davis-like solo. The title track is an exquisite, for old-times-sake duet, in which the two horns, unaccompanied, blend perfectly. Getz is, of course, the stronger of the two in terms of technical resources, but here all is sweetness and harmony. The tenor player's joyful, inventive work throughout this set, nicely recorded, shows just why he remains at the top of the tree.

DIZZY GILLESPIE
(b. Cheraw, South Carolina, 21 October 1917)

Still the most influential trumpeter since Louis Armstrong, John Birks 'Dizzy' Gillespie was, with Charlie Parker, the prime instigator of the be-bop revolution. As Leonard Feather wrote in 1949: 'He has figured so prominently . . . the stories of Bird, Monk, Klook and the others all dovetail into Dizzy's biography.'

Soon after his family moved north to Philadelphia in 1935, Gillespie got his first professional job with Frank Fairfax, and in 1937 Teddy Hill, who had seen him play in Philly, hired him as a like-sounding replacement for Roy Eldridge. In Cab Calloway's band from late 1939, he lived up to his reputation for on-stage clowning, and was fired for throwing a spitball behind the leader's back (for once, he was innocent). From late 1941 he worked with Ella Fitzgerald, Benny Carter, Charlie Barnet and Les Hite before joining Earl Hines' touring band where he met Charlie Parker. He joined Billy Eckstine's new band in June 1944, but early in 1945 cut his first records as leader, including *Groovin' High*, his first record with Parker. A first attempt to launch a big band failed, but in 1946 his second big band proved a success, with Kinny Dorham, Sonny Stitt, Leo Parker, John Lewis, Ray Brown, Milt Jackson and Kenny Clarke in its ranks. By 1947, Gillespie was introducing Afro-Cuban rhythms with the help of the conga player Chano Pozo. Disbanding in 1950, Gillespie started recording with small groups on his own Dee Gee record label, which lasted until 1953. He then signed with Norman Granz, and made some excellent big band sides for Verve in September 1954. When the State Department sponsored a 'jazz ambassadors' overseas tour in 1956, Gillespie created a big band which lasted until the end of 1957.

During the 1950s Gillespie also recorded with Sonny Rollins and Sonny Stitt (*Duets*) and with Stitt and Stan Getz (*For Musicians Only*). In the 1960s and '70s he continued to tour and record prolifically. In the 1980s he has been seen and heard with musicians ranging from Herbie Hancock to the Cuban (Gillespie-influenced) trumpeter Arturo Sandoval, and with symphony orchestras. Gillespie's ability to entertain on all levels may have sometimes obscured his artistic vitality, but future generations will no doubt give him full credit for his incalculable contribution to Afro-American music.

DEE GEE DAYS (THE SAVOY SESSIONS)
Tin Tin Deo/Birks' Works/We Love To Boogie/Lady Be Good/Love Me Pretty Baby/The Champ/I'm In A Mess/Schooldays/Swing Low Sweet Cadillac/Bopsie's Blues (2 takes)/I Couldn't Beat The Rap/Caravan (2 takes)/Nobody Knows/The Bluest Blues/On The Sunny Side Of The Street/Stardust/Time On My Hands/Blue Skies/Umbrella Man/Confessin' (Pops)/Ooh-Shoo-Be-Doo-Be/They Can't Take That Away From Me
1–3 Dizzy Gillespie (tp), John Coltrane (as, ts), Milt Jackson (vib), Kenny Burrell (g), Percy Heath (b), Kansas Fields (d), Freddy Strong (voc), March 1951; 4–6 Gillespie (tp), J. J. Johnson (tb, Budd Johnson (ts), Jackson (p, vib), Heath (b), Art Blakey (d), Joe Carroll (voc 4), Melvin Moore (voc, 5) April 1951; 7–12 Gillespie (tp, voc 9), Bill Graham (bars), Jackson (p), Heath (b), Al Jones (d), Carroll (voc 7, 8), Moore (voc 10–12), August 1951; 13–19 Gillespie (tp, voc 15, 17), Graham (bars), Stuff Smith (vln), Jackson (p, org, vib), Heath (b), Art Blakey (d), Joe Carroll (voc 4), Melvin Moore (voc, 5) April 1951; 7–12 Gillespie (tp, voc 9), Bill Graham (bars), Jackson (p), Heath (b), Al Jones (d), Carroll (voc 7, 8), Moore (voc

10–12), August 1951; 13–19 Gillespie (tp, voc 15, 17), Graham (bars),, Stuff Smith (vln), Jackson (p, org, vib), Heath (b), Al Jones (d), Carroll (voc, 15, 17), October 1951; 20–24 Gillespie (tp, voc 20), Graham (bars), Wynton Kelly (p), Bernie Griggs (b), Jones (d), Carroll (voc 20–23), July 1952.
Savoy ZD70517
AAD Running time: 73.02
Performance: ★ ★ (★ ★ ★)
Recording: ★ ★

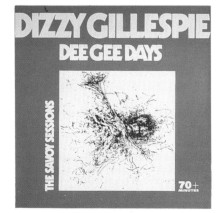

DIZZY GILLESPIE
DEE GEE DAYS
THE SAVOY SESSIONS
70+ MINUTES

When Gillespie's Dee Gee record company folded early in 1953, the masters were acquired by Savoy. This set, available for some years as a double LP, contains all the Dee Gee tracks on which Dizzy performed himself. Seventeen of the twenty-two titles (two alternate takes bring the track total to twenty-four) have vocals, and though these range from the appealingly modernised jump-band blues shout of Freddy Strong '(we love to boogie, and re-bop and be-boppin' too . . .') to the too-mannered Eckstine-style baritone of Melvin Moore, most of the singing is by Joe Carroll, whose work ranges from the enjoyably hip (*Bluest Blues*) to a deadly accurate but affectionate Armstrong parody (*Confessin'*), to the dated and actually flat (*Lady Be Good*).

On the instrumental side, this period saw Gillespie developing material that he continued to use for many years. Milt Jackson features prominently, providing the Milt Buckner-type piano on *Bopsie's Blues*, and Bill Graham's baritone sax lends weight to *The Champ* and (with Stuff Smith) the exotic *Caravan*. Gillespie's own playing is often astounding, and the recording quality is fundamentally good. An essential disc, if a candidate for 'Favourite Track Selection'!

DIZZY IN PARIS
Hurry Home/Afro Paris/Say Eh!/I Cover The Waterfront/She's Funny That Way/Cripple Crapple Crutch/Dizzy Song (Lady Bird)/Somebody Loves Me/Wrap Your Troubles In Dreams/Sweet Lorraine/Everything Happens To Me/I Don't Know Why/Always/Mon Homme/Watch Out/Moon Nocturne/This Is The Way/S'Wonderful/Oo Bla Dee
1–5 Dizzy Gillespie (tp), Don Byas (ts), Arnold Ross (p), Joe Benjamin (b), Bill Clark (d), Humberto Canto (cga), Paris, March 1952; 6–12 Gillespie (tp), Bill Tamper (tb), Hubert Fol (as), Byas (ts), Raymond Fol (p), Pierre Michelot (b), Pierre Lemarchand (d), Paris, April 1952; 13–19 Gillespie (tp), Nat Peck (tb), Wade Legge (p), Lou Hackney (b), Al Jones (d), Joe Carroll (voc), Paris, February 1953.
Vogue 600047
AAD Running time: 59.15
Performance: ★ ★ ★   Recording: ★

On the first of the three Paris studio sessions included here, Gillespie and Byas were joined by Lena Horne's rhythm section to produce a quietly effective quintet, Gillespie sounding happy and unusually lyrical on the ballads. Recording with a French group the following

month, Gillespie opened by singing the burlesque blues *Cripple Crapple Crutch*, and on the other numbers produced a series of fine solos over the efficient if sometimes rather tick-tock rhythm section. Sound quality from this date is variable, with Gillespie's trumpet sometimes blasting out while the other instruments form a mushy fog.

The final session, from the following year's tour, features Gillespie's own musicians, except for baritone saxist Bill Graham, who had disappeared at the time and so was replaced by trombonist Peck. Vocals come from the band (on *Always*) and from Carroll (*Oo Bla Dee*), while *S'Wonderful* opens with a Dixieland parody before doubling the time in a be-bop version. Also outstanding instrumentally is *Mon Homme* (or *My Man*, either way a big hit for Gillespie with the French). Despite an often muzzy sound, this disc has much to offer and is a valuable addition to Gillespie's live French recordings (*Pleyel Concert*) and his US studio dates of the period.

A PORTRAIT OF DUKE ELLINGTON
In a Mellow Tone/Things Ain't What They Used To Be/Serenade To Sweden/Chelsea Bridge/Upper Manhattan Medical Group/Do Nothin' Till You Here From Me/Caravan/Sophisticated Lady/Johnny Come Lately/Perdido/Come Sunday
Dizzy Gillespie (tp), Bennie Green (tb), Robert de Dominica (fl), Stan Webb, Paul Ritchie, John Murtaugh, Ernest Bright (woodwinds), Richard Berg, Ray Alonge, Joe Singer (fr h), John McAllister (tuba), George Devens (vib), Hank Jones (p), George Duviver (b), Charlie Persip (d), Clare Fischer (arr), April 1960.
Verve 817 107
AAD Running time: 41.42
Performance: ★ ★   Recording: ★ ★ ★

Gillespie's readings of these Ellington tunes have an unexpected sound, mainly because the 16-piece orchestra is not a conventional big band; in place of the usual ranks of trumpets and saxophones are woodwinds, French horns, a flute, tuba and vibraphone. Perhaps the instrumentation seemed appropriate in a 'portrait' of one who extracted such very different tone colours from the conventional jazz horns (if not in conventional combinations), and in the case of *Caravan* the effect actually is that of a slightly pallid Ellington group.

Elsewhere, the results are sometimes intriguing, sometimes not; for example, Gillespie drastically slows down *Things Ain't What They Used To Be* (usually a medium-fast blues played with a train rhythm), making it rather aimless and lacking in punch. Some of the other numbers also seem to invite unfavourable comparison with the work of earlier Gillespie big bands, but this might be to miss the point; Gillespie himself excels against this lighter, woodier background in *Do Nothin' Till You Hear From Me*, *Sophisticated Lady* and the mid-tempo swinger (usually associated with Hodges), *Johnny Come Lately*. Gillespie also gives a virtuoso workout on *Perdido*, and plays *Come Sunday* in his best rhapsody open-horn style. This may not be one of Gillespie's great recordings, but it is one that improves with listening.

DIZZY GILLESPIE AND THE DOUBLE SIX OF PARIS (FEATURING BUD POWELL)
Emanon/Anthropology/Tin Tin Deo/One Bass Hit/Two Bass Hit/Groovin' High/Oo-Shoo-Be-Do-Be/Hot House/Con Alma/Blue'n' Boogie/The Champ/Ow!
1–6, 8, 10–12 Dizzy Gillespie (tp), Bud Powell (p), Pierre Michelot (b), Kenny Clarke (d), Mimi Perrin, Claudine Barge, Christine Legrand, Ward Swingle, Robert Smart, Eddy Louis, Jean-Claude Briodin (voc), Lalo Schifrin (arr), Paris, July 1963; 7, 9 add James Moody (as), Kenny Barron (p), Chris White (b), Rudy Collins (d) replace Powell, Michelot, Clarke, Chicago, September 1963.
Philips 830 224-2
AAD Running time: 39.12
Performance: ★ ★   Recording: ★ ★

Putting words to be-bop was hard enough in English but here, using favourite Gillespie tunes of the 1940s, the incredibly accomplished Double Six did it in French. The results are at once peculiar and appealing. Lyrics were provided by Mimi Perrin, chief vocal soloist, who based most of them on science fiction or fantasy themes; thus *The Champ* becomes *Robie Le Robot* while *Blue And Boogie* becomes *Le Monde Vert*. Recording quality is helpfully clear if sometimes over-bright, and the vibrant sound of the vocal group impresses with sheer speed on *Anthropology*. The rich and softening effect of Schifrin's arrangement provides telling accompaniment on *Tin Tin Deo*, which is fascinating also for Powell's solo. The comfortable European feeling about this disc really takes it almost out of the jazz sphere, and it is clearly not a record for those who loathe the Swingle Singers, but it does show that Gillespie, ever ready to experiment, was once again ahead of his time.

THE GIANT
Manteca/Alone Together/Brother K/Wheatleigh Hall/Stella By Starlight/I Waited For You/Girl Of My Dreams
Dizzy Gillespie (tp), Johnny Griffin (ts),Kenny Drew (p), Neils Henning Orsted Pedersen (b), Humberto Canto (cga)
Accord 139217
AAD Running time: 53.52
Performance: ★ ★ ★
Recording: ★ ★ ★

With the great Kenny Clarke, fellow expatriates Griffin and Drew, and veteran conga player Canto, not to mention the virtuoso bassist Pedersen, this should have been a classic Gillespie date; and as it turns out, there are few disappointments. *Manteca* kicks the set off with a fantastic funk-influenced rhythm from Clarke. On the second tune Pedersen plays arco to introduce Gillespie, whose tone is now characteristically broad and slightly fuzzy on this lovingly-sustained ballad. Gillespie puts in a mute for *Mr K*, a feature also for Drew, and with an appealing solo by Griffin; while on the ultra-fast *Wheatleigh Hall*, Griffin solos superbly over a simply breathtaking performance by Clarke. *Stella* is a little less successful somehow, the rhythm becoming merely busy. But this is a disc containing some excellent music by a group of not-so-old masters, very well recorded too.

NEW FACES
Birks' Works/Lorraine/Tin Tin Deo/Tenor Song/Ballad/Fiesta Mojo/Every Mornin'
Dizzy Gillespie (tp), Branford Marsalis (ts, ss), Kenny Kirkland (p), Lonnie Plaxico (b), Robert Ameen (d), Lincoln Gains (el b 7), Steve Thornton (perc 3, 6), 1984.
GRP GRP-D-9512
AAD Running time: 43.02
Performance: ★ ★   Recording: ★ ★ ★

An avowed part of GRP's policy is to record the jazz giants of an older generation whenever the opportunity presents itself. This well-planned recording of Gillespie with a group of younger musicians turned out to be an almost unqualified success, as perhaps it should have been bearing in mind the quality of the sidemen; at the time, Kirkland was the pianist in Wynton Marsalis' group, Plaxico Art Blakey's bassist. Ameen is the only member of this group drawn from GRP's own artist roster, Branford Marsalis is excellent throughout; he provides a deep, baritone-like tenor sound on a rhythmically-updated but convincing *Birks' Works*, and with a real 'edge' in Gillespie's playing, the often-imitated minor-key blues theme comes through as strong as ever over a near-rock beat.

On *Lorraine*, Marsalis provides a perfectly-intoned soprano solo and later adds an attractive harmony part to Gillespie's reprise of the theme, Kirkland solos with cascades of notes. *Tin Tin Deo* does not seem to have come as naturally; entering after the usual rhythm-section intro, Gillespie's trumpet has been given a lot of echo and sounds artificially distant. You are just getting used to the sound of this when, after eight bars, Branford's soprano takes over the tune; the two horns play together in the release, but the effect is rather strange.

Again, there are fine solos from Marsalis and Kirkland, as there are on most tracks. Gillespie seems to have discovered the secret of eternal youth as he dances with equal delight over the Latin beat of *Fiesta Mojo* and the brash jazz-rock of *Every Mornin'*. Ameen must be partly responsible for the pronounced GRP flavour which pervades the disc, but this is perhaps mainly due to the production. The sound, almost clinical and with any natural ambience suppressed, gives the impression of having been meticulously assembled in the control room, and consequently (depending on taste) the listener can feel distanced from the performers; but they, without a doubt, did a good job.

BENNY GOODMAN
(b. Chicago, Illinois, 30 May 1909; d. 13 June, 1986)

It was as a bandleader that Goodman became 'King of Swing' but he may be remembered primarily as a surprisingly influential soloist, who undoubtedly helped set new technical standards, and for his remarkable small groups, which first engendered the description 'chamber jazz'.

Aged ten, Benny enrolled in the local synagogue band along with his older brothers Harry and Freddie, and started formal clarinet lessons with Franz Shoepp, who taught Buster Bailey and Jimmy Noone. He was soon performing Ted Lewis imitations and by thirteen was playing in dance bands. By the end of 1923, he had worked in river boat bands, and played with Jimmy McPartland, Dave Tough and Art Hodes. Still not quite sixteen, he joined Ben Pollack in 1925, first recorded with him in 1926, and was touring with the Pollack band for most of the next three years. He recorded with Red Nichols in 1929, while 1931 brought Goodman's own 'Charlestown Chasers' session and the classic Venuti-Lang session with Jack Teagarden.

Teagarden was also the vocalist when Benny assembled a studio band for John Hammond in October 1933, to provide 'hot' records for the European market. Further sessions used Billie Holiday (her first record date) in November, and Mildred Bailey in February 1934. In June 1934, Goodman assembled a band for a residency at Billy Rose's Music Hall, and from December the band gained national exposure with weekly radio broadcasts. A national tour followed, unsuccessful

KING OF SWING
Watch What Happens/Windy/Love Theme From 'Romeo And Juliet'/You Made Me So Very Happy/I'll Never Fall In Love Again/Bluesette/Good Morning Starshine/Aquarius/Spinning Wheel/Monday, Monday/Both Sides Now/Up, Up And Away
1-5, 7-9, 11, 12 Benny Goodman Orchestra; 6 Benny Goodman Sextet featuring Toots Thielmans (harmonica); 10 Benny Goodman Sextet, October 1969
Bridge 100.021
AAD Running time: 41.04
Performance: ★　Recording: ★ ★ ★

An educated glance at the titles could date this set to within a year or two; some make better vehicles than others. Perhaps the most unlikely is *Monday, Monday*, by the Sextet, based on a very 'dirty' electric blues guitar sound and chunky electric bass. Against this crass accompaniment, the subtle exposition of the rather ordinary tune, by muted trombone backing Goodman's clarinet, is rather lost.

I'll Never Fall In Love Again comes

perilously close to Muzak despite a fine arrangement and, in spite of a neat guest appearance by the composer on harmonica, this brisk 4/4 rendering of *Bluesette* still seems a little shapeless. *Aquarius* has a Goodman solo over drums reminiscent of *Twilight In Turkey*. Other big band tracks, for example *Good Morning Starshine* and *Up, Up And Away*, are successful, with an infectious beat, punchy and extremely well played arrangements, and the expected quicksilver of the leader's clarinet. There is a touch of graininess in the treble, but generally the sound quality (like the music) is enjoyable enough.

LIVE AT CARNEGIE HALL: 40th ANNIVERSARY CONCERT
Let's Dance/I've Found A New Baby/Send In The Clowns/Loch Lomond/Stardust/I Love A Piano/Roll 'Em/King Porter Stomp/Rocky Raccoon/Yesterday/That's A Plenty/How High The Moon/Moonglow/Oh! Lady Be Good/Jersey Bounce/Seven Come Eleven/Someone To Watch Over Me/Please Don't Talk About Me When I'm Gone/Benny Goodman Medley/Sing, Sing, Sing; Christopher Columbus/Goodbye
Victor Paz, Warren Vache, Jack Sheldon (tp), Wayne Andre, George Masso, John Messner (tb), George Young, Mel Rodnon (as), Buddy Tate, Frank Wess (ts), Sol Schlinger (bars), Jimmy Rowles, John Bunch (p), Cal Collins, Wayne Wright (g), Michael Moore (b), Connie Kay (d); guest artists Martha Tilton, Debi Craig (voc), Mary Lou Williams (p), Lionel Hampton (vib), January 1978.
London 820 349
DDD Running time: 107.36 (2 discs)
Performance: ★ ★　Recording: ★ ★ ★

To say that this was a special occasion would be almost an understatement. With an already star-studded band, Goodman brought on four guests whose presence at first but turning into now-legendary triumph at the Palomar Ballroom, Los Angeles. By now, the Benny Goodman Trio, the prototype 'band within a band', brought in Teddy Wilson on piano and featured Gene Krupa. It became a quartet when, in Hollywood in 1936 to film *The Big Broadcast of 1937*, Goodman discovered and recruited Lionel Hampton. In March 1937, at the paramount Theatre, New York, audiences went wild in the first scenes of 'Goodmania', and in January 1938 the band played the first 'swing' concert at Carnegie Hall. In contrast, later that year Goodman recorded Mozart's Clarinet Quintet with the Budapest String Quartet.

With the great guitarist Charlie Christian, whose work with Goodman between 1939 and 1941 makes up the bulk of his recorded legacy, the 'band within a band' became a sextet. Although Wilson, Krupa, Hampton and trumpet star Harry James all left to form their own bands, personnel changes did little to slow the band's success. In later years Goodman appeared in many films, and successfully led both large and small bands, as well as performing and recording as a classical soloist. Touring the world in the 1960s and 1970s, he also hosted and performed in a star-studded commemorative concert at Carnegie Hall in 1978.

turned the evening into a historic reunion. With the possible exception of Goodman's own lachrymose singing (*I Love A Piano*), the performances are excellent Connie Kay maintaining that light-footed swing throughout.

Goodman did not attempt to repeat the programme of the original 1938 Carnegie Hall concert, but presented a careful mixture of old favourites and newer numbers; the latter range from *Send In The Clowns* and *Yesterday*, with Goodman's clarinet at its most liquid and lyrical, to The Beatles'

Rocky Raccoon, sung in an appropriate and surprisingly appealing country style (after a few introductory jokes) by Jack Sheldon. The old favourites are slick and effective; Mary Lou Williams excels on the boogie-woogie *Roll 'Em* while Hampton is evocative on *Moonglow* and exciting on *Jersey Bounce* and *Seven Come Eleven*. Recording quality is excellent, the balance good, the live feeling conveyed well. Sadly, although the liner notes make lighthearted reference to plans for a 50th Anniversary concert, Benny Goodman will not be there.

DEXTER GORDON
(b. Los Angeles, California, 27 February 1923)

Innovator of a rugged bop tenor style, Dexter Gordon's acting experience uniquely qualified him for the starring role in 'Round Midnight', the 1986 French film loosely based on the character of his primary musical influence, Lester Young, and on the life of his one-time colleague, Bud Powell.

The son of a doctor (who numbered Duke Ellington and Lionel Hampton among his patients), Gordon was taught by Lloyd Reese (who also taught Charles Mingus). In December 1940, he went on the road with Lionel Hampton, whose star tenorist was then Illinois Jacquet, and in 1944 played with Fletcher Henderson and even with Armstrong. He then replaced Lucky Thompson in the Billy Eckstine band.

With Gene Ammons, he recorded the first of many frenetic tenor duels, *Blowin' the Blues Away*, then in 1945 appeared on Dizzy Gillespie's *Blue 'n' Boogie* (Guild) and did *Blow Mr Dexter* for Savoy. Back in LA in 1946, he formed a two-tenor team with Wardell Gray and cut *The Chase*, while 1947 saw more Savoy sides with Tadd Dameron and Fats Navarro. Back on the Coast, he worked with Helen Humes in 1950, and in 1952 re-did *The Chase* with Gray, but then, after a narcotics bust, spent most of 1953–4 in Chino open prison. He was seen (although the sound was dubbed by another player) in a film about the institution.

After some 1955 Bethlehem recordings with Kenny Drew, there was a gap until 1960, when Gordon's playing and acting role in the LA production of Jack Gelber's *The Connection* (a play about junkies) led to new recordings. Gordon went to Europe in 1962, and has lived in Copenhagen ever since, recording many albums with Scandinavian musicians. *Round Midnight* is Gordon's biggest-ever comeback, and no doubt this time he is back to stay.

GO
Cheese Cake/Guess I'll Hang My Tears Out To Dry/Second Balcony Jump/Love For Sale/Where Are You/Three O'Clock In The Morning
Dexter Gordon (ts), Sonny Clarke (p), Butch Warren (b), Billy Higgins (d), 1962
Blue Note CDP 7 46094
AAD Running time: 37.50
Performance: ★ ★ ★   Recording: ★ ★ ★

A currently successful reissue in the wake of the film 'Round Midnight,' Go was originally the third in a series of three Blue Note albums (following *Doin' Allright* and *Dexter Calling*) which Dexter made in 1961 and 1962 after his West Coast appearance in *The Connection*. It is essentially a straightforward record, with Gordon blowing long, relaxed and expansive solos over a rhythm section dominated by the varied, sometimes explosive, always interesting and always urgently propulsive drumming of Billy Higgins. The dependable Butch Warren remains firmly in the background.

Gordon's theme in the opener, *Cheese Cake*, built on a basically minor-key sequence, is a bit like an idiosyncratic, updated *Topsy*, a flexible blowing vehicle; rather like a stone faced giant for once grudgingly showing signs of tender emotion, Gordon allows himself some vibrato on a resonant ballad treatment in *Guess I'll Hang My Tears Out To Dry*.

Sonny Clarke's solos keep things moving but seldom seem inspired; he seems to have really hit his stride, only to falter again with thin-sounding repetitions, in *Love For Sale*, a tune which once more lends itself to Gordon's 'sixties uptempo manner, keeping the pressure on through the sheer power and weight of his tone while maintaining an almost leisurely approach to the chords. *Second Balcony Jump*, a busy jump tune originating with Earl Hines and his 1940s big band, has Gordon sounding at first like the earlier Sonny Rollins, punching the notes out but still with a slightly softer approach (evoking Lester Young) than his own 'tough' style of the 1940s.

Wit appears in the eccentric treatment of *Where Are You*, and in the jaunty 'chimes' effect and miscellaneous quotes of *Three O'Clock In The Morning*, which nonetheless has a compulsive swing. This remains something of a Gordon classic, and sound quality is excellent.

OUR MAN IN PARIS

Scrapple From The Apple/Willow Weep For
Me/Broadway/Stairway To The Stars/A
Night In Tunisia/Our Love Is Here To Stay/
Like Someone In Love
Dexter Gordon (ts except 7), Bud Powell (p),
Pierre Michelot (b), Kenny Clarke (d), Paris,
May 1963.
Blue Note CDP7 46394
AAD Running time: 50.13
Performance: ★ ★ ★   Recording: ★ ★

From the first bars of the first number, there
is real vitality in this set; Gordon launches a
full-bodied and vibrant attack on the
archetypal bebop theme, spurred on by the
still-potent fireworks of the great Kenny
Clarke. He wraps up his solo with a final
burst of speed, and then as they trade fours,
matches Clarke's ebullience with a
sardonically-repeated *Tea For Two*
fragment.

The other period piece from this gathering
of bop-era giants is the less striking but still
effective *Night In Tunisia*, where Gordon
takes a simpler route and does not attempt to
re-create the interplay of the original lines;
more gripping is the quintessentially
percussive, authoritative solo of Bud Powell
in *Willow Weep For Me*.

On *Broadway*, Gordon alternates his more
strident version of Lester Young, complete
with repeated honks, with eighth-note
flurries in truer bop style. Added reverb
gives him a still dense but somehow foggy
tone in *Stairway To The Stars*; and Gordon
sounds positively nasal in *Our Love Is Here
To Stay*, which gets its usual medium-swing
treatment. It is understandable that this and
the trio number *Someone In Love*, where
Powell's crushed notes and brittle, dissonant
chords produce the effect of distortion, were
omitted from the vinyl release. Though these
add only marginally to its value, the disc has
much to recommend it.

BITING THE APPLE

Apple Jump/I'll Remember April/Georgia
On My Mind/Blue Bossa/Skylark/A La
Modal
Dexter Gordon (ts), Barry Harris (p), Sam
Jones (b), Al Foster (d), November 1976
Steeplechase SCCD-31080
AAD Running time: 56.30
Performance: ★ ★   Recording: ★ ★ ★

Sounding supremely relaxed, this quartet
session dates from a year when Gordon, long
based in Europe, made one of his periodical
returns to the USA. He is well supported
here, and Detroit-born pianist Harris offers
attractive solos, especially over the supple
arco bass of Jones on *Skylark*. The other

ballad here is a lovely *Georgia*, and this, along with a workmanlike and bouncy *Blue Bossa*, are the two previously unissued tracks which give a generous running time. Gordon's smooth, creamy tone reveals a firm centre, rather than a hard edge, in his soaring, masterful performance on the Coltrane-inflected *A La Modal*, where it has to be said that the relatively gentle pianist seems less effective; more characteristic, perhaps, are the first two tracks, both of which allow long and comfortable blowing. Sound quality on this disc is hard to fault, the acoustic fairly dry but the instruments nicely distanced to produce a satisfying balance and weight. Good value.

THE OTHER SIDE OF ROUND MIDNIGHT

Round Midnight/Berangere's Nightmare 2/ Call Sheet Blues/What Is This Thing Called Love/Tivoli/Society Red/As Time Goes By/ It's Only A Paper Moon/Round Midnight
1 Dexter Gordon (ts), Wayne Shorter (ss), Palle Mikkelborg (tp), Herbie Hancock (p), Ron Carter (b), Mads Vinding (b), Billy Higgins (d); 2 Freddie Hubbard (tp), Hancock (p), Carter (b), Tony Williams (d); 3 Shorter (ss), Hancock (p), Carter (b), Higgins (d); 4 Bobby McFerrin (voc), Hancock (p); 5 Gordon (ts), Mikkelborg (tp), Ceder Walton (p), Vinding (b), Higgins (d); 6 Gordon (ts), Hubbard (tp), Walton (p), Carter (b), Williams (d); 7 Gordon (ts), Hancock (p), John McLaughlin (g), Pierre Michelot (b), Higgins (d); 8 Bobby Hutcherson (vib), Hancock (p), Michelot (b), Higgins (d); 9 Hancock (p), Summer 1985.
Blue Note CDP 7 46297
AAD Running time: 51.18
Performance: ★   Recording: ★ ★ ★

This title is a nice way of describing material that was not used for the *Round Midnight* soundtrack. In the opening version of the title theme here, Shorter, then Mikkelborg (muted) and Gordon give a superbly atmospheric introduction and Carter then plays the theme on the upper reaches of his bass, giving way to a truly sonorous interlude from Gordon. There is also a Miles-like solo here, but the powerful Hubbard leaves off the mute for his blistering, trilling lead in *Berangere's Nightmare No 2*; here Hancock stokes the fires with tumbling cascades of notes over a stabbing left hand.

Call Sheet blues, a spontaneous jam. kicked off by Carter while the musicians were waiting on the set, becomes effectively a feature for Shorter, as does *Tivoli*, which in this version fades during an attractive piano solo (recording stopped when no more was needed for the film). *Society Red* is a grimly-determined kind of soul blues, complete with rolling piano from Hancock, Blakey-style rolls and sections of fourth-beat rim-shots from Higgins. McLaughlin contributes some little lifting chords behind Gordon's lag-along interpretation of *As Time Goes By*, before proffering a short solo; *It's Only A Paper Moon*, featuring Bobby Hutcherson, sounds pleasant but a little flimsy on a moody Latin beat with switches to straight 4/4, and the title theme, this time a florid, rambling solo by Hancock, brings this rather assorted collection to a close. It really is a mixed bag; momentum is often lost, and there is a tendency to drift into a stylistic limbo. But it is still full of interest, well recorded and enjoyable enough, if with only snatches of Gordon at his majestic best.

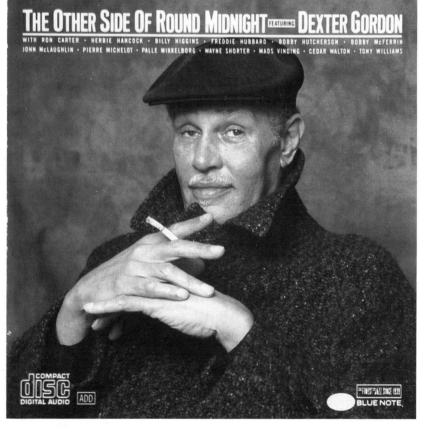

STEPHANE GRAPPELLI
(b. Paris, France, 26 January 1908)

Outside his native France, Grappelli's earliest fame came as the distinctive and technically-adept foil to the guitar genius Django Reinhardt in the Quintette du Hot Club de France recordings of the 1930s; subsequent decades have seen him continue to develop and refine his violin style in a long and distinguished career.

The young Grappelly (as he then spelled his name) learned several instruments, and became a good pianist, but by the age of twelve he was firmly started on the violin. His professional career started with jobs in Paris theatre bands, and by the early 1930s he was playing in the polite tea-dance orchestra led by accordionist and bassist Louis Vola. But American jazz was already exerting a powerful influence on the members of Vola's band, and when the jazz enthusiast Hugues Panassié and his friends formed their Hot Club de France, they found the Quintette almost ready made.   War broke out while the group was in London, and Grappelli, having no family reasons to return to France, stayed in London. Playing with local musicians, he became a popular figure in the London club scene. He returned to Paris in 1946.

Touring throughout Europe, his popularity with theatre, club and festival audiences continued to increase in the 1960s and 1970s, and since *Violin Summit*, with Stuff Smith, Jean Luc-Ponty and Svend Asmussen (1966), he has once more become a prolific recording artist.

AFTERNOON IN PARIS
This Can't Be Love/Time After Time/ Undecided/You Were Only Passing By/ Tangerine/Chicago/Manoir De Mes Reves/ Daphne/Misty/Afternoon In Paris/Autumn Leaves
Stephane Grappelli (vln), Marc Hemmeler (p), Eberhard Weber (b), Kenny Clare (d), Villingen, West Germany, March 1971.
MPS 821 865
AAD Running time: 42.10
Performance: ★ ★   Recording: ★

Working energetically through a programme of well-varied standards, Grappelli displays dazzling form on the faster numbers; for example, he breathes life into the corny old tune *Undecided. This Can't Be Love* is typical uptempo Grappelli, as he throws in all his usual phrasing devices, and is followed effectively by a fine ballad performance, *Time After Time*; here, sympathetically accompanied, Grappelli's treatment somehow seems to retain the depth so often lost in his renditions of familiar tunes. It is more effective than either *Misty* or the lovely Reinhardt tune *Manoir de Mes Reves*, which gets an incredibly skilled but almost peremptory run-through as a sort of intro to the Hot Club's anthem, *Daphne*.

Grappelli's wonderful urbanity is demonstrated on *Chicago*, and on John Lewis's nostalgically evocative city-streets theme *Afternoon In Paris*, but interest flags a little through the repetitive chord cycles of *Tangerine*. The set ends well with a solid if predictable *Autumn Leaves*.

Unfortunately, particularly when subjected to the scrutiny of Compact Disc on a modern hi-fi system, the recording balance leaves a lot to be desired. The initially-appealing resonance of Grappelli's violin becomes overpowering after a while, while Weber's bass is overpowering in the opposite sense, recorded with an airless closeness which makes it sound lumbering and too loud. A shame, because the playing on this disc is extremely good.

PABLO LIVE
It's Only A Paper Moon/Time After Time/ Let's Fall In Love/Crazy Rhythm/How Deep Is The Ocean/I'll Remember April/I Can't Get Started/I Get A Kick Out Of You.
Stephane Grappelli (vln), Joe Pass (g), Neils Henning Orsted Pedersen (b), Denmark, July 1979.
Pablo J33J 20041
AAD Running time: 44.42
Performance: ★ ★   Recording: ★ ★ ★

Without piano or drums, this string trio presents true salon jazz, which is after all Grappelli's *métier*. Pedersen, comprehensive to the point of being busy, provides the foundation and in fact, through his very 'close' amplified bass sound, is rather too omnipresent. Pass, as ever, displays inexhaustible reserves of invention and technique, and a light touch in chord work as well as in his bursts of contrapuntal accompaniment to Grappelli.

Among the best numbers are the fastest (*Crazy Rhythm* and *I'll Remember April*), though the spectacular mastery of the players leads to audience applause after every solo, and this becomes a little irritating after a while. Others (*Let's Fall In Love, I Get A Kick Out Of You*) fall into an over-comfortable, rather plunking mid-tempo rhythm which is only saved from banality by the virtuosity of the participants. Yet this itself seems to work against the overall effect when Grappelli drops out for the slow ballad *How Deep Is The Ocean*, a duet in which Pedersen and Pass sometimes seem to be merely competing to see who can put in the most notes. Pedersen's solo is impressive rather than appealing, and here even Pass seems to sacrifice lyricism for instant effect.

Elsewhere Grappelli demonstrates the polished, instantly recognisable style which has retained its vitality since before the war. Sound quality is good, being bright, smooth and clear; fans of Pass and particularly of Grappelli will find this recording well up to standard.

DAVE GRUSIN
(b. Denver, Colorado, 26 June 1934)

Now almost a father figure in fusion, Dave Grusin is a remarkably prolific pianist and keyboard player, composer and arranger. In recent recordings on his own label, GRP (which he co-owns with former drummer Larry Rosen) he has often figured as a catalyst, providing a context for the work of other established or developing stars.

Encouraged to take up music by his father, who was a watchmaker and a keen violinist, Grusin started the piano early. In his late teens, he was set for a career in veterinary medicine but changed his mind at the last minute; instead of veterinary college, he took up piano studies at Colorado University, and later moved to Manhattan School of Music. He had intended to continue in music teaching, but after taking a job as pianist on tour with singer Andy Williams, he became musical director on Williams' successful TV show. Film writing followed (Grusin has produced scores for 'The Graduate', 'Heaven Can Wait'. 'On Golden Pond' and many other movies) and he continued to write for TV while becoming a sought-after session pianist and producer.

Grusin and Rosen Productions was formed in 1976, and though initially releasing product through other companies, GRP soon became a fully-fledged independent label. In the days before the term 'New Age' had taken on its current specific and not always positive connotation, GRP's stated aim was to 'document the new age in jazz'. The long list of fusion players associated with GRP includes Lee Ritenour, Grover Washington and Sadao Watanabe; artists recently recorded on GRP also include Dizzy Gillespie and Gerry Mulligan, as well as singers Diane Schuur and Phoebe Snow.

ONE OF A KIND
Modaji/The Heart Is A Lonely Hunter/
Catavento/Montage/Playera.
1 Grover Washington Jr (ss), Dave Grusin (el p), Francisco Centeno (el b), Steve Gadd (d), Ralph MacDonald (perc), Don Elliot (mellophone, voc); 2 Grusin (p, el p), Ron Carter (b); 3 Grusin (el p), Dave Valentin (fl), Centeno (el b), Gadd (d), MacDonald (perc); 4 Grusin (p, el p, synth), Valentin (fl), Anthony Jackson, Centeno (el b), Gadd (d), MacDonald (perc), Larry Rosen (triangle); 5 Washington (ss), Grusin (p, el p, perc), Carter (b), Gadd (d). String section concert master Paul Gershman; 1977.
GRP GRP-D-9514
ADD Running time: 36.13
Performance: ★ ★ Recording: ★ ★ ★

Recorded orginally for Polydor in the early days of GRP, but later bought back by Grusin and Rosen for their own label, One Of A Kind is something of a fusion classic. Opening with the slapped funky bass of Centeno, Grusin's tune Modaji is an ideal vehicle for the unmistakable soprano of Grover Washington, the modern sounds set in a beautifully-distanced cloud of strings. Grusin weaves a florid piano line in The Heart Is A Lonely Hunter, while rich and resonant strings well up behind, but as the piece goes on, in suspension almost on the pedal points provided by Carter, you can't help feeling that this is a backdrop for something that didn't happen. Montage is rich in synthesiser sounds, bubbling over a driving beat; Grover Washington returns quite majestically in the final number.

This is an attractive disc, sonically as well as mechanically; perhaps the sound does not have the cut-glass detail of GRP's later all-digital recordings, but it is still enjoyable.

MOUNTAIN DANCE
Rag Bag/Friends and Strangers/City Lights/
Rondo/Mountain Dance/Thanksong/
Captain Caribe/Either Way.
1-5, 7, 8 Jeff Miranov (g), Dave Grusin (p, el p), Marcus Miller (el b), Ed Walsh, Ian Underwood (synth), Marcus Miller (b), Harvey Mason (d), Rubens Bassini (perc); 6 Grusin (p), 1981.
GRP D-9507
DDD Running time: 39.36
Performance: ★ ★ Recording: ★ ★ ★

Grusin and Rosen describe the making of Mountain Dance as a two-fold challenge. Pushing at what were then the frontiers of technology, they opted for direct-to-digital recording, using the Soundstream system, so there could be no overdubs and no remixing after the session; the music had to be peformed live in the studio and mixing had to be done live too.

Grusin opens the album acoustically with an almost raggy piano intro, and offers a continuing interplay between acoustic piano and electronic sounds with the entry of a high, piping synth line. Miranov adds a brief but gutsy solo. City Lights sets a mood with a typically lush piano opening from Grusin, then settles down to a springy four-bar riff. The title track is reminiscent of Keith Jarrett or Chick Corea, but despite the bright, plangent piano sound, the contours of the theme are too regular for this; on another level, it really is a dance, with an appealing kind of movement. Thanksong provides a pleasant acoustic interlude before the uptempo Captain Caribe, on which Miranov solos. Either Way ends the set in a floating, undemanding soft-soul groove. Bright, clean and immediate in sound quality, this whole disc exhibits perfect craftsmanship.

CHARLIE HADEN
(b. Shenendoah, Missouri, 6 August 1937)

Finding a new role for the bass in the context of Ornette Coleman's revolutionary 'free' jazz of the late 1950s, Haden has gone on to become a uniquely respected and influential player.

Working with Coleman's original group from 1958 to 1960, Haden abandoned the conventional time-keeping and harmonic roles of the bass, responding instead to the instantaneous demand of collective free improvising. After leaving Coleman, he did work briefly in the mainstream group of vibes player Red Norvo, then joined another leader of the *avant garde* Archie Shepp before going back to Coleman in 1966; by this time, the altoist had added his young son Denardo on drums, providing a further challenge for the bassist.

In 1969, he drew on the ranks of Carla Bley's JCOA to form the large group which produced the Impulse album *Liberation Music Orchestra*, making use of Spanish and other folk material and highlighting politically-inspired compositions such as *Song For Che*. He worked with Bley on her *Escalator Over The Hill*, but soon afterwards joined Keith Jarrett's trio. Later in the 1970s, he recorded a series of duets, featuring Coleman, Jarrett and Shepp among others, which have been acclaimed as his finest work; but Haden's most recent work, ranging from his work with Mingus Dynasty to his playing on Metheny and Coleman's *Song X*, shows that he is still a vital force.

MAGICO
Bailarina/Magico/Silence'/Spor/Palhaco
Jan Garbarek (ss, ts), Egberto Gismonti (p, g), Charlie Haden (b), June 1979, Oslo.
ECM 823 474
AAD Running time: 43.50
Performance: ★ ★ Recording: ★ ★ ★

After Gismonti's sumptuous guitar introduction, and sharp-toned yet lyrical playing from Garbarek, the first section of *Bailarina* gives way to a rippling, dancing rhythm that turns at one stage into a furious insect buzz; after a brief (wordless) vocal interlude, Garbarek re-enters with his most mournful, keening sound, taking the piece to another level and giving way, again, to a highly-charged bass/guitar duo. With busy, tumbling rhythm from the guitar, Haden again gives perfect support as Garbarek soars and swirls; subtle dynamic shading reveals the great empathy in this trio. With no loss of freshness or vitality, Gismonti adds a tender solo over the existing parts.

Gismonti's guitar glistens and glints on *Spor*; in *Palhaco*, as so often elsewhere, Haden steps back to contribute a subtle but vital underpinning. With relatively few instruments to deal with, the recording is superb here, open and clean with that cleverly-contrived feeling of space which makes the ECM sound so distinctive.

THE BALLAD OF THE FALLEN
Els Segadors/The Ballad Of The Fallen/If You Want To Write To Me/Grandola Villa Morena/Introduction To People/The People United Will Never Be Defeated/Silence/Too Late/La Pasionaria/La Santa Espina
Michael Mantler (tp), Don Cherry (pocket tp), Gary Valente (tb), Sharon Freeman (fr h), Jack Jeffers (tu), Jim Pepper (ts, ss, fl), Steve Slagle (as, ss, cl,/fl), Dewey Redman (ts), Carla Bley (p, glockenspiel), Mike Goodrick (g), Charlie Haden (b), Paul Motian (d, perc), November 1982.
ECM 811 546
DDD Running time: 51.56
Performance: ★ ★ ★ Recording: ★ ★ ★

CHARLIE HADEN
THE BALLAD OF THE FALLEN
CARLA BLEY

DON CHERRY
SHARON FREEMAN
MICK GOODRICK
JACK JEFFERS
MICHAEL MANTLER
PAUL MOTIAN
JIM PEPPER
DEWEY REDMAN
STEVE SLAGLE
GARY VALENTE

While the title is that of a recent song from El Salvador (and of course a poem, which is given in translation from the Spanish in the liner booklet), this recording also makes use of songs from the Spanish Civil War and the Chilean resistance movement in its theme of protest and revolt against oppression. The group is Haden's re-formed Liberation Music Orchestra, which in its original form had grown out of Bley's and Mantler's Jazz Composers Association Orchestra. The arrangements are by Bley, who provides arresting treatments of these folk or popular tunes; for example, *Grandola Vila Morena*, is a song led by flutes over an insistent march rhythm, associated with the Portugese army revolt of 1974.

This is followed almost seamlessly by Bley's own *Introduction To People*, using flutes and brass over a rippling piano, which pre-figures the darker, more powerful brass of *The People United Will Never Be Defeated*. Haden's *Silence*, fuller-sounding than the trio version on *Magico*, is thoughtfully scored for brass, with stately piano from Bley. *Too Late* is an absorbing, Spanish-sounding duet for Haden and Bley; Goodrick's Spanish guitar introduces the Civil War song *La Pasionaria*. Recorded to ECM's usual impeccable standard, this disc should be heard.

LIONEL HAMPTON
(b. Louisville, Kentucky, 12 April, 1909)

Before Lionel Hampton, the xylophone's electric cousin was little more than a novel addition to the percussionist's armoury. Hampton made the vibraphone his own, and remained its unchallenged genius until the advent of Milt Jackson.

Hampton was raised in Birmingham, Alabama, before moving with his family to Chicago in 1919. He played drums in the celebrated Chicago Defender Newsboys Band, and got his first xylophone tuition from bandleader Jimmy Bertrand. Working with various Chicago bands, he got stranded on tour in Hastings, Nebraska, and settled in California about 1927. After a stint with Paul Howard's Quality Serenaders, Hampton joined the Les Hite band, and appeared as the masked drummer in the film *Pennies from Heaven*.

He was leading his own band at the Paradise Cafe, Hollywood, when he was 'discovered' by Benny Goodman, and joined Teddy Wilson and Gene Krupa in the Benny Goodman Quartet. In 1939, Goodman added the electric guitarist Charlie Christian, and the Sextet recordings (the sixth member was bassist Artie Bernstein) offer fine examples of Hamp's dazzling melodic invention and rhythmic drive. Meanwhile, Hampton made many Victor recordings with 'all star' studio groups, often marred by his singing, which has, in the words of Charles Fox, 'the dreariness of lukewarm water'.

Hampton left Goodman in July 1940, and returned to California to form his own big band, which, with a few breaks, has toured successfully ever since. A majority of the bop-era horn players cut their teeth in the Hampton ranks but despite its 'modern' flavour, the later-1940s band specialised in a loping boogie-based blues style which now sounds terribly dated. Hampton's showmanship extended to taking over the drums or, in a two-fingered adaptation of his vibraphone style, the upper half of the piano. The most enduring example of Hampton's pianism is the early *Central Avenue Breakdown*, recorded with Nat Cole's Trio in 1940.

In later years, the band was still full of fine musicians, and Hamp's vibraphone solos, now well recorded, seemed to swing the whole band. Hamp retained Goodman's small-group 'band within a band' idea, and also recorded sessions with Oscar Peterson and Art Tatum. More successful, perhaps were some reunion sessions with Wilson and Krupa in July 1955, during the filming of 'The Benny Goodman Story'.

Still touring, Hampton has been fairly well captured by recordings in recent years, but musically his band has remained static. The few Compact Discs so far issued hardly do justice to his recording career, and it is to be hoped that his most creative phases will soon be better covered on CD.

THE COMPLETE PARIS SESSION
September In The Rain/Free Press Oui/
Always/Real Crazy/More Crazy/More And
More Crazy/Completely Crazy/I Only Have
Eyes For You
1, 3, 8 Lionel Hampton (vib), Billy Mackel
(g), William Montgomery (el b), Paris
September 1953; 2, 4-6, Walter Williams
(tp), Al Hayse, James Cleveland (tb), Milton
'Mezz' Mezzrow (cl), Clifford Scott, Alix
Combelle (ts), Hampton (vib), Claude
Bolling (p), Mackel (g), Montgomery (el b),
Curley Hamner (d), September 1953; 7 as 2,
Combelle out.
Vogue VG651 600029
AAD Running time: 54.42
Performance: ★   Recording: ★ ★

Now issued complete, this session is a
historical curiosity, actually laughable at
times, but it offers enough good playing by
Hampton to make up for almost all its
shortcomings. Recorded for the Hot Club of
France during Hampton's European tour, the
session is a prolonged and often directionless
jam session in which the French pianist/
composer Claude Bolling and well-known
sax player Alix Combelle sat in with a
nucleus of Hampton musicians, along with
the clarinettist Mezz Mezzrow, before a
small invited studio audience. Vogue's liner
note reference to 'the best soloists from his
band, now seems slightly ludicrous since the
Hampton orchestra's young rising stars
Clifford Brown, Quincy Jones and Gigi
Gryce are conspicuously absent from these
sessions.

On the three trio tracks, where Hampton
is accompanied only by guitar and bass, you
do have a chance to hear his vibes at unusual
length. All three are attractive performances,
perhaps the heavily tremolo-laden solo of *I*

Only Have Eyes For You being the most striking. *Free Press Oui* is a predominantly minor-key 32-bar sequence which gives Mackel and Combelle a chance to solo effectively (it is hard to believe the pianist here is Bolling), Williams and Mezzrow stridently.

All the *Crazy* tracks are mid-tempo jamming blues, with Bolling contributing a middle-of-the-road sort of boogie piano, while there are simple but attractively swinging phrases from Mackel, and some typically querulous and unfinished-sounding solos from Mezzrow, all this being backed up by some hastily improvised riffs from Hampton's hornmen, Williams, Hayse and Cleveland. Things only come to life when Hampton solos, as he exercises his apparently miraculous power of making the whole band swing behind him. Whether the excellent playing from Hampton will make up sufficiently for the disorganised and often un-swinging character of the rest of the music is a matter of personal taste; but in any case, it is a refreshingly simple recording, catching the zestful sound of Hamp's vibes to remarkable effect.

LIONEL HAMPTON PRESENTS GERRY MULLIGAN
Apple Core/Song For Johnny Hodges/Blight Of The Fumble Bee/Gerry Meets Hamp/ Blues For Gerry/Line For Lyons/Walking Shoes/Limelight
Gerry Mulligan (bars), Lionel Hampton (vib), Hank Jones (p), Bucky Pizzarelli (g), George Duvivier (b), Grady Tate (d), Candido Camero (cga), October 1977.
Kingdom CD GATE 7014
AAD Running time: 53.29
Performance: ★ ★   **Recording:** ★ ★

LIONEL HAMPTON PRESENTS
GERRY MULLIGAN
with
LIONEL HAMPTON
HANK JONES
BUCKY PIZZARELLI
GEORGE DUVIVIER
GRADY TATE
CANDIDO

The intention of this disc was to feature Mulligan rather than Hampton, but it presents Hampton effectively too. The opening *Apple Core*, based on the chords of *Love Me Or Leave Me*, is a perfect up-tempo vehicle for Hamp, and the versatile Mulligan falls happily into what is essentially a swing-era groove. *Gerry Meets Hamp* is a fast riff-based tune which has the frenetic precision of the Goodman Sextet, while Mulligan's tune *Blight Of The Fumble Bee* really moves along, Camero adding a 'soul' punctuation to the beat laid down by Tate. Hamp is prominent in Mulligan's *Line For Lyons* (sound quality is a bit peculiar here), but drops out of the more boppish *Limelight*. Pizzarelli uses the now dated sound of the wah-wah pedal in the rock-tinged *Walking Shoes*, but both Mulligan and Hampton look back affectionately in the moving slow ballad *For Johnny Hodges*. In general, sound quality is average for a modern recording, but the music is better than that.

LIONEL HAMPTON
THE COMPLETE PARIS SESSION

Vogue

HERBIE HANCOCK
(b. Chicago, 12 April 1940)

By the time he became a key figure in the fusion movement of the late 1960s and early 1970s, Herbie Hancock had spent several years as one of the most sought-after jazz pianists; and in recent years he has begun a parallel performing life with a series of returns to acoustic music. Conservatory-trained, the versatile Hancock remains one of the most respected keyboard players in the whole of the popular music field.

A true child prodigy, Herbert Jeffrey Hancock performed Mozart piano concertos with the Chicago Symphony at the age of eleven. When barely out of his teens he went to New York with the encouragement of trumpeter Donald Byrd, who took him to Blue Note records. He scored an immediate success with his 1961 debut album, *Takin' Off*, which featured Freddie Hubbard and Dexter Gordon; it included, among several Hancock compositions, his hit 'soul' tune *Watermelon Man*. The follow-up album *My Point Of View* and a piano trio album *Succotash* established Hancock's early keyboard style, in which distinctively chunky passages were relieved by effortless runs. He now became virtually the house pianist at Blue Note, and was soon involved in music by some of the more adventurous artists on the label, ranging from Sam Rivers and Bobby Hutcherson to Wayne Shorter and Tony Williams. Along with Shorter (whom Miles 'stole' from Art Blakey) and Williams, Hancock ended up as a member of Miles Davis' group, recruited only after what was apparently a casual and last minute invitation to play on *Seven Steps To Heaven* in 1963.

After this recording date (according to Miles' biographer Ian Carr), Hancock was invited to play a live gig and, uncertain of his status asked Miles whether he was in the group or not. 'You made the record, didn't you?' Miles replied. A few months later Hancock was recorded live with Miles at the particularly memorable Philharmonic Hall concert, an occasion which yielded two albums, *Four And More* and *My Funny Valentine*.

In the Davis quintet with bassist Ron Carter and the virtuoso drummer Williams, Hancock found a freer, more interactive way of playing with the rhythm team, and in the end his four years with Davis completely transformed his own approach. By the time he left in 1968 he was using electric piano almost exclusively. He formed his own sextet, with first Joe Henderson, then Bennie Maupin on tenor, but the next few years saw him develop a complete mastery of keyboard electronics as he moved steadily deeper into the pop field. The bass-riff funk formula of *Headhunters* brought enormous commercial success, but in 1976, as a side venture, Hancock was joined in a co-operative touring group called VSOP by Hubbard, Shorter, Williams and Carter, playing straight jazz. In 1978 Hancock played an extremely successful duo concert with Chick Corea, but around the same time showed that he had not lost his grip on the pop market; the 1978 single *I Though It Was You* was a huge hit for Hancock and briefly popularised the peculiar sound of the Sennheiser Vocoder voice-synthesiser.

A 1984 concert tour under the name VSOP II successfully featured the Marsalis brothers; and though continuing also to thrive as a fusion artist, Hancock has since made many appearances in what could rather stiffly be called a 'legitimate' jazz context, notably in the film *Round Midnight*.

While albums like *Headhunters* cannot rate many stars in the present context, they stand out from the mass of disco material; the sheer polish and unbeatable rhythmic compulsion that Hancock can achieve demand acknowledgement.

StEREO
BST 84279
BLUE NOTE

CP32-5219

SPEAK LIKE A CHILD

Riot/Speak Like a Child/First Trip/Toys/
Goodbye To Childhood/The Sorcerer
1, 2, 4 Thad Jones (flug), Peter Philips (b tb),
Jerry Dodgion (a fl), Herbie Hancock (p),
Ron Carter (b), Mickey Roker (d); 3, 5, 6
Hancock (p), Carter (b), Roker (d), 1968
Blue Note BST 84279
AAD Running time: 37.01
Performance: ★ ★   Recording: ★ ★ ★

On this 'limited edition' CD can be heard the
fruits of some later Blue Note sessions, with
a well-balanced group including Thad Jones
on flugelhorn; but the horns play quite
subsidiary roles, setting the scene for
Hancock in a series of explorations on his
own themes. The exception to this, and quite
different in feel, is a trio track *First Trip*;
written by Ron Carter, this is introduced by
the bassist as a deceptive two-beat swinger,
then exercises a set of subtle changes.
Hancock is bluesily reminiscent of Red
Garland or even Wynton Kelly here.
   Riot is a more typical Hancock
composition, an urgent ensemble
introduction giving way to a finely-
controlled solo in which Hancock's notes
sometimes seem to rain down like clear
drops, while snarling horns return behind.
The title track sets a sweet, almost hypnotic
mood, while *Toys* has some interesting
writing for the brass and more Garland-like,
light-tripping blues-inflected phrases from
Hancock. *Goodbye To Childhood* is a truly
evocative piece, conveying trepidation, then
sadness, then resignation; *The Sorcerer*, a
Hancock theme which provided the title for
a 1967 Miles Davis album, is a confident,
absorbing trio performance here. Recorded
sound quality is excellent; this is a disc which
offers some very fine playing.

HEADHUNTERS

Chameleon/Watermelon Man/Sly/Vein
Melter
Bennie Maupin (ts, ss, b cl, a fl), Herbie
Hancock (el p, clavinet, Arp synths), Paul
Jackson (el b), Harvey Mason (d), Bill
Summers (perc), 1974.
CBS CDCBS 65928
AAD Running time: 41.54
Performance: ★   Recording: ★ ★

With almost endlessly repeated riffs as a
principal feature, *Headhunters* is to be
regarded as a classic example of mid-1970s
funk rather than as any kind of jazz album.
Yet although its mannerisms now sound
dated, it has great strengths.
   Hancock's old composition *Watermelon
Man* is the basis for an extended piece in
which the theme just surfaces lazily through
the atmospheric tropical-night effects.
Chameleon, at over fifteen minutes, makes
hypnotic use of Jackson's bass riff; but
Hancock demonstrates true virtuosity in his
handling of the synthesizers. *Sly* sparkles
with an intricate tracery of synth parts,
while the slow and menacing *Vein Melter*
contains fine playing by Maupin, and almost
convincing synthesizer strings.

FEETS DON'T FAIL ME NOW

You Bet Your Love/Trust Me/Ready Or
Not/Tell Everybody/Honey From The Jar/
Knee Deep
Herbie Hancock (key, voc), Eddie Watkins
(b), James Gadson (d), Bill Summers (perc),
Julia Tillman Waters, Maxine Willard
Waters, Oren Waters and Luther Waters
(background voc), 1979.
CBS CDCBS 83491
AAD Running time: 40.42
Performance: ★   Recording: ★

This album is among Hancock's purest disco-pop offerings, making extensive use of the appalling Vocoder, which allows a voice to articulate the notes from an electronic instrument, giving the impression of a robot-like but pitch-perfect vocalist; *Feets Don't Fail Me Now* was in fact the follow-up to the immensely successful *Sunlight* album, which contained the Vocoder-based single hit *I Thought It Was You*, and deserves inclusion here only as an example of Hancock's multiple skills as tunesmith and keyboard manipulator. The tunes are fine (*Trust Me*, particularly), the trashy, tinselly disco beat done to perfection (*Ready Or Not*) and the funk is the funkiest, if now rather horribly dated (*Tell Everybody, Honey From The Jar*).

Once again, a low 'performance' rating only because of the virtually zero jazz content, but as far as the 'recording' part is concerned, on this Compact Disc the sound quality could have been better; the

undemanding electronics all sound fine, but the background vocals ought to be more intelligible.

FUTURE SHOCK
Rockit/Future Shock/TFS/Earthbeat/Autodrive/Rough
1, 4 Herbie Hancock, Michael Beinhorn (synths), Bill Laswell (b), Grand Mixer D.ST (turntables), Daniel Ponce (Bata); 2 Hancock, Beinhorn (synths), Pete Cosey (g), Laswell (b), Sly Dunbar (d, bgo), Dwight Jackson, Jr, Bernard Fowler (voc); 3, 5 Hancock, Beinhorn (synths), Laswell (b); 6 as 1, add Lamar Wright, Roger Trilling, Nicky Skopelitis, Fowler, D.ST, (voc), 1983.
CBS CDCBS 25540
AAD Running time: 38.02
Performance: ★ ★   Recording: ★ ★

This last helping of Hancock's pop/fusion output takes its title from Curtis Mayfield's powerful message song, covered effectively here with a vocal from Dwight Jackson, and a predictably violent and anarchic guitar solo by Pete Cosey. Real drums appear here, in the inimitable hands of Sly Dunbar, but on most other tracks the percussion sounds are all emulated; Hancock by 1983 had added the Fairlight to his armoury, and had Michael Beinhorn to help with programming so could theoretically mimic almost any instrumental sound through his keyboards. This does not really happen, but the rap style *Rockit*, with scratching by Grand Mixer D.ST is a classic of its kind; the intensely hypnotic *Rough* also deserves a mention. Perhaps Hancock's VSOP efforts (unavailable, at the time of writing, on CD) will stand the test of time better, but we shall have to wait and see.

COLEMAN HAWKINS

(b. St Joseph, Missouri, 21 November 1904 (possibly 1901); d. New York City, 19 May 1969)

Though far from being the first saxophonist in jazz, Coleman Hawkins finally liberated the tenor sax from its subservient or semi-comic roles, making it an emotionally effective as well as a dominant solo voice. In his best rhapsodic vein, Hawkins' tone was (to quote Noel Hendrick): 'a luscious sweetmeat with an unexpected and delicious hard centre', and he produced music which never grows stale.

As a child, Hawkins studied piano and cello, then took up the saxophone at nine. Hired by vaudeville blues singer Mamie Smith in 1921, he toured with her Jazz Hounds until 1923. In New York, he joined Fletcher Henderson's band in 1924 and stayed almost ten years. Henderson recordings aside, Hawkins 'hot' style (not yet perfected) is featured on *Hello Lola* from the famous 1929 small-group session with comb-and-paper player Red McKenzie's Mound City Blue Blowers; while *One Hour*, from the same date, introduces Hawkins' ballad method.

Later Henderson sides reveal Hawkins' playing at its first mature peak, but in 1934 he left for Europe (recording a session in London on the way) to join Jack Hylton's band. Leaving Hylton (the Nazis would not let him enter Germany) he worked with some of the best European dance bands, notably The Ramblers in Holland. He returned to the US in July 1939, and in October that year his recording of *Body and Soul* became an unexpected hit; fronting his own short-lived big band in 1940–1, Hawkins was billed as 'the body and soul of the saxophone'.

In 1943–4 he produced a classic series of small group recordings for the small Signature and Keynote labels, but was soon working and recording with the 'modernists', notably Howard McGhee, Milt Jackson, and Thelonious Monk. With his superb technique and deep

With justification, Coleman Hawkins has been called 'the father figure of the tenor saxophone'. For some forty years, he was its pre-eminent exponent.

theoretical knowledge, he was comfortable with extended harmonic ideas, though relatively untouched by the rhythmic revolution of bop. From 1946, he played Norman Granz's JATP concerts, and in 1948 and 1949 visited Europe again.

The early 1950s were years of disillusionment, and his playing became simplified in approach, harsh and aggressive in manner, but later recordings, particularly with his long-term front-line partner, Roy Eldridge, and with one-time tenor disciple Ben Webster, were effective. Notable among many 'guest star' record dates was *Duke Ellington Meets Coleman Hawkins* (1962). He continued to tour almost to the end, and though failing health made him an erratic performer in his last few years, he did begin again to enjoy fuller recognition as a major influence. Currently, there is little enough of Hawkins on CD; perhaps future issues will do him better justice.

**THE CHOCOLATE DANDIES AND
LEONARD FEATHER'S ALL STARS, 1940
AND 1943**
Smack (2 takes)/I Surrender Dear (2 takes)/I
Can't Believe That You're In Love With Me
(2 takes)/Dedication/Esquire Bounce (2
takes)/Boff Boff [Mop Mop] (2 takes)/My
Ideal (2 takes)/Esquire Blues (2 takes)
1-7 Roy Eldridge (tp), Benny Carter (as),
Coleman Hawkins (ts), Bernard Addison (g),
John Kirby (b), Sid Catlett (d), May 1940;
8-15 Cootie Williams (tp), Edmond Hall (cl),
Hawkins (ts), Art Tatum (p), Al Casey (g),
Oscar Pettiford (b), Catlett (d), December
1943.
Commodore 8.204056 ZP
AAD Running time: 50.26
Performance: ★ ★   Recording: ★ ★

There tends to be something artificial about
any kind of 'all-star' studio date, but in the
case of these two sessions, any such doubts
are blown away by the quality and gusto of
the solo work. The Chocolate Dandies of
1940, assembled by Leonard Feather, are not
to be confused with the 1930 group of the
same name, an almost legendary assemblage
which also included Hawkins and Benny
Carter but was completed by other members
of the great Fletcher Henderson band of the
time.

The 1940 titles start with a fast vamp
number named for Henderson (*Smack* was
his nickname), in which Carter, Roy Eldridge
and Hawkins solo against the energetic
backing of 'Big Sid' Catlett and John Kirby,
filled out by the flowing rhythm chords of
Bernard Addison. After an appealingly
quicksilver solo by Carter and a fine,
swaggering one from Eldridge, Hawkins
settles straight into the groove with amazing
drive. In the second take he offers a more
aggressive, simplified line in his tenor solo,
and this time round the rideout by the

ensemble of the three horns is also, quite
noticeably more rousing.

Hawkins' mid-tempo swing style is well
demonstrated by the two versions, one fairly
fast and the other steady, of *I Can't Believe
That You're In Love With Me*, a number he
was using around the same time in his own
short-lived big band. *I Surrender Dear* (with
support from an uncredited pianist) produces
a notably fine Hawkins ballad treatment in
both takes (although the alternative has
slight fluffs and moments of uncertainty),
complementing a bravura performance by
Roy Eldridge.

Things had changed by 1943, when
Feather assembled *Esquire* magazine's poll
winners for the Esquire All-Stars date.
Esquire Bounce is a blasé-sounding swing
theme; in the first, rather restrained take,
Hawkins injects more drive and swing by
constructing a solo from riffs, but in the
second all the solos are rather wilder. *Boff
Boff (Mop Mop)* resembles Tiny Grimes'
Tiny's Tempo recorded the following year,
and is sharpened by a foretaste of the coming
bop revolution, but as far as Hawkins' solo
is concerned, it is a vehicle for another
urgent, bustling swing-era solo, as is the final
Esquire Blues.

The session generally is also remarkable
for contributions from the others,
particularly Art Tatum and Al Casey (who
support Hawkins so beautifully in the ballad
My Ideal); in this case, the 'All Stars' tag is
no exaggeration at all. Sound quality is
acceptable, apparently well transferred for
CD, and since the alternate takes show
considerable differences, this disc is good
value; it will remain an essential one, at least
until the greatest Hawkins records of the
1930s and 1940s are on Compact Disc. The
European sessions, though, Carter and
Django Reinhardt (*qv*), are worth seeking
out.

until the greatest Hawkins records of the 1930s and 1940s are on Compact Disc. The European sessions, though, with Carter and Django Reinhardt (qv), are worth seeking out.

THE GENIUS OF COLEMAN HAWKINS

I'll Never Be The Same/You're Blasé/I Wished On The Moon/How Long Has This Been Going On/Like Someone In Love/My Melancholy Baby/Ill Wind/In A Mellotone/There's No You/The World Is Waiting For The Sunrise/Somebody Loves Me/Blues For Rene
Coleman Hawkins (ts), Oscar Peterson (p), Herb Ellis (g), Ray Brown (b), Alvin Stoller (d), October 1957.
Verve 825 673
AAD Running time: 47.26
Performance: ★ ★   Recording: ★ ★ ★

Familiar ballads, played at middle tempos, make up most of the programme here, and the rest of the group is in effect a Verve house rhythm section consisting of the Oscar Peterson Trio with the addition of Alvin Stoller on drums. But the music is not as unvaried as that might imply, since although the other players had only supporting roles, they were the best available; and although the format may not appear to offer much variety, Hawkins' playing does.

Hawkins opens on an almost strutting *I'll Never Be The Same* with the slightly baggy tone that was characteristic of his work in the mid 1950s; it is a tone that could become almost scrawny, as in *Somebody Loves Me*. On *I Wished On The Moon* his sound has a delicate, almost fragile quality which contrasts strongly with the rumbustious and choleric effect he so often produced. *In A Mellotone* starts in rather a stock fashion, but Hawkins' solo is full of interest, sounding momentarily like one of his own devotees, Sonny Rollins, as he inserts some angular double-time phrases. At a really fast tempo, *The World Is Waiting For The Sunrise* allows Hawkins to blow a simple line over the pulse; other touches which vary the accompaniment come with Peterson's old-timey semi-stride style in *How Long Has This Been Going On*, and Ellis's delicate intro to *Like Someone In Love*. At the slowest tempos Peterson's chords can become syrupy and bland, but all trace of this is blown away with the closing *Blues For Rene*, not a blues but a lively 32-bar original by Hawkins, where his long, effortlessly structured and fiercely inventive solo demonstrates how firmly he was still in command.

COLEMAN HAWKINS ENCOUNTERS BEN WEBSTER

Blues For Yolande/It Never Entered My Mind/Rosita/You'd Be So Nice To Come Home To/Prisoner Of Love/Tangerine/Shine On Harvest Moon
Coleman Hawkins, Ben Webster (ts), Oscar Peterson (p), Herb Ellis (g), Ray Brown (b), Alvin Stoller (d), October 1957.
Verve 823 120
AAD Running time: 36.32
Performance: ★ ★ ★   Recording: ★ ★ ★

With an accompanying group again consisting of the Peterson trio with Stoller added on drums, this justly-celebrated 'encounter' gets off to a free-wheeling start as Peterson's lazy-tempo barrelhouse piano, against Stoller's powerful backbeat, introduces a wonderfully lush-sounding harmonised riff from the two tenors. After a shouting solo from Hawkins, the inflappable Webster, showing his mastery of tension and dynamics, enters from a quieter level, then builds his own solo to a climax.

In a similar relaxed vein is *Shine On Harvest Moon*, where the tenors freely trade phrases and underpin each other. A further moment of perfect rapport comes in *Rosita*, where, after a rhapsodic theme statement from Hawkins, Webster joins in to produce a lovely, delicate tenor duet; when the number breaks from its Latin beat into a light but punchy straight 4/4, it is Webster who provides the wispy solo. On the Richard Rodgers' ballad *It Never Entered My Mind*, it is Webster's turn to set the pace, which he does with a superb, ravishing statement of the theme; Hawkins follows, and then, in a deep, mellow but muscular solo, puts forward a concise statement which just for a moment makes Webster's airy rhapsodising seem like so much fluff.

Hawkins, fittingly perhaps, becomes the dominant partner each time, playing with depth, power and authority, yet Webster too is at his breathy best as he introduces a swinging *You'd Be So Nice To Come Home To*. The recording has clarity, naturalness and space, though with heavy reverberation giving life and a rounded punch to the two horns.

It is a pity that all two-tenor collaborations have not been as successful as this exceptional date; the contents of this particular disc offers some of the most attractive examples of Hawkins' work from the 1950s, and with the added attraction of Webster's contribution it becomes sheer enjoyment.

BILLIE HOLIDAY
(b. Baltimore, Ohio, 7 April 1915; d. New York City, 17 July 1959)

Billie Holiday, in some senses the first or even the only true jazz singer, remains the greatest. She set out, as she said, to use her voice like a horn, but her natural and lucid phrasing made her one of the most imitated as well as one of the most moving singers ever.

After a deprived childhood and adolescence, Eleanora 'Billie' Holiday began singing in her late teens and was heard at Monette Moore's club by John Hammond, who arranged for her to record with Benny Goodman in late 1933. She sang two numbers, *Your Mother's Son In Law* and *Riffin' The Scotch*, which reveal only the raw ingredients of her style, but in 1935 she made the first of many record dates with groups led and directed by Teddy Wilson, for release on the American Record Company's low-price Brunswick label. Wilson picked the best musicians available, so by the end of 1936 Billie had recorded with Johnny Hodges, Harry Carney, Ben Webster, Artie Shaw and Bunny Berigan. In January 1937, the group included five men from the Basie band, and among them was the tenor player Lester Young. *This Year's Kisses* marked the beginning of a fabled studio partnership that lasted on an off for three years.

Billie joined the Basie band in March 1937, but left after less than a year, joining Artie Shaw only to leave that before the end of 1938 because of racial harassment. In 1939 she was featured at the newly-opened Cafe Society, New York, and gained new stature as a solo artist; by 1944 she was able to record with strings.

In 1946 Billie appeared in the film 'New Orleans' with Louis Armstrong, but in May 1947 was arrested on a narcotics charge and detained until February 1948. Studio recordings in 1948–50 used various orchestras, while Billie usually sang live with a pianist or trio. In 1952 she signed for Clef (later Verve) for the first of a long series of recordings with generally compatible jazz groups, which the label later collected and reissued under the title *The Voice of Jazz*.

Her recording career reached its last phase with *Lady In Satin* (Columbia), recorded with the large orchestra of Ray Ellis in 1958, but her voice had now deteriorated so much that listening to this, and the final Ellis sessions of early 1959, is a deeply saddening experience. While some of the best of Billie Holiday is now available on CD, we are still waiting for her incomparable pre-war recordings.

FINE AND MELLOW: 1939 and 1944
Strange Fruit (2 takes)/Yesterdays (2 takes)/ Fine And Mellow/ I Gotta Right To Sing The Blues (2 takes)/How Am I To Know? (2 takes)/My Old Flame (2 takes)/I'll Get By (2 takes)/I Cover The Waterfront (2 takes)
1,2, 5-7 Billie Holiday (voc), Frank Newton (tp), Tab Smith (as), Kenneth Hollon, Stanley Payne (ts), Sonny White (p), Jimmy McLin (g), John Williams (b), Eddie Dougherty (d); 3, 4 Holiday (voc), Smith (as), White (p), McLin (g), Williams (b), Dougherty (d), April 1939; 8-15 Doc Cheatham (tp), Vic Dickenson (tb), Lem Davis (as), Eddie Heywood (p), Teddy Walters (g), John Simmons (b), Big Sid Catlett (d), March 1944.
Commodore 8.24055
AAD Running time: 46.07
Performance: ★ ★ ★   Recording: ★

A powerful poem of protest about lynching ('. . . black bodies swinging in the southern breeze . . .'), *Strange Fruit* marked a turning point in Billie Holiday's career; her performance of the song at Cafe Society in New York and this subsequent recording for record store proprietor and enthusiast Milt Gabler led to a new popularity among the white liberal intelligentsia. However untypical, it became a key item in her repertoire, which retained its power to the end. Here, as with all but one of the other titles in this Commodore set, there are two takes and, as with most of her performances, the differences are not great - Holiday was working with experienced and sympathetic musicians - but it is usually fairly easy to guess which take was the one originally chosen for the issue.

The 20 April 1939 date was remarkable; it produced a near-definitive *Yesterdays*, as well as the archetypal Billie Holiday blues *Fine And Mellow*, which (not surprisingly) didn't need a second take. A mid-tempo, bittersweet *I Gotta Right To Sing The Blues* is almost in the spirit of the great Teddy Wilson records. Without the tenor saxes, the 1944 sessions have a less richly-balanced group sound, and Holiday's approach has subtly changed; sung this time without the verse, *I Cover The Waterfront* makes an interesting comparison with the version recorded with Wilson in 1941. Sound quality is not up to the best standards of the time, and these transfers sound boxy with some 'surface'. But the voice is well projected, which is what really matters.

THE LEGEND OF BILLIE HOLIDAY
That Ole Devil Called Love/Loverman/
Don't Explain/Good Morning Heartache/
There Is No Greater Love/Easy Living/
Solitude/Porgy/My Man/Them There Eyes/
Now Or Never/T'Ain't Nobody's Business If
I Do/Somebody's On My Mind/Keeps On A
Rainin'/You're My Thrill/God Bless The
Child
Billie Holiday (voc), with orchestra directed
by: 1, 2, 8, 9, 10 Toots Camerata, October/
November 1944; 3 Bob Haggart, August
1945; 5-7 Bob Haggart, February 1947; 4 Bill
Stegmeyer, January 1946; 11-14, Sy Oliver,
August/September 1949; 15 Gordon Jenkins,
October 1949; 16 Gordon Jenkins, March
1950.
MCA DBH TV1
AAD Running time: 50.01
Performance: ★ ★ ★   Recording: ★

With the Decca label, Billie Holiday's
recordings entered a new phase; she was at
last able to have her own way and record
with strings. This collection, compiled in
1985, starts with the then recently-covered
Ole Devil Called Love and includes a string
of classic tracks taken from a large number
of sessions which took place between 1944
and 1950. Brightest and brashest of the
accompanying orchestras is Sy Oliver's,
effective if rather overdone on *Them There
Eyes*. The band's brassy show-time effect
does not swamp the singer, whose inimitable
mastery of the beat gives her almost a quiet
authority over these noisy accompanying
forces. Oliver's accompaniment does less for
Billie in two numbers which do not really
suit her, the Louis Jordan-styled *Now Or
Never* and the almost sleazy *Keeps A
Raining*. At the opposite extreme are Gordon
Jenkins' subtle, supportive arrangements;
moody, mysterious *cine noir* strings and
flute on *You're My Thrill* and the rather
corny but effective choir on her own terse
statement of realistic philosophy, *God Bless
The Child*. The other Holiday song here,
'Tain't Nobody's Business, actually does
stand out as the only one to feature a jazz big
band (led by the great arranger, Buster
Harding). It goes without saying that this is
essential Billie Holiday.
   Unfortunately, the sound quality is a
travesty, since despite having previously
issued the tracks in mono, MCA have seen
fit to impose the grossest kind of fake 'stereo'
effect here. Anyone who does not regard this
as a criminal act should listen to just the
right channel, which sounds like a telephone.
An amplifier with a mono switch will cancel

this effect, but unfortunately still leaves the
music sounding hard, forward and lacking
subtlety compared with the better (mono) LP
reissues of this material (for example, *16
Classic Tracks* and *Volume II*, MCA
MCL1688 and 1776), which themselves
seldom seem to have been prepared with the
care that these performances deserve.

THE BILLIE HOLIDAY SONGBOOK
Good Morning Heartache/My Man/Billie's
Blues/What A Little Moonlight Can Do/
Don't Explain/Lady Sings The Blues/Lover
Man/God Bless The Child/Fine And
Mellow/I Cried For You/Strange Fruit/
Stormy Blues/Trav'lin' Light/I Cover The
Waterfront
1, 6, 8, 13 Billie Holiday (voc), Charlie
Shavers (tp), Tony Scott (cl), Paul
Quinichette(ts), Wynton Kelly (p), Kenny
Burrell (g), Aaron Bell (b), Larry McBrowen
(d), June 1957; 2 Holiday (voc), Joe Newman
(tp), Quinichette (ts), Oscar Peterson (p),
Freddie Green (g), Ray Brown (b), Gus
Johnson (d), July 1952; 3 Holiday (voc), Roy
Eldridge (tp), Coleman Hawkins (ts), Carl
Drinkard (p), Burrell (g), Carson Smith (b),
Chico Hamilton (d), November 1956; 4
Holiday (voc), Shavers (tp), Peterson (p),
Herb Ellis (g), Brown (b), Ed Shaughnessy
(d), April 1954; 5 as 3 Eldridge and Hawkins
out, November 1956; 7 Buck Clayton (tp),
Mal Waldron (p), Milt Hinton (b), Don
Lamond (d), September 1958; 9, 14, as 5 add
Clayton (tp), Mal Waldron (p), Milt Hinton
(b), Don Lamond (d), September 1958; 9, 14,
as 5 add Clayton (tp). Scott and Quinichette
out, June 1956; 12 Harry 'Sweets' Edison
(tp), Willie Smith (as), Bobby Tucker (p),
Barney Kessel (g), Red Callander (b),
Hamilton (d), September 1954
Verve 823 246
DDD Running time: 45.46
Performance: ★ ★ ★   Recording: ★ ★

The idea of a Holiday songbook is a slightly
spurious one, but although only six of the
songs here credit the singer as composer, the
other eight (*I Cover The Waterfront* and *I
Cried For You* are not included in the vinyl
version of this title) are all songs she had
long since 'made her own'. All the November
1956 tracks are live recordings from her
Carnegie Hall concert, and these are
outstanding; she was clearly in very good
voice, and the concert was a personal
triumph. This gripping *Billie's Blues* is
unequalled, as is the slow, deeply moving
Don't Explain; while *Strange Fruit* seems
only to have grown in the strength and

coherence of its message. The singer floats her voice easily over a light, fast and swinging accompaniment, her first chorus followed by an appealing Peterson solo. Among the studio tracks, only *Lady Sings The Blues* (the same title had just been used for Billie's heavily-ghosted autobiography) seems contrived, settling down uneasily after Shavers' bravura trumpet intro; but on others Billie's voice has an undeniably heavy, almost dulled quality compared with the Carnegie Hall recordings. On the other hand, the very late *Lover Man* is a fine performance, well captured in a live recording.

Despite the choice of material, it would be pointless to compare these interpretations with those of earlier years, although *Good Morning Heartache,* for instance, closely follows the previously-recorded arrangement. With good sound quality (despite a fair amount of tape hiss on the studio tracks) this fairly generous disc does contain some very fine examples of the singer's later work.

THE SILVER COLLECTION
I Wished On The Moon/Moonlight In Vermont/Say It Isn't So/Our Love Is Here To Stay/Darn That Dream/But Not For Me/Body And Soul/Comes Love/They Can't Take That Away From Me/Embraceable You/Let's Call The Whole Thing Off/Gee Baby Ain't I Good To You/All Or Nothing At All/We'll Be Together Again
1-7 Billie Holiday (voc), Harry 'Sweets' Edison (tp), Ben Webster (ts), Jimmy Rowles (p), Barney Kessel (g), Red Mitchell (b), Alvin Stoller (d), January 1957; 8 as 1 but Joe Mondragon (b), Larry Bunker (d), replace Mitchell, Stoller, January 1957; 9-12 as 1 but Bunker (d), replaces Stoller, January 1957; 13, 14, as 1 but Mondragon (b), replaces Mitchell, August 1956.
Verve 823 449
AAD Running time: 65.21
Performance: ★ ★ Recording: ★ ★

With the most sympathetic backing imaginable, Billie Holiday worked through a large number of standards on a series of studio dates in January 1957, and the ones included here do not duplicate any of the selections issued as *Songs For Distingue Lovers*; on *The Silver Collection,* the extended playing time is filled out by a couple of tracks from August 1956. Apart from a different studio balance, these are of similar character, but their inclusion may explain why the whole disc is in mono. Only

those new to Billie Holiday will be surprised by the deteriorated quality of her voice at this period, highlighted with unintentional cruelty by sumptuous playing and admirable recording quality. For the most part, the tragic failings of her vocal equipment are artfully and courageously overcome, so that the listener is still drawn irresistibly in to the performance. Though the accompaniment as a whole reaches a rare standard of excellence, Ben Webster is outstanding and at his very best here. In many ways this disc does offer good value.

SONGS FOR DISTINGUE LOVERS
Day In, Day Out/A Foggy Day/Stars Fell On Alabama/One For My Baby/Just One Of Those Things/I Didn't Know What Time It Was
1, 2, 6 Billie Holiday (voc), Harry Edison (tp), Ben Webster (ts), Jimmy Rowles (p), Barney Kessel (g), Red Mitchell (b), Alvin Stoller (d), January 1957; 3-5 as 1 but Joe Mondragon (b), Larry Bunker (d), replace Mitchell, Stoller, January 1957.
Verve 815 055
AAD Running time: 33.02
Performance: ★ ★ Recording: ★ ★ ★

Selected from the January 1957 sessions which are now covered (without duplication) by *The Silver Collection,* this disc comes with a fascimile of the original album cover, which itself echoed one of Sinatra's (though on *Songs For Swinging Lovers* the liner note did not need to apologise for the choice of adjective in the title). Unlike the compilation CD, this is in impressive stereo, the sound being airy, spacious and beautifully detailed throughout. *Day In, Day Out* opens confidently, and Billie Holiday's vocal is followed by a crisp string of solos from Edison, Kessel, Rowles and Webster.

Few could argue that *A Foggy Day* was really a very good choice for Billie Holiday at this stage, but *One For My Baby* comes over extremely well. Particularly on *Just One Of Those Things,* the singer is buoyed up by the fine swinging rhythm section. The routine here features a string of solos culminating again in one from Webster, who also takes first turn at adding the subtly-weaving obbligato behind her vocal on *I Didn't Know What Time It Was,* where the singer sounds impossibly frail and vulnerable. Somehow, despite this aspect, and having barely half the playing time, this established title has to be rated more highly than *The Silver Collection,* though it is not the place to start a collection of Holiday.

FREDDIE HUBBARD
(b. Indianapolis, Indiana, 7 April 1938)

One of the fastest trumpeters ever, Freddie Hubbard combines immense technical resources with a sheer power and intensity of expression that continues to dazzle audiences everywhere.

By the time he was 20 had already worked with Sonny Rollins and Max Roach. He moved to New York in 1958, joining Slide Hampton's band the following year; in 1960 he was a member of J J Johnson's quintet, then toured Europe with Quincy Jones' big band. Summer 1961 saw him in the ranks of Art Blakey's Jazz Messengers, and he appeared on Blue Note dates with Dexter Gordon, Herbie Hancock, fellow-Messenger Wayne Shorter and ex-Messenger Jackie McLean; Though he worked briefly with Ornette Coleman, a switch to Atlantic Records produced a series of 'soul' influenced albums. In the 1970s, his recordings for CTI and Columbia embraced a commercial disco approach, but as the market climate has grown less hostile to jazz, Hubbard has re-emerged as a major performer in a purer idiom, and as one of the most exciting horn players to be seen.

BORN TO BE BLUE
Gibraltar/True Colours/Born To Be Blue/ Joy Spring/Up Jumped Spring.
Freddie Hubbard (tp), Harold Land (ts), Billy Childs (p), Steve Houghton (d), Buck Clark (perc), 1982.
Pablo 3112-6
DDD Running time: 41.39
Performance: ★ ★   Recording: ★ ★

On this Pablo recording, Hubbard leads a very fine sextet, essentially the classic quintet line-up with additional percussion. The music is mainly undiluted hard bop, and the playing throughout is of the highest standard. The other horn in the group is Harold Land, the fine West Coast saxophonist who worked with the Brown-Roach Quintet in the early 1950s; after that his style had absorbed much of the influence of John Coltrane, which is evident here particularly in the fast *True Colours*.

Although the reading of Clifford Brown's *Joy Spring* is accurate, affectionate and effective, it is no mere recreation on the part of Hubbard (although he does sound like Brown) or of Land (who was there at the time); both blow forceful and well-structured solos. On this track Buck Clark adds a 'klook-a-mop' and a conga solo; he contributes perhaps more effectively to the opening *Gibraltar*, though he does add some incidental rattles and tinkles to the title track, which is a big-toned feature for Hubbard's flugelhorn. Hubbard is a little like a much robuster middle-period Miles in the pretty jazz-waltz *Up Jumped Spring*, which includes an excellent solo from Billy Childs.

Sonically, with bass, drums and piano all in proportion, and not too much reverberation on the horns, this is a clean if not particularly warm recording, which repays repeated listening.

SWEET RETURN
Sweet Return/Misty/Whistling Away The Dark/Calypso Fred/Heidi-B/The Night Has A Thousand Eyes.
Freddie Hubbard (tp, flug), Lew Tabackin (ts, fl, alto fl), Joanne Brackeen (p), Eddie Gomez (b), Roy Haynes (d), Hector Manuel Andrade (perc 2-4), Craig Haynes (tambourine 4, 5), June 1983.
Atlantic 80108
DDD Running time: 48.09
Performance: ★ ★   Recording: ★ ★

The 'All Stars' captured on this disc were assembled by impresario George Wein in the summer of 1983 to do the rounds of the American and European jazz festivals; their appearance in the studio also marked the occasion of Freddie Hubbard's return to Atlantic records after an absence of more than a decade. The music turned out to be well-finished, enjoyable and usually far from being merely 'festival jazz'.

Founded on an easygoing rhythm, the title track is almost in danger of becoming sickly-sweet, with gentle piano and echoing flute, but is saved by a Hubbard solo that is both powerful and logical. In *Misty*, Hubbard stays fairly close to the tune, with his own characteristic, almost impatient-sounding bounce, still with traces of Clifford Brown. Tabackin takes a mellow voiced, agile tenor solo.

The next track is a sophisticated jazz-waltz, with excellent Hubbard, Tabackin warm and melodious again, Joanne Brackeen's solo rhythmic and stimulating. Brackeen's *Heidi B* is a chant-like tune built on a hypnotic, repeating piano figure in 7/4, which also features a fine, swirling solo from the composer, an atmospheric flute solo from Tabackin and some astounding playing by Gomez. *Calypso Fred* is an erudite piece of good-time music while the Caribbean flavour is maintained in a slick, pleasantly swinging *Night Has A Thousand Eyes*, with has an outstanding, light but fiery solo from Hubbard. Sound quality from this all-digital production is clean and bright, the music often sparkling too.

MILT JACKSON
(b. Detroit, Michigan, January 1, 1923)

Jackson was the first modern vibes player, and is a true virtuoso. He creates the illusion that bars and beats can impose no limits on the length and complexity of his lines; and within his own solid, blues-based bop tradition, his playing seems to spring from a completely unfettered imagination.

As a child, Jackson learned several instruments before turning to vibes, then played his first professional gig at sixteen, with tenor player Lucky Thompson and drummer Art Mardigan. Still in Detroit, he was discovered by Dizzy Gillespie in 1945, and in the Gillespie band met John Lewis, Ray Brown and Kenny Clarke. Recordings with Gillespie followed, and in 1948 Jackson recorded *Epistrophy* and *Misterioso* with Thelonious Monk. Apart from a Gillespie sextet date, Jackson's 1951 recordings included his own Quartet dates (for Dee Gee, later on Savoy) with Lewis, which presaged the Modern Jazz Quartet (*q.v.*); April 1952 saw the definitive Blue Note quintet recording of *Bags' Groove*. (Jackson's nickname came, prosaically, from the bags under his eyes.) Later that year came the first MJQ date, for Prestige. The group was a co-operative, but since Lewis provided and arranged the material, he soon became leader in effect.

Outside the MJQ, Jackson recorded extensively, playing dates with Miles Davis in 1954 and 1955, reuniting with tenor man Lucky Thompson in 1956, guesting with John Coltrane (Atlantic) and Wes Montgomery (Riverside) in 1961, then making the first of many with Oscar Peterson in 1962 (*Very Tall*, Verve). In 1975, a year after the official (but not final) break-up of the MJQ, he was the sensation of the 1975 Montreux Festival and in the last decade has continued to delight audiences wherever he appears.

FROM OPUS DE JAZZ TO JAZZ SKYLINE
Opus de Funk/You Leave Me Breathless/Opus And Interlude/Opus Pocus/Lover/Can't Help Lovin' That Man/The Lady Is A Tramp/Angel Face/ Sometimes I'm Happy/What's New
1-4 Frank Wess (fl, ts), Milt Jackson (vib), Hank Jones (p), Eddie Jones (b), Kenny Clarke (d), October 1955; 5-10 Lucky Thompson (ts), Jackson (vib), Jones (p), Wendell Marshall (b), Clarke (d), January 1956.
Savoy ZD70815
AAD Running time: 71.49
Performance: ★ ★ ★   **Recording:** ★ ★

Compiled from the two albums named in the title, this reissue offers almost as much music as it is possible to get on one disc, but it is the quality not the quantity which makes it exceptional. This is, of course, the 'other' Milt Jackson, away from the dinner-jacketed sobriety of the MJQ; on the 1955 *Opus de*

Jazz session he is heard in dazzling form with one of the best of rhythm sections, as Eddie Jones, sometime Basie alumnus, adds a springy bounce to the pulse so flawlessly laid down by the great Kenny Clarke. Jackson, who has of course recorded with dozens of 'all star' groups, can seldom have had more freedom than here; Wess on flute provides a perfect foil and, on the medium blues *Opus Pocus*, offers an obliquely glancing tenor solo.

With his old associate, the underrated tenor Lucky Thompson, Jackson twists some old standards into new shapes; *Lover* switches from a whimsical merry-go-round 3/4 to a very fast 4/4. The closing ballad, *What's New*, is Thompson's feature, and he plays ravishingly. Like most of the Savoy discs, this one preserves the fine recording balance of the original sessions. It really is a joy.

MILT JACKSON PLUS COUNT BASIE PLUS THE BIG BAND, VOLUME TWO
9.20 Special/Moonlight Becomes You/Shiny Stockings/Blues For Me/Every Tub/Easy Does It/Lena And Lenny/Sunny Side Of The Street/Back To The Apple/I'll Always Be In Love With You.
Wayman Reed, Lyn Biviano, Sonny Cohn, Pete Minger (tp); Bill Hughes, Mel Wanzo, Fred Wesley, Dennis Wilson (tb); Bobby Plater (as), Danny Turner, Eric Dixon, Kenny Hing (ts), Charlie Fowlkes (bars), Milt Jackson (vib), Count Basie (p), Freddie Green (g), John Clayton (b), Butch Miles (d), Sarah Vaughan (voc 7), January 1978.
Pablo J33J 20054
AAD Running time: 42.30
Performance: ★ ★ ★   **Recording:** ★ ★ ★

In Volume One Jackson featured with the band in a selection of numbers including Hefti's *Li'l Darlin'* along with Freddie Green's best known contribution to the Basie Book, *Corner Pocket*. But it is Volume Two which essays Basie favourites from all eras. The riff-like theme of *9.20 Special* emerges fresh and sparkling as Jackson joins the ensemble, then provides a long, crisply telling solo; less successful is *Every Tub*, a flag-waver from the great 1930s Basie band. Here, despite the swing generated by the band, Jackson's work seems detached from, rather than propelled by, the familiar series of riff variations; but when, on *Blues For Me*, Basie's down-home piano delves even further into the past (to an era, in fact, when the vibraphone had yet to be invented) it meshes perfectly with Jackson's passionate modern blues style.

Easy Does It gives Jackson another chance to demonstrate speed, dexterity and perfect taste against the gentle backdrop of the Basie rhythm section. *I'll Always Be In Love With You* is a another delightful small group performance, at an easier tempo than a rather predictable *Sunny Side Of The Street*, which nonetheless makes effective use of the band behind the chief soloist. Outstanding are *Shiny Stockings* and the slow *Lena and Lenny*, with Sarah Vaughan adding an impromptu wordless vocal like another horn part in an already rich ensemble sound underpinned by Fowlkes' smoky baritone sax. There are moments on this album when you suddenly notice the stylistic gulf between Basie's swing rhythm and the elastic modernism of Jackson's style, but these are few. Altogether, getting Jackson into a studio with Basie was one of Granz's better ideas, and as he says in the liner note, *'if you like this, why not try Volume One?'*

AIN'T BUT A FEW OF US LEFT
Ain't But A Few Of Us Left/Stuffy/A Time For Love/Body and Soul/If I Should Lose You/What Am I Here For.
Milt Jackson (vib), Oscar Peterson (p), Ray Brown (b), Grady Tate (d), November 1981.
Pablo 3112-13
AAD Running time: 43.38
Performance: ★ ★   Recording: ★ ★ ★

A soloist could hardly ask for a finer accompanying group than Peterson, Brown and Tate, whose hard-swinging,rock-solid beat lifts the quartet throughout this set. *Body and Soul* serves as an example of the level of sheer musicianship and rapport within the group. Brown, with a funky solo introduction, Tate with a pseudo-samba beat and an utterly superb Jackson with his most beautiful tremolo tone, take the tune to the limits of credibility before switching the rhythm and getting down to an infectiously swinging runthrough; Peterson out-doubles Jackson's high-speed solo, after which Jackson and the rhythm section bring down the tempo and return to the opening riff, closing the number as smoothly, neatly and effortlessly as a chauffeur parking a limousine.

Coleman Hawkins' tune from the 1940s, *Stuffy*, becomes superbly jaunty in the hands of Jackson and Peterson, while Jackson's ballad style blossoms (admittedly with a slightly busy accompaniment from Peterson) in *A Time For Love*. (The order of tracks is as above, not as on the outside liner note).

Despite some wonderful playing, there does sometimes seem to be a feeling of showiness, a lack of light and shade, but the absence of a third star in the rating is meant as an assessment relative only to the very best efforts of these unequalled musicians.

Some may think this too harsh a judgement, since this really is an excellent disc; Ray Brown alone would make it worth listening to. The recording quality, unstrained, silky smooth and clear throughout, is very fine indeed.

JACKSON, JOHNSON, BROWN & COMPANY
Jaybone/Lament/Our Delight/Bags' Groove/Watch What Happens/My One And Only Love/Jumpin' Blues.
J J Johnson (tb), Milt Jackson (vib), Tom Ranier (p), Ray Brown (b), John Collins (b), Roy McCurdy (d), May 1983.
Pablo J33J 20002
AAD Running time: 38.54
Performance: ★ ★   Recording: ★ ★ ★

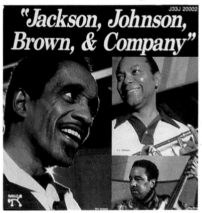

Rather like Jackson, J J Johnson became the peerless be-bop exponent of an instrument which in other hands could sound clumsy or inappropriate to the idiom, and became a star soloist who could shine given even an approximately suitable background. Here, the bassist is once more the endlessly swinging and dependable Ray Brown (more resonantly-recorded than on some recent Pablo discs), while pianist Tom Ranier provides a more restrained background than the soloists would have got from Oscar Peterson. As it turns out this is not such a bad thing. The opener, not surprisingly, is a medium-paced blues, but it is a stodgy, lacklustre performance merely thickened by the guitar chords of Collins.

Lament, though, is a beautiful track, a showcase for Jackson, who uses all his delicacy of touch and sustaining vibrato. His solo is complemented by a lovely, wistful muted chorus from Johnson before the tempo gently picks up. Equally successful is *Our Delight*, a spacious, bouncy and relaxed performance hitting exactly the right tempo on Tadd Dameron's classic be-bop theme, with a typical long-legged solo from Jackson followed by a witty Johnson. Collins is mixed so far down as to be almost inaudible here; he gets just a brief chance to solo, even then being upstaged by Brown, in *Bags' Groove*, but does contribute an attractive unaccompanied chord solo on the theme of *My One And Only Love*, introducing and closing another sweet-toned Jackson ballad.

KEITH JARRETT
(b. Allentown, Pennsylvania, 8 May 1945)

Despite his contribution, while with Miles Davis, to the development of electrified jazz/rock, Keith Jarrett has become a champion of the acoustic piano and has produced some of the most widely-heard solo piano music ever.

Starting on piano at the age of three, Jarrett showed early signs of wanting to improvise and compose; he began lessons in composition at fifteen. His first significant professional job was a tour with Fred Waring's Pennsylvanians, after which he gained a scholarship to Berklee. Leaving there after a year, he stayed in Boston for a while, then moved to New York, working briefly during 1965 with Art Blakey's Jazz Messengers and with Roland Kirk. His three-year association with the psychedelic era's most popular jazz saxophonist, Charles Lloyd, began early in 1966; with Lloyd's group Jarrett visited many European countries including Russia.

Jarrett formed his own trio in 1969, with bassist Charlie Haden and ex-Bill Evans drummer Paul Motian. He later added saxophonist Dewey Redman, who, like Haden, had established his style while with Ornette Coleman. The following year, Miles Davis asked Jarrett to join his group, supplementing, and then replacing Chick Corea. Jarrett's energy and virtuosity, often sounding like two men as he played a keyboard with either hand, was for a while a major feature of the band, but by 1971 he had decided to concentrate on solo piano. Joining the ECM label, he recorded an enormous amount of solo work during the early 1970s.

Though an uncompromised improvising soloist playing his own compositions might seem an unlikely candidate for commercial success, Jarrett's dedication to live performance, his attractive sound, limitless invention, control of dynamics and pace, and the underlying sincerity of his work, helped win huge album sales. In the 1970s he did also make group recordings, a notable collaborator being Jan

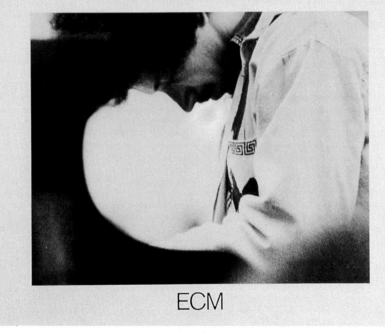

KEITH JARRETT
THE KÖLN CONCERT

ECM

Garbarek, who appeared first on *Belonging* and later on *My Song*. Most of Jarrett's work has featured his own compositions, but when, after more than a decade, he once more formed a 'conventional' jazz trio with Gary Peacock and Jack DeJohnette, he also reintroduced the convention of the standard repertoire.

Technically brilliant but never showy, Jarrett continues to offer uniquely accessible and enjoyable piano music.

THE KÖLN CONCERT
Part I/Part IIa/Part IIb/Part 11c
Keith Jarrett (p),January 1975
ECM 810 067
AAD Running time: 66.08
Performance: ★ ★ ★   Recording: ★ ★ ★

Devoting himself to solo performance, Jarrett in the 1970s made many extended recordings of unaccompanied piano. Of these, *The Köln Concert* double album became one of the best known and the biggest seller. The venue, Köln (Cologne) Opera House, gives a sense of space to the recording and seems to have been ideally suited to Jarrett's vibrant, ringing keyboard style. Like several other Jarrett performances, it consists of untitled parts, and here Part I is the longest at just over 26 minutes – in vinyl terms, a whole LP side. It begins in an out-of-tempo, rhapsodic vein, sometimes beginning to hint at a descending minor chord sequence, but settles down to a pattern which simply alternates between two related tonalities. Underneath, a pulse gradually develops, helped along by tapping noises,until eventually Jarrett reaches a stately 4/4 beat and introduces some ballad-like changes, then discards the beat to rhapsodise once more; then finds the pulse again for a final development over a highly rhythmic repeated bass.

Part IIa is in many ways typical Jarrett, building up the hypnotic effect of an endlessly repeated bass pattern, this time an urgent rhythm played on one note; his right hand dances freely above,sometimes throwing in a glancing barrelhouse phrase, and drawing on country, soul and gospel elements. After nearly six minutes, a threatened modulation dissipates but provides a transition into a stronger, darker sound. The bass is truly thunderous until Jarrett breaks stride to enter a deep and muscular lyrical section, which he accompanies at one point with solemn whacks on the soundboard. Jarrett's music here is as difficult to categorise as it is to describe; but repetition and extended playing time are important to the experience, and to this extent the sheer running time of Compact Disc is as much an advantage as any sonic benefit to the rich and almost-too-sonorous piano sound captured on ECM's very fine original master tape.

ARBOUR ZENA
Runes/Solara March/Mirrors
Jan Garbarek (ts, ss), Keith Jarrett (p), Charlie Haden (b), members of Stuttgart Radio Symphony Orchestra, conducted by Mladen Gutesha; Ludwigsburg, October 1975
ECM 825 592
AAD Running time: 53.01
Performance: ★ ★
Recording: ★ ★ ★

Not the first Jarrett project to involve the Norwegian saxophonist Garbarek, this was nonetheless one of the most ambitious. In three extended pieces, Jarrett, Haden and Garbarek are the solo voices against the expansive background provided by a superb string orchestra. Haden opens *Runes*, his muscular sound unmistakeable in front of the delicate curtain of strings. Jarrett enters with concerto-like interplay; then Garbarek's alto-like tenor saxophone, softer at first than usual, blends subtly with the violin timbre before soaring in solo voice. Garbarek features more typically in *Mirrors*; here, the inner sections incorporate Jarrett's use of repeated rhythmic figures as well as some striking, glossy string writing. Recording quality, as you would expect from ECM at Ludwigsburg, is superb, if a little hard-edged; musically, this disc has much to commend it but would hardly be a first choice as an introduction to Garbarek, Haden or Jarrett himself.

MY SONG
Questar/My Song/Tabarka/Country/ Mandala/The Journey Home
Jan Garbarek (ts, ss), Keith Jarrett (p, perc), Palle Danielsson (b). Jon Christiensen (d), November 1977
ECM 821 406
AAD Running time: 48.35
Performance: ★ ★   Recording: ★ ★ ★

In this 1977 collaboration, Garbarek and Jarrett mesh perfectly, the saxophonist displaying a lyrical delicacy which would come as a surprise if you had only heard him with his own group. On a number like *Country*, where Jarrett provides an appropriately down-home, semi-gospel beat, Garbarek plays the melody with a swing and simplicity almost reminiscent of Grover Washington. *Mandala*, with Daniellson and Christiansen attempting (not quite convincingly) a driving pulse in the Elvin Jones manner, is a bit more challenging. In *My Song* itself, Jarrett draws on many influences but a Spanish Flamenco feeling permeates the whole performance, the pianist supported ably by Danielsson, whose bass playing is responsive, technically adept but never too busy.

Much of the album has the bright, reverberant quality of Jarrett's solo work, this produced partly by the recording technique and partly by Jarrett's individualistic use of the pedal. The pianist also demonstrates his subtlest touch, sometimes playing fast runs with such even volume and so little attack that he seems to have been barely stroking the keys. Sonically, the recording is as sweet and silky as anyone could wish.

STANDARDS, VOLUME 1
Meaning Of The Blues/All The Things You Are/It Never Entered My Mind/The Masquerade Is Over/God Bless The Child
Keith Jarrett (p), Gary Peacock (b) Jack DeJohnette (d), January 1983
ECM 811 966
AAD Running time: 45.38
Performance: ★ ★ Recording: ★ ★ ★

This album is the first of several to document Jarrett's return to the standard repertoire. Often gentle and meandering, sometimes swinging hard, Jarrett's use of these tunes is seldom predictable and never trite. With *All The Things You Are*, he uses part of the tune as an almost desultory intro, then gathers up the rhythm section to provide accelerating, loose-fingered variations over a wonderfully rushing beat. Peacock solos woodily over DeJohnette's fleet and shimmering cymbal pulse, then Jarrett returns at halved tempo, winding down to a gentle ending.

Rodgers' and Hart's *It Never Entered My Mind*, once a vehicle for Miles Davis, is here given a two-beat treatment by the trio before Jarrett starts his solo with a stretched-out, lag-along version of the theme; Jarrett plays *God Bless The Child* with a reflective sort of soul beat and chiming gospel chords. Peacock is excellent throughout, DeJohnette is supple, subtle and always a delight to listen to; this is indeed a disc that grows on you.

STANDARDS, VOLUME 2
So Tender/Moon and Sand/In Love In Vain/Never Let Me Go/If I Should Lose You/I Fall In Love Too Easily
Keith Jarrett (p), Gary Peacock (b), Jack DeJohnette (d), January 1983
ECM 825 015
AAD Running time: 45.13
Performance: ★ ★ Recording: ★ ★ ★

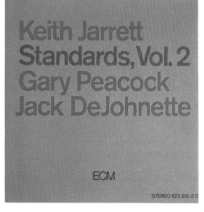

Another six titles from the same January 1983 trio sessions make up this *Volume 2*; if anything, the overall mood is even easier and more relaxed, and although the tunes may actually be less familiar, the result is a set of melodic, accessible performances. There is a consistent and enjoyable feeling of intimacy throughout, and the tempo remains moderate most of the time. Nonetheless DeJohnette provides a solid swing on *In Love In Vain*, Peacock subtle arco support in *Never Let me Go*; and from the light tripping of *If I Should Lose You* to the wistful *I Fall In Love Too Easily*, Jarrett is in lucid form. Certainly, this easy-going collection could fairly be said to live up to the promise of *Volume 1*.

STANDARDS LIVE
Stella By Starlight/The Wrong Blues/Falling In Love With Love/Too Young To Go Steady/The Way You Look Tonight/The Old Country
Keith Jarrett (p), Gary Peacock (b), Jack DeJohnette (d), July 1985
ECM 827 827
AAD Running time: 54.23
Performance: ★ ★ ★ Recording: ★ ★ ★

You might not immediately recognise Jarrett's solo introduction to *Stella By Starlight*, which refrains from the usual tendency to luxuriate in the harmony, but then, with the trio, he delivers a firm and confident reading of the tune.

The trio take *Falling In Love With Love* with a lilt, Dejonette's cymbals light and precise, Peacock's bass spare and springy. A bright-sounding *Too Young To Go Steady* seems saturated with the flavour of *It Never Entered My Mind*; then, propelled by an almost gong-like cymbal and encouraging clunks from DeJohnette, Jarrett delivers some long, well-argued lines which take the performance to a new level. Jarrett plays *The Way You look Tonight* with asymmetrical phrasing over an ultra-fast pulse, while *The Old Country* is smoothly eloquent, moderately fast but wistful as it shifts into the minor key. On the whole, this varied set does not offer spectacular pianism for its own sake, but captures the varied work of Jarrett's trio on what must have been a good night. Recording quality is excellent, smooth yet intimate in character, the piano mellow, Peacock's bass unexaggerated and naturally resonant, DeJohnette's drum sound clear and his cymbals almost singing. On most counts this disc is hard to fault.

QUINCY JONES
(b. Chicago, Illinois, 14 March 1933)

As a producer, arranger and composer, Quincy Jones is a major figure in the music industry; his distinguished contribution to jazz represents only one facet of an utterly remarkable career.

Jones' family moved to Seattle when he was ten, and it was there that he took up the trumpet and met his lifelong friend Ray Charles. He gained a music scholarship to Schillinger House, later to become Berklee, and soon had a reputation as an arranger. He toured Europe with Hampton in 1953, and the following year worked with Gillespie. He returned to Paris as musical director for Barclay Records.

When Jones formed his own big band, it turned out to be musically superb, but, unfortunately, an economic disaster for its leader. However, he was appointed vice president at Mercury Records and became the producer and arranger of dozens of hit records during the 1960s; by this time he had also started writing film scores. Moving to A&M, he produced a new series of big-selling records including *Body Heat* in 1974; but his career was brutally interrupted when he suffered two aneurisms and had to undergo brain surgery.

He was back to work by 1976, when he launched the Brothers Johnson, and Randy Crawford. Since then his productions and have achieved phenomenal record sales for Michael Jackson.

BIRTH OF A BAND
The Birth Of A Band/Moanin'/I Remember Clifford/Along Came Betty/Tickle Toe/Happy Faces/Whisper Not/The Gypsy/A Change Of Pace/Tuxedo Junction/Daylie Double/The Midnight Sun Will Never Set.
Joe Newman, Ernie Royal, Harry 'Sweets' Edison, Joe Wilder, Clark Terry (tp), Billy Byers, Jimmy Cleveland, Urbie Green, Quentin Jackson, Melba Liston, Tom Mitchell (tb), Julius Watkins (fr h), Phil Woods, Frank Wess, Benny Golson, Zoot Sims, Jerome Richardson, Sam 'The Man' Taylor, Sahib Shihab, Danny Bank (reeds), Patti Bown or Moe Wechsler (p), Kenny Burrell (g), Milt Hinton (b), Osie Johnson or Charlie Persip (d), Jimmy Crawford (perc), February/May 1959.
EmArcy 822 469
AAD Running time: 41.34
Performance: ★ ★ ★   Recording: ★ ★ ★

Jones' title track makes it an explosive birth; opening with a fanfare, it is a fast, exciting riff blues, a brilliant showcase for the precision and flair of brass and reed sections, with a 'chase' section for the tenors of Zoot Sims and Jerome Richardson.

Subtle scoring maintains the spontaneous catchiness of *Moanin'*, while a fast, bouncy *Tickle Toe* (arranged here by Al Cohn and featuring a very Prez-like Zoot Sims) and a springy *Tuxedo Junction* (with an impeccable muted Harry Edison on trumpet and a wailing, 'Lockjaw' Davis-like Sam 'The Man' Taylor on tenor) shows how effectively this sophisticated unit could put over the big band standards of years gone by. Three of the numbers are Benny Golson's, including *I Remember Clifford* (the lead taken, rather too idiosyncratically, by Clark Terry) and *Whisper Not*. Jones' own medium-paced *Daylie Double* is a not too distant relative of *Jersey Bounce*, while Sonny Stitt's *Happy Faces* is an exhilarating fast blues, mellow brass, Jones' tune *The Midnight Sun Will Never Set* features Kenny Burrell, and brings an impressively varied and well thought-out package to a close.

THE GREAT WIDE WORLD OF QUINCY JONES
Lester Leaps In/Ghana/Caravan/Everybody's Blues/Cherokee/Airmail Special/They Say It's Wonderful/Chant Of The Weed/I Never Has Seen Snow/Eesom.
Ernie Royal, Jimmy Maxwell, Art Farmer, Lee Morgan, Nick Travis, Lennie Johnson (tp), Jimmy Cleveland, Frankrehak, Urbie Green, Billy Byers (tb), Julius Watkins (fr h), Phil Woods, Porter Kilbert (as), Jerome Richardson (ts, fl, piccolo), Budd Johnson (ts), Sahib Shihab (bars), Patti Bown (p), Les Spann (g, fl), Buddy Catlett (b), Don Lamond (d), November 1959.
EmArcy 822 470
AAD Running time: 36.41
Performance: ★ ★   Recording: ★ ★ ★

For this follow-up to *Birth Of A Band*, the choice of material showed if anything a greater emphasis on material of past decades, with arrangements mainly by Ernie Wilkins.

A version of Don Redman's *Chant Of The Weed* moodily effective, while the opening *Lester Leaps In* drives along well, as Les Spann introduces the tune on guitar before the band comes in to give a unison replica of Lester Young's original solo; *Caravan* is appealing enough, and has a fine solo by Jimmy Cleveland, but despite a tantalisingly brief solo by Lee Morgan, *Air Mail Special* does not really stand up against the version recorded by Hampton's band in 1955.

Cherokee, the swing-era tune whose intriguing modulations made it a staple of the bebop era too has a busy run-through here with a rather quiet muted solo from Art Farmer, an agile but odd-toned one from Porter Kilbert on alto, and a brief entry by Spann on guitar. On the other hand, the arresting *Ghana* (written by Wilkins) has a fine baritone solo by Sahib Shihab.

Recorded with clarity, space and smoothness if not with quite the exaggerated glamour of *The Birth Of A Band*, this disc does not perhaps quite live up to the extraordinary promises of that album, but does contain some very fine music.

STANLEY JORDAN
(b. Palo Alto, California, 1960)

It remains to be seen how profound an influence the brilliant Stanley Jordan will have on guitarists in general, but it is clear that his two-handed approach to the instrument is a revolution in electric guitar technique.

Trained as a pianist from the age of six, Stanley Jordan took up guitar at eleven after hearing records of Jimi Hendrix. He listened to many other guitarists during his teens, absorbing influences ranging from Barney Kessel and Wes Montgomery to Larry Coryell and John McLaughlin; he had been attracted by the articulation and expressive phrasing that was possible on the guitar, but he still wanted to be able to produce the texture and harmonic movement that was possible on piano. By the age of sixteen he was tuning the guitar completely in fourths (the top two strings raised to C and F), which made the position of octaves consistent across all the strings and opened up new chord possibilities. Eventually, he perfected his 'tapping' technique, in which the fingers of either hand produce notes or chords independently, without the need for a plectrum; each string is started vibrating as it hits the fret. It is a method only possible on the electric instrument, demanding extreme delicacy of touch from both hands.

Jordan studied music at Princeton University, graduating in 1981, and was soon selling copies of a privately-recorded album, *Touch Sensitive*, at his gigs. Moving to New York in early 1984, he found it hard to get into the club scene and was reduced to playing for small change in the street until an audition with impresario George Wein led to an unannounced appearance at the 1984 Kool Jazz Festival, which in turn led to a booking at the Montreux Festival and a recording contract with Blue Note. Jordan's arrival fortunately coincided with the revival of new recording activity by the famous label, and he also appeared on Blue Note's 1985 video *One Night With Blue Note*. The two albums released so far will no doubt be followed by many more.

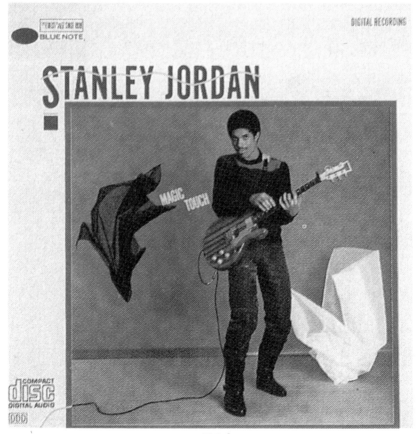

MAGIC TOUCH

Eleanor Rigby/Freddie Freeloader/'Round Midnight/All The Children/The Lady In My Life/Angel/Fundance/New Love/Return Expedition/A Child Is Born

1, 3, 4, 6, 7, 8, 10 Stanley Jordan (g), Sammy Figueroa (perc); 2 Jordan (g), Charnett Moffett (b), Peter Erskine (d); 5 Jordan (g), Wayne Braithwaite (el b), Onaje Allan Gumbs (key), Omar Hakim (d); 9 Jordan (g), Moffett (b), Figueroa, Bugsy Moore (perc), Al DiMeola (cymbals), 1985.

Blue Note CDP7 46092
DDD Running time: 53.57
Performance: ★ ★ **Recording:** ★ ★ ★

Covering a wide range of material in this debut album, Stanley Jordan used his two-handed technique to create a suitable variety of treatments. His own tunes include the pretty, dance-like *All The Children*, a solo in which he produces an effect rather like a 12-string guitar, using a repeated Alberti-type bass figure; the jazzy *Fundance*, a happy up-tempo blues in which he plays a walking bass line under his own boppish solo, even throwing in chords as well; he is joined by an (uncredited) flautist and rhythm section on the appealingly sunny, Latin-tinged *New Love*, with a fast and fluent solo; then the full, supple bass of Moffett along with percussion and cymbals sets up the moody *Return Expedition*, in which Jordan's incredibly fluid, long-lined solo is a beautifully structured *tour de force*. Here, and even more so in the convincing *Freddie Freeloader*, Jordan's left-hand chords produce the effect of a piano comping behind his own free-flying solo.

Produced by Al Dimeola, the disc has fine sound quality, though it cannot perhaps be described as natural since Jordan's guitar appears in a the haze of echo effects, which apart from anything else help smooth over the edges in the solo pieces; this disc as a whole has certainly served to showcase Stanley Jordan's amazing talent.

STANDARDS VOL 1

The Sound Of Silence/Sunny/Georgia On My Mind/Send One Your Love/Moon River/Guitar Man/One Less Bell To Answer/Because/My Favourite Things/Silent Night

Stanley Jordan (g), 1986.

Blue Note CDP7 463332
DDD Running time: 47.38
Performance: ★ ★ **Recording:** ★ ★ ★

Few of these tunes are standards in the usual jazz sense, ranging as they do from the Duane Eddy hit *Guitar Man* to *Silent Night*, which, like *Georgia On My Mind*, is turned almost completely into a blues; but all are among Jordan's longstanding favourite tunes. He fragments *Moon River* in a somehow slightly disappointing way, and (inspired by Coltrane) takes *My Favourite Things* at a furious tempo, adding a rhythm part which becomes an end in itself.

He starts *Because* with a little intro in octaves, then some little flurrying runs before he plays the tune over gently-arpeggiated chords, and this is one of the nicest tracks on the disc. Recorded with rather less reverberation and a consequently more intimate and ruthlessly revealing sound, this follow-up album does not fulfil all the promise of Jordan's astounding first appearance on record; but as he put it himself in a recent interview: 'forget about the technique, listen to the songs'.

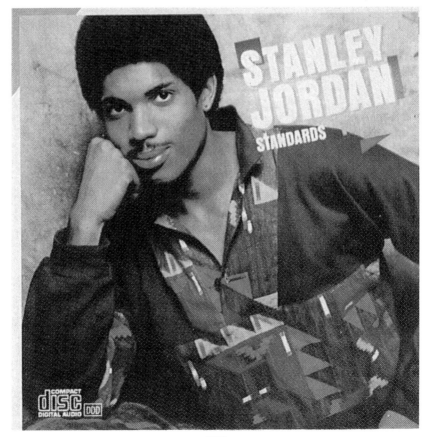

B B KING
(b. Itta Bena, Mississipi, 16 September 1925)

Following, then rapidly outshining, the guitar and vocal stylings (and the band-leading showmanship) of T-Bone Walker and Lowell Fulsom, B B King became one of the greatest blues instrumentalists, and certainly the most widely influential. As a singer and lyricist, his variations gave new, scope to the familiar blues verse pattern.

Raised on the farm where his parents were sharecroppers, King made his home in Indianola, but went to Memphis to track down and learn from his cousin, blues artist Bukka White. After this he returned to Indianola for a while, but on his second trip to Memphis he met Sonny Boy Williamson II (Rice Miller) and through him landed a spot on the local radio station WDIA; he worked at the station for three years as a disc jockey and performer of commercials and requests.

In 1949 he cut four titles in the WDIA studio with Tuff Green's band, but in 1950 he was signed up by the Bihari brothers' Modern Records for their RPM label, topping the R&B charts in December 1951 with his first version of the Lowell Fulsom number *Three O'Clock Blues*. He remained with the Biharis (on their Crown and Kent labels) throughout the 1950s, then in 1961 signed for ABC Paramount. Record releases included some outstanding live performances (notably the *Live At The Regal* album of 1964) but by the end of the 1960s these were balanced by a studio output involving more rock-based musicians and an 'updated' sound.

This was a period in which the blues as pioneered by King in earlier years had ceased to be widely fashionable even with white audiences, and King was compelled to use clogging, overblown backgrounds and sometimes unsuitable material, but his ability to communicate emotion remained undimmed.

In more recent years, King has benefited from a renewed appreciation by more jazz-orientated listeners. He continues to front an impressive band and is still one of the great performers.

THE BEST OF B B KING VOL 1

You Upset Me Baby/Every Day I Have The Blues/Five Long Years/Sweet Little Angel/Beautician Blues/Dust My Broom/Three O'Clock Blues/Ain't That Just Like A Woman/I'm King/Sweet Sixteen (part 1)/Sweet Sixteen (part 2)/Whole Lotta Lovin'/Mean Ole Frisco/Please Accept My Love/Going Down Slow/Blues For Me/You Don't Know/Early Every Morning/Blues At Sunrise/Please Love Me
B B King (g, voc) with 1, 2 possibly including Floyd Jones (tp), George Coleman (as, ts), Bill Harvey (ts), Connie McBooker (p), James Walker (b), Ted Curry (d) 1954/1955; 3-19 variously including Kenny Sands or Henry Boozier (tp), Lawrence Burdine (as), Johnny Board (ts), Floyd Newman, Herman Green, Fred Ford or Barney Hubbard (bars), Millard Lee (p), Duke Jethro (org), Jymie Merritt (b) or Marshall York (el b), Curry (d), 1956-60; 20 as 1, 1953 (additional instruments added later on some tracks)
Ace CDCH 908
AAD Running time: 57.16
Performance: ★ ★ ★ **Recording:** ★

This first selection from King's recordings on the Modern labels includes his first hit *Three O'Clock Blues*, in its raw, unadorned and most effective studio form with King backed only by piano, organ and rhythm section. Some of the other early recordings were later remixed with additional horns, bass and drums to update the sound; King's voice and guitar are surrounded by brass and the beat becomes an open kind of swing rather than the tight, intense shuffle of the early R&B style. On the other hand, a number like *Beautician Blues*, heard here without this treatment, may surprise those who know it from other reissues, on which the horns respond too neatly to King's guitar.

However, there are plenty of numbers, like the outstanding *You Don't Know*, which show how effectively King could use the big-band sound he has always been so fond of. He was always ready to adapt his style, as in the uncharacteristic fast shuffle of *Mean Ole Frisco* and the amazing straight-ahead rocking beat of *Early In The Morning*.

Sound quality is understandably variable, but the transfer appears to be excellent.

THE BEST OF B B KING VOL 2

Bad Luck Soul/Get Out Of Here/The Jungle/Sugar Mama/Ten Long Years/Bad Case Of Love/House Rocker/Sneakin' Around/Shut Your Mouth/The Letter/I've Got A Right To Love My Baby/The Woman I Love/You Done Lost Your Good Thing Now/Did You Ever Love A Woman/B B Rock/Rock Me Baby/It's My Own Fault/You Know I Love You /Low Rider/You're Gonna Miss Me
B B King (g, voc) with unknown personnels, probably including Kenny Sands or Henry Boozier (tp), Lawrence Burdine (as), Johnny Board (ts), Floyd Newman, Herman Green, Fred Ford or Barney Hubbard (bars), Millard Lee (p), Duke Jethro (org), Jymie Merritt (b) or Marshall York (el b), Ted Curry or Sonny Freeman (d), 1956-60
Ace CDCH 199
AAD Running time: 59.28
Performance: ★ ★ ★ **Recording:** ★ ★
Drawing on the same resources as *Vol 1*, this is very far from being a second-best

collection. The opening *Bad Luck Soul* and the superbly swinging *Get Out Of Here* typify the way King (with the help of arranger Maxwell Davis) had perfected a sophisticated but still gutsy presentation of his work by 1959-60. Yet *The Jungle*, electrifying with King's angry, shouting vocal style and a consummate guitar solo, the steady rock of an excellent rhythm section and spare yet driving horn riffs, make this the archetypal urban blues performance, immeasurably more intense.

Perhaps King's best-ever blues-ballad performance *Sneaking Around* comes here without the unnecessary extra horns and outstanding among the remaining numbers (despite its rather peculiar sound quality) is *Rock Me Baby*; this disc must rank as even more essential than *Vol 1*.

THE BEST OF B B KING

Hummingbird/Cook County Jail Introduction/How Blue Can You Get/Caldonia/Sweet Sixteen/Ain't Nobody Home/Why I Sing The Blues/The Thrill Is Gone/Nobody Loves Me But My Mother
B B King (g, voc) with: 1 Leon Russell (p), Joe Walsh (g), Brian Garofalo (el b), Russ Kunkel (d), Sherlie Matthews, Merry Clayton, Clydie King, Vonetta Fields (background voc), orchestra arr, cond Jimmie Haskell, June 1970; 2 spoken introduction; 3 John Browning (tp), Booker Walker (as), Louis Hubert (ts), Ron Levy (p), Wilbert Freeman (el b), Sonny Freeman (d), September 1970; 4 Jim Price, Ollie Mitchell (tp), Chuck Findley (tb), Bobby Keys (ts), Bill Perkins (bars, cl), Duster Bennett (harmonica), Gary Wright (org), Rick Wright (el p), Klaus Voorman (el b), Jim Gordon (d), June 1971; 5 as 3 Earl Turbinton (as) replaces Walker, add Joe Burton (tb), Mel Brown (g), March 1971; 6 Price (tp, tb), Keys (ts), Gary Wright (org), Jerry Ragovoy (p), John Uribe, David Spinozza (g), Voorman (b), Jim Keltner (d), Joshie Armstead, Tasha Thomas, Carl Hall (background voc), June 1971; 7 Paul Harris (p), Hugh McCracken (g), Gerald Jermott (el b), Herbie Lovelle (d); 8 as 7, orchestra arr and cond Bert DeCoteaux, 1969. 9 King (p, voc), 1972.
MCA CMCAD 31040
AAD Running time: 40.29
Performance: ★ ★ **Recording:** ★

The swamp-rock beat of Leon Russell and friends stultifies *Hummingbird*, while *Ain't Nobody Home*, despite the elaborate horns and background vocals, is feeble (with a thin and irritatingly fuddled sound quality); but King's powerful, serious vocal and searing guitar redeem the lumbering funk of the rhythm section in *Why I Sing The Blues*, and in *The Thrill Is Gone* (a single hit, from the album *Completely Well*) the rock elements are at last successfully brought into balance with an enduring performance. Despite strong efforts by King, this run-through of Louis Jordan's *Caldonia* suffers from a flabby beat and too many players just ineptly joining in; by way of contrast, both *How Blue Can You Get* (from *Live At Cook's County Jail*) and *Sweet Sixteen* (in which King updates the lyric 'my brother's in Korea . . .' to 'I just got back from Vietnam . . .!') are great, solid performances by King with his own band.

ROLAND KIRK
(b. Columbus, Ohio, 7 August 1936; d. Bloomington, Indiana, 5 December 1977)

Simply because he was an unforgettable performer, the late Rahsaan Roland Kirk's pioneering use of two or three horns at once sometimes unjustly overshadows other aspects of his great talent.

Blinded in a accident as a baby, Kirk took up the tenor saxophone at an early age, was playing with an R&B band at eleven and leading his own by the time he was fourteen. By the time he was in his early twenties he was experimenting with the idea of playing more than one horn at a time, apparently following a dream he had in his childhood of playing three saxophones at once; he discovered the obscure stritch (which sounds like an alto) and manzello (resembling a soprano sax) and these became part of his musical equipment. He also developed the technique of circular breathing (inhaling while still pushing air through the instrument) to a remarkable degree and was known to hold a note for twenty minutes. But of all Kirk's innovations, perhaps the most widely copied was his bluesy vocalised flute style, in which he sang across the mouthpiece while blowing, producing in a natural way the singing-instrument effect which, fifteen years later, keyboard players emulated with the Vocoder voice synthesizer.

Kirk adopted the name Rahsaan after being instructed to, he said, in a dream. To an extent he appealed to the same audience as the 'free' jazz players of the 1960s, and he could and did play in a 'free' context from time to time, but Kirk's music was deeply and relatively conventionally rooted in the jazz and blues traditions.

In 1976 he suffered a stroke, which left one hand paralysed, but he continued to perform with amazing fluency one-handed while exercising to regain the use of the other hand. In 1977 a second stroke proved fatal, cutting short the life of a great original talent, a man who had shown immense courage and determination in the face of personal adversity, and had produced moving as well as exciting music.

WE FREE KINGS

Three For The Festival/Moon Song/A Sack Full Of Soul/The Haunted Melody/Blues For Alice (2 takes)/We Free Kings/You Did It, You Did It/Some Kind Of Love/My Delight.
1, 2, 7-9 Rahsaan Roland Kirk (ts, fl, manzello, stritch, siren), Hank Jones (p), Wendell Marshall (b), Charlie Persip (d), 3-6, 10 as 1 but Richard Wyands (p) and Art Davis (b) replace Jones and Marshall; August 1961.
EmArcy 826 455
AAD Running time: 43.12
Performance ★ ★ ★   Recording ★ ★ ★

As a bonus, the CD buyer gets an additional take of Charlie Parker's archetypal bop 12-bar *Blues For Alice*, not present on the vinyl LP; but this set would be good value anyway. Kirk's amazing sax 'section' is heard steaming in to good effect on the fast opening blues, which is propelled with great drive by Persip. The mid-paced *Moon Song* contains a fine tenor solo, while the pretty *Some Kind Of Love* is affectionately tongue-in-cheek but again provides the vehicle for some fine soloing; *Haunted Melody* is a moving ballad. Kirk's *My Delight* is a catchy tune, like a smoothed-out bop theme (the title, of course, echoes Tadd Dameron's *Our Delight*), which the saxophonist uses to launch some wilder excursions.

The title track makes use of the similarly-named Christmas carol, swinging in 6/8 time, again with an impressive sax ensemble effect, this quite quickly, giving way to a flute solo which moves effectively from purity to blues inflections, with Kirk switching to manzello before returning once again to flute for the fade.

But the blues remains Kirk's predominant starting point, with *A Sack Full Of Soul* representing the gospel-soaked, foot-tapping kind of blues you would expect from the title, with Kirk on tenor, then on the soprano-like manzello, in superb unhurried form over an exciting, marching beat. His unison/harmony playing makes this a *tour de force*, but it is in *You Did It, You Did It*, the stirring flute blues, that Kirk intones the words of the title across the mouthpiece to produce the sound which, for better or worse, he will be best remembered. Yet to appear on Compact Disc is Kirk's great 1965 album *Rip, Rig And Panic*, so for now this superbly-recorded and always enjoyable disc appears to be the only example of his music available in digital form.

GENE KRUPA
(b. Chicago, Illinois, 15 January 1909; d. Yonkers, New York, 16 October 1973)

With a unique drum sound, unbeatable showmanship and good looks, Krupa was the first drummer to become a star in his own right. He was the driving force in the Benny Goodman band, and in the earliest of Goodman's small groups, and later a successful leader.

At sixteen, he worked with Al Gale's band, then in several Chicago groups. His first record date, in 1927, was with Red McKenzie and Eddie Condon's Chicagoans, but he moved to New York in 1929, playing there in theatre bands directed by Red Nichols. He worked in various dance bands before joining Benny Goodman in January 1934. He stayed until February 1938, when he left to form a successful band of his own, which featured trumpet star Roy Eldridge and singer Anita O'Day. Unfortunately the band broke up in May 1943 because of Krupa's brush with the law (he had been arrested for possession of marijuana), and in September that year he rejoined Goodman. In 1944, after a spell with Tommy Dorsey, he formed a new big band, at first overburdened with a string section, but later of normal size.

However, big bands generally were becoming uneconomic, and in 1951 he disbanded to tour with Norman Granz's 'Jazz At The Philharmonic' (JATP) package. Recordings for Granz included 'drum battles' with Buddy Rich (generally acknowledged to have been the winner) and Louie Bellson. In 1954 Krupa co-founded a drum school with Cozy Cole, while 1955 brought a film appearance in 'The Benny Goodman Story', and reunion recordings of the Goodman Quartet, in February 1956, he went into the studio with Eldridge and O'Day to re-create his early-1940s hits. He appeared in 'The Gene Krupa Story', filmed in 1959, but retired soon after this because of heart trouble. He returned to musical activity in 1963, but during his last years each live appearance represented a courageous fight against leukaemia, to which he eventually succumbed.

DRUMMER MAN
Let Me Off Uptown/Rockin' Chair/Opus 1/ Fish Fry/Drummin' Man/Drum Boogie/ Boogie Blues/Leave Us Leap/Slow Down/ Wire Brush Stomp/That's What You Think/ After You've Gone
Roy Eldridge (tp, voc 1), Joe Ferrante, Bernie Glow, Ernie Royal, Nick Travis (tp), J J Johnson, Kai Winding, Fred Ohms, Jimmy Cleveland (tb), Sam Marowitz (as), Hal McKusick (as, ss), Eddie Shu (ts), Aaron Sachs (ts, cl), Danny Bank (bars), Dave McKenna (p), Barry Galbraith (g), John Drew (b), Gene Krupa (d), Anita O'Day (voc 1, 3, 5, 7, 9, 11), Quincy Jones (arr except 4, 6, 8), Manny Albam (arr 4), Nat Pierce (arr 6), Billy Byers (8), February 1956.
Verve 827 843
AAD Running time: 39.39
Performance: ★ ★   Recording: ★ ★ ★

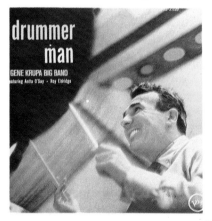

The idea of this 1956 recording was to re-create the hits of Krupa's great band of the early 1940's, which had Roy Eldridge as featured soloist and Anita O'Day as vocalist. With fresh-sounding, mildly-updated arrangements by Quincy Jones (on all but the three tracks where arranger credits go to Manny Albam, Nat Pierce and Billy Byers), it at least partly succeeds in that intention.

Krupa's biggest features are of course *Drummin' Man, Drum Boogie* and *Wire Brush Stomp*, where he energetically demonstrates his unique drum sound, which in some aspects dates back to the Chicago school of the pre-swing years. Eldridge plays a whole batch of excellent, exciting solos, from the rich post-Armstrong bravura style of *Rockin' Chair* (not a vocal here!) and the outstanding *After You've Gone*, to the superb muted playing on *That's What You Think*, where he sounds to modern ears just like his greatest follower, Gillespie. This number is one of the best features for Anita O'Day, who caresses the lyric and baby-talks her scat part with utter sensuality. She is also excellent on *Boogie Blues* and *Slow Down*; but fluent, versatile and thoroughly professional as O'Day is, she not surprisingly cannot really do much with the dated and even irritating *Opus 1*. However, along with Eldridge, she just manages to sound convincing on the patter of the famous *Let Me Off Uptown*, though this is equally dated in content. The band is a fine one, notable among other things for the presence of the two virtuoso trombonists, J J Johnson and Kai Winding, and sound quality (mono) is very good too.

WYNTON MARSALIS
(b.New Orleans, 18 October 1961)

Supremely gifted, the trumpeter Wynton Marsalis actively combines the inheritance of the 'great tradition' of jazz with a stated commitment to formal musical excellence. An astonishingly mature artist while still in his late teens, Marsalis became, in his early twenties, the living symbol of a 1980s jazz revival.

Wynton's father, Ellis Marsalis, is well known in New Orleans as a pianist and music teacher; at one time he worked with Cannonball Adderley's group, but could not be persuaded to leave New Orleans to go on the road. Wynton was given a trumpet at six, but did not take it up seriously until he was 12. He then set his sights on the school's classical solo competition, for which a trumpeter was an unlikely entrant, and at fourteen, confounding his critics, he won the chance to perform with the New Orleans Philharmonic. He was the soloist in the Haydn Trumpet Concerto; two years later he played Bach's Brandenburg Concerto No 2 with them. While in high school he had been playing with the New Orleans Civic Orchestra, and at 17 he was admitted to the Berkshire Music Centre at Tanglewood, which made a special exception to its usual minimum acceptance limit of 18. Marsalis later said that he shocked Gunther Schuller, on the staff at the Centre, by revealing that he could also play jazz!

At eighteen he went to Juilliard, played with the Brooklyn Philharmonic and worked in a theatre pit orchestra, then joined Art Blakey's Jazz Messengers; the following summer he was invited to join Herbie Hancock's quartet; and this led to his first album, *Wynton Marsalis*, produced by Hancock. Wynton and his brother Branford (his senior by one year), on tenor and soprano sax, both toured with Hancock's VSOP II in 1983.

In the same year, after he had formed his own group with Branford, Wynton's jazz album *Think Of One* was released simultaneously with his *Trumpet Concertos*, an unprecedented feat. The 1984 album of standards *Hot House Flowers*, with a large string orchestra, was

followed in 1985 by the rather more hard-hitting personal statement of *Black Codes*, featuring what was now a well-established quintet. Following this with the quartet performances of *J Mood*, he continues to record for CBS.

Marsalis has always been proud to describe himself as a product of the jazz tradition; and as more and more musicians have turned or returned to the traditional values, the passage of time seems so far only to have strengthened and justified the stance of this remarkable musician.

AN AMERICAN HERO
One By One/My Funny Valentine/'Round Midnight/E.T.A./Time Will Tell/Blakey's Theme
Wynton Marsalis (tp), Bobby Watson (as), Billy Pierce (ts), Jimmy Williams (p), Charles Fambrough (b), Art Blakey (d), October 1980.
Kingdom CD GATE 7018
AAD Running time: 42.53
Performance: ★ ★ ★   Recording: ★ ★

Subtitled 'The Best Of His First Recordings', this is a selection taken from the tapes of a Blakey gig at Bubba's Jazz Restaurant, Fort Lauderdale, Florida, which has already yielded *Art Blakey: Live At Bubba's* (CD GATE 7003). All the tunes here are more or less Marsalis features, but *My Funny Valentine* is truly exceptional, a fine example of sheer control as he first establishes the classic lines of a trumpet ballad and then negotiates a faster interlude. *'Round Midnight* uses a 'traditional' Parker-style intro by Watson but soon displays some typical Blakey twists, with stops, breaks and tempo changes. Marsalis, caressing the melody, is completely at ease through all this.

On Wayne Shorter's tune *One By One*, again a characteristic Messengers performance driven at a strutting pace by Blakey's offbeat, Marsalis takes the first solo, pausing only to quote laconically from *Squatty Roo* before plunging into a series of double-time runs; but his fastest playing comes in *Blakey's Theme* , where his solo (played, impressively, as if he had quite a few more bars per minute in hand) follows an eel-like Watson and a slightly breathless Pierce. Sound is good, clean and full of impact, although lacking some 'air', and perhaps some of the live atmosphere has disappeared in the remixing (there seems to be an edit after Marsalis' solo on the last track), which was done, long after the event, in 1985.

THINK OF ONE
Knozz-Moe-King/Fuchsia/My Ideal/What Is Happening, Here (Now)?/Think Of One/The Bell Ringer/Later/Melancholia
1-6 Wynton Marsalis (tp), Branford Marsalis (ts, ss), Kenny Kirkland (p), Phil Bowler (b), Jeffrey 'Tain' Watts (d); 7, 8 Ray Drummond (b), replaces Bowler, 1983.
CBS/SONY 35DP 75
DDD Running time: 44.38
Performance: ★ ★ ★   Recording: ★ ★ ★

For this second CBS album, Marsalis had formed his own quintet, and the music had gone somewhat beyond string-of-solos formulae; here, in each number, the parts seem to go together like a watch. On the very fast (horribly titled!) opener, the trumpeter is magnificent, and Branford follows adeptly on tenor; yet his Traneisms, though beautifully played, come off as rather lightweight. But Branford's soprano is first cool and elegant, then soaring and expressive on *Fuchsia*, an attractive tune by Kirkland, with plinking flower-like piano and cymbals.

My Ideal begins as a ballad with a beautiful solo from the trumpeter, who soon swings into a 4/4 beat with rhythmic excursions, prodded by Kirkland, whose own solo alternates legato runs with dense but lightly-struck chord passages. The title tune strips down the idea of a unison theme to a series of staccato chords, dynamically shaded from a whisper to a shout, the whole thing carrying strong echoes of Thelonious Monk. The intricate and superbly executed ensemble playing (trumpet, tenor and piano) in the theme of *The Bell Ringer* gives just one example of the group's collective technical abilities and musical coherence. *Later*, at a fast but relaxed hard-bop tempo, has an appealing loose-sounding solo from Wynton and a soft-toned, scale-exploring one from Branford; and finally, the ballad-like *Melancholia* is almost sentimental, a pensive, muted Marsalis backed by beautifully-placed, luminous piano chords.

With excellent sound quality, this disc must also be praised for excellent playing throughout, even though, despite the variety of material, it may leave the feeling of a certain lack of substance.

HOT HOUSE FLOWERS
Stardust/Lazy Afternoon/For All We Know/When You Wish Upon A Star/Django/Melancholia/Hot House Flowers/I'm Confessing That I Love You
Wynton Marsalis (tp), Branford Marsalis (ts), Kent Jordan (alto fl), Kenny Kirkland (p), Ron Carter (b), Jeffrey 'Tain' Watts (d), orchestra directed by Bob Freedman, 1984.
CBS/Sony 32DP 183
DDD Running time: 41.56
Performance: ★ ★   Recording: ★ ★ ★

The orchestral arrangements provided for (and partly by) Marsalis here are vastly superior to those some of his predecessors had to work with. One of the strengths of this disc is that you never get the feeling that the trumpeter has merely found himself standing in front of a curtain of string sounds, struggling to find something to say.

However, as *Stardust* has been a standard choice for trumpet features for well over 40 years, Marsalis does try to do something different with it. *When You Wish Upon A Star*, with a beat, is a virtuoso piece of arranging, and contains fine playing by Branford. *Django* is a little fragmented, while *I'm Confessing That I Love You* is perhaps pushing things a little too far, but the astonishing standard of musical craftsmanship overcomes any quibbles.

BLACK CODES

Black Codes/For Wee Folks/Delfeayo's Dilemma/Phryzzinian Man/Aural Oasis/Chambers Of Train/Blues
1-4, 6, 7 Wynton Marsalis (tp), Branford Marsalis (ts, ss), Kenny Kirkland (p), Charnett Moffett (b), Jeffrey 'Tain' Watts (d), 5 as 1 but Ron Carter (b), replaces Moffett, 1985.
CBS/Sony 32DP 276
DDD Running time: 51.15
Performance: ★ ★ ★   Recording: ★ ★ ★

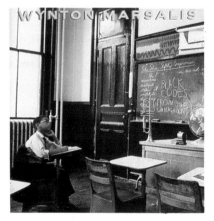

With this album, Marsalis' playing takes in much more of the potent, enriching influence of Miles Davis than was heard before. The title track has an intricate theme which gives on to a 'modal' blowing section, where Marsalis plays with vigour, power and conviction. In *For Wee Folks*, the brothers share the theme, soprano sax and muted trumpet alternating phrases against the

incredibly accurately-controlled cymbal sounds of Watts; they duet in conventional unison and harmony on the theme of *Phryzzinian Man*, which turns out to be another fast vehicle for Wynton's trumpet, Kirkland keeping up the pressure with almost squirted chords behind him. Branford's solo is softer, less urgent at first, but builds effectively.

In *Aural Oasis*, a piano figure echoes *Black Codes* while Marsalis displays a deep, Miles-like, echo-boosted trumpet. Finally, on *Blues*, he duets with Moffett's bass, throwing out the usual 12-bar sequence but keeping the feel of altered blues changes, spinning out longer and longer lines. The number finishes with an archly casual little off-mike coda from Marsalis, as if he is walking away up a corridor. In the end, this is a more satisfying disc than *Think Of One*, and again demonstrates fine musicianship; though Kirkland occasionally runs out of solo steam and the youthful Moffett lacks authority and power.

J MOOD

J Mood/Presence That Lament Brings/Insane Asylum/Skain's Domain/Melodique/After/Much Later
Wynton Marsalis (tp), Marcus Roberts (p), Robert Leslie Hurst III (b), Jeffrey 'Tain' Watts (d),
Columbia CK 40308
DDD Running time: 42.54
Performance: ★ ★ ★   Recording: ★ ★ ★

For this quartet recording Marsalis retains only the drummer, 'Tain' Watts, from his previous line-up. The pianist is Marcus Roberts, whose style is virile, relatively spare, yet with a subtle control of dynamics; his work seems to bring a sense of space into the music, and the high level of his rapport with Marsalis is obvious. In the absence of Branford, Wynton seems at one point (on *Presence That Lament Brings*) to be producing a soprano-like sound on his trumpet; but this is just another small facet of his apparently endless versatility.

Generally, his playing on this disc has a solid, completely unhurried quality which seems new here. The influence of early-to-mid period Miles is again very clear, notably in the quiet little tune, *Melodique*, where Roberts begins to take on the guise of a less-filigreed Red Garland. *After*, so slow as to be nearly static, offers delicate interplay between Harmon-muted trumpet, piano, and sensitively-controlled cymbals; *Much Later* wraps things up at a fine bustling tempo.

JOHN McLAUGHLIN
(b. Doncaster, Yorkshire, England, 4 January 1942)

Taking the achievement of speed on the guitar to almost unbelievable lengths, John McLaughlin was an influential figure in early-1970s fusion, and has continued to experiment.

Influenced in his early teens by an elder brother's blues records, McLaughlin soon became part of the earliest wave of 'British blues' in the 1960s, with The Graham Bond Organisation, Alexis Korner and Georgie Fame; but later in the decade he became absorbed in 'free' jazz, working with baritonist John Surman and bassist Dave Holland.

McLaughlin travelled to the USA in February 1969; Miles Davis' astonishing young drummer, Tony Williams, ready to leave and form his own group, had heard a tape of McLaughlin and been impressed enough to invite him over. Within two weeks of his arrival, Williams had invited him along to the Davis recording session which produced *In A Silent Way*.

Working with Miles made McLaughlin's reputation, and in 1971 he, too was ready to form his own group, the Mahavishnu Orchestra, whose title and music (at least on *The Inner Mounting Flame*) reflected McLaughlin's involvement with Eastern religious thinking in the shape of the guru Sri Chinmoy. Ego clashes broke up the group in 1974, leaving McLaughlin to form Shakti, an acoustic quartet with Indian musicians L Shankar (violin), Zakir Hussain (tabla) and T H Vinayakram (percussion).

In 1978, McLaughlin began working with Paco de Lucia and Larry Coryell, who was soon replaced by Al DiMeola to create the popular guitar trio which produced the album *Friday Night In San Francisco* in 1980. Only in 1985 did McLaughlin reform the Mahavishnu orchestra, which in most recent form included the young saxophonist Bill Evans.

BETWEEN NOTHINGNESS AND ETERNITY
Trilogy: The Sunlit Path: La Mere De La Mer; Tomorrow's Story Not The Same/ Sister Andrea/Dream
John McLaughlin (g), Jerry Goodman (vln), Jan Hammer (key), Rick Laird (b), Billy Cobham (perc), 1973.
CBS CDCBS 69046
AAD Running time: 42.23
Performance: ★   Recording: ★ ★

For all its faults, this live recording seems to capture the essence of the Mahavishnu Orchestra. Opening with a portentous (real) eastern gong, *The Sunlit Path* develops through attractive guitar arpeggios (sounding to the irreverent like The Beatles' *Dear Prudence*) into a rock section where McLaughlin trades high speed runs with Hammer; this gives in turn on to the quiet opening of *La Mère De La Mer*, in which Goodman solos first over shimmering, *gamelin*-like guitar, before McLaughlin switches to a heavy rock sound to join in exchanges with Goodman and Hammer as Cobham's accelerating beat brings the section to a furious climax.

With *Sister Andrea*, McLaughlin's heavily distorted guitar has all the speed but none of the grace of Jimi Hendrix; more absorbing is the suite-like *Dream*, which on vinyl occupied the whole of side two. Here McLaughlin starts with a series of incredibly fast flamenco-influenced runs, then duets effectively with Hammer; a driving rock beat develops, propelling Goodman's violin solo, until we hear the riff from Cream's *Sunshine Of Your Love* and the start of a duet section between McLaughlin and Cobham which is the most compelling part of the album.

BIRDS OF FIRE
Birds Of Fire/Miles Beyond/Celestial: Terrestrial Commuters/Sapphire Bullets Of Pure Love/Thousand Island Park/Hope/ One Word/Sanctuary/Open Country Joy/ Resolution
John McLaughlin (g), Jerry Goodman (vln), Jan Hammer (key), Rick Laird (b), Billy Cobham (perc), 1973.
CBS CDCBS 65321
AAD Running time: 40.18
Performance: ★   Recording: ★ ★

With Cobham's heavily-phased cymbal sound doing service as a gong, *Birds Of Fire* opens gently before Hammer and McLaughlin bring in first an insistent riff and then a soaring theme in virtuosic unison. Brooding electric piano opens *Miles Beyond*, with McLaughlin's guitar chords over Cobham's splashing cymbal work sounding momentarily like the Hendrix of the *Band Of Gypsies* period, the impetus building with a McLaughlin solo at machine-gun speed over a crisp, rapid-fire Cobham.

Celestial: Terrestrial Commuters has some typical exchanges between Hammer (using all his effects) and a searing McLaughlin, while the few seconds of *Sapphire Bullets* introduce some flamenco-like guitar and almost acoustic-sounding piano, over an urgent pulse. Cobham's versatility comes through as he switches from exhilarating drive (on *One Word*) to subtle pulse (*Sanctuary*), while McLaughlin moves from folky/country licks (*Open Country Joy*) back to electric intensity (*Resolution*).

On the whole the recording is good, but sometimes the group's sound, 'heavy' with electronic grunge, seems just too inherently dated.

PAT METHENY

(b. Lee's Summit, Missouri, 12 August 1954)

Long respected by other musicians, Pat Metheny has now most emphatically reached the 'wider audience'; though he has varied the context of his playing, this commercial success seems to have come accidentally, not through any perceptible change of artistic stance. Metheny's music may be accessible, but it is not compromised.

Taking up the guitar at fourteen, Metheny's progress was rapid. He first wanted to emulate the Beatles, but soon started to discover jazz in the form of Miles Davis, John Coltrane and Ornette Coleman. He became a guitar teacher on leaving school, first at the University of Miami and then at Berklee, but then, still only nineteen years old, joined Gary Burton's group on tour. He joined Burton in signing for the ECM label, and by 1975 was recording under his own name with other members of Burton's group; but his music took on a new dimension when he began working with the brilliant and compatible young keyboard player Lyle Mays.

While developing a distinctive, atmospheric synthesizer-based music with Mays, Metheny also took an opportunity to record with Dewey Redman, Michael Brecker, Charlie Haden and Jack DeJohnette; the result was the intense *80/81* double album, followed a couple of years later by the trio *Rejoicing*, again featuring Haden. This aspect of Metheny's work should have made his recent landmark collaboration with Ornette Coleman, *Song X*, less of a surprise.

Metheny continues to expand his horizons, and while he has made many excellent studio recordings, the live double album *Travels* stands as some indication of his true stature as a performer.

BRIGHT SIZE LIFE
Bright Size Life/Sirabhorn/Unity Village/ Missouri Uncompromised/Midwestern Night's Dream/Unquity Road/Omaha Celebration/Round Trip; Broadway Blues
Pat Metheny (g), Jaco Pastorius (el b), Bob Moses (d), Ludwigsburg, Germany, December 1975.
ECM 827 133
AAD Running time: 37.12
Performance: ★ ★   Recording: ★ ★ ★

PAT METHENY   BRIGHT SIZE LIFE

STEREO 827 133-2   ECM

Recorded when the guitarist had been playing with Gary Burton for two years but was still only twenty-one, this early ECM recording is a remarkable precursor of Metheny's later big-selling ECM albums. Bassist Jaco Pastorius and drummer Bob Moses, also members of Burton's group of the time, provide flexible and sympathetic support.

From the start, Metheny demonstrates the guitar sound, clean and bright yet full-bodied, which characterises most of his work. Sometimes he dubs in a second guitar

part to fill in harmony or rhythm, but whether Metheny is throwing in chords or playing runs in single notes, the agile bass of Pastorius often provides all the harmonic movement and rhythmic propulsion needed. Pastorius gets a human tone from the electric instrument and never seems hurried; he plays an exceptional solo in *Midwestern Night's Dream*.

Omaha Celebration, changing the mood completely, couples some introductory country licks with a slippery jazz improvisation on a fast 4/4, provides another neat solo from Pastorius and ends with a deft unison passage between guitarist and bassist; they demonstrate their speed and rapport in unison again on the final tune, Ornette Coleman's *Round Trip-Broadway Blues*. Recording quality has most of the ECM virtues, though it sounds a little 'soft' or even veiled by today's most up-front standards. Playing time is short, and there are none of the 'orchestral' effects heard on later Metheny albums, but this one still deserves a second listen.

AS FALLS WICHITA, SO FALLS WICHITA FALLS
As Falls Wichita, So Falls Wichita Falls/ Ozark/September Fifteenth (dedicated to Bill Evans)/'It's For You'/Estupenda Graca
Pat Metheny (g), Lyle Mays (p, synth, org, autoharp), Nana Vasconcelos (d, perc, voc), September 1980.
ECM 821 416
AAD Running time: 43.38
Performance: ★ ★ ★   Recording: ★ ★ ★

Collaborating with keyboardist Lyle Mays, Metheny was able to create lush textures and effects, often using lovingly-crafted tones drawn out over insistently repeated rhythms to give a feeling of time itself slowing down with abstract yet almost tangible sounds that seemed to hang in space or rumble across a cosmic backdrop.

Such is the feeling of the title track, which seems redolent of Pink Floyd, but *Ozark* brings a bright contrast, as Mays' bustling piano bubbles and sparkles; then the keyboardist provides a background of 'strings' for the opening of Metheny's tribute *September Fifteenth*, the guitarist stating the theme in poignant single notes and then in chords played with superb delicacy, complemented by Mays' gentle but firmly stated piano. 'It's For You' contrasts strumming twelve-string with synth bass and strings, then with an echo-laden electric guitar lead. *Estupenda Graca* is a tune which is more than familiar under its English name, but here gets a somewhat expanded instrumental treatment as well as an ethereal vocal from Vasconcelos. Vaguely animal noises in the background provide a faint echo of the distant crowd noise that opened the set.

It is a beautiful production, a sonic delight as well as musically coherent, and whatever *Wichita Falls'* relation to jazz, both Metheny and Mays display superb musicianship on this universally-appealing and deservedly successful disc.

REJOICING
Lonely Woman/Tears Inside/Humpty Dumpty/Blues For Pat/Rejoicing/Story From A Stranger/The Calling/Waiting For An Answer
Pat Metheny (g), Charlie Haden (b), Billy Higgins (d), November 1983
ECM 817 795
AAD Running time: 43.56
Performance: ★ ★   Recording: ★ ★

For the opening number Metheny uses a near-acoustic Ovation-type guitar sound, playing mainly in chords to give almost the sound of a piano trio in a tuneful, sensitive, quietly effective version of Horace's Silver's song; then the full electric sound of *Tears Inside* almost evokes the shade of Wes Montgomery. His soft-edged echoing lines make the moderate-paced *Blues For Pat* relaxed and swinging (and there is a fine solo by Haden), while *Rejoicing* is an ultra-fast workout with be-bop ancestry.

With *The Calling*, Metheny uses a synthesiser to produce wailing and dissonant horn sounds (almost like traditional middle-eastern trumpets), while in the rather slight final track, *Waiting For An Answer*, more gently mysterious distant sounds produce the feeling of space and depth Metheny so often creates on other albums. An interesting and well varied collection, but recorded with space and atmosphere traded, perhaps, for the last ounce of clarity.

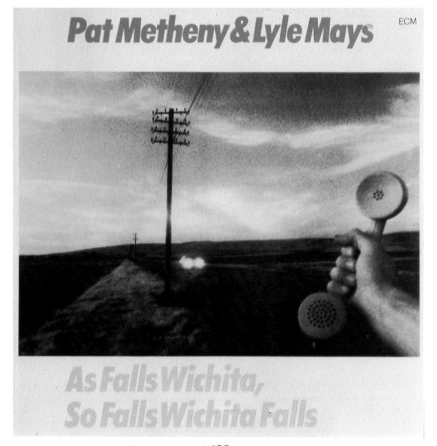

CHARLES MINGUS
(b. Nogales, Arizona, 22 April 1922; d. Cuernavaca, Mexico, 5 January 1979)

With formidable technique and a huge sound, Mingus could have been just a great bass player. Instead, he became a great leader, composer, creator and innovator, whose work nonetheless reflected a deep feeling for the jazz tradition.

At sixteen, Mingus had cello and bass lessons from jazz bassist Red Callender, which were followed by five years formal study with a former New York Philharmonic bassist. Meanwhile, he joined Lee Young's group in 1940, then spent two years with Louis Armstrong before joining Lionel Hampton's band. Hampton gave Mingus a chance to write, and recorded his *Mingus Fingers* in 1947. In 1950, he joined the Red Norvo trio, which at that time also included the great guitarist Tal Farlow, but left in 1951 with much bitterness because (he later claimed) discrimination had prevented him from playing with the group on television.

After this, he actually worked for the US Post Office for several months, before joining Billy Taylor's trio. In 1953 he organised the Jazz Society of Toronto's all-star concert with Dizzy Gillespie, Charlie Parker, Bud Powell and Max Roach, and taped it for his own Debut label to produce the classic *Jazz at Massey Hall* album (now on Fantasy). In the same year, he started a composers' workshop (recording *Jazz Composers Workshop No 1* on Savoy), with Teddy Charles, Teo Macero and John LaPorta, adopting the means of arranging he afterwards always used, bringing in only sketched outlines of the music and then telling the musicians the kind of feeling he wanted. In 1955 he recorded the duet *Percussion Discussion* with Max Roach (Prestige), but first drew real attention with *Pithecanthropus Erectus* (1956, Atlantic).

During the new few years, his music introduced earthy gospel elements, using them in a more profound and penetrating way than the 'soul' jazz brigade, and his approach to collective playing

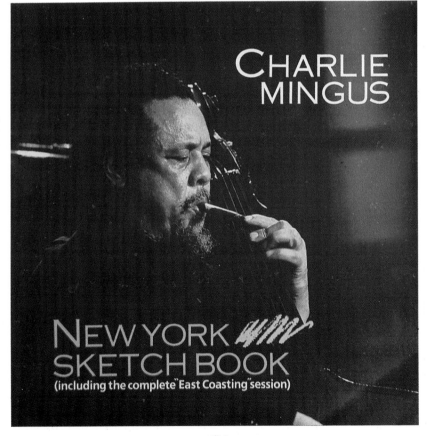

CHARLIE MINGUS

NEW YORK SKETCH BOOK
(including the complete 'East Coasting' session)

anticipated the 'free' movement of the early 1960s. He assembled some excellent soloists who developed his compositions in a spontaneous way, rather as Ellington's had done, and, like Duke's sidemen, they tended to become indelibly associated with the leader's music.

The early 1960s saw Mingus experimenting with a very large band, and with his regular group, embarking on more extended works, including *The Black Saint and the Sinner Lady*, featuring altoist Charlie Mariano. The Mingus quartet of 1964, with Eric Dolphy, Clifford Jordan and Dannie Richmond, is captured at length in the three-album set *The Great Concert*, recorded in Paris. In the 1970s Mingus again gathered great soloists around him, including pianist Don Pullen and tenor player George Adams. Before his death, Mingus had written his autobiography, *Beneath the Underdog* and had also collaborated on an album with singer Joni Mitchell that ended up being a tribute, but his musicians kept his memory alive by recording as the Mingus Dynasty. But a lot more CD issues will be needed to do justice to the scope of Mingus' own work.

NEW YORK SKETCHBOOK
Memories Of You/East Coasting/West Coast Ghost/Celia/Conversation/Fifty First Street Blues/Scenes In The City/Duke's Choice/New York Sketchbook
1–6 Clarence Shaw (tp),Jimmy Knepper (tb), Shafi Hadi (as, ts), Bill Evans (p), Charles Mingus (b), Dannie Richmond (d), August 1957; 7 Bob Hammer replaces Evans, add Melvin Stewart, narration; 9 add Horace Parlan (p), Stewart out; 8 Hammer out, October 1957.
Affinity CD CHARLY 19
AAD Running time: 65.51
Performance: ★ ★ ★   Recording: ★ ★ ★

Like most Affinity discs, this one offers a longer programme than previous LP issues. It adds *New York Sketchbook* and two other tracks to the complete *East Coasting* session, which has the added bonus of Bill Evans on piano. The opening tune, Eubie Blake's *Memories of You*, had just had a popular revival thanks to its inclusion in the film *The Benny Goodman Story*. By setting it against new and dissonant chords, Mingus stripped the tune of sentimentality and made it a vehicle for deeply-felt playing by the hornmen. *East Coasting*, its title a reference to Mingus' feeling that he was really a visitor to the New York scene, is a virile bop vehicle which demonstrates the Mingus group's ability to retain great freedom of individual expression in the midst of a complex ensemble passage. The almost wistful *West Coast Ghost* is the cooler side of the coin. But *Scenes*, *Sketchbook* and *Duke's Choice* complete the set well.

THE BLACK SAINT AND THE SINNER LADY
Solo Dancer/Duet Solo Dancers/Group Dancers/Trio And Group Dancers; Single Solos And Group Dance; Group And Solo Dance
Rolf Ericson, Richard Williams (tp), Quentin Jackson (tb), Jerome Richardson (bars, ss, fl), Charles Mariano (as), Dick Hafer (ts, fl), Don Butterfield (tuba), Jaki Byard (p), Jay Berliner (g), Charles Mingus (b, p), Danny Richmond (d), January 1963.
MCA Impulse MCAD 5649
AAD Running time: 39.30
Performance: ★ ★ ★   Recording: ★ ★ ★

As will be gathered from his own liner note, Mingus felt that with Impulse he had at last found a record company that would allow him to ignore the idiocy of the critics and present his music as he wanted it to be heard. The first Impulse release, *Mingus Mingus Mingus Mingus Mingus* was followed by this recording, which as it turned out was virtually the final flowering of this particular creative phase. Mingus used the talents of altoist and writer Charlie Mariano as well as his regular line-up; *The Black Saint And The Sinner Lady* is a complete and complex work, presented as a set of dances, which draws on many sources, most obviously the earlier music of Ellington.

The opening *Solo Dance* features a repeated frog-like 'pedal point blast' (as Mingus himself calls it from Don Butterfield on contrabass trombone, a wild and jungly baritone from Richardson, and an ever-accelerating beat of irresistible physical power. After this urgent introduction comes *Duet Solo Dancers*, beginning with an Ellington-style piano intro, Mariano's alto smooth, glassy and Hodges-like over an almost languid ensemble; the jungle wah-wahs and growls close in darkly again. *Group Dancers* (subtitle: 'Freewoman and Oh, This Freedom's Slave Cries') introduces a lovely, hypnotic flute theme which recurs later, as does Berliner's flamenco-style guitar.

The last three dances (a single long track as far as the CD is concerned) complete the work with new rhythms, making further use of Mingus accelerating effects, and returning also to make more use of material already established, with constantly shifting tempos and orchestral colours. Sound quality lacks the ultimately panoramic quality that could have been hoped for with stereo recording, but is on the whole open, well balanced and generally good enough to do justice to this extraordinary music.

MINGUS REVISITED
Take The 'A' Train/Prayer For Passive Resistance/Eclipse/Mingus Fingus No 2/ Weird Nightmare/Do Nothin' Till You Hear From Me/Bemoanable Lady/Half Mast Inhibition
1-3, 5, 6 Ted Curson (tp), Jimmy Knepper (tb), Joe Farrell, Booker Ervin (saxes), Yusef Lateef, Eric Dolphy (fl), Roland Hanna or Paul Bley (p), Charles Mingus (b), Danny Richmond (d), Lorraine Cousins (voc 3, 5), May 1960; 4, 7, 8 Marcus Belgrave, Hobart Dotson, Clark Terry, Curson, Richard Williams (tp), Slide Hampton, Charles Grenlee, Eddie Bert, Knepper (tb), Eric Dolphy, John LaPorta, William Barron, Jr, Joe Farrell, Yusef Lateef, Danny Bank (saxes), Robert Di Domenica (fl), Harry Shulman (oboe), Don Butterfield (tu), Hanna (p), Mingus (b), Charles McCracken (cello), Richmond, George Scott, Sticks Evans (perc), Gunther Schuller (cond 8), May 1960.
EmArcy 826 498
AAD Running time: 35.12
Performance: ★ ★ ★   **Recording:** ★ ★

When first issued, this album was called *Pre-Bird*, a title more descriptive of some of the music, or at least of the strands of influence Mingus was working with in 1960. Though recorded on consecutive days, the two

sessions which produced this material were really quite different. The May 24 date used an orchestra of up to 22 pieces not counting the additional percussionists, and up to a point worked within the long-established conventions of big-band jazz. *Mingus Fingus No 2* is basically a reworking of the number Mingus had written while with Lionel Hampton's band in the late 1940s, and features a gritty, belting tenor solo by Joe Farrell, followed by Lateef also on tenor, and then by a chorus of fours in which the five trumpet players can all be heard all taking their turn.

Bemoanable Lady has Ellington associations, but is a feature for Eric Dolphy on alto sax, his astringent tone cutting through the mock-1940s richness of the arrangement. With Gunther Schuller brought in to conduct (since Mingus could not play bass and conduct at the same time), the extended composition *Half Mast Inhibition*, making use of cello and woodwinds, has a coherence and validity absent from other efforts to introduce European elements to jazz. In both Ellington titles, two tunes are heard at once; *Exactly Like You* is interpolated into *Take The 'A' Train* (which was based on similar, if not identical, chords), while in the case of *Do Nothin' Till You Hear From Me*, the secondary theme is another Ellington one, *I Let a Song Go Out Of My Heart*.

Two vocal tracks have rather demanding lyrics and vocal lines written by Mingus, but these are well handled by Lorraine Cousins. Recording quality is good, generally open and natural, though with a slight distortion on piano at times; musically, this disc conveys just how multi-faceted was Mingus' work at that time.

THE MODERN JAZZ QUARTET

(1952-1974, re-formed 1981)

The beginnings of the MJQ can be traced back to 1942, when pianist John Lewis met drummer Kenny Clarke while serving in the US Army. Both joined Dizzy Gillespie's 1946 big band and there encountered vibraphonist Milt Jackson and bassist Ray Brown. The rhythm section often played long passages on its own, mainly because the horns needed to rest; and this gave Jackson a chance to solo freely.

The Milt Jackson Quartet, including Lewis, Brown and Clarke, had recorded for Dee Gee and (with Percy Heath already replacing Brown) for Blue Note, when the first Modern Jazz Quartet session took place in late 1952. Bob Weinstock of Prestige wanted to call the group The New Jazz Quartet, to tie in with his subsidiary New Jazz label, but the group held out for 'Modern'. This coincidentally preserved the original leader's initials, though the group was now run as a co-operative venture. When Clarke left in 1955 to live in France, he was replaced by Connie Kay.

By 1956, when the group moved to Atlantic Records, its musical identity was firmly established. Lewis, as musical director, provided the themes, while the tirelessly inventive Jackson wove ringing, rippling lines around them. Wearing evening dress, the MJQ was soon playing to polite concertgoers, rather than to the denizens of seedy nightclubs or to over-excited college kids, and Lewis' compositions took on a classical guise too. As he told Nat Hentoff: *'the audience for our work can be widened if we strengthen our work with structure. If there is more reason for what's going on, there'll be more overall sense, and therefore more interest for the listener . . .*

After ten successful years, MJQ agreed to disband for six months in every twelve, so that members could follow other pursuits. After another decade or so, in 1974, Jackson left and the MJQ broke up, but a festival reunion in 1981 was followed by renewed activity, with extensive touring and recording.

LONGING FOR THE CONTINENT
MODERN JAZZ QUARTET

LONGING FOR THE CONTINENT
Animal Dance/Django/England's Carol/
Bluesology/Bags' Groove/ Sketch 3/
Ambiquite/Midsommer
John Lewis (p), Milt Jackson (vib), Percy
Heath (b), Connie Kay (d), probably 1958,
6, 7 additional French musicians led by
André Hodeir
Denon 33C38-7678
AAD Running time: 39.20
Performance: ★ ★   Recording: ★

Yet again, Denon are unsure of the
discographical details, which hardly matters
in the case of the first five numbers, since the
MJQ's personnel did not change after 1955.
Recording quality is only fair, with some
semblance of stereo and a just acceptably
natural balance, still favouring Kay more
than Lewis (whose piano sounds mushy) and
Heath (whose bass is soggy) or Jackson,
whose vibraharp is thin here compared with
the sound in studio recordings.

After a spirited up-tempo opener, *Django*
starts with great deliberation (and a rather
'clangy' recorded sound) and though imbued
with Jackson's usual easy grace, is not
outstanding among the group's many
recordings of this theme. But *England's
Carol*, which like *Animal Dance* bears a
resemblance to *Hallelujah*, really swings.
The next two are features for Jackson, but
unfortunately his loudest sustained notes
sound distorted.

After these live tracks, we hear an
enlarged group, with 'Third Stream'
connections, playing two Lewis originals, in
a detailed if boxy-sounding studio recording.
The final track is an effective Quartet
version of another Lewis piece, composed for
symphonic forces. A mixed bag.

ECHOES
That Slavic Smile/Echoes/The Watergate
Blues/The Hornpipe/Connie's Blues/Sacha's
March.
John Lewis (p), Milt Jackson (vib), Percy
Heath (b), Connie Kay (d), March 1984.
Pablo 3112-41
DDD Running time: 45.19
Performance: ★ ★   Recording: ★ ★ ★

The 1981 reunion had become more or less
permanent, and the MJQ was working
together nine or ten months of the year by
the time this recording was made in 1984; the
manager of the group was now the great
bassist Ray Brown.

This set opens with a minor-key theme
that may strike as trite or even twee, and
only seems mildly 'Slavic' in character, but is
given an atmospheric treatment and a
punchy solo from Jackson. *The Watergate
Blues* and *Hornpipe* are both in 3/4, both
with an element of humour in their jokey
themes, but both compellingly effective.
After milking the minor-key melodrama
effects, *Hornpipe* includes some outstanding
playing by Lewis. The title track is based on
bluesy changes, while *Connie's Blues*
actually is a 12-bar, and is really a
straightforward feature for Jackson; the
drummer features most obviously on the
closing *Sacha's March,* again a near-novelty
tune redeemed by precision playing.

Recording quality is excellent, Jackson's
vibes achieving their full sonority, Kay's
drum-kit sounding crisp and multi-faceted,
and (as you might expect with Brown as
producer), a satisfyingly full and natural
bass sound from Percy Heath. Sonically
exceptional, this disc offers music with some
fine moments and impeccable craftmanship.

THELONIOUS MONK
(b. Rocky Mount, North Carolina, 10 October 1917; d. Englewood, New Jersey, 17 February 1982)

In at beginning of modern jazz, Thelonious Monk was nonetheless never quite part of the bop movement, and the oddness of his music led people to ask whether he could really play. But as saxophonist Steve Lacy put it: 'If technique is the art of making sense, then he's got more technique than anybody.'

While he was still a small child, Monk's family moved to New York City, where he was raised by his mother. His first musical job was with a travelling evangelist, but by 1940 he was working as resident pianist at Minton's Playhouse, the after-hours spot usually described as 'the cradle of modern jazz'. Monk can be heard on recordings made there in 1941-2.

His first real record date was in late 1944 with Coleman Hawkins. Monk's ideas already ran counter to the current be-bop piano style, and late 1940s Blue Note recordings document his first famous tunes, *Round Midnight, Ruby My Dear* and *Straight No Chaser*. In 1951, a drugs bust (Monk was innocent) led to the loss of his cabaret card, which meant he was prohibited from playing New York clubs. Switching to Prestige, he recorded only spasmodically. His last date for the company was on Christmas Eve 1954, when his studio clash with Miles Davis was captured in the tragi-comic solo battle of *The Man I Love*.

After this, Monk moved to Riverside, and having recorded some Ellington numbers and standards, he produced an album of his own tunes, *Brilliant Corners*, at the end of 1956. In 1957 he regained his NYC cabaret card and took on John Coltrane for a summer engagement at the Five Spot Cafe, and this proved to be the upward turning point in Monk's fortunes. He appeared with his trio in the CBS TV special *Sounds of Jazz* and recorded an album with Gerry Mulligan; subsequent Monk quartets made effective use of Johnny Griffin and Charlie Rouse. Monk also recorded with Thad Jones (*Five by Monk by Five*) and with his own big band (*At Town Hall*).

It was the recordings of the Riverside period, as a liner note claims, which 'finally put to rest the long-fixed image of Monk as an eccentric plunker'. Monk, who died of a stroke in 1982, had few direct imitators in his lifetime. But, as James Lincoln Collier has pointed out, all jazz players have listened to him, and carried something away with them.

THE UNIQUE THELONIOUS MONK
Liza/Memories Of You/Honeysuckle Rose/
Darn That Dream/Tea For Two/You Are
Too Beautiful/Just You, Just Me
1, 3-7 Thelonious Monk (p), Oscar Pettiford
(b), Art Blakey (d); 2 Monk (p), March/
April 1956.
Riverside CA/802/98.942
AAD Running time: 38.39
Performance: ★ ★   Recording: ★ ★ ★

Monk's career had been at a low ebb when he joined Riverside, and like *Thelonious Monk Plays Duke Ellington*, this album of standards was intended to get people listening to him again. If the idea was Riverside's, the choice of tunes was Monk's; although this is a trio album, the outstanding track really is the deeply-felt solo *Memories Of You*, which bears endless re-hearing. Monk extracts poignancy from *Darn That Dream*; and *You Are Too Beautiful* is played disarmingly straight until he sharpens the sweetness with a characteristic dissonance.

On an uptempo tune his clashing, dissonant approach can sound initially perverse, but the Monk's own logic soon takes hold; in *Honeysuckle Rose*, for example, he leaves the first half of the second chorus to Pettiford, then plays a bridge that consists simply of two of his splintery-sounding downward runs. *Tea For Two*, as the most hackneyed tune, receives the most severe dissection, and as well as Monk's explorations, there is a freely-quoting bass solo from the empathetic Pettiford. *Just You, Just Me* seems to lapse into routine, but generally this is a stimulating disc, the sound quality excellent.

RIVERSIDE   CARRERE
                   DISTRIBUTION

BRILLIANT CORNERS

Brilliant Corners/Ba-lue Bolivar Ba-lues-are/
Pannonica/I Surrender Dear/Bemsha Swing
1-3 Ernie Henry (as), Sonny Rollins (ts),
Thelonious Monk (p), Oscar Pettiford (b),
Max Roach (d); 4 Monk (p); 5 Clark Terry
(tp), Rollins (ts), Monk (p), Paul Chambers
(b), Roach (d), December 1956.
Riverside VDJ-1526
AAD Running time: 42.52
Performance: ★ ★ ★   Recording: ★ ★ ★

The most famous and enduring of Monk's
tunes to be included here is *Pannonica*
(named for Baroness Pannonica de
Koenigswarter, who had befriended many
musicians in New York). Here it gets a
celeste-style introduction before the saxes
state the theme; next follows a superb solo
by Rollins, one of the few horn players able
to get right inside Monk's compositions
without apparent effort, and then Monk
offers his own set of variations, using the
celeste again.

Bemsha Swing is another Monk standard,
a robust and superficially simple theme,
propelled by its own momentum almost
despite the interjections of Terry and Rollins.
Of the other three numbers, *I Surrender
Dear* is a solo ballad performance by Monk,
craggy but tender; the title track is one of
Monk's more menacing tunes, succeeding
through the superb rhythmic foundation
provided by Roach, who also plays a
gripping solo. *Ba-lue Bolivar Ba-lues-are* is
just what its title says (imagine Monk
announcing it), a very sardonically-inclined
but nonetheless powerful blues. With fine
sound quality (aside from an easily-ignored
trace of tape hiss), this is an album of
compelling music.

MONK'S MUSIC

Abide With Me/Well, You Needn't/Ruby,
My Dear/Off Minor/Epistrophy/Crepescule
With Nellie
1 Ray Copeland (tp), Gigi Gryce (as);
Coleman Hawkins, John Coltrane (ts); 2, 4-6
add Thelonious Monk, Wilbur Ware (b), Art
Blakey (d); 3 Hawkins (ts), Monk (p), Ware
(b), Blakey (d), June 1957.
Riverside CA 802 98.948
AAD Running time: 38.42
Performance: ★ ★ ★   Recording: ★ ★ ★

Despite the relatively short running time,
and the fact that two performances (*Off
Minor* and *Epistrophy*) are duplicated on
Thelonious Monk With John Coltrane, this
original collection from Monk's 1957 septet
date retains its validity. Following the brief
opening hymn, which runs less than a

minute and is played by the horns only, *Well
You Needn't* has an easy, bounding swing
which proves once again how compatible
were Monk and Blakey; *Ruby My Dear*
receives an absorbing interpretation from
Hawkins, which, of course, makes an
interesting comparison with Coltrane's (from
the following year). *Crepescule With Nellie*
opens with a firm treatment from Monk,
very lightly accompanied by Blakey's
brushes, before the ensemble states the theme
with a new solidity and depth. Value for
money may be problematical, but this is a
disc that must be heard.

THELONIOUS MONK WITH JOHN COLTRANE

Ruby, My Dear/Trinkle, Tinkle/Off Minor/
Nutty/Epistrophy/Functional
1, 2, 4 John Coltrane (ts), Thelonious Monk
(p), Wilbur Ware (b), Shadow Wilson (d),
Spring 1958; 3, 5 Ray Copeland (tp), Gigi
Gryce (as), Coltrane, Coleman Hawkins (ts),
Ware (b), Art Blakey (d), June 1957.
Riverside VDJ-1510
AAD Running time: 37.55
Performance: ★ ★ ★   Recording: ★ ★ ★

When Coltrane became a member of Monk's
quartet for an engagement at the Five Spot
cafe in the summer of 1957, Riverside were
unable to record the group because of
Coltrane's contract with Prestige. In April
that year, before the Five Spot quartet was
formed, Monk had already recorded one
track for Riverside with Coltrane and bassist
Wilbur Ware; this was *Monk's Mood*, a
gripping performance which was included in
the otherwise all-solo album *Thelonious
Himself*. The two numbers with Hawkins,
Gryce and Copeland were recorded (in
stereo) for *Monk's Music*.

But early in 1958, hoping that Coltrane
would soon leave Prestige and anxious to
capture Monk and Coltrane together before
it was too late, Orrin Keepnews of Riverside
reconstituted the previous summer's quartet
in the studio, producing the remaining three
tracks here. Coltrane's improvisation fitted
perfectly into the spaces Monk's conception
allowed, and he played Monk's compositions
with conviction and absolute precision.
Coltrane often spoke later of how much he
had learned from Monk, and the rapport is
obvious, on *Ruby, My Dear*, he plays a solo,
then imperceptibly lays back until the
listener realises that he is playing an
obbligato to Monk's lead.

With the larger group, it is fascinating to
hear Hawkins playing Monk's tunes. His

solo in *Off Minor* reveals his effortless grasp of Monk's harmonic and rhythmic language even though he has not updated his own style completely. Copeland is an effective trumpeter in the Clifford Brown mould, sounds ordinary in this company. The final track, filling out the playing time here, is *Functional*, a somewhat boogie-influenced blues, slightly resembling *Blue Monk*, played as a solo. A near-essential disc, if poor value compared with the old Riverside double LP *Monk/Trane*, which offered *Monk's Mood* as well.

THELONIOUS ALONE IN SAN FRANCISCO
Blue Monk/Ruby, My Dear/Round Lights/Everything Happens To Me/You Took The Words Right Out Of My Heart/Bluehawk/Pannonica/Remember/There's Danger In Your Eyes, Cherie/Reflections
Thelonious Monk (p), October 1959
Riverside VDJ-1549
AAD Running time: 41.06
Performance: ★ ★ ★   Recording: ★ ★ ★

Recorded not in a 'dead' studio but on the stage of an empty hall, this set of solo performances has a special quality of its own; there is a kind of intimacy, absent from Monk's studio group recordings. The contents of this album also seem to have a greater artistic coherence and sense of conviction than the earlier solo set, *Thelonious Himself* (the track with Coltrane excepted). Apart from four standards, all the tunes are Monk's own; *Blue Monk* and *Ruby My Dear* are definitive performances which, along with a lovely *Pannonica*, are enough to make this an essential record. *Round Lights* (Monk got the title by looking up at the chandeliers) and *Bluehawk* are blues, slow and moderate respectively; and as always in Monk's solos, the beat, however obliquely referred to by the notes actually being struck, is there, heard as clearly and firmly as if a drummer were hammering it out.

Of the standards, perhaps the most familiar (probably to the pianist as well as to us) and perhaps the most effective, is *Everything Happens To Me*, which Monk illuminates with dissonance. The gentle, appealing *There's Danger In Your Eyes, Cherie* is Monk's unique, inspired read-through. Sound quality is excellent, the simply-miked piano sounding very natural, if a little brighter on CD, with tape hiss obvious but not serious. As with other Fantasy single-album reissues, this CD can

hardly compete, in actual running time for the money, with the special-price 'twofer' package which offered *Thelonious Himself* as well; but *Thelonious Alone In San Francisco* remains a classic.

THELONIOUS MONK AND MAX ROACH: EUROPEAN TOUR
Blue Monk/Light Blue/Evidence/To Lady/Stop Motion
1–3 Thad Jones (tp), Charlie Rouse (ts), Thelonious Monk (p), John Ore (b), Billy Higgins (d), late 1950s, Europe; 4, 5 Tommy Turrentine (tp), Julian Priester (tb), Stanley Turrentine (ts), Bob Boswell (b), Max Roach (d), France, 1960.
Denon 33C38-7683
AAD Running time: 55.41
Performance: ★ ★   Recording: ★ ★

Not, as you might think at first sight, a recording of two leaders together, but two separate sets recorded by Monk and Roach with their respective sidemen. Liner-note writer Fujimoto speculates, rather wildly, that the *Blue Monk* here could be from Monk's 1959 big band Town Hall concert; and there do indeed seem to be more than two horns in the opening ensemble. After this the pianist is silent (perhaps absent, rather than dancing) while Jones (if it is he) plays a long solo in a shouting blues vein, which isn't really Monk's. Rouse, on the other hand, meshed perfectly with Monk's conceptions and his tersely-argued work on the other two tracks is typical. These feature just the quartet; recording quality is atmospheric and very good, though on some CD players and systems Rouse might sound a little too abrasive.

Roach's piano-less quintet, apparently recorded in France, plays in a style still clearly descended from that of the great Clifford Brown-Max Roach groups, but more concentrated and, in a sense, introvert. Brown's influence pervades the agile playing of Tommy Turrentine, while Stanley displays great technique and inventiveness in a way that recalls Harold Land. Though Priester shows technique, his solos lack the structure to sustain interest. But Roach himself, propelling the music with smooth, vital force, and producing lean, muscular solos, makes it all worthwhile. This disc is very far from being an essential one, and it will not appeal to those who prefer to know exactly where the music has come from and who is playing it, yet it does have something to say about both the great modern jazz pioneers featured on it.

WES MONTGOMERY
(b. Indianapolis, Indiana, 6 March 1925; d. Indianapolis, 15 June 1968)

Of all the guitarists who, in the 1940s, had followed Charlie Christian, one turned out to be the innovator who took up where Christian left off. Christian had shown that the guitar could be used like a horn; Montgomery came still nearer to the horn-player's natural, vocalised expression.

John Leslie Montgomery was a late starter. He did not take up the guitar seriously until he was nineteen, and did not record under his own name until he was well into his thirties. Inspired initially by records of Christian, he found that he couldn't get the sound he wanted with a pick, and used his thumb instead. This unorthodox approach gave him a unique, warm and personal sound. He toured with Lionel Hampton's band in 1948–50, but then returned home to a day job and local club work. His brothers Buddy and Monk moved to the West Coast and achieved some success as The Mastersounds, but Wes was already the father of a family and stayed behind. He did make one successful record with his brothers (*The Montgomery Brothers and Five Others*, World Pacific), but was back in Indianapolis, working with his own trio at an after-hours club called The Missile Room when he was 'discovered' by Cannonball Adderley in 1959. This led to recordings on Riverside, first with the trio, then with established rhythm sections and star soloists. The Riverside albums provide most of Montgomery's best work, with solos that shift effortlessly from supple, blues-inflected single-note lines, to runs in octaves, then to block chords.

His career took a new direction when he joined Verve Records in 1964. Most of his subsequent studio work featured him in lush orchestral or big band arrangements, which provided a string of big selling albums. His final recordings for A&M followed the same formula, the material being the hit tunes of the day. Sadly, he did not live to enjoy financial success for very long, but died of a heart attack

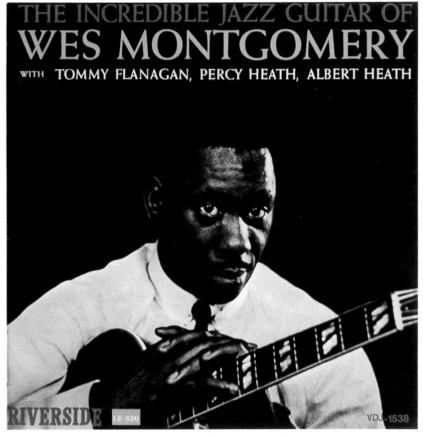

THE INCREDIBLE JAZZ GUITAR OF
WES MONTGOMERY
WITH TOMMY FLANAGAN, PERCY HEATH, ALBERT HEATH

RIVERSIDE

at the age of forty-three. Jazz fans at the time may have been disappointed at the 'commercial' nature of some of the later material, but even the most banal moments in that 'pop' part of his output cannot detract from the enormous contribution Montgomery made to the guitar in jazz.

THE INCREDIBLE JAZZ GUITAR OF WES MONTGOMERY
Airegin/D-Natural Blues/Polkadots And Moonbeams/Four On Six/West Coast Blues/In Your Own Sweet Way/Mister Walker/Gone With The Wind
Wes Montgomery (g), Tommy Flanagan (p), Percy Heath (b), Albert Heath (d), January 1960).
Riverside VDJ-1538
AAD Running time: 44.19
Performance: ★ ★ ★   Recording: ★

When Riverside first took Montgomery into a New York studio with an established rhythm team (though not the most exciting he was to work with), this was the fairly astonishing result. The material is a judicious blend of jazz tunes (like the opener), standards (like *Polkadots*, where he produces a magically tender tone in octaves and stays just this side of sentimentality) and intriguing originals, like the enduring *Four on Six*. The music lives up to the title, with Montgomery's uniquely fluid single lines, octaves and chords falling together perfectly. Sound quality remains a bit of a disappointment, with a muzzy, veiled quality and a rather peculiar stereo effect, but for any serious listener to Montgomery, the musical content makes this an essential disc.

FULL HOUSE
Full House/I've Grown Accustomed To Her Face/Blue'n'Boogie/Cariba/Come Rain Or Come Shine/S.O.S.
Johnny Griffin (ts), West Montgomery (g), Wynton Kelly (p), Paul Chambers (b), Jimmy Cobb (d), June 1962.
Riverside VDJ-1508
AAD Running time: 44.13
Performance: ★ ★ ★   Recording: ★ ★ ★

Riverside Records were fortunate in being able to set up and record a gig at the Tsubo Coffee House, Berkeley, in which the participants were their star guitarist, one of the fastest and most exciting tenor players around, and Miles Davis' rhythm section; the set swings irresistibly from the start. *Full House* is a tough, soulful jazz-waltz, in which, behind Kelly's forceful solo, Montgomery demonstrates his matchless ability to comp at any tempo and still assist rather than clog the beat. *I've Grown Accustomed To Her Face* is a perfect sample of what he could do unaccompanied, the tone lucid and beautiful, the chords full and flowing.
Then comes *Blue'n'Boogie*, fast, clean and building on the groove from chorus to chorus, solo to solo; Montgomery, Kelly and Griffin all thrive on the amazing pace set by Chambers and the rock-solid Cobb. It is a miraculous example of what live jazz recordings should be all about, and this track alone almost justifies the price of the disc. Sound quality is exemplary conveying the atmosphere well.

ROUND MIDNIGHT
Wes Montgomery (g), Harold Mabern (p), Arthur Harper (b), Jimmy Lovelace (d), Johnny Griffin (ts) on 'Round About Midnight' only.
March 27, 1965
Four On Six/Impressions/To When/Mister Walker/Here's That Rainy Day/'Round About Midnight
Affinity CD Charly 13
AAD Running time: 50.24
Performance: ★ ★ ★   Recording: ★ ★

Montgomery continued to work with small groups even when his studio performances were backed by large ensembles. This 1965 quartet recording captures a concert in Paris, one of the dates on the guitarist's only European tour. The recorded sound quality is clean enough, if rather lacking in 'sparkle', dynamics and spaciousness, but the programme contains a lot of excellent music, which rewards repeated listening. Like most Affinity CDs, this offers more playing time than a single LP, and in fact includes most of the contents of Affinity's *Impressions* and *Round Midnight* albums.
Impressions is the kaleidoscopic John Coltrane composition, based on the chords of Miles' *So What*, which provides Montgomery with a vehicle for effortless flight; such is his mastery of the instrument that he sounds relaxed even at this headlong tempo, more so in fact than Harold Mabern. Admirable as it is, this performance does not reach the heights of the one Wes recorded a couple of months later at the Half Note in New York, with the unbeatable rhythm section of Kelly, Chambers and Cobb. *Here's That Rainy Day* (a tune popularised by Stan Getz) is an attractive if not absolutely slick bossa nova, which makes for interesting comparison with the orchestrally-backed version on Verve 821 985. But the highlight of the set is the title track, with Griffin, gruff and wryly humorous by turns, the perfect foil for Wes. A thoroughly enjoyable disc.

THE SILVER COLLECTION
If You Could See Me Now/Impressions/Four On Six/Unit 7/Mellow Mood/James And Wes/What's New/Misty/13 (Death March)/Here's That Rainy Day
1-4, 7 Wes Montgomery (g), Wynton Kelly (p), Paul Chambers (b), Jimmy Cobb (d), August 1965; 5, 6 Montgomery (g), Jimmy Smith (org), Grady Tate (d), September 1966; 8 as 1 with additional brass and woodwinds arranged and conducted by Claus Ogerman; 9 as 5 with orchestra arranged and conducted by Oliver Nelson, 1966; 10 Montgomery (g), Roger Kellaway (p), Bob Cranshaw (b), Tate or Helcio Milito (d), Margaret Ross (harp); 13 strings arranged and conducted by Don Sebesky, March 1965.
Verve 823 448
AAD Running time: 67.16
Performance: ★ ★ ★   Recording: ★ ★ ★

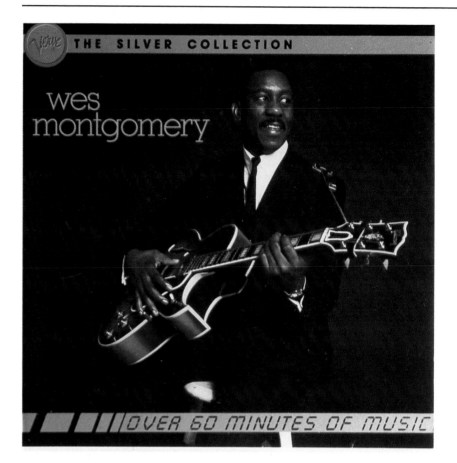

Though dating from a period when he had started recording with large orchestras, most of these tracks feature Montgomery with small groups. The live performances with the ex-Miles Davis rhythm team of Kelly, Chambers and Cobb are all superb, and very well recorded, but particularly good is the exultant *Impressions*, an exciting, uplifting recording which perhaps also reveals some of the potential Montgomery would have fulfilled had he lived to continue recording with small groups for a few more years. The group also produces an intensely swinging version of Wes's rhythmically-deceptive *Four On Six*, but unfortunately *Misty* was subsequently defiled by the tasteless editing-in of brass and woodwinds, and it is in this form that it is included here. This is annoying, especially as Verve has previously reissued this track with the offending orchestra removed and even patted itself on the back for doing so (*The Small Group Recordings*). *Portrait of Jenny* (to which the same remarks would apply) is listed in error on the liner; track nine is actually *Death March* from the *Dynamic Duo* album with Jimmy Smith.

This aside, the programme is hard to fault; with Smith, Montgomery becomes part of the truly superior organ trio represented by the Latin-tinged *Mellow Mood* and the superb blues *James And Wes*, while *Here's That Rainy Day* really is among the best of his orchestral recordings, Montgomery's economical and beautifully logical interpretation of the melody line backed effectively by the strings. Both these last-named tracks are duplicated on other discs (see the review of *The Dynamic Duo*, but that hardly alters the fact that this simply offers the most Wes for your money.

MOVIN' WES
Wes Montgomery (g) with Orchestra arranged and conducted by Johnny Pate: Ernie Royal, Clark Terry, Snooky Young (tp), Jimmy Cleveland, Urbie Green, Quentin Jackson, Chauncey Welsh (tb), Jerome Richardson (ww), Don Butterfield or Harvey Philips (tu), Bobby Scott (p), Bob Cranshaw (b), Grady Tate (d), Willie Bobo (per). Produced by Creed Taylor.
November 11 and 16, 1965.
Caravan/People/Movin' Wes: Part 1/Moca Flor/Matchmaker/Movin' Wes Part 2/The Phoenix Love Theme/Theordora/In And Out/Born To Be Blue/West Coast Blues
Verve 810 045
AAD Running time: 36.15
Performance: ★ **Recording:** ★ ★ ★

On his first LP for Verve, Wes Montgomery's guitar has a richer, deeper and fuller-bodied studio sound than ever before. Balanced effectively against the bright, brassy orchestration (there are no saxes), the result is just as intended – a truly exciting sound. Montgomery's playing is often inspired. On the opener, 'Caravan', he slams into the tune with sliding octaves and chords, riding the crests of a suitably frenetic arrangement. His solo in single notes floats beautifully over the hustling rhythm. The same tough, glittering, chunky sound is effective on the bluesy 'Movin' Wes', but less so on 'West Coast Blues', a rather stilted version of the catchy 6/4 time number Wes had recorded twice in 1960. The pop-Latin style of 'Moca Flor' is appealing if dated, but the only real low point is the tinkling, Floyd Cramer-styled piano on 'Matchmaker'. Creed Taylor's production is superb, the guitar in front and retaining command in front of the powerful forces behind. The transfer to CD helping to make the bass more solid and well defined and maintaining clarity of the horn parts even at their loudest.

BUMPIN'

Wes Montgomery (g) with Orchestra arranged and conducted by Don Sebesky: Arnold Eidus, Lewis Eley, Paul Gershman, Louis Haber, Julius Held, Harry Lookofsky, Jos Malignaggi, Gene Orloff, Sol Shapiro (violins), Harold Coletta, David Schwartz (violas), George Ricci, Charles McCracken (cellos), Margaret Ross (harp), Roger Kellaway (p), Bob Cranshaw (b), Helcio Milito or Grady Tate (d), Candido Camero (bongo, conga). Produced by Creed Taylor.
May 1967
Bumpin'/Tear It Down/A Quiet Thing/Cn Alma/The Shadow Of Your Smile/Mi Cosa/Here's That Rainy Day/Musty
Verve 821 985
AAD Running time: 31.43
Performance: ★ Recording: ★ ★ ★

With strings added by Sebesky, this 1967 album represents the final phase of Montgomery's career, when the arrangements would cross the fatal line between lush and mush, and when the tunes he played became so simple that, the guitarist's contribution was little more than a sound, a flavour in the orchestration, and as Chris Albertson wrote, 'to those of us who had heard him swing, it was tantamount to hearing Horovitz play "Chopsticks" '. But on this album, although the actual tone is somehow thinner, more polite, less dramatic, he still really does play. You get some fine improvisation on 'Tear It Down', some lovely unaccompanied chord work

leading into the admittedly schmaltzy 'Mi Cosa', the often-imitated 'Shadow of Your Smile' and the superbly atmospheric 'Here's That Rainy Day', using a Shearing-style piano/guitar unison effect over a bossa beat. 'Musty' though, is a sort of sanitised 'Birks' Works', which in this case doesn't, really.

JIMMY AND WES: THE DYNAMIC DUO

Jimy Smith (org), Wes Montgomery (g), with Orchestra arranged and conducted by Oliver Nelson: Jimmy Maxwell, Joe Newman, Ernie Royal (tp), Clark Terry (fh, tp), Richard Hixon, Jimmy Cleveland, Quentin Jackson (tb), Tony Studd (btb), Jerry Dodgion (cl, as, fl), Jerome Richardson, Phil Woods (cl, fl), Bob Ashton (cl, ts, fl), Danny Bank (bs), Richard Davis (b), Grady Tate (d). produced by Creed Taylor.
September 1986
Down By The Riverside/Night Train/James and Wes/13 (Death March)/Baby Its Cold Outside
Verve 821 577
AAD Running time: 36.31
Performance: ★ ★ Recording: ★ ★ ★

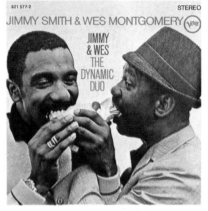

The principals do live up to the title here. In 'Down By . . .' the tune gets a quick, derisive big-band working over and is then forgotten for several minutes while Smith gets down to blowing a fast blues, Montgomery feeding riffs. They end up trading fours, before the theme returns, an exuberant irrelevance. 'Night Train' is of course another blues, Nelson's arrangement extracting the most from the classic theme, leaving solo space for a thoughtful Montgomery and a typical climax-building Smith.

Of a similar mid tempo, but a different feeling entirely, is the wonderful trio blues 'James and Wes' with Grady Tate but without orchestra – an eight-minute development which shows perfect rapport and make you wonder whether that orchestra was just sound and fury signifying nothing. '13', with echoing flutes and mock-Bossa beat, now sounds just too rooted in the sixties. 'Baby Its Cold Outside' is another trio number, not so quite so striking but still effective, with Tate somehow producing an appropriate sleigh bell cymbal sound.

Despite the high standard of these trio tracks, the scantiness of the other material and moderate running time mean that this is less than overwhelmingly good value. Those who like the orchestral Wes should also try two other recordings on CD: *Goin' Out Of My Head* (Verve 825 676) and *California Dreaming* (Verve 827 842).

JELLY ROLL MORTON

(b. Gulfport, Louisiana, 20 October 1885 (possibly 1890); d. Los Angeles, California, 10 July, 1941)

Morton was not, as he claimed, the inventor of jazz, but his Red Hot Peppers band recordings prove that he was one of the first masters of jazz composition and arrangement.

The young Ferdinand Joseph LeMenthe (Morton was a stepfather's name) scandalised his respectable Creole family by playing piano in the 'sporting houses' of Storyville, but left New Orleans about 1906. Moving from town to town, he earned a living as a pool shark, card sharp and possibly as a pimp (hence 'Jelly Roll') as well as by playing piano. He reached New York about 1911 and Chicago about 1914. His travels continued until about 1921, when he settled back in Chicago. He appeared on some 1923 records by the New Orleans Rhythm Kings, and in the next two years recorded 'King Porter Stomp' with King Oliver, a string of piano solos on the Gennett label and a trio session with clarinettist Johnny and drummer Baby Dodds.

But it was in 1926 that he cut the first of the Red Hot Peppers sessions. He generally used the classic New Orleans instrumentation of trumpet, clarinet, trombone and rhythm, but the musicians followed his written arrangements, except for solo breaks. Morton moved to New York in 1928, but the more advanced black bands of the early 1930s made his New Orleans style sound very old fashioned, and he sank into obscurity.

Morton was back in the limelight early in 1938, when he challenged a statement on Ripley's 'Believe It Or Not' radio show that W C Handy was the originator of jazz, stomps and blues. Morton claimed to have invented the lot, and told his story in words and music at the piano, to folksong collector Alan Lomax in a series of recordings made at the Library of Congress between May and July 1938.

At the end of 1938, Morton returned to York and recorded for Victor again. In the cold winter of 1940, he packed up and drove to California, but the move came too late to mend his health or his fortunes. He died a few months later of heart trouble.

GREAT ORIGINAL PERFORMANCES

Black Bottom Stomp/The Chant/Dead Man Blues/Grandpa's Spells/Original Jelly Roll Blues/Beale Street Blues/Ham And Eggs/You Need Some Loving/Kansas City Stomps/Shoe Shiner's Drag/Deep Creek/Pretty Lil/New Orleans Bump/Ponchartrain/Blue Blood Blues/I'm Alone Without You
1, 2 George Mitchell (cnt), Kid Ory (tb), Omer Simeon (cl),Jelly Roll Morton (p, arr, voice 3), Johnny St Cyr (bj, voice 3), John Lindsey (b), Andrew Hilaire (d), September 1926; 3 as 1, add Barney Bigard, Darnell Howard (cl), December 1926; 4, 5 as 1, December 1926; 6 Mitchell (cnt), Gerald Reeves (tb), Johnny Dodds (cl), Stump Evans (as), Morton (p, arr), Bud Scott (g), Quinn Wilson (tu), Baby Dodds (d), June 1927; 7, 8 Johnny Dunn (cnt), Herb Fleming (tb), Garvin Bushell (cl), Morton (p), John Mitchell (bj), Harry Hull (tu), Mort Perry (d), March 1928; 9, 10 Ward Pinkett (tp), Geechie Fields (tb), Omer Simeon (cl), Morton (p, arr), Lee Blair (bj), Bill Benford (tu), Tommy Benford (d), June 1928; 11 Ed Anderson, Edwin Swayzee (tp), William Kato (tb), Russell Procope (cl, as), Paul Barnes (ss), Joe Garland (ts), Morton (p, arr), Blair (g), William Moore (tu), Manzie Johnson (d), December 1928; 12, 13 Walter Briscoe or David Richards, Red Rossiter (tp), Charlie Irvis (tb), George Bacquet (cl), Barnes (ss), Walter Thomas (as), Joe Thomas (ts), Morton (p, arr), Barney Alexander (bj),

Harry Prather (tu), William Laws (d), July 1929; 14, 15 Pinkett, Bubber Miley (tp), Wilbur De Paris (tb), Ernie Bullock or Jerry Blake (cl), Morton (p, arr), Bernard Addison (g), Bill Benford (b), Tommy Benford (d), March/July 1930; 16 Wingy Manone (tp), Dicky Wells (tb), Artie Shaw (cl), Morton (p), Frank Victor (g), John Kirby (b), Kaiser Marshall (d), August 1934.
BBC CD 604
AAD Running time: 50.53
Performance: ★ ★ ★   Recording: ★ ★

Whatever the delights of Morton's piano solos and trios, the recordings he made for Victor with his band remain his greatest achievement; this disc offers a generous helping. The numbers are presented chronologically, starting with the archetypal *Black Bottom Stomp*, a foot-tapping miracle of orchestration using the traditional New Orleans instrumentation.

The next four are all classics, from the 'hokum' of *Dead Man Blues* (which closes with the superb clarinet trio section from Simeon, Bigard and Howard), to the stop-time breaks of *Grandpa's Spells* and *Original Jelly Roll Blues*. The slow and affecting *Beale Street Blues*, remarkable for the contributions of the Dodds brothers, is something of a departure, being arranged as a string of solos, but the real change in style comes with *Ham And Eggs*, first of the recordings made after Morton's move to New York. The great Ward Pinkett provides a suppler lead than the brash and ultimately uninteresting trumpet of bandleader Johnny Dunn; excellent though these tracks are, the ensemble no longer has quite that surging, natural bounce that Morton and his musicians had brought from New Orleans to Chicago.

Quite different again is the final cut, from the one-off 1934 session with Wingy Manone's band, where Morton contributes only a brief and not especially distinguished piano solo. Aside from this non-essential, the selection is hard to criticise, except that it would be nice to have *Sidewalk Blues* and of course *Dr Jazz*, which compiler Robert Parker had already used on the *New Orleans* and *Chicago* samplers. Parker's fake stereo and added echo is in evidence, though the results are not nearly so gross as with his Louis Armstrong collection. The original sound quality achieved by Victor in these Morton recordings was exceptionally good for the time (as evidenced by the earliest LP reissues), and there is now at least the faint hope that the success of Parker's discs will encourage RCA to offer a definitive, unprocessed Morton reissue on CD. The music certainly deserves it.

NEW ORLEANS MEMORIES PLUS TWO
Sporting House Rag/Original Rags/The Crave/The Naked Dance/Mister Joe/King Porter Stomp/Winin' Boy Blues/Buddy Bolden's Blues/The Naked Dance (originally issued take)/Don't You Leave Me Here/Mamie's Blues/Michigan Water Blues
Jelly Roll Morton (p, voc 7, 12), December 1939.
Commodore 8.24062
AAD Running time: 34.06
Performance: ★ ★ Recording: ★ ★

Dating from the end of the year following his 'rediscovery' and the long series of recordings made by Alan Lomax at the Library Of Congress, this set of Commodore recordings also features Morton, solo, at the piano and musically recalling his early days.

The addition of *Sporting House Rag* and the previous-unissued version of *The Naked Dance* explain the *Plus Two* in the title of this 1979 compilation. These extended the running time to respectable LP length, although neither of them is really among the most essential listening here; the originally-issued *Naked Dance*, cut two days later, is very different, being faster and more flowing, while more substantial than *Sporting House Rag* are the other Morton originals including a powerful *King Porter Stomp* (by now already a big-band standard), *Mr Joe* with its glancing melodic feel and stop-time breaks, and the dark, intriguing habañera flavour of *The Crave*. Morton's light-toned, arrestingly tuneful but always blues-saturated singing is heard to best advantage in the superbly off-handed *Winin' Boy* and the beautiful slow *Mamie's Blues* (Morton's piano style here being one familiar from Jimmy Yancey's records), and the steadily-driving *Michigan Water*. The sophisticated vocal sob of *Don't You Leave Me Here* (which contains some of his most delightful piano playing at slow tempo), and the semi-recitative of *Buddy Bolden* reveals just how supremely practised was Morton in the art of entertaining alone at the piano, which in itself reveals the tragic decline in the fortunes of Morton the bandleader.

Sound quality is perhaps just a little dry and strident, but this reissue carries some of Morton's most enjoyable late recordings and should not be missed.

· GREAT · ORIGINAL · PERFORMANCES · 1926–1934 ·

GERRY MULLIGAN
(b. Queen's Village, Long Island, 6 April 1927)

Master of the baritone saxophone, Mulligan achieved fame with his West Coast piano-less quartet in the early 1950s, but his primary concerns have always been composition and arrangement.

After early piano lessons, Mulligan learned clarinet, alto, tenor, and finally baritone sax. His family lived in various towns before eventually settling in Philadelphia, where Gerry, while still in High School, sold a couple of arrangements to a local radio station house band, and later found regular work with Elliot Lawrence. In 1946-7 he worked for Gene Krupa, providing arrangements for *Disc Jockey Jump* and *How High The Moon*. Moving to the Claude Thornhill band in 1947, he met Gil Evans, and collaborated in the Miles Davis sessions now known as *The Birth of the Cool*.

Mulligan's real breakthrough came in 1952, after he had moved to Los Angeles. Richard Bock heard Mulligan and set up recordings for his new Pacific Jazz record company. Mulligan's piano-less group (Chet Baker, trumpet; Carson Smith, bass; Chico Hamilton, drums) was an instant success. Mulligan saw the quartet as the smallest possible unit that he could write for, and in the absence of a piano, he could work closely with the bass.

A setback came in September 1953, when Mulligan was arrested on a narcotics charge, and spent three months in prison. In 1954, he formed a new quartet with valve trombonist Bob Brookmeyer. Mulligan's 1958 quartet, seen in the film *Jazz on a Summer's Day*, featured Art Farmer on trumpet. By this time he had already begun the long series of *Mulligan Meets . . .* recordings, on which he guested with a staggering variety of musicians, from Thelonious Monk (1957) to Johnny Hodges.

By the end of the decade, Mulligan was able to realise a long-held ambition in the creation of his Concert band, a thirteen-piece aggregation which featured trumpeter Doc Severinson and recorded for Verve in 1961. More recently he has been largely occupied in writing for film and television, but also recording jazz again; CD now offers a good range of his work.

THE SILVER COLLECTION: GERRY MULLIGAN MEETS THE SAXOPHONISTS
Chelsea Bridge/Tell Me When/Bunny/18 Carrots For Rabbit/Come Rain Or Come Shine/Red Door/Scrapple From The Apple/This Can't Be Love/Line For Lyons/Body And Soul
1, 2 Ben Webster (ts), Gerry Mulligan (bars), Jimmy Rowles (p), Leroy Vinnegar (b), Mel Lewis (d), November 1959; 3, 4 Johnny Hodges (as), Mulligan (bars), Claude Williamson (p), Buddy Clark (b), Lewis (d), November 1959; 5 Don Ferrara, Nick Travis, Conte Candoli (tp), Bob Brookmeyer (valve tb, p), Wayne Andre, Alan Ralph (tb), Gene Quill, Dick Meldonian (as), Zoot Sims (ts), Mulligan (bars), Gene Allen (bars, b cl), Clark (b), Lewis (d), 1960; 6 Sims (ts), Mulligan (bars), Brookmeyer (p), Clark (b), Lewis (d), 1960; 7, 8 Stan Getz (ts), Mulligan (bars), Lou Levy (p), Ray Brown (b), Stan Levey (d), October 1957; 9, 10 Paul Desmond (as), Mulligan bars, Joe Benjamin (b), Dave Bailey (d), August 1957.
Verve 827 436
AAD Running time: 64.16
Performance: ★ ★ ★ Recording: ★ ★ ★

Taken from the long series of 'Mulligan Meets . . .' sessions which the baritonist made in the late 1950s, this is another *Silver Collection* which offers an unbeatable amount of music on one disc. The superbly evocative *Chelsea Bridge* is a true one-off, a small masterpiece in which, while an incomparable Ben Webster unveils the theme, Mulligan's foggy baritone provides an almost visible river haze in the background, before wreathing his own delicately-balanced solo around the Strayhorn tune.

Mulligan's own *Tell Me When* also proved an excellent vehicle for a duet with Webster, but the formula of two saxophonists and rhythm does not always work so well; the piano-less combination of Mulligan's gruff baritone with the light-toned Paul Desmond now sounds merely nasal on *Line For Lyons*, though the altoist is entrancingly airy on *Body And Soul*; Mulligan, probing rather than rhapsodic, shows his versatility here as much as in *Bunny*, a tune which though credited to Mulligan, contains typical Hodges mannerisms and sounds just like the kind of tune the Ellington alto star created for his own small group sessions. The execution is bouncy but perhaps a little 'polite'; ultimately more successful is the joyously contrapuntal workout, with a hard-swinging Stan Getz, on *This Can't Be Love*.

Mulligan's Concert Jazz Band features on the first of the two well-recorded live tracks with Zoot Sims, *Come Rain Or Come Shine*, which offers a rather abrupt change of mood but it is a very fine performance. On the other hand, the small-group *Red Door* has the clean, nervily-swinging sound of earlier West Coast jazz. Remastering is excellent throughout this disc (the producer was not afraid to mix mono and stereo tracks here), and it has to be rated as very good value.

NIGHT LIGHTS

Night Lights/Morning Of The Carnival (from 'Black Orpheus')/In The Wee Small Hours Of The Morning/Prelude In E-Minor/ Festival Minor/Tell Me When/Night Lights
1-6 Art Farmer (tp, flug), Bob Brookmeyer (valve tb), Gerry Mulligan (bars, piano 1), Jim Hall (g), Bill Crow (b), Dave Bailey (d), September 1963; 7 Mulligan (cl), Pete Jolly (p), Jond Grey (g), Jimmy Bond (b), Hal Blaine (d), ten strings directed by Harry Bluestone, 1965.
Mercury 818 271
AAD Running time: 34.10
Performance: ★ ★ ★   Recording: ★ ★ ★

Sumptuously recorded, the Mulligan sextet here provides gentle, deceptively simple, often exquisite music. Mulligan's title tune, which has a faint echo of *I Loves You Porgy*, allows Art Farmer space to demonstrate the sheer clarity and beautiful purity of tone that makes his playing so consistently enjoyable. Brookmeyer follows, while Mulligan accompanies on piano. Farmer opens an excellent *Manha de Carnaval*, supported by a simple, swinging Samba beat from Bailey and judicious, warm-voiced chords from Hall, and followed by convincing, atmospheric solos from Mulligan and Brookmeyer; Farmer returns with a bright-sounding solo, followed by a plangent Hall, the piece ending with a sweet and plaintive brass.

The guitarist contributes a brilliantly lucid solo to *Wee Hours*, but reverts to soft chording in the next track, where Mulligan uses a Chopin melody against a bossa nova beat. On this version of *Tell Me When*, Mulligan adds a breathy vibrato which makes it seem for a moment that he is substituting for Ben Webster. *Festival Minor* is a straightforward performance, with excellent solos including slightly bluesy ones from Hall and Brookmeyer. The final track, a second *Night Lights* which appears only on the Compact Disc, is quite different from the opening sextet version; here the result is rather over-sentimental as Mulligan plays a liquid-toned clarinet against a string section.

Without this rather sugary bonus, this would be a very short disc indeed, but it is hard to fault in other respects.

GERRY MULLIGAN

Jeru/Festive Minor/Rose Room/North Atlantic Run/Taurus Moon/Out Back Of The Barn
1 Gerry Mulligan (bars), Buddy Clarke (b), Mel Lewis (d), probably 1960; 2 Art Farmer(tp), Mulligan (bars), Dave Bailey (d), probably 1958-9; 3 Ruby Braff (tp), Bud Freeman (ts), Billy Taylor (p), Benny Moten (b), Osie Johnson (d), date unknown; 4-6 Mulligan (bars, ss), Dave Samuels (vib), Mike Santiago (g), George Duvivier (b), Bob Rosengarden (d), probably 1976.
Denon 33C38-7682
AAD Running time: 38.32
Performance: ★   Recording: ★

Material licenced from LRC once more provides appealing music combined with an infuriating lack of recording details.

However, it does provide intriguing glimpses of Mulligan at work in an amazing variety of settings. At one extreme is *Rose Room* with Ruby Braff, where through the murk of a faded recording that sounds as if it had been deliberately aged, Mulligan is heard just about managing to fit in with the revivalist/Chicago style ensemble. This comes as something of a culture shock after this loose, relaxed version of *Jeru* and the cool *Festive Minor* (which has a nice solo by Farmer). It is difficult to give this disc many stars, but it has its moments.

WALK ON THE WATER

For An Unfinished Woman/Song For Strayhorn/42nd & Broadway/Angelica/ Walk On The Water/Across The Track Blues/I'm Getting Sentimental Over You
Laurie Frink, Barrie Ries, Tom Harrell, Mike Davis, Danny Hayes (tp), Keith O'Quinn, Dave Glenn, Alan Raph (tb), Gerry Mulligan (ss, bars, arr), Ken Hitchcock (as, ts), Gerry Niewood (as), Gary Keller (ts), Ralph Olsen, Seth Brody, Eric Turkel (saxes), Joe Temperly (bars), Mitchel Forman (p), Jay Leonhart, Mike Bocchicchio (b), Richie Derosa (d), September 1980.
DRG CDSL 5194
AAD Running time: 39.12
Performance: ★ ★   Recording: ★ ★

Featuring soprano almost as often as baritone sax, Mulligan is an impressive soloist on this recording, but it is his melodies and always-innovative arrangements which helped it win a Grammy Award. Mulligan at this point had clearly moved with the times, and the music strongly echoes his film and TV writing. Yet while, for example, pianist Forman's *Angelica*, built on a pedal point effect, becomes almost a sing-along tune, Mulligan's superficially-similar *Song For Strayhorn* is much more substantial, as his baritone builds up to a passionate lyricism. *For An Unfinished Woman* opens with a repeated motif passed from piano to muted brass, Mulligan's baritone introducing the almost languorous theme over a firm pulse. After O'Quinn's delicately-handled trombone solo, Forman contributes a Jarrett-like piano; a bass solo from Bocchicchio leads in to a rousing final ensemble.

The title track has a kind of fresh-air optimistic feeling, a soprano-led ensemble carrying the bright tune over a slightly whimsical waltz rhythm. *Across The Tracks* is written, affectionately, in the now traditional language of big-band blues, though displaying Mulligan's gift for arranging an ensemble to sound, melodically, like a solo; the same goes for *Getting Sentimental Over You*, a seemingly impossible choice of material but one with a harmonic structure still interesting enough to build on. There are brief solos (after Mulligan's) from Ries, Hitchcock and Keller, but individual voices are in effect outdone by the swinging ensemble. Throughout the disc recording quality is clean, but has a pinched, 'small' or even tinny effect, which tends to rob the music of some of its warmth.

LITTLE BIG HORN
Little Big Horn/Under A Star/Sun On Stairs/Another Kind Of Sunday/Bright Angel Falls/I Never Was A Young Man
1, 4 Marvin Stamm, Alan Rubin (tp), Keith O'Quinn (tb), Lou Marini (as), Michael Brecker (ts), Gerry Mulligan (bars), Dave Grusin (p, el p), Anthony Jackson(el b), Buddy Williams (d); 2, 6 Mulligan (bars), Grusin (el p, synth 2, el p 6), Leonhart (el b, b 6), Williams (d); 3 Mulligan (bars), Grusin (p), Leonhart (el b), Butch Miles (d); 5 Mulligan (bars), Grusin (el p), Richard Tee (p), Jackson (el b), Williams (d), 1983.
GRP GRP-D-9503
DDD Running time: 36.36
Performance: ★ ★   Recording: ★ ★ ★

On this ground-breaking disc, Mulligan appears with a rhythm section led by GRP founder Dave Grusin, who plays synth and electric piano as well as the acoustic instrument. In the opener, which steams along with a typical GRP fusion beat, he

solos against a background provided by a six-piece virtuoso horn section lead by fusion virtuoso Michael Brecker. *Another Kind Of Sunday*, at a sort of lope-along tempo, is a successful combination of a Mulligan melody with a heavily rock-tinged backing. On the other hand, *Under A Star* features the metallic, all-too-predictable sound of Grusin's Rhodes piano which begins alternately to detract from Mulligan's beautiful melody, or to echo it too obviously.

For *Sun On Stairs*, a jaunty, lightweight tune very reminiscent of *Brotherhood of Man*, the electronic instruments are put away; with Grusin contributing some deftly funky piano, the whole thing flies along (with the punch of former Basie band drummer Butch Miles). By contrast, *Bright Angel Falls*, with Richard Tee guesting on piano, really gets back to the GRP house sound.

The disc ends with the novelty of a Mulligan vocal; the lyric is a good, clever one, but maybe it should have stayed written on paper. Recording quality is up to the usual digitally-polished GRP standard; overall, this disc is full of excellent musicianship, though Mulligan in this context may not appeal to all his fans.

SOFT LIGHTS AND SWEET MUSIC
Soft Lights and Sweet Music/Gone/Do You Know What I See/I've Just Seen Her/Noblesse/Ghosts/Port Of Baltimore Blues
Scott Hamilton (ts), Gerry Mulligan (bars), Mike Renzi (p), Jay Leonhart (b), Grady Tate (d), January 1986.
Concord CCD-4300
AAD Running time: 42.51
Performance: ★ ★   Recording: ★ ★ ★

Subtitled *Gerry Mulligan Meets Scott Hamilton*, this recording certainly has Mulligan in congenial, relaxed and thoroughly compatible company. Hamilton is an agile, fairly light-toned tenor player, who can combine phrasing of Getz-like precision with the gutty swing of Zoot Sims or Flip Philips; this is well displayed in the title track, a mid-tempo mainstream swinger, and in the neatly-turned chase choruses of the faster *Gone*. At other times, as on the dreamy Mulligan ballad *Noblesse* (with all credit to Renzi and Leonhart for setting the scene), he comes in with a lusher, breathier sound, or, over the gospel/soul-type changes of *Ghosts*, gets a bluesy edge. Mulligan's playing, miraculously full of melodic invention as always, has a deeply resonant, almost grainy tonal quality here.

Finally, there is the sophisticated blues duet (as with *Ghosts*, it is not actually a 12-bar) which is somehow reminiscent of the slower sort of vehicle Ellington constructed for his saxes in the 1950s; perhaps for a moment Tate sounds like Sam Woodyard, but in fact the easy-going effect of the music belies the great subtlety of his drumming, which makes the whole album swing. Recording quality is fine, the horns coming over with great realism, though Renzi's piano somehow sounds a little thin and lacking in body; Tate is well captured, while Leonhart's bass, again, sounds rather light and insubstantial. Not quite as soft-centred as the title and packaging might have you believe, this is an enjoyable disc.

DAVID MURRAY
(b. Berkeley, California, 19 February 1955)

Now recognised as an important new voice on tenor saxophone, David Murray gained early experience at home on the West Coast before moving to New York and becoming active in the 'loft scene'.

Though he also studied piano, Murray took up the saxophone at the age of nine, and was playing in R&B bands by his mid-teens, later joining the Black Music Infinity Band of Arthur Blythe and Bobby Bradford. He went to New York in 1975 mainly with the intention of completing his college saxophone thesis, but was soon sitting in with musicians like Anthony Braxton, Cecil Taylor, Sunny Murray and Don Cherry.

He was the youngest of the four players who, in 1977, formed the World Saxophone Quartet. With Murray in the WSQ were Hamiet Bluiett, Julius Hemphill and Oliver Lake, producing music strong in counterpoint and dazzling unison work as well as solos. In 1978, Murray launched a big band whose music paid tribute to the greats of past generations past, while his first album *Flowers For Albert*, was dedicated to the memory of his most telling influence, Albert Ayler, who died in 1970.

Now seen as Ayler's successor, Murray has worked with an octet but has most recently (1986) toured with John Hicks (piano), Ray Drummond (bass) and Ed Blackwell (drums).

HOME
Home/Santa Barbara And Crenshaw Follies/
Choctaw Blues/Last Of The Hipmen
Olu Dara (tp), Lawrence 'Butch' Morris
(cnt), George Lewis (tb), Henry Threadgill
(as, b fl), David Murray (ts), Anthony Davis
(p), Wilber Morris (b), Steve McCall (perc),
October/November 1981.
Black Saint BSR-0055CD
AAD Running time: 36.56
Performance: ★ ★   Recording: ★ ★ ★

Dense and richly-textured, through the use
of an unusually sonorous instrumentation
and mutes, the ensemble in *Home* alternates
a predominantly restful feeling with short
flares of slightly disturbing dissonance, and
gives way to an astonishingly deep and
mellifluous solo by Threadgill on bass flute.
Murray takes flight on the Mingus-
influenced *Santa Barbara And Crenshaw
Follies*, with its joyfully dissonant ensemble
driven by a springy and relentless McCall.
Wilber Morris produces a striking, skreakily
'vocalised' bass sound as he opens with a
solo over a 'jungle' sound in *Choctaw Blues*,
while the horns come in behind with a series
of 'urban' figures suggesting a kind of
defocused jazz-funk.
Last Of The Hipmen also contains
elements of parody, opening, straight-faced,
with bland expansive chords from the horns,
which give way to a straighter solo spot
from the bassist, then to a bouncy, poppy
theme, then to a powerful, heavy-toned solo
from Murray. Finally, *3-D Family* offers an
intricate though spontaneous-sounding
theme, creating steps for solo leaps by
Murray, 'Butch' Morris, Threadgill and a
tight-rope walk by Lewis.
  The music is strong, dissonant, but with
moods that are playful rather than intense,
and is meant to be enjoyed. The recording
quality is fine, free of the claustrophobic
sense of strain often heard in 1980s studio
work, and this in itself is a commendable
feature.

MORNING SONG
Morning Song/Body And Soul/Light Blue
Frolic/Jitterbug Waltz/Off Season/Duet
David Murray (ts, b cl), John Hicks (p),
Reggie Workman (b), Ed Blackwell (d),
September 1983.
Black Saint BSR 0075CD
AAD Running time: 42.17
Performance: ★ ★   Recording: ★ ★ ★

David Murray Quartet

Morning Song

Here Murray, with the impeccably
responsive support of Workman and
Blackwell, takes an affectionate and often
virtuoso look back to the saxophone
tradition; he opens *Body And Soul* with a
tone of rare purity and beauty, running
through the classic ornamentations of the
rhapsodist as he gradually introduces more
modern thoughts. This sort of pattern is
repeated in *Jitterbug Waltz*, where, over an
easy-going rhythm, Murray plays the jaunty
theme with delicacy and precision on his
sweet-sounding bass clarinet, exploiting the
rich, woody sound of the instrument to the
full. *Light Blue Frolic* is well titled, an
attractive almost frothy theme with a solid
centre provided by Murray's gutsy tenor
solo. Recording quality is perhaps a little
'close' and dry, but this supremely intelligent
and agile quartet is well captured.

CHARLIE PARKER
(b. Kansas City, Kansas, 29 August 1920; d. New York City, 12 March 1955)

Certainly the most profoundly influential musician since Louis Armstrong, Charlie 'Bird' Parker remains arguably the greatest instrumental soloist in jazz.

Parker was brought up in Kansas City by his mother, who bought him an old alto sax when he was eleven, and as a teenager he saw the Count Basie band with Lester Young. He was humiliated (by his own account) in his first attempt to sit in at a Kansas City jam session, but he spent the summer of 1937 with singer George E. Lee in the resorts of the Ozarks, taking a pile of Basie records on the trip, and came back with Young's solos 'down cold'. After this he joined Jay McShann's band briefly and worked with altoist Buster Smith.

In autumn 1939, he first met Dizzy Gillespie, passing through with the Cab Calloway band, and by the end of the year Parker was in New York, jamming at Monroe's Uptown House. He rejoined McShann to tour through 1940 and 1941, making his first appearance on records. In 1942, he played tenor in the Earl Hines band, which also contained Gillespie, then worked briefly with Andy Kirk and Noble Sissle before joining the ex-Hines men who made up the Billy Eckstine band.

Though he recorded with guitarist Tiny Grimes in 1944, Parker's first date as leader was the historic November 1945 session for Savoy. Soon after this, Parker accompanied Gillespie to Hollywood for a season at Billy Berg's Club. Be-bop did not go down well on the Coast, but the group cut *Diggin' Diz* for Dial records before returning.

Parker, however, missed the plane and stayed in California, and a March 28 Dial session produced the superb *Ornithology, Yardbird Suite* and *Night In Tunisia*. But Parker's difficulties obtaining narcotics and subsequent attempt to kick the habit 'cold turkey' contributed to a complete breakdown following the infamous *Loverman* date in July. After six months' rehabilitation in Camarillo State Hospital, he made a couple more Dial sessions in February 1947, then returned to New York, to form a quintet including Miles Davis, Duke Jordan, Tommy Potter and Max Roach. Dial relocated in New York and recorded this group in the autumn.

A trip to Europe for the 1949 Paris Jazz Festival was followed by another happy visit to Sweden in 1950. At the end of 1948, Parker had signed a 14-year contract with Norman Granz (the records appeared on Mercury, then on Granz's own Clef and Verve labels), and now Parker recorded with strings and with Machito's Latin orchestra.

Finally, the years of dissipation caught up with him. Suffering from cirrhosis of the liver and stomach ulcers, he died of heart failure, aged thirty-four. His vast recorded legacy includes dozens of broadcasts and illicit club recordings, on which he usually plays at greater length and more adventurously than in the studio.

BIRD/THE SAVOY RECORDINGS
(MASTER TAKES)
Tiny's Tempo/Red Cross/Warming Up A Riff/Billie's Bounce/Now's The Time/Thriving On A Riff/KoKo/Donna Lee/Chasin' The Bird/Cheryl/Milestones/Little Willie Leaps/Half Nelson/Another Hair-Do/Bluebird/Klaunstance/Bird Gets The Worm/Barbados/Ah-Leu-Cha/Constellation/Parker's Mood/Perhaps/Marmaduke/Steeplechase/Merry-Go-Round
1, 2 Charlie Parker (as), Clyde Hart (p), Tiny Grimes (g, voc), Jimmy Butts (b, voc), Harold 'Doc' West (d), September 1944; 3–7 Miles Davis (tp), Charlie Parker (as), Dizzy Gillespie (tp 7, p), Sadik Hakim (Argonne Thornton) (p 7), Curley Russell (b), Max Roach (d), November 1945. 8–10 Davis (tp), Parker (as), Bud Powell (p), Tommy Potter

(ts), John Lewis (p), May 1947; 11–13 Davis (tp), Parker (ts), John Lewis (p), Nelson Boyd (b), Roach (d), August 1947; 14–17 Davis (tp), Parker (as), Duke Jordan (p), Potter (b), Roach (d), December 1947; 18–25 Davis (tp), Parker (as), Lewis (p), Russell (b), Roach (d), September 1948.
Savoy ZD70737
AAD Running time: 71.26
Performance: ★ ★ ★   Recording: ★ ★

Rome wasn't built in a day, but Savoy's claim that its 26 November 1945 session laid the foundations of modern jazz was not without a grain of truth. This date gave the world *Billie's Bounce* and *Now's The Time*, both to become standard themes, as well as *KoKo*, Parker's definitive improvisation on the chords of *Cherokee*. It also produced a beautiful ballad fragment, *Meandering*, on the chords of *Embraceable You*, which was the only serious casualty, apart from *Buzzy* (a May 1947 blues) when Savoy squeezed a double album on to a single Compact Disc. Few will miss the vocal novelty *Romance Without Finance*, from the opening Tiny Grimes session.

Most of the later tunes were written, on the blues or *I Got Rhythm* changes, by Parker, who just showed them to the other musicians when they got to the studio; but Davis contributed *Donna Lee* and the sinuous *Milestones*, which clearly indicated his own future direction. It seems to have been a happy accident that Parker played tenor on this session, since it gave a softer balance that suited Davis' tunes. There were also experiments with counterpoint (*Ah-Leu-Cha*). Although Savoy caught the magnificent slow blues *Parker's Mood*, the greatness of Parker's ballad playing at this period is revealed only in the Dial recordings, not yet on CD. But if this Savoy collection does not quite give you everything, it comes as close as can be expected in a single silver disc. Apart from the barely noticeable presence of 78 'surface', the excellence of the original studio recording quality has been retained in the transfer.

BIRD AND DIZ
Bloomdido/An Oscar For Treadwell (2 takes)/Mohawk (2 takes)/My Melancholy Baby (2 takes)/Leap Frog (4 takes)/Relaxin' With Lee (2 takes).
Dizzy Gillespie (tp), Charlie Parker (as), Thelonious Monk (p), Curly Russell (b), Buddy Rich (d), June 1950.
Verve 831 133
AAD Running time: 40.41
Performance: ★ ★ ★   Recording: ★ ★ ★

With this studio reunion, Parker and Gillespie were able to recreate some of the impact of their earlier recordings together. To complete the group, Parker hired Thelonious Monk (who had not recorded since 1948) and Curly Russell, who at the time was the house bassist at Birdland; producer Norman Granz picked Buddy Rich, whose presence added excitement of a sort but who was very far from being a bebop drummer.

This quintet could hardly be described as a cohesive unit, but the two principals, solidly supported by Russell, seem to have carried on regardless, with a series of original lines based, as usual, on the blues or *I Got*

Rhythm chords. In the end the music was excellent, and is essential listening.

For the Compact Disc reissue, playing time has been extended with the addition of two further unreleased takes of *Leap Frog* (which are as astounding as the two already available) and one (inferior to the master but still intriguing) of *My Melancholy Baby*. As to technical quality, Phil Schaap's liner note states that further research has provided the best source material for the CD issue, and this is borne out by the sound quality here, which is excellent.

NOW'S THE TIME
The Song Is You/Laird Baird/Kim (2 takes)/Cosmic Rays (2 takes)/Chi-Chi (4 takes)/I Remember You/Now's The Time/Confirmation.
1-6 Charlie Parker (as), Hank Jones (p), Teddy Kotick (b), Max Roach (d), December 1952; 7-13 Parker (as), Al Haig (p), Percy Heath (b), Max Roach (d), August 1953.
Verve 825 671
AAD Running time: 39.19
Performance: ★ ★ ★   Recording: ★ ★

From the later of the two dates represented here comes a free-blowing version of one of Parker's best known blues lines, *Now's The Time*; not surprisingly, it bears little resemblance to the intense 1945 quintet recording of the same tune on Savoy. The session also produced a studio version of *Confirmation* (a tune which can be heard on a Parker broadcast from 1947), and four takes of a fast blues called *Chi-Chi*, one of which is issued for the first time on this Compact Disc, which as a set actually do make fascinating listening.

Parker, sounding happy and comfortable, delivers a fine performance on a mid-to-fast *I Remember You*. The sound is marked or marred (depending on personal taste) by heavy echo; though somewhat artificial, this makes the music sound 'big', smooth-flowing and exciting, and avoids any danger of the mild hardness which characterises the sound of the dry 1952 recording. This earlier session produced Parker's masterly *The Song Is You*, a Kern song whose unusual changes made it an interesting vehicle when played fast, and the incredibly fast *Kim (I Got Rhythm* chords), and two more blues lines. Again, this is among the best of the Verve sessions, with Max Roach providing the vital drive with that characteristically effortless command and speed which allows Bird to fly on the fast numbers. This disc may not be absolutely essential, but it comes close.

JOE PASS
(b. New Brunswick, New Jersey, 13 January 1929)

Though he began as a disciple of Django Reinhardt, Joe Pass absorbed the influences of Charlie Christian and the modern horn players to become one of the most accomplished and versatile of all jazz guitar players.

Starting on the guitar at the age of nine, Pass (originally Passaloqua) had only about a year's formal tuition, but he soon began playing local gigs and actually played truant from school to go on tour with Tony Pastor's band. He worked in clubs around New York, then joined the Marines, where he played cymbals in the marching band and guitar in the NCOs' club. Released from the service, he moved west and played hotels in Las Vegas, but his career was disrupted by personal problems and there were long periods of non-musical employment before the end of the 1950s, when he found himself rehabilitating at Synanon House, Santa Monica. Here he was discovered by Dick Bock of World Pacific Records, who recorded the Synanon House musicians. Pass later made the delightful tribute *For Django* (1964), an album of tunes associated with Reinhardt.

However, the career of Pass really blossomed when he began recording for Pablo in the early 1970s. He first worked with Oscar Peterson in 1973, becoming an intermittent member of Peterson's trio, and also recorded with many other artists, notably Stephane Grappelli, Milt Jackson, Ella Fitzgerald and Zoot Sims. In 1974, he made an album of guitar duets with Herb Ellis (*Two For The Road*) and followed this with the solo records *Virtuoso* and *Virtuoso No 2*. No doubt further issues will soon complete the CD picture.

VIRTUOSO
Night And Day/Stella By Starlight/Here's That Rainy Day/My Old Flame/How High The Moon/Cherokee/Sweet Lorraine/Have You Met Miss Jones/Round Midnight/All The Things You Are/Blues For Alican/The Song Is You.
Joe Pass (g), 1974.
Pablo 3112-15
AAD Running time: 53.34
Performance: ★ ★ ★ **Recording:** ★ ★ ★

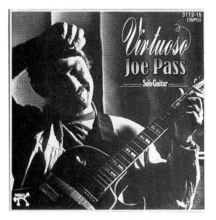

With this, the first of his solo albums, Pass demonstrated more clearly what should have been discernible from his earlier records; that he could do without other instruments altogether. Here Pass explores the melody and harmony of nearly a dozen standards (one of the twelve tracks is a slow blues), producing endlessly subtle chords often supported by a cunningly-wrought bass line; when he is not playing the melody in chords, he will break off to insert a breathtaking run. Often tender, sometimes beautiful and always impressive, this disc will for some listeners (and particularly on some numbers) have the effect of constant interruption; but others will find that renewed listening reveals an unstated constancy beneath the embellishment. Sound quality is excellent.

CHECKMATES
What's Your Story Morning Glory/So Rare/As Long As I Live/Marquita/Stardust/We'll Be Together Again/Can't We Be Friends/'Deed I Do/T'is Autumn/God Bless The Child.
Joe Pass (g), Jimmy Rowles (p), January 1981.
Pablo 3112
DDD Running time: 44.26
Performance: ★ ★ **Recording:** ★ ★

Guitar and piano are not always the easiest instruments to combine in a duo, since their abilities overlap; but in the case of this collaboration between Joe Pass, who had long worked with Oscar Peterson, and the distinctive Jimmy Rowles, always a sensitive accompanist, problems of demarcation never arise. Instead, and remarkably considering that the two men had neither worked together regularly nor rehearsed for the date, there is a rapport and an unforced ability to keep things going interestingly.

Pass seldom dazzles with virtuosity here, but instead offers great lyrical depths (*Stardust*) or switches to bass-line accompaniment (*'Deed I Do*), or provides rhythm chords to assist Rowles in generating an easy swing (*T'is Autumn*). Recording quality is attractive too, with an appropriate distance and space around the instruments. Listening to this disc really is a bit like overhearing a conversation, and though it may be a quiet, intimate and seldom earthshaking one, it is quickly obvious that both participants have a lot to say.

ART PEPPER

(b. Gardena, California, 1 September 1925; d. Los Angeles, 15 June 1982)

A direct and intense emotional impact sets the work of Art Pepper apart from the school of white Lester Young-influenced saxophonists to which, geographically, he seems to belong.

Pepper started on clarinet at the age of nine, and took up the alto saxophone at thirteen; by November 1943, when he joined Stan Kenton's orchestra, he had already worked around LA in the bands of Gus Arnheim, Lee Young and Benny Carter. Drafted in February 1942, he was released from the army in May 1946, and freelanced for a while before rejoining Kenton in September 1947, becoming a featured soloist. He also worked and recorded with Shorty Rogers And His Giants, but by 1952 started to record with small groups under his own name.

Recognised as one of the finest exponents of his instrument, with an emotional power that transcended the 'West Coast' label, Pepper should have become an established star, but was held back by the problems associated with his narcotics addiction.

For much of the 1960s, he was effectively out of the music scene, his career completely disrupted by ill-health and imprisonment, but this period ended with rehabilitation at Synanon House, Santa Monica, and with an emotional 'comeback' album, *Living Legend*, made in 1975.

Media attention followed the publication of his gripping autobiography *Straight Life* in 1979, but the extended international tour of 1981 was to be his last. Art Pepper, who had survived so much, succumbed to a brain haemorrhage, just as he was beginning to receive the recognition he undoubtedly deserved.

STRAIGHT LIFE/THE SAVOY SESSIONS
Straight Life/Chili Pepper/Cinnamon/Tickle Toe/Suzy The Poodle/Everything Happens To Me/Nutmeg/Deep Purple/What's New/Thyme Time/Art's Oregano/The Way You Look Tonight/Straight Life
2, 4–6 Art Pepper (as), Russ Freeman (p), Bob Whitlock (b), Bobby White (d), October 1952; 1, 3, 7–13, Pepper (as), Jack Montrose (ts), Claude Williamson (p), Monte Budwig (b), Larry Bunker (d), August 1954.
Savoy ZD70820
AAD Running time: 42.16
Performance: ★ ★ ★   Recording: ★ ★ ★

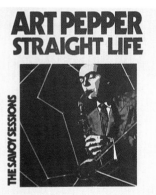

Pepper's second 1952 date as leader, for the Discovery label, produced the four quartet sides here. Pepper and pianist Russ Freeman demonstrate tremendous rapport in the fast and tricky unison theme statements of *Chili Pepper* (over *Tea For Two* chords) and *Tickle Toe* (the Basie number). *Suzy The Poodle* (on *Indiana* changes) is another flagwaver, but Pepper demonstrates a slightly edgy if muscular ballad approach

with *Everything Happens To Me.*

He plays even better on the quintet date, with the soft, nasal-sounding, deftly competent but relatively ordinary tenor of Montrose, who he'd worked with many times, as a sympathetic foil. They harmonise naturally and effortlessly on the themes and support each other in solos. Pepper is bursting with energy on the two takes of his anthem *Straight Life* (an ultra-fast be-bop tune on the chords of *After You've Gone*) and the other uptempo numbers; this time he is clean-lined and lucid on the ballad, *What's New* slipping effortlessly in and out of double time. Williamson, Budwig and Bunker offer excellent support throughout. Recording quality is clean and well balanced for the time, though Budwig's bass could have been captured better. It is a pity that the extra CD running time could not have been used to include the first Discovery session (with Hampton Hawes on piano), but in any case this disc covers some historic Pepper.

ART PEPPER MEETS THE RHYTHM SECTION
You'd Be So Nice To Come Home To/Red Pepper Blues/Imagination/Waltz Me Blues/Straight Life/Jazz Me Blues/Tin Tin Deo/Star Eyes/Birks' Works/The Man I Love.
Art Pepper (as), Red Garland (p), Paul Chambers (b), Philly Joe Jones (d), January 1957.
Contemporary VDJ-1556
AAD Running time: 50.48
Performance: ★ ★ ★   Recording: ★ ★ ★

By his own account Pepper was quite unprepared for this session with a trio of Miles Davis' sidemen; his striking and beautiful line on the opening *You'd Be So Nice To Come Home To* was, he later said, just the nearest he could get to the tune from memory.

This may just be the self-criticism of the perfection.st, for however Pepper recollected it, the session produced results which now sound excellent. Material which gets effective treatment by Pepper ranges from the classic minor-key blues *Birks' Works* to the well-contoured ballad *Imagination,* and with this rhythm section behind him, he really flies on *The Man I Love* and his own up-tempo theme *Straight Life.* Only on *Waltz Me Blues* is there an audible failure of Pepper's rapport with the trio; the 3/4 variant was presumably thought up as being less corny than the 'normal' 4/4 *Jazz Me Blues,* though this itself comes off very well in the hands of the quartet.

A truly memorable album, superbly recorded and balanced in natural-sounding stereo, and well transferred to Compact Disc.

MODERN JAZZ CLASSICS: ART PEPPER PLUS ELEVEN

Move/Groovin' High/Opus De Funk/ 'Round Midnight/Four Brothers/Shawnuff/ Bernie's Tune/Walkin' Shoes/ Anthropology/Airegin/Walkin' (3 takes)/ Donna Lee (2 takes), March/May 1959. 3, 4, 8, 10 Pete Candoli, Jack Sheldon (tp), Dick Nash (tb), Bob Enevoldsen (v tb, ts), Vince de Rosa (fr h), Art Pepper, Herb Geller (as), Bill Perkins (ts), Med Flory (bars), Russ Freeman (p), Joe Mondragon (b), Mel Lewis (d), March 1959; 2, 6, 9, 14, 15 as 3 but Al Porcino (tp), Bud Shank (as), replace Candoli, Geller, March 1959; 1, 5, 7, 11-13 as 2 but Charlie Kennedy (as), Richie Kamuca (ts), replace Shank, Perkins, May 1959.
Contemporary VDJ-1578
AAD Running time: 54.45
Performance: ★ ★ ★   Recording: ★ ★

These recordings, which feature Pepper in the front line of an excellent twelve piece band, were undoubtedly among the highlights of the altoist's career. The three sessions that produced *Art Pepper Plus Eleven* made fluent use of a dozen numbers that had already become jazz standards, masterfully arranged by Marty Paich.

The collection concentrates on the work of the bebop masters, but ranges from Horace Silver's *Opus De funk,* in which the comparatively formal horn lines do seem to smooth out the 'funk' intended by Silver, back in time to the classic of 1940s bop influenced big-band swing, *Four Brothers,*

which in a sense is closer to Pepper's roots. Pepper is in outstanding form on most of the fast numbers (from *Shawnuff* to *Donna Lee),* but he also offers a solo of great power and beauty on *'Round Midnight,* in the spacious if somewhat consciously dramatic setting provided by Paich.

Musically an essential recording, this disc (with the running time extended for CD by the addition of alternate takes) displays a clean and enjoyable sound, which, with just a slight boxiness and rolled-off extreme top end, which gives the impression of being an accurate transfer from the admirable master tapes.

THE MILCHO LEVIEV QUARTET: BLUES FOR THE FISHERMAN

True Blues/Make A List, Make A Wish/Sad, A Little Bit/Ophelia/Goodbye/Blues For The Fisherman.
Art Pepper (as), Milcho Leviev (p), Tony Dumas (b), Carl Burnett (d), London, June 1980.
Mole CD MOLE 1 PLUS
AAD Running time: 70.21
Performance: ★ ★ ★   Recording: ★ ★ ★

Billed under Leviev's name for contractual reasons, the quartet which Art Pepper brought to Ronnie Scott's club in the summer of 1980 was a superb group by any standards. The long opening blues starts conventionally, at a moderate bounce tempo, yet Pepper's characteristically spare and angular line immediately lifts the performance out of the ordinary; stark, probing, Pepper's playing is an individual expression which never merely follows the groove.

In the Romanian-born Leviev, mastery of jazz idioms is strengthened, not diluted, by the background influence of other cultures. He is also the composer of *Sad, A Little Bit,* a ballad which here is a feature for Pepper. The altoist plays the tune out of tempo first, with a melancholy, arrestingly beautiful sound, then continues with a very gentle *bossa* beat.

Early on, Leviev proves that he was perhaps the most compatible pianist for Pepper; not only does he play themes in unison with the altoist to produce the effect of a second horn, but in his solos, like Pepper, he takes the blues off into unexpected territory, with a positive drive and superb technique.

On his own *Make A List, Make A Wish,* Pepper blows at length over simple two-chord change, but in practice, however long Pepper's solos are, they remain cogently expressive. On the bounce-tempo *Ophelia,* Pepper alternates telling fragments with long and supple phrases, and Leviev, as usual, nimbly catches up the strand of Pepper's improvisation before weaving his own. The final blues (the title track) is a real slow drag, which despite the inevitable passing nod to *Parker's Mood,* shows just how great an individualist Pepper was.

Recording quality is quite good, with the excellent Dumas slightly under-recorded but still clear; Burnett's cymbals sometimes come through a little to strongly and the piano sound could be better, but the overall effect is of naturalness and realism. The quality of the music is such that this must not be missed.

OSCAR PETERSON
(b. Montreal, Canada, August 15 1925)

No rival can now challenge the pre-eminence of Oscar Peterson as complete master of traditionally-developed piano jazz. The sheer gloss and polish of his performances, combined with his essential conservatism, has sometimes led to criticism, but his best work offers, in the words of Benny Green, 'jazz which is perfect but not soulless'.

As a child, Peterson received tuition from his sister, an accomplished classical pianist, and at fourteen won $250 in a talent contest, which enabled him to buy his own piano. Around this time he first heard the music of his greatest influence, Art Tatum.

In 1950 he toured with JATP and began recording for Granz. He found a natural partner in Ray Brown, and completed a trio by adding Irving Ashby on guitar. Barney Kessel replaced Ashby in 1952, and after a year was replaced in turn by the subtle Herb Ellis.

Peterson reverted to a piano, bass and drums format when Herb Ellis left in 1958. Gene Gammage joined briefly, but in spring 1959 the trio really gelled with drummer Ed Thigpen. After a long series of successful albums, Peterson left Verve in 1964, and made the first complete recording of his *Canadiana Suite* for Mercury.

In the early 1970s, Norman Granz reappeared on the scene with his new Pablo label, and was soon recording Peterson again. Although the pianist had once said 'you can't replace Ray Brown', he had by now found a new virtuoso bassist, Neils-Henning Orsted Pedersen.

A JAZZ PORTRAIT OF FRANK SINATRA
You Make Me Feel So Young/Come Dance With Me/Learnin' The Blues/Witchcraft/The Tender Trap/Saturday Night (Is The Loneliest Night Of The Week/Just In Time/It Happened In Monterey/I Get A Kick Out Of You/All Of Me/Birth Of The Blues/How About You.
Oscar Peterson (p), Ray Brown (b), Ed Thigpen (d), Paris, May 1959.
Verve 825 769
AAD Running time: 34.55
Performance: ★ ★ ★   Recording: ★ ★

Although none of the tunes here are among the list of standards that usually crop up in jaz, they all reflect Sinatra's well-documented ability to pick quality material; and the result of this 1959 session was a complete jazz course in how to play popular tunes. For numbers like *Learnin' The Blues, Witchcraft* and *The Tender Trap,* Peterson had evolved a style of playing the melody in light, brightly-voiced chords, often with a subtle added harmony underneath, and when introducing rhythmic variation he could rely on the responsive, flexible teamwork of his matchless rhythm section.

For *Just In Time,* he comes in over Thigpen's brushes, to set a deliberate steady-paced groove which in the hands of a lesser trio would become turgid; even Peterson avoids going into improvised choruses with this number, which lasts less than two minutes, but, on the other hand, he clearly enjoys *It Happened In Monterey.* Peterson's apparently endless keyboard resources are revealed in many small touches; his softened, delicate sound in *I Get A Kick Out Of You,* his insertion of some barrelhouse effects in the breathing spaces of *Birth Of The Blues,* and, of course, his turn-laden treatment (almost tongue in cheek) of *You Make Me Feel So Young.*

Recording quality on the piano is a little brash and 'glamourised' with slight reverb, but the clarity of bass and drums means that there is little to complain of here.

VERY TALL
Green Dolphin Street/Heartstrings/Work Song/John Brown's Body/A Wonderful Guy/Reunion Blues.
Milt Jackson (vib), Oscar Peterson (p), Ray Brown (b), Ed Thigpen (d), September 1961.
Verve 827 821
Running time: 40.53
Performance: ★ ★ ★   Recording: ★ ★ ★

Many guest stars recorded with the Oscar Peterson Trio during his years on Verve, but few such meetings have resulted in such effortlessly foot-tapping music as this first encounter with Milt Jackson, who establishes his characteristic relaxed swing from the start. After the mid-paced *Green Dolphin Street,* an arco introduction from Brown and a softly-comping Peterson (who seems to have modified his often florid style to suit the occasion) allow the vibraharpist to weave a ballad spell with *Heartstrings,* while *Work Song* is a natural vehicle for him.

After a droll *John Brown's Body* and a first gently-, then rapidly-waltzing *Wonderful Guy,* comes a blues, whose theme is an archetypal Jackson line and whose sharp mid-tempo beat brings the set to a satisfying close. Like the two main soloists, Brown and Thigpen are well recorded here.

WE GET REQUESTS

Quiet Nights Of Quiet Stars (Corcovado)/
Days Of Wine And Roses/My One And
Only Love/People/Have You Met Miss
Jones/You Look Good To Me/The Girl
From Ipanema/D&E/Time and Again/
Goodbye J.D.
Oscar Peterson (p), Ray Brown (b), Ed
Thigpen (d), 1965.
Verve 810 047
Running time: 40.02
Performance: ★ ★ ★   **Recording:** ★ ★ ★

The stated intention of this album was to
offer the kind of tunes that people always
requested at live appearances, and at least six
of the ten numbers fulfil the brief. They
include Jobim's delicately reflective
Corcovado (played rather robustly here) as
well as *The Girl From Ipanema*; Mancini's
deceptively-simple, deservedly enduring
Days Of Wine And Roses (again, given a
fairly bright treatment) and Merrill and
Styne's *People*. The last third of the album is
given over to John Lewis's *D&E* blues
(Peterson hinting at the simpler,
rhythmically-bland piano style of the MJQ
leader), an almost plinkingly sentimental
Time and Again (written by Stuff Smith),
and finally, the fast and funky *Goodbye J.D.*
(addressed to Verve producer Jim Davis).
This set shows just how broad Peterson's
appeal could be, but there is no real
compromise in quality; and the dynamic
control and support provided by Brown and
Thigpen offer further evidence that, in many
ways, this was his greatest-ever trio.

'SATCH' AND 'JOSH'

Buns/These Foolish Things/RB/Burning/
Exactly Like You/Jumpin' At The
Woodside/Louie B/Lester Leaps In/Big
Stockings/S & J Blues.
Count Bassie (p, org 10), Oscar Peterson (p),
Freddie Green (g), Ray Brown (b), Louie
Bellson (d), December 1974.
Pablo J33J 20013
AAD Running time: 51.46
Performance: ★   **Recording:** ★
The title here refers not to musician's
nicknames, but, according to Norman
Granz's liner notes, to a baseball story, told
by Basie as a parable for the session. The
point of the story is that, once out on the
field, no quarter is given or received, even
among the best of friends. So, in stereo, we
have the pianos of Peterson on the left and
Basie on the right, managing at least for
some of the time to keep out of each other's
way. The rhythm section is perfect for the

job; the quiet but vital rhythm chords of
Freddie Green's acoustic guitar add the true
Basie flavour to the already unbeatable
combination of Brown and Bellson, to
provide a beat that is always neo-swing, not
modern.
   Despite all this, there are moments when
the effect is confusion, notes splattering
around ineffectually, as in the stride-style
blues *Big Stockings*, with the rhythm section
out; the problem is solved in the slow *S&J
Blues*, where Basie plays organ to great
effect. There is some good music on this disc,
and recording quality would be fine but for a
strange distortion, presumably due to
overload in the mastering, on the loud
passages of *Lester Leaps In*. But despite the
modern benefit of having one piano per
stereo speaker, parts of this album are
inescapably reminiscent of the duos and trios
recorded by Albert Ammons, Pete Johnson
and Meade Lux Lewis, thrown together by
fame but each so much more effective on his
own.

THE OSCAR PETERSON BIG SIX AT THE
MONTREUX JAZZ FESTIVAL 1975

Toots Thielemans (harm), Milt Jackson
(vib), Joe Pass (g), Oscar Peterson (p), Neils
Henning Orsted Pedersen (b), Louis Bellson
(d), July 1975.
Pablo J33J 20050
AAD Running time: 51.15
Performance: ★ ★ ★   **Recording:** ★ ★

Parker's blues theme *Au Privave*, at a very
high speed, opens this long-running slice of
top-quality festival jazz. Harmonica player
Thielemans produces a fast and fluent solo,
followed by an incredibly fast one from
Pass, then a solo of driving, hammering
swing from Jackson; then comes Peterson,
apparently throwing everything in. Pedersen
follows, his mastery of the bass making it
sound easy, then Peterson, Jackson, Pass and
Thielemans trade fours, each competing to
get the most notes into his four bars, then
return joyously to the theme.
   After a nice opening, *Here's That Rainy
Day* gets into a fast chug-along beat, which
nonetheless allows Jackson to take off in his
most free-flowing manner. Thielemans' wild
solo, impressive as it is, has the effect of
leaving the tune in tatters, and Peterson's
somewhat barrelhouse-tinged contribution
does little to repair it; but in the slow *Poor
Butterfly*, after several great choruses by
Jackson and a Thielemans solo, Petersen
gives a breathtaking display of what can be
done on this hoary old chord sequence when
you have a command of every piano style
since it was written. Pass, wistful and
melodic, is also excellent here.
   The set ends with an extremely fast pop-
influenced blues, with another virtuoso solo
from Pass; while Bellson, who keeps time
with his usual superhuman (some might say
mechanical) precision throughout, solos here
also. In terms of sound quality, the disc has
an appealing live feel, though the balance is
imperfect, with Jackson too quiet. Though
hardly of great emotional depth, the music
on this disc is as good an illustration as any
of the utterly astounding technical standards
now set by the leading jazz musicians, and
particularly by Peterson, who had gathered
around him men of equally extraordinary
abilities.

BUD POWELL
(b. New York City, 27 September 1924; d. New York City, 31 July 1966)

As the creator of a genuine bebop piano style, Earl 'Bud' Powell influenced almost every pianist who followed, though his drive and emotional power were seldom if ever equalled.

After working for about three years with Cootie Williams, he emerged as a key sideman with Gillespie and Don Byas, recording with J J Johnson and Kenny Clarke, as well as with Parker (on Savoy) and with his own trio in 1947. In the next few years, he recorded with Sonny Stitt, Fats Navarro and Sonny Rollins, and in 1953 played in a trio set as well as the quintet performances at the famous Massey Hall concert in Toronto (*The Quintet Of The Year*). In 1959, he moved to Paris, where *Our Man In Paris* with Dexter Gordon was among his first recordings.

Further sessions included a set with Johnny Griffin and trio dates, though the last of these (including the 1964 New York recordings to be found on *Paris-New York*, Vogue VG651 600046) show a tragic loss of pianistic command. Powell made his permanent return to New York in early 1966, but died only a few months later.

MONK AND BUD
'Round Midnight/Eronel/Reflections/We See/Well You Needn't/Hackensack/ Evidence/Smoke Gets In Your Eyes/Off Minor/I'll Remember April/Everything Happens To Me/Indiana/I Should Care/ Nice Work If You Can Get It/Off Minor/ Buds Bubble/Somebody Loves Me
1-9, Thelonious Monk (p), Paris, June 1954; 10-17 Bud Powell (p), Curley Russell (b), Max Roach (d), January 1947.
Vogue VG651 600101
AAD Running time: 51.12
Performance: ★ ★ ★   Recording: ★

About half the running time of this disc is devoted to solo recordings made by Monk when he spent a week in Paris during the summer of 1954.

Pre-dating the more celebrated Riverside solo recordings, they are strong, absorbing, typically architectural performances of Monk's own tunes, with Kern's *Smoke Gets In Your Eyes* getting a fairly predictable (with hindsight!) but enjoyable treatment. Despite the thin, watery sound quality (as if using a tape recorder with quite severe flutter) the disc would be worth having for these Monk tracks alone: but the eight Bud Powell trio titles make it essential.

He displays his quintessential bebop right hand style on *Indiana* and his own theme *Bud's Bubble*, and produces a driving version of Monk's *Off Minor*; inventive left hand figures propel *I'll Remember April*, while *Nice Work If You Can Get It* is a fast and matchlessly rhythmic interpretation of this lively standard, alternating single line runs and chord passages to state the theme.

Somebody Loves Me contains a typical example of the 'locked hands' style, later developed by Milt Buckner, as well as characteristically free-running and expressive horn-like single note passages. *I Should Care* is a slow ballad in the manner which Powell derived largely from Tatum and which was smoothed and polished by Oscar Peterson.

Sound quality is not good but this is soon forgotten as Powell's music takes hold.

THE SCENE CHANGES
Cleopatra's Dream/Duid Deed/Down With It/Danceland/Borderick/Crossin' The Channel/Comin' Up/Gettin' There/The Scene Changes/Comin' Up (alternate take)
Bud Powell (p, Paul Chambers (b), Art Taylor (d), December 1958.
Blue Note CDP 7 46529
AAD Running time: 45.35
Performance: ★ ★   Recording: ★ ★ ★

Here Powell's playing still has much of the vital force of his work in the 1940s and in terms of material, this session clearly looked back to the bebop era. The title track is a fast boppish theme which Powell plays in octaves, as is *Crossin' The Channel*; the opening *Cleopatra's Dream* also uses occasional octave passages as well as a flowing single-note line over a simple minor-key chord sequence, while *Duid Deed*, again in a minor key, has overtones of Monk. *Danceland*, yet another minor-key theme, resembles a simplified, squared-up version of *Topsy*.

With *Comin' up*, which runs over seven minutes, Powell offers a surprisingly gripping exploration over a steady mambo beat, with a string of intriguing quotes and constantly renewed rhythm interest. On this disc Powell, characteristically, sometimes seems to convey all the elements of bebop group performances himself, playing first a short piano introduction, then an octave theme statement like two horns in unison, then a flying single-note line like a horn solo.

Recording quality is excellent, and musically, as an example of the richness and emotional directness of Powell's work, this disc must be rated very highly.

DJANGO REINHARDT

(b. Liberchies, Belgium, 23 January 1910; d. Samois, France, 15 May 1953)

Jean Baptiste 'Django' Reinhardt was born into the tradition of gipsy music, but by blending this with the jazz idiom became the only European musician to influence the American jazz scene.

Reinhardt's earliest recorded solo is a short break on *Si J'aime Suzy*, with L'Orchestre du Theatre Daunou, from 1933, the year he first played with Stephane Grappelli, in Louis Vola's Hotel Claridge Orchestra. This band was the basis of the Quintet of the Hot Club of France, originally a jam session group encouraged by Hot Club founders Hugues Panassié and Charles Delaunay. They persuaded Ultraphone to record *Dinah* and *Tiger Rag* in December 1934.

When war broke out, the quintet were in London. While Grappelli stayed in England, Reinhardt returned to Paris and soon formed a new group with the great clarinettist Hubert Rostaing. This association continued with post-war recordings. By 1949, he was being seen as old-fashioned, but made a comeback at the Club St Germain in 1951, playing electric guitar with a 'modern' group. Still at the height of his powers, Reinhardt died suddenly of a stroke.

COLEMAN HAWKINS AND BENNY CARTER

I'm Coming, Virginia/Farewell Blues/Blue Light Blues/Sweet Georgia Brown/Out Of My Way/What'll It Be/Cadillac Slim/Blue Moon/Avalon/What A Difference A Day Made/Stardust/Honeysuckle Rose/Crazy Rhythm/Out Of Nowhere/Sweet Georgia Brown
1, 2 Benny Carter, Fletcher Allen (as), Bertie King, Alix Combelle (ts), Yorke De Souza (p), Django Reinhardt (g), Len Harrison (b), Robert Montmarche (d), Paris, March 1938; 3 as 1 but Carter (tp), March 1938; 4-7 Buck Clayton (tp), Carter (as), Al Grey (tb), Ben Webster (ts), Sonny White (p), John Simmons (b), 'Big' Sid Catlett (d), August 1946; 8-10 Arthur Briggs, Noel Chiboust, Pierre Allier (tp), Andre Ekyan,Charles Lisee (as), Coleman Hawkins, Alix Combelle (ts), Stephan Grappelli (p), Reinhardt (g), Eugene D'Hellemmes (b), Maurice Chaillou (d), Michel Warlop (leader), Paris, March 1935; 11 Hawkins (ts), Grappelli (p), Reinhardt (g), March 1935; 12, 13 Carter, Ekyan (as), Hawkins, Combelle (ts), Grappelli (p), Reinhardt (g), D'Hellemmes (b), Tommy Benford (d), Paris, April 1937; 14, 15, as 12 but Carter (tp), Paris, April 1937.
DRG CDSW 8403
AAD Running time: 46.39
Performance: ★ ★   Recording: ★ ★ ★

Reinhardt is absent from the four American 1946 recordings (which have excellent playing from Clayton and Webster), but on the other tracks it is fascinating to hear how he had responded to contact with Hawkins and Carter, two giants of American jazz. He throws everything into his solo on *Avalon*; could any other (acoustic) guitarist at the time have competed so effectively with the powerful forces of the Warlop big band? On the trio recording of *Stardust* he has the difficult job of following Hawkins, which he does with power and energy, though the recording regrettably thins his tone. It can be argued that Hawkins is not at best here, though Carter probably is; but this well-transferred and attractive, informatively-packaged disc (though note that the track order is above, not as the liner) is essential for anyone even vaguely interested in the jazz of this period.

DJANGO REINHARDT

Improvisation/Honeysuckle Rose/Eddie's Blues/Bill Coleman Blues/Minor's Swing/Swingin' With Django/Christmas Swing/I Got Rhythm/Younger Generation/Tears/Swing 41/Nuages/Les Nuages/Les Yeux Noirs/La Cigale Et La Formi
Django Reinhardt (g), unknown personnel, 1937-1944.
Pathe 746 5012
AAD Running time: 57.44
Performance: ★ ★   Recording: ★

The track listing, quoted above, is incorrect; the first two numbers are respectively accordion and vocal features, which will be of little interest; tracks 3 and 4 are actually *Rosetta* (Reinhardt on brilliant form, with violin and piano) and *Limehouse Blues* (a very fast, perhaps 'speeded up' Hot Club version), and so it goes on. However, tracks 11 to 13 are classic Reinhardt performances from 1940, with clarinettists Hubert Rostaing and (except *Nuages*), Alix Combelle. Track 14 is a vocal by Charles Trenet; 15, 16 and 17 are big band numbers (which now sound almost quaint); 18 is a post-war live recording with unknown saxophonist, while the final number is a duet with Grappelli on one of Django's most moving tunes.

Whether this disc's moments of pure delight will make up for the frustrating nature of the package is debatable! It is unfortunate that an earlier Hot Club Quintet CD collection no longer seems to be available.

BUDDY RICH
(b. New York City, 30 June 1917; d. Los Angeles, 2 April 1987)

One of the most exciting drummers ever, Buddy Rich combined tremendous speed with an unrelenting drive, which led to accusations of insensitivity or excessive showmanship when playing with a small group. It is true that he was most at home demonstrating his almost unrivalled ability to swing a big band.

A true child of show business, Buddy Rich was onstage in his parents vaudeville act 'Wilson and Rich' before he was two years old. At four he was playing drums and tap dancing, at six he was billed as 'Traps the Drum Wonder', and at eleven he led a band. Rich worked with bass player Art Shapiro about 1936, but first attracted real attention when he sat in with 'Hot Lips' Page's band the following year. He worked with Joe Marsala, Artie Shaw and Bunny Berigan before starting the first of several stints with Harry James, in December 1938. He moved to the Tommy Dorsey band in 1939, staying until 1942, when after a spell with Benny Carter, he went into the US Marines.

Released in 1944, he rejoined Dorsey, but formed his own band late in 1945. He disbanded at the beginning of 1947 to undertake the first of many JATP tours. In the early 1950s he recorded several small-group sessions for Norman Granz, but he was soon working for the big bands of James (1953-4) and Dorsey (1954-5), and James again (1956-7). While on tour with his own quintet in 1959, he suffered a mild heart attack, but was soon back at work.

From 1961, he played with the James band again, also making innumerable 'guest star' appearances, then in 1966 formed a new big band of his own. The band played successfully all over the world, and jazz/rock with *A Different Drummer* (RCA, 1971). A serious heart attack in 1983 demanded open-heart surgery, but even this did not keep Rich off the road for long, and he continued to tour with a band fronted by virtuoso sax player Steve Marcus; sadly, he died in hospital while recovering from another operation in early 1987. Though he appears as a sideman on many other discs, the essential Buddy Rich is well represented by the titles recorded with his own band.

Never less than exciting to hear and watch, Buddy Rich toured right up to his death in 1987.

TUFF DUDE
Donna Lee/Chameleon/2nd Avenue Blues/ Jumpin' At The Woodside/Sierra Lonely/ Nica's Dream/Billie's Bounce
1-3, 5-7 Sonny Fortune (as, ss), Sal Nistico (ts), Jack Wilkins (g), Kenny Barron (p), Anthony Jackson (b), Jimmy Maelen (per), Buddy Rich (d); 4, Mike Abene replaces Barron, May 1974.
Denon 33C38-7972
AAD Running time: 62.39
Performance: ★ ★   Recording: ★ ★ ★

It has been said that Buddy Rich is better driving a big band than overpowering a small group, and it has also been said that he is better live than on record. But here Rich's own medium-sized band was recorded live in his own club, Buddy's Place, which does indeed provide an effective showcase for him. In fact, Rich's drums are well captured in a recording which also conveys the feel of a club stage rather well. The opener is a rather raggedy workout on the Parker-Davis bop line over *Indiana* chords, *Donna Lee*,

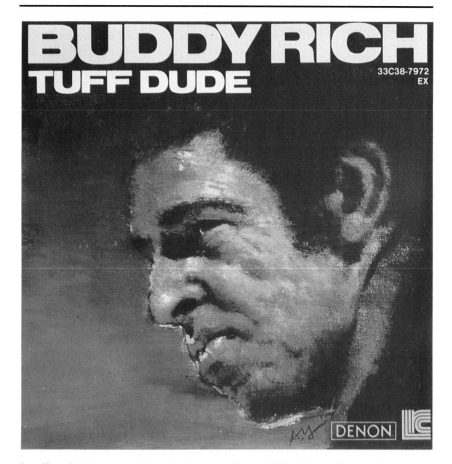

but *Chameleon* turns out to be a dated, nearly themeless piece of funk, complete with electric keyboard and wah-wah guitar sounds. For some reason there is no applause at the end of this track, which doesn't sound as if it could really have been part of the live set anyway.

The flute-led *Sierra Lonely* is a more interesting fusion effort. The slow *2nd Avenue Blues* is actually a string of rather over-indulgent solos (the eclectic Wilkins is impressive as he runs the gamut from Wes Montgomery to Albert King). Obviously effective in the club, it sounds a bit laboured on record.

Rich gets into a more characteristic uptempo groove with *Jumpin'*, and excellent sax and guitar solos make this about the best track on the disc apart from the fast, exciting and tightly-played *Nica's Dream*. Rich never was really a be-bop drummer, but he is a joy to listen to on the closing *Billie's Bounce*.

This set's long running time reflects the inclusion of some weak tracks, but the recording itself does have a satisfying immediacy about it, and this will be good value for Rich fans.

LIONEL HAMPTON PRESENTS BUDDY RICH
Moment's Notice/Giant Steps/Buddy's Cherokee/Take The 'A' Train/I'll Never Be The Same/Buddy's Rock/My Funny Valentine/Latin Silk
Steve Marcus (ts, ss), Gary Pribek (ts), Paul Moen (ts), Lionel Hampton (vib), Barry Kiener (p), Tom Warrington (b), Buddy Rich (d), Candido Camero (cga), 1977
Kingdom CD GATE 7011
AAD Running time: 48.12
Performance: ★ ★ ★   Recording: ★ ★ ★

In 1977 Rich, along with Mingus, Mulligan and others, made recordings for Lionel Hampton's own now-obscure Gate label; for each album, Hampton's idea was to present a star talent in an uninhibited, enjoyable programme. In this series Hampton, whose approach was firmly rooted in the swing era, proved capable of bridging almost any stylistic gaps, though the freedom of the Mingus band did leave him sounding rather stiff. Such criticisms could hardly apply to a collaboration with Rich, who despite his successful adaptation to other and later styles, was at heart a big band drummer and leader too.

But with three tenor players on hand, it is not surprising to see that the first two numbers are tunes written by Coltrane, and demonstrate his almost overwhelming influence. *Moment's Notice* is taken at a blistering pace, and includes a string of effective solos from Marcus, Pribek and Moen. Although the saxists (particularly Pribek in his fine opening solo) do evoke JC, *Giant Steps* soon becomes a swing vehicle for Rich, trading fours with Hampton and then with conga player Camero. More predictably, the next two titles strongly feature Hamp, and the balance of the disc is made up of two attractive ballads, the slick and appealing *Latin Silk* in which a rather heavy-handed Rich is augmented effectively by Camero; and *Buddy's Rock*, a funk/rock number typical of what jazzmen felt obliged to do in the mid to late 1970s, and on which Hampton is almost amusingly adrift. This aside, this is a fine disc, swinging, exciting and well recorded. If not quite the most fitting tribute to the great drummer, it at least offers a chance to hear him at length, and at his best.

MAX ROACH
(b. Brooklyn, NY, 10 January 1925)

Undoubtedly the finest drummer to emerge from the whole 'modern jazz' movement in the 1940s and early 1950s, Max Roach set new standards of speed, precision, intelligence and taste.

Leaving school in 1942, Roach was soon playing at Monroe's Uptown House, where the bebop pioneers often jammed. His main influence was Kenny Clarke, who he closely resembles on early recordings he spent the late 1940s freelancing in New York, playing and recording extensively with Charlie Parker, Tadd Dameron and other leading figures of modern jazz. In 1954 he invited the young trumpeter Clifford Brown to join him with the status of co-leader, and the Brown/Roach quintet became one of the greatest of all small jazz groups. Later, 'with *We Insist! Freedom Now Suite*, Roach's music began to express the commitment to the Civil Rights movement which resulted in his being blacklisted by the major studios in the 1960s. But in recent years, he has worked in many contexts, and written for theatre, TV and video productions.

IN THE LIGHT
In The Light/Straight No Chaser/Ruby My Dear/Henry Street Blues/If You Could See Me Now/Good Bait/Tricotism.
Cecil Bridgewater (tp, flug),Odean Pope (ts), Calvin Hill (b, el b), Max Roach (d), July 1982.
Soul Note SN-1053CD
AAD Running time: 42.22
Performance: ★ ★ ★   Recording: ★ ★ ★

In keeping with Roach's views of tradition, this 1982 quartet recording includes two compositions by Monk and two by Tadd Dameron. But the little track is a powerful performance too, with constant interplay between the sonorous Pope and the quicksilver Bridgewater. *Straight No Chaser*, again demonstrates the importance of group interaction rather than soloing, for although there are solos, these are better described as exchanges; after the simple but punchy *Henry Street Blues* and *If You Could See Me Now* (with a smoky, deep-toned Pope) comes Oscar Pettiford's *Tricotism*, with Hill agile on electric bass. For some reason the otherwise excellent recording quality becomes boxy here.

BIRTH AND REBIRTH
Birth/Magic And Music/Tropical Forest/Dance Griot/Spirit Possession/Softshoe/Rebirth
Anthony Braxton (as, ss, sopranino s, cl), Max Roach (d), 1978.
Black Saint BSR 0024 CD
AAD Running time: 43.20
Performance: ★ ★ ★   Recording: ★ ★ ★

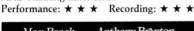

BIRTH AND REBIRTH

From Braxton's subtle, high-pitched but full bodied introduction, this recording has a vibrancy and musical coherence which is sustained to the end. After the quiet start, Roach's drums, especially well recorded on this disc, burst in, while Braxton plays a furious yet intricate and purposefully-argued obbligato with a nasal sound resembling that of North African trumpets, scarcely pausing and giving the feeling of swirling, fervid creation, while Roach builds his uncannily melodic variations.

With an almost whimsical sopranino opening by Braxton, the rapport on *Magic And Music* extends to the subtlest conversational nuances. Roach produces his most gripping rhythms in *Spirit Possession*, while Braxton interjects sharply, then weaves dancer-like around him, on clarinet. The final *Rebirth* mirrors the opening of this disc, which is sonically flawless.

SURVIVORS
Survivors/The Third Eye/Billy The Kid/JasMe/The Drum Also Waltzes/Sassy Max/The Smoke That Thunders.
Gillermo Figueroa (1st vln), Donald Bauch (2nd vln), Louise Schulman (viola), Christopher Finckel (cello), Max Roach (d, perc), October 1984.
Soul Note SN 1093
AAD Running time: 43.01
Performance: ★ ★   Recording: ★ ★

At the 1958 Monterey Jazz Festival, Max Roach appeared as soloist with a full orchestra in Peter Philips' 'Concerto For Max'; a quarter of a century later, Roach and Philips collaborated on this album, in which Roach is joined by a string quartet. Accounting for almost exactly half the running time of the disc, *Survivors* itself pits angular chords from the quartet against the fluid, expressive pulse of Roach's snares and tom-toms, building to a stark climax.

The other tracks are solo performances: *The Third Eye* based on a deceptively simple two-note bass-drum pattern, over which exchanges between other parts of the kit take place; *Billy The Kid* sets up a looser, more swinging framework, while *The Drum Also Waltzes* provides intricate variations on a 3/4 basis. Those who blench at the idea of a disc composed almost entirely of drum solos should remember that Max Roach is no ordinary drummer.

SONNY ROLLINS
(b. New York City, 7 September 1930)

'My playing calypsos is mainly due to my mother coming from the Virgin Islands' said Rollins. 'I went with her to a lot of Calypso dances and heard these songs at a fairly early age.' But the Caribbean flavour of *St Thomas* is only one aspect of his contribution to jazz.

Theodore Walter Rollins originally wanted to be a painter. Only after his first recording session, in 1948, with singer Babs Gonzales (Capitol), did he decide to become a full-time musician. By 1949, when he recorded with Bud Powell, Fats Navarro and J J Johnson, the influence of Louis Jordan had been overlaid by that of Parker. In 1951, he recorded with Miles Davis and as a leader, but it was in June 1954 that he reached the brink of real fame by recording his own tunes *Oleo, Doxy* and *Airegin* as a member of Miles' quintet.

Then, in late 1954, Rollins left the scene, having decided to shake off narcotics. He went to Chicago, placed himself under a doctor and took a job as a janitor. After a year, he reappeared as a member of the Brown/Roach quintet. In 1956 his *Saxophone Colossus* was the subject of a learned *Jazz Review* dissection by Gunther Schuller, while Whitney Balliet in *The New Yorker* described Rollins as having a musical imagination that probably equalled Parker's.

A few days after the *Colossus* date came the car crash that killed Clifford Brown and the quintet's pianist Richie Powell. Rollins left Roach in May 1957; after a brief spell with Miles, he formed his own group, again without a pianist ('I couldn't find any piano players I liked') and recorded for at least half a dozen different labels.

In 1959 Rollins 'retired' again. He returned in 1961, to a lucrative RCA contract, but the changes that had taken place during his two-year 'sabbatical' left him looking a little old-fashioned. Nonetheless, Rollins was by now a major figure in jazz, a fact which was unaltered by his next disappearance, this time for five years, in the mid-1960s. Since then he has worked and recorded mainly in Europe.

SAXOPHONE COLOSSUS
St Thomas/You Don't Know What Love Is/
Strode Rode/Moritat/Blue Seven
Sonny Rollins (ts), Tommy Flanagan (p),
Doug Watkins (b), Max Roach (d), June
1956.
Prestige VDJ-1501
AAD Running time: 39.56
Performance: ★ ★ ★   Recording: ★ ★ ★

Still striking in its fresh, uncluttered approach, this classic Prestige album marked the final arrival of Sonny Rollins as a solo star. It was the somewhat Miles-like *Blue Seven*, a confident, satisfying improvisation against the blues pattern of ambiguous tonality cleanly laid down by Watkins, which attracted the academic attention of Gunther Schuller; but *Saxophone Colossus* also introduced the West Indian tune *St Thomas* and an attractive *Moritat* ('Mack The Knife'), idiosyncratic but not eccentric. In *You Don't Know What Love Is*, Rollins displays a style embracing virtually all that had gone before him, yet stripped of inessentials, the tone full and generous, the melodic approach just hinting at the rhapsodic tradition but lean and unsentimental; for *Strode Rode* he produced the archetypal lean and virile drive of hard bop. With fine solo work from the often under-rated Flanagan as well as the peerless Roach, this session was balanced and recorded by Rudy Van Gelder, whose fine original engineering has made for an excellent sound on Compact Disc.

SONNY ROLLINS PLUS FOUR
Valse Hot/Kiss And Run/I Feel A Song
Coming On/Count Your Blessings/Pent-Up
House
1-3, 5 Clifford Brown (tp), Sonny Rollins
(ts), Richie Powell (p), George Morrow (b),
Max Roach (d); 4 Brown out, March 1956.
Prestige VDJ-1524
AAD Running time: 32.38
Performance: ★ ★ ★   Recording: ★ ★

Though under Rollins' nominal leadership, this Prestige date used the Max Roach/Clifford Brown quintet, which otherwise recorded for Mercury/EmArcy. Here, as on other Roach/Brown recordings, the group always sounds coherent and well integrated, in happy contrast to many rather fragmentary Prestige sessions of the period. The opener, *Valse Hot* is pretty, a sentimental tune subjected to a hip reworking which itself now seems nostalgic, yet this track seems almost lumbering against the next two selections, where both Rollins and Brown are on superb form. Rollins had now learned the language of Charlie Parker but was clearly already a master in his own right. His sumptuously melodic *Count Your Blessings* provides a fitting change of pace before *Pent Up House*, which allows Rollins the kind of space he was soon to exploit more fully. Sound quality, intimate if a little 'boxy', is fine for the period and (for audio enthusiasts at least) makes an interesting comparison with the smooth, slightly distant EmArcy sound.

SONNY ROLLINS BRASS/SONNY ROLLINS TRIO
Who Cares/Love Is A Simple Thing/Grand Street/Far Out East/What's My Name/If You Were The Only Girl In The World/Manhattan/Body And Soul
1-4 Clark Terry, Reunald Jones, Ernie Royal (tp), Nat Adderley (cnt), Billy Byers, Jimmy Cleveland, Frank Rehak (tb), Don Butterfield (tu), Sonny Rollins (ts), Dick Katz (p), Rene Thomas (g), Henry Grimes (b), Roy Haynes (d), Ernie Wilkins (cond, arr); 5-7 Rollins (ts), Grimes (b), Wright (d); 8 Rollins (ts), July 1958.
Verve 815 056
AAD Running time: 35.27
Performance: ★ ★ **Recording:** ★ ★ ★

Halfway to being a big band, the thirteen piece group of the *Brass* session leaves Rollins as the only reed player; and the only soloist, apart from Rene Thomas' excellent but hardly fiery guitar, and an almost thin-sounding cornet (on *Grand Street*) from Nat Adderley. The *Trio* tracks reflect the format Rollins used in club dates, and his free, expansive approach on these make his work with the brass sound constricted, anxious and over-busy. *If You Were The Only Girl In The World* exemplifies Rollins' effective use of apparently absurd material, while in *Manhattan* his intentions toward the tune seem to be edging into satire.

WAY OUT WEST
I'm An Old Cowhand/Come, Gone/There Is No Greater Love/Way Out West
Sonny Rollins (ts), Ray Brown (b), Shelly Manne (d), March 1957.
Contemporary CA/802/98.600
AAD Running time: 43.23
Performance: ★ ★ ★ **Recording:** ★ ★ ★

Doing without a piano was not quite a new idea, nor was it just a gimmick when Rollins took time out from a tour with the Max Roach group to record this trio album. In any case, Brown provided all the harmonic foundation necessary. The Western theme extends to the choice of *I'm An Old Cowhand* and *Wagon Wheels* (the hooves supplied by Manne sound as if they belonged to a three-legged horse). The two ballads are a pensive *Solitude* and *There Is No Greater Love*, dissected and thoughtfully reassembled by Rollins, who is not afraid to lean toward the breathiness of Webster. Brown's well-recorded solo here is a delight. With only three instruments and a simple recording set-up the sonic qualities of this disc have worn at least as well as its content.

SONNY ROLLINS ON IMPULSE
On Green Dolphin Street/Everything Happens To Me/Hold 'Em Joe/Blue Room/Three Little Words
Sonny Rollins (ts), Ray Bryant (p), Walter Booker (b), Mickey Roker (d), July 1965.
MCA Impulse MCAD 5655 JVC 458
AAD Running time: 34.34
Performance: ★ ★ **Recording:** ★ ★ ★

On Green Dolphin Street would seem a natural vehicle for Rollins, though the way he used it here in 1965 differs strikingly from what he might have done with it before or since; he stretches and compresses the theme with slides and slurs, then blows long, shaped notes over a pulsing beat. *Everything Happens To Me* is reshaped with similar logic, if greater tenderness, *Hold 'Em Joe* is a by-then fairly typical Rollins calypso, while *The Blue Room* is simplified and hardened-up into angular phrases which display the rhythmic subtlety which ultimately prevents anything Rollins plays from becoming banal. After this, the almost Parker-like intro and fast bop tempo of *Three Little Words* comes almost as a surprise; buoyed up by the rhythm team, Rollins throws out a few hints of just how much technique he really has in hand. Sound quality is good, capturing the peculiarities of Rollins' tone as effectively as the fast-fingered piano of Ray Bryant or the full-blooded drums of Mickey Roker.

SUNNY DAYS, STARRY NIGHTS
Mava Mava/I'm Old Fashioned/Wynton/Tell Me You Love Me/I'll See You Again/Kilauea
Clifton Anderson (tb), Sonny Rollins (ts), Mark Soskin (keyboards), Russell Blake (el b), Tommy Campbell (d), January 1984.
Milestone FCD-604-9122
AAD Running time: 39.01
Performance: ★ ★ **Recording:** ★ ★

For this generally happy-sounding album, Rollins goes back to his Caribbean roots, with three out of the six titles hitting a sunny, good-time beat derived from West Indian island music. *Mava Mava* bursts upon the listener with a joyous feeling, the tune reminiscent of *St Thomas*, the sound dominated by the drums of Campbell, who seems to fill-in a bit too comprehensively. More swinging, almost Latin in feel, is another near calypso, *Tell Me You Love Me*, full of vibrant life and with a fine rocking beat effectively heightened by Campbell's solo breaks. Rollins uses an expressively dirty 'R&B' tone, diving down to a honk, then wheezing and whistling up into the very highest register. *Kilauea* is almost more of the same, but with the wild shouting theme given a second strand by Anderson, and a strong underpinning by Campbell.
Playing the waltz-time theme of the unexpected *I'll See You Again* are multiple dubbed saxes, on which Rollins duets with himself in counterpoint. Rollins is clearly in good, boisterous form on this disc, but though he seems determined to have a good time, the results are a bit overpowering, with loud, busy and closely-recorded drumming from Campbell combined with an electric bass that comes over as bloated rather than authoritative, producing a sound that is incoherent, messy and claustrophobic at times.

ARCHIE SHEPP
(b. Fort Lauderdale, Florida, 27 May 1937)

Linked with the most overtly political aspects of the 'free' music movement of the 1960s, Archie Shepp was also active as a poet and playwright. His earliest recordings were with Cecil Taylor in 1960, but two years later he had formed a quartet with trumpeter Bill Dixon, recording an album for Savoy. He co-founded the New York Contemporary Five in 1963, but by 1967 his music, like that of his primary influence Ornette Coleman, met with audience hostility since it rejected the established jazz forms in favour of a violent and direct political message; it is ironic that in more recent years Shepp has suffered critical attacks for returning in his work to the music of earlier decades.

In Paris in 1969-70, Shepp came into contact with the Art Ensemble Of Chicago, and recorded with Anthony Braxton, Sunny Murray, Roscoe Mitchell and others. Back in the US, he became a college professor and drifted away from the music scene until he returned, in the mid 1970s, with a style which while not denying the 'free' revolution, became dominated by elements of bebop; in Shepp's view a re-examination that was a legitimate part of his creative quest.

BALLADS FOR TRANE
Soul Eyes/You Don't Know What Love Is/ Wise One/Where Are You/Darn That Dream/Theme For Ernie.
Archie Shepp (ts, ss), Albert Dailey (p), Reginald Workman (b), Charles Persip (d), May 1977.
Denon 35C38-7264
DDD Running time: 38.26
Performance: ★ ★   Recording: ★ ★

ON GREEN DOLPHIN STREET
On Green Dolphin Street/Enough/The Scene Is Clean/In A Mellow Blues/I Thought About You
Archie Shepp (ts, ss) Walter Bishop, Jr (p), Sam Jones (b), Joe Chambers (d), November 1977.
Denon 38C38-7262
DDD Running time: 42.27
Performance: ★ ★   Recording: ★ ★

On this 1977 date, Shepp had the support of sympathetic musicians, and, it would seem from the results, freedom from distractions or time pressures; he seems to simply give each number as long as it takes. Outstanding are *Wise One* (written by Coltrane) where Shepp uses all registers of the tenor and deploys the full range of tonal qualities above the stern arco bass of Workman. *You Don't Know What Love Is* receives a firm and virile treatment; *Where Are You* is lighter, almost casual. On soprano, he introduces *Darn That Dream* with a flurry of arpeggios but makes this a lyrical if hard-edged treatment as he sticks (as is not the case on other numbers here) fairly close to the original line. Well recorded, this is not a disc for those who always seek variety, rather it is for those who want to hear Shepp playing consistently and with direct emotional appeal.

Though Shepp has recorded prolifically, the Denon issues are at time of writing the only ones available on silver disc.

Shepp strides purposefully into *Green Dolphin Street*, hammering home the theme and then entwining it in some characteristic twists of sour tonality. He switches to soprano for *Enough*, floating almost whimsically over a Latin beat, exploiting the squeaks of the instrument with his usual perfect control. The next two tracks, respectively a Tadd Dameron bop classic and a slow blues, feature Shepp's full, slightly rasping and furry tenor sound at its best. The final ballad is a powerful, evocative soprano performance with excellent support from Bishop, whose own solo quotes wittily from *Straight No Chaser* and demonstrates most effectively the art of swinging at a slow tempo.

Recording quality is fine, though the sound does reveal the separate treatment given to each instrument (the light reverb on Shepp's sax tends to divorce it from the rest of the group). But musically, Shepp's sheer authority gives this set a refreshing sense of purpose and direction.

JIMMY SMITH

(b. Norristown, Pennsylvania, 8 December 1925)

Jimmy Smith, best-known exponent of the Hammond organ, both inside and outside jazz.

Though he also learned to play bass, Jimmy Smith started out as pianist, modelling his style first on Bud Powell and then on Horace Silver. But in the early 1950s he made the switch to the instrument he virtually re-invented; the Hammond organ. When Smith emerged on disc in 1956, he had developed a command of the instrument that gave his playing variety, excitement and above all, soul. His early Blue Note records brought an almost immediate rush of imitators; yet Smith's style was a personal blend which combined speed and energy with a subtle control of the organ stops (registrations) and ultimately proved inimitable.

Eventually, despite the efforts of such able players as Brother Jack McDuff and Richard 'Groove' Holmes, the organ craze ran its course and the once novel and exciting Hammond sound became the lowest common denominator of R&B; but when the followers had all but disappeared, there was still room for the one original master.

BACK AT THE CHICKEN SHACK

Back At The Chicken Shack/When I Grow Too Old To Dream/Minor Chant/Messy Bessie/On The Sunny Side Of The Street. Stanley Turrentine (ts), Jimmy Smith (org), Kenny Burrell (g), Donald Bailey (d), April 1960.
Blue Note CDP 7 46402
AAD Running time: 43.51
Performance: ★ ★ Recording: ★ ★

Recorded when Smith had already established himself as a solo attraction and as an exciting sideman on Blue Note, this unhurried 'blowing' album exemplifies the label's approach of the time. Smith kicks off the classic groove of the title track, Turrentine is always inventive too, and there is an excellent solo from Burrell in *On The Sunny Side Of The Street*; Smith's subtle, softened tone in *Messy Bessie* is appealing and he is stirring in *Minor Chant*.

The organist displays constant drive and swing, while his ceaselessly inventive variations communicate a thoroughly happy spirit; but in the end there is a feeling of some lack of substance, which despite a reasonable running time makes this disc seem less than exceptional value.

THE CAT

Theme From 'Joy House'/The Cat/Basin Street Blues/Main Title From 'The Carpetbaggers'/Chicago Serenade/St Louis Blues/Delon's Blues/Blues In The Night. Ernie Royal, Bernie Glow, Jimmy Maxwell, Marky Markowitz, Snooky Young, Thad Jones (tp), Ray Alonge, Jim Buffington, Earl Chapin, Bill Correa (fr h), Billy Byers, Jimmy Cleveland, Urbie Green (tb), Tony Studd (b tb), Don Butterfield (tu), Jimmy Smith (org), Kenny Burrell (g), George Duvivier (b), Grady Tate (d), Lalo Schifrin (arr, cond) April 1964.
Verve 810 046
AAD Running time: 33.08
Performance: ★ ★ ★ **Recording:** ★ ★

Clearly thriving on the huge scale of the orchestra around him, Smith does not disappoint when the brass builds up the excitement for his entry (as on the outstanding *St Louis Blues*) or feeds him

stop-time breaks to fill (as on the title track). In *Chicago Serenade*, Burrell produces a guitar sound like that of Wes Montgomery's pop numbers, but is usually occupied adding a funky rhythm part; *The Carpetbaggers* film theme is a showpiece for moody, menacing urban brass, but despite the success of such efforts it is the quite simply-arranged mid-paced *Blues For Delon* that offers quintessential Smith. Sound quality is excellent.

OFF THE TOP

Off The Top/Endless Love/Mimosa/I'll Drink To That/Theme From M.A.S.H./Ain't Misbehavin'/Jimmy Smith Rap. Stanley Turrentine (ts), Jimmy Smith (org), George Benson (g), Ron Carter (b), Grady Tate (d), Errol Crusher Bennett (perc 2, 3), June 1982.
Elektra Musician 60175
AAD Running time: 39.49
Performance: ★ ★ **Recording:** ★ ★ ★

This was a jazz reunion of musicians then involved in music where little jazz content remains. It's a varied, gentle programme, with smooth work from Turrentine, and (particularly on *Theme From M.A.S.H.*) outstanding playing from Benson; the material ranges in age from the near-current *Endless Love* (by Lionel Richie) to the venerable *Ain't Misbehavin'* of Fats Waller, and in style from the MOR Latin touch of *Mimosa* to the funkiness of *I'll Drink To That*, but it all swings. A rather short set is rounded off by the words of Smith, who suggests that he might not get the chance to do this kind of album again; fortunately, he did, as witness the recent Blue Note issue (CDP7 46297) *Go For Whatcha Know.*

SONNY STITT

(b. Boston, Massachusetts, 2 February 1924; d. New York City, 23 July 1982)

Four years younger than Charlie Parker, Edward 'Sonny' Stitt's style was so similar that he long seemed condemned to live in the great altoist's shadow. Stitt claimed to have developed his style independently of Parker, and in 1949 he even switched to tenor for a while, presumably to escape the wearisome comparisons.

Stitt, who was brought up in Saginaw, Michigan, and later Detroit. He learned piano and clarinet before starting the saxophone; his father was a professor of music, while his mother taught piano and organ. Still in his teens, he went on the road with Tiny Bradshaw's band.

By 1945 he was in New York, and recorded with Gillespie the following year; he was soon appreciated as the first player capable of playing a style convincingly similar to Parker's. His Prestige recordings of 1949 (under J J Johnson's leadership) and 1951 (under his own name established him as a fine and consistently exciting player, sometimes using baritone sax as well as tenor and alto.

In 1950 he also recorded with Gene Ammons, later his partner in some spectacular two-tenor 'battles'. He then recorded a notable album with Art Blakey's Jazz Messengers (*In Walked Sonny*), and in the last years of his life continued to be a truly prolific recording artist as well as a dependably popular jazz festival star. Stitt died of cancer in 1982, but by then he had long outlived the early accusations that he was merely a technically-gifted copyist and his passionate, intelligent and melodic playing will be long remembered.

POW!

I Want To Be Happy/Love On The Rocks/ Blue Lights/Scramble/Up And Over/Pride And Passion/'Nuff Guff
Sonny Stitt (as), Benny Green (tb), Kirk Lightsey (p), Herman Wright (b), Roy Brooks (d), 1966.
Roulette RCD 59049
AAD Running time: 44.43
Performance: ★ ★   Recording: ★ ★ ★

sonny stitt.. **POW!**
with benny green, kirk lightsey, herman wright, roy brooks

In harmonious partnership, Stitt and Green provide a varied but generally hard-driving programme here. Stitt gets straight down to it on a very fast *I Want To Be Happy*, soaring over a rhythm section that 'cooks' in the best tradition. *Love On The Rocks* is slow and voluptuous, a relaxed rapport apparent as Green and Stitt harmonise the lazy, moody theme.

Blue Lights is a mid-tempo blues, with Lightsey essaying the loose Wynton Kelly style to introduce the horns' theme, Stitt sometimes extremely Bird-like; Green follows, unhurried and effective. Stitt soars again on the ultra-fast *Scramble* (which rapidly hints at *Ornithology*), demonstrating speed, passion and precision. On the bright

Up And Over Green's solo is again easy and relaxed, while Stitt is fluid, again using direct quotes from Parker, and the efficient rhythm section never flags. Wrapped up by another quite powerful 'ballad' performance in *Pride And Passion* and the final bounce blues *'Nuff Gruff*, this disc presents a generous sample of Stitt's straightforward, no-nonsense blowing with an unremitting and infectious swing, a well-rounded package that is meant simply to be enjoyed.

MOONLIGHT IN VERMONT

West 46th Street/Who Can I Turn To?/ Moonlight In Vermont/Flight Cap Blues/It Might As Well Be Spring/Constellation/ Blues for PCM
Sonny Stitt (as, ts), Barry Harris (p), Reggie Workman (b), Tony Williams (d); 4, Walter Davis replaces Harris, 1983.
Denon 38C38-7046
DDD Running time: 38.15
Performance: ★ ★   Recording: ★ ★

Kicking off with a punchy mid-tempo blues, this set conveys life and excitement from the first few bars. Stitt's pre-eminence as a hard-blowing 'tough' tenorist (or altoist for that matter), is proven yet again, and *Flight Cap Blues* is a strong blowing vehicle in the good old hard-bop manner.

The three ballads here show that there is another side to Stitt. *Moonlight* is a solid treatment in which Stitt soars lyrically, yet with a satisfying bite, but he applies a softer touch to *It Might As Well Be Spring*. Charlie Parker's all-pervading influence appears in *Constellation* and *Blues for PCM*, which, despite the digital-era dedication, is really *Parker's Mood*, and none the worse for that. It is hard to fault the recording, and although the fairly 'close' bass and piano sound are occasionally a little oppressive, this is really a matter of taste. More important, Stitt plays superbly throughout this disc and is well supported, too.

ART TATUM
(b. Toledo, Ohio 13 October 1910; d. Los Angeles, California, 5 November 1956)

Fats Waller's often-quoted introduction: 'Ladies and gentlemen, I play piano, but God is in the house tonight!' obscures the fact that Waller himself had been one of Tatum's greatest influences. But Tatum in turn influenced or inspired a whole generation of musicians, including Parker and other modernists.

Suffering from cateracts, which left him with only partial vision in one eye, Art Tatum attended the Cousino School For The Blind in Colombus, Ohio, where he studied piano and violin. He studied at the Toledo School of Music, but around 1926 formed his own small band, working Toledo clubs. In mid-1929 he started a residency (with a day-time spot on radio WSPD, but continued to play local clubs until 1932, when Joe Turner (the pianist) heard him and recommended him to singer Adelaide Hall. He made his first recordings (apart from the early *Tiger Rag* of 1932) for Decca in 1933.

Tatum continued working mainly as a soloist either in Hollywood or New York (though he recorded with a small group in 1941), until 1943 when he formed a trio with Tiny Grimes on guitar and 'Slam Stewart on bass. In the last few years of his life, Tatum recorded enough solos to fill the thirteen long-playing discs currently known as *The Tatum Solo Masterpieces*.

THE TATUM GROUP MASTERPIECES
(with Ben Webster, Red Callender, Bill Douglass)
Gone With The Wind/All The Things You Are/ Have You Met Miss Jones/My One And Only Love/ Night And Day/My Ideal/ Where Or When
Ben Webster (ts), Art Tatum (p), Red Callender (b), Bill Douglass (d), 1955.
Pablo J33J 20034
AAD Running time: 39.44
Performance: ★ ★   Recording: ★ ★ ★

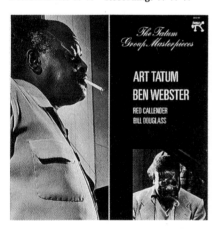

Piano solos make up the bulk of Tatum's recorded work, so the currently-available Conpact Discs are in a sense unrepresentative. This one features some particularly urbane playing from Ben Webster, as well as the discreet and often almost-forgotten rhythm section, which consists of Tatum's sometime regular bassist Red Callender and drummer Bill Douglass.

Gone With The Wind starts in rather restrained fashion, Tatum pushing and pulling subtly against the steady beat; after Webster has played the theme almost straight, Tatum returns for a chorus of more urgent-sounding arabesques, then Webster re-enters with the bridge to take the tune out. This is more or less the pattern for most of the numbers, Webster firmly unhurried, if not actually languorous, over what might

otherwise have seemed rather tumultuous accompaniments from Tatum. On the whole, this is one of the smoothest if hardly the most invigorating of the Tatum group recordings.

THE TATUM GROUP MASTERPIECES
(with Red Callender, Jo Jones)
Just One Of Those Things/More Than You Know/Some Other Spring/If/Blue Lou/Love For Sale/Isn't It Romantic/I'll Never Be The Same/I Guess I'll Have To Change My Plan/ Trio Blues
Art Tatum (p), Red Callender (b), Jo Jones (d), January 1956.
Pablo J33J 20035
AAD Running time: 42.46
Performance: ★ ★ ★   Recording: ★ ★ ★

In the 1940s, Tatum had used a piano/ guitar/bass trio format, creating excitement and variety with spectacular interplay between the instruments, but this 'conventional' trio is something quite different; from the beginning there is in Tatum's playing a freedom and 'life' not apparent in all the group recordings.

Just One Of Those Things, at a bright tempo, eventually becomes almost a duet in which the sparkling brush-work of Jones perfectly complements the flashing brilliance of Tatum. In *Love For Sale*, Jones again makes a solo contribution but is mostly in the background, generating an incredibly compulsive swing with graceful economy of effort. At a steady tempo, *Isn't It Romantic* illustrates Tatum's lush harmonic approach to a ballad, heightened with chromatic interludes and references to the blues.

I'll Never Be The Same seems at first a return to the earlier manner, only a discreet bowed bass note audible behind an introduction which has the fresh magic of pre-war Tatum; he brings out the melody exquisitely in *I Guess I'll Have To Change My Plan*. Finally, with Tatum's own sophisticated absorption of the Chicago blues and boogie pianists, *Trio Blues* rounds off a superbly-recorded (mono) disc which will reward much repeated listening.

CECIL TAYLOR
(b. New York City, 15 March 1933)

Overtaken later, in terms of recognition, by figures like Ornette Coleman, the pianist Cecil Taylor was in 1957 the true pioneer of the *avant garde*. In contrast to Coleman, his approach was backed by conservatory training and an astonishing instrumental facility.

Starting piano lessons at five, Cecil Taylor also had the opportunity to study percussion with his piano teacher's husband, who was an orchestral tympanist. After school, he went to the New York College of Music, and then spent three years at the New England Conservatory studying piano, composition and theory.

From his academic standpoint, Taylor was reluctant to adopt an improvisational approach, but by 1954 he was playing occasional jobs with name jazz musicians and at the same time developing a small following for his own music. He was soon joined by soprano saxophonist Steve Lacy, and formed a quartet including Lacy, bassist Buell Neidlinger and drummer Dennis Charles: with this group, Taylor produced his first album, *Jazz Advance*, in 1956.

Though some 1959-60 record dates produced indifferent results, by the early 1960s Taylor had teamed up with altoist Jimmy Lyons and free drummer Sunny Murray and the later 1960s saw the emergence of his most characteristic work.

CONQUISTADOR!
Conquistador/With (Exit)
Bill Dixon (tp), Jimmy Lyons (as), Cecil Taylor (p), Henry Grimes, Alan Silva (b), Andrew Cyrille (d), October 1966.
Blue Note CDP 7 46535
AAD Running time: 37.20
Performance: ★ ★   Recording: ★ ★ ★

WINGED SERPENT (SLIDING QUADRANTS)
Taht/Womb Waters Scent Of The Burning Armadillo Shell/Cun-Un-Un-Un-An/Winged Serpent
Cecil Taylor (p) and his Orchestra of Two Continents
Soul Note SN 1089
AAD Running time: 43.16
Performance: ★ ★   Recording: ★ ★ ★

It was Taylor's indisputable technical mastery that forced the critics to take him seriously in the 1950s, and listeners new to him today may have much the same experience; Taylor's music may seem impossible or disturbing at first but *Conquistador!*, on which Taylor's group includes Bill Dixon on trumpet as well as altoist Lyons, while second bassist Silva contributes violin-like high register arco playing, is as good a place to start as any.

The title piece opens with some typical precision flurries from Taylor, then the ensemble develops an almost buzzing effect, while Taylor produces waves and surges from behind. After a quieter central section, *Conquistador* ends on an almost quizzical note. *With*, almost tempoless, opens with remarkable collective playing, the group's dynamics controlled in a gripping way, and develops with inexorable power. Recording quality (by Van Gelder) is superb, with a relaxed, open clarity to the sound.

Opening with an ensemble of interwoven horn calls, which gradually resolve into a long-held, frenetic tremolo effect from piano and trumpet, *Taht* builds up to an almost incredible pace, a rushing tide created mainly by Taylor himself but fuelled by lithe and energetic drumming. *Womb Waters Scent Of The Burning Armadillo Shell* starts on a simple motif, but uses a greater variety of horn effects, with the resonant bass clarinet underpinning cacophanous treble sounds. *Cun-Un-Un-Un-An* begins with African percussion and chanting, which gives way to a horn ensemble without piano, a frog-like saxophone bass note acting as a drone.

In *Winged Serpent*, the ensemble is somehow charged up to another level by the entry of Taylor's unremittingly forceful piano. Intense music, which for many people will still prove uncomfortable, recorded to high sonic standards.

SARAH VAUGHAN
(b. Newark, New Jersey, 27 March 1924)

While Ella Fitzgerald commands universal respect as the ideal all-round singer, Sarah Vaughan inspires devotion as an incomparable stylist.

Musically precocious, Sarah Vaughan began piano studies at seven and was soon playing organ in her local church as well as singing in the choir. In October 1942, legend has it for a dare, she took part in a talent contest at the Apollo in Harlem with a rendition of *Body And Soul* which won her a week's engagement at the theatre. She was heard there by Billy Eckstine, the vocalist with Earl Hines, who was so impressed that he immediately recommended her to Hines. Still aged only nineteen, she joined the band and soon appeared at the Apollo again, as Hines' second vocalist and second pianist. In the ranks of the Hines orchestra she met Charlie Parker and Dizzy Gillespie, and with them joined Eckstine's short-lived breakaway band at the end of 1943.

After the break-up of the Eckstine band, she cut some appealing records with a small group led by Teddy Wilson (*September Song*), but most of her early recordings, such as those with Gillespie (*Loverman*) or with Tadd Dameron (*If You Could See Me Now*) showed the influence of the bebop pioneers as well as that of Eckstine. From the late 1940s she toured extensively with her own group.

In the 1950s she made some memorable small group recordings, but after her hit *Brokenhearted Melody* it was her series of duets with Billy Eckstine which continued to bring commercial success.

SARAH VAUGHAN
Lullaby Of Birdland/April In Paris/He's My Guy/Jim/You're Not The Kind/Embraceable You/I'm Glad There Is You/September Song/It's Crazy.
Clifford Brown (tp), Herbie Mann (fl), Paul Quinichette (ts), Jimmy Jones (p), Joe Benjamin (b), Roy Haynes (d), Ernie Wilkins (cond), 1955.
EmArcy 814 641
AAD Running time: 46.06
Performance: ★ ★ ★ **Recording:** ★ ★

Despite the sleeve credit to Ernie Wilkins, this recording really features Sarah Vaughan and her regular trio of the time, with the more or less *ad hoc* addition of the three hornmen. Routines were worked out in the studio, so arranged ensemble passages are few, but there are many memorable exchanges. Sarah scat-sings alternate 'fours' (on more than equal terms) with all three horns on *Lullaby Of Birdland*, then improvises the last eight bars of the 32-bar chorus before scooping up the tune again, to take it out in triumph. She also scats memorably in unison with Mann's flute to introduce *Jim*. Here, and on *He's My Guy*,

Quinichette provides the kind of wistful obbligato his model, Lester Young, might have offered to Billie Holiday had they recorded again together in the 1950s. All solo effectively here too; though in general Mann's solos tend to occasional harshness, Quinichette's to diffidence. Yet all provide excellent support at one moment or another, notably in *April In Paris*, where Vaughan provides a definitive interpretation; Mann adds evocative birdsong, Quinichette follows a subtle 'locked-hands' chord solo from Jimmy Jones with a gentle eight bars, Brown provides an eight bar solo and a sensitive obbligato. Sarah's vocal perfection is breathtaking here, but *Embraceable You* and *September Song* reach similar heights. Fortunately sound quality is good too. The disc certainly contains some of Sarah Vaughan's finest work.

SARAH VAUGHAN AND BILLY ECKSTINE SING THE IRVING BERLIN SONGBOOK
Alexander's Ragtime Band/Isn't This A Lovely Day/I've Got My Love To Keep Me Warm/All Of My Life/Cheek To Cheek/You're Just In Love/Remember/Easter Parade/The Girl That I Marry/Now It Can Be Told
Sarah Vaughan (voc except 4, 10), Billy Eckstine (voc), orchestra arr and cond Hal Mooney, featuring Harry Edison (tp), 1957
EmArcy 822 526
AAD Running time: 37.13
Performance: ★ ★ ★ **Recording:** ★ ★ ★

Though now retitled to become one of EmArcy's 'Great American Songbooks', this album was originally released as *Sarah Vaughan and Billy Eckstine Sing The Best Of Irving Berlin*; Sarah Vaughan had already recorded an album of Gershwin tunes and this joyful collaboration with Eckstine made a spectacular follow up.

It was Eckstine, with Earl Hines, who had

really started her career, and his singing style had been an early influence. Teaming up again in the 1950s, they seemed made for each other; here Sarah's supple voice weaves round Eckstine's warm, virile baritone like ivy round a solid oak. Their most breathtaking displays, technically, are on the opening *Alexander's Ragtime Band*, in which both the singers and Hal Mooney set out to completely outshine even the brightest and gutsiest of the many previous versions; and on *I've Got My Love To Keep Me Warm*, where their bop variations seem effortless, natural and apt. More straight-forwardly romantic duets are to be found in plenty, standouts being *Now It Can Be Told* and the lovely *Always*.

Recorded with the high gloss of Mercury's best studio practice, a classic of its kind.

CRAZY AND MIXED UP
I Didn't Know What Time It Was/That's All/Autumn Leaves/Love Dance/The Island/Seasons/In Love In Vain/You Are Too Beautiful
Sarah Vaughan (voc), Joe Pass (g), Roland Hanna (p), Andy Simpkins (b), Harold Jones (d), March 1982.
Pablo J33J 20043
AAD Running time: 33.43
Performance: ★ ★   Recording: ★ ★

An unusual Pablo release, in that the 'producer' credit goes not to Norman Granz, but to the singer herself; this time, the choice of musicians and tunes was Sarah's. It was, obviously enough, a straight-ahead jazz date, and the high spot, in improvisational terms, is Sarah's urgent, uninhibited 'scat' solo on *Autumn Leaves*, in which she shows who is really the boss of this difficult art.

The other songs all have words, and are a mainly unhackneyed selection; some will find Sarah's treatment of *I Didn't Know What Time It Was* affected, or will think the slow, drawn out *Love Dance* too self-indulgent (and the indulgence does almost reach the point of self-parody as she squeezes out the notes on *You Are Too Beautiful*), but few could deny the effective emotional use she makes of her technical recources in the heartfelt *That's All*, or the nicely put-over *In Love In Vain*.

Hanna's unfussy piano, the always-appropriate guitar of Pass and a fine rhythm team make excellent partners; recording quality is good as far as singer, bass and drums are concerned, though the guitar sound lacks top and Hanna's piano sound is rather thin and brittle.

THE RODGERS AND HART SONGBOOK
My Funny Valentine/Little Girl Blue/A Tree In The Park/It's Got To Be Love/A Ship Without A Sail/Bewitched/Thou Swell/It Never Entered My Mind/It's Easy To Remember/Why Can't I/My Romance/My Heart Stood Still.
1 Sarah Vaughan (voc), orchestra arr and cond Richard Hayman, February 1954; 2-6, 8, 12 Vaughan (voc), orchestra arr and cond Hal Mooney, October 1956; 7 Vaughan (voc), Rannell Bright (p), Richard Davis (b), Roy Haynes (d), March 1958; 9 Vaughan (voc), orchestra arr and cond Don Costa, March 1954; 10 Vaughan (voc), Ernie Royal, Bernie Glow (tp), J J Johnson, Kai Winding (tb), Julian 'Cannonball' Adderley, Sam Marowitz (as), Jerome Richardson (ts, bars), Jimmy Jones (p), Turk van Lake (g), Joe Benjamin (b), Roy Haynes (d), arr and cond Ernie Wilkins, October 1955; 11 Vaughan (voc), orchestra arr and cond Hal Mooney, April 1955.
EmArcy 824 864
AAD Running time: 37.42
Performance: ★ ★ ★   Recording: ★ ★ ★

As the track details reveal, this 'songbook' has been assembled for this issue from Mercury/EmArcy recordings Sarah Vaughan made between 1954 and 1958. Hal Mooney's orchestrations may be lush (on the superb and moving *Ship Without a Sail*) or brash (on the weaker *It's Got To Be Love*), but they provide perfect support on *A Tree In The Park*, a wonderful *It Never Entered My Mind*, and the beautiful *My Romance*.

THE DIVINE
Perdido/Sermonette/The Man I Love/The Good Life/When Lights Are Low/Moanin'/'Round Midnight/Midnight Sun/Baby Won't You Please Come Home/Solitude/I Can't Give You Anything But Love/Stormy Weather/A Taste Of Honey
1 Sarah Vaughan (voc), Count Basie orchestra; 2, 4, 6-9, 13, Vaughan (voc), arr and cond by Gerald Wilson; 3, 10, 11 Vaughan (voc) with orchestra arr and cond by Benny Carter; 5 Vaughan (voc), Barry Kessel (g), Joe Comfort (b); 12 Vaughan (voc), orchestra arr and cond by Jimmy Jones
Roulette VG 651 600017
AAD Running time: 46.07
Performance: ★ ★   Recording: ★ ★

Nine of these thirteen 1960s tracks were recorded with a group led by organist Gerald Wilson, who provides a generally undemanding but often effective setting.

The three Benny Carter arrangements offer a more challenging environment and are effective. On the opener *Perdido*, an out-and-out bash with the Basie band, her scat singing becomes alarmingly uninhibited, while *Stormy Weather* on the other hand leans to the soporific.

Clearly programmed with the most impressive numbers first, this set does have a hidden treasure in *When Lights Are Low*, recorded in 1962 with Barney Kessel and Joe Comfort, two musicians who somehow provide all the accompaniment needed. Sarah Vaughan disciples will not dispute the divinity of this collection (not the only disc to use this title), but it is a relatively patchy one.

DINAH WASHINGTON
(b. Tuscaloosa, Alabama, 29 August 1924; d. 14 December 1963)

Despite her affinity with Billie Holiday, Dinah Washington was less clearly categorisable as a jazz singer though her mannered and dramatic style proved so compatible with jazz backgrounds.

Raised in Chicago, Dinah (then still known as Ruth Jones) sang gospel and played piano, and at fifteen won a talent contest at the Regal Theatre, singing blues. This led to jobs at the Flame Show Bar and at the Garrick Bar, where she was seen in 1943 by Henry 'Red' Allen, with the result that she was hired by Lionel Hampton. She recorded four sides on a date with some Hampton sidemen, but nothing happened. She stayed with the band until 1946, when a second record date (organised, like the first, by Leonard Feather) produced *Blow Top Blues*. Three years later, she recorded the searing blues *Baby, Get Lost*, which reached No 1 in the R&B charts in 1949, and followed up in 1950 with *Long John*. In the next ten years, there were many more hits; and when she re-recorded them for Mercury's stereo catalogue they still sounded just as good.

Her death, at the age of thirty-nine, was a tragic accident caused by the combination of alcohol with a drug she was taking to lose weight. While 'Jazz On A Summer's Day' captures a stunning performance on film, current CDs do offer most of the best of Dinah Washington, though not always strictly in a jazz context.

Dinah Washington – always at home with jazz ensembles.

DINAH JAMS
Lover Come Back To Me/Alone Together/ Summertime/Come Rain Or Come Shine/ No More/I've Got You Under My Skin/ There Is No Greater Love/You Go To My Head.
1, 8 Dinah Washington (voc), Clifford Brown, Maynard Ferguson, Clark Terry (tp), Herb Geller (as), Harold Land (ts), Richie Powell, Junior Mance (p), Keeter Betts (b), George Morrow (b 1), Max Roach (d); 2 Land (ts), Powell (p), Morrow (b), Roach (d); 3 Ferguson (tp), Powell (p), Morrow (b), Roach (d); 4 Washington (voc), Powell (p), Morrow (b), Roach (d); 5 Washington (voc), Mance (p), Betts (b), Roach (d); 6 Washington (voc), Brown, Ferguson, Terry (tp), Mance (p), Morrow (b), Roach (d); 7 Washington (voc), Mance (p), Morrow (b), Roach (d), August 1954.
EmArcy 814 639
AAD Running time: 38.59
Performance: ★ ★ ★   Recording: ★ ★ ★

If this disc has the clean quality of a studio recording with the atmosphere of a live performance before an audience, this is because that is exactly what it is. On August 14, 1954, EmArcy gathered together eleven musicians, including Dinah Washington, for a well-organised but still exciting 'jam session'. Not all the musicians participated in all the numbers; while previous issues have failed to give more details, Kiyoshi Koyama's notes to this CD give the somewhat speculative personnel details above. The idea was not to feature a large group, but to encourage competitive solo blowing; in the fast *Lover Come Back To Me*, Dinah Washington is at her blistering, fervent best as she rides the crests provided by an eager ensemble. Her chorus is followed by a string of trumpet solos, an exchange of fours between the two bassists and then a chorus shared by the two pianists. Though sound quality is good by the standards of the time, it is not always easy to sort this out, especially without the benefit of stereo. Given the fairly 'woolly' bottom-end recording quality, the two bassists do tend to sound pretty similar.

The next three numbers make up a medley of short solo features, Land with a velvety, brooding *Alone Together*, Ferguson playing to the gallery with a rather harsh, bravura *Summertime*, and Washington with an enigmatic *No More*. *I've Got You Under My Skin* is a fine performance, switching from Latin for Dinah's vocal to straight 4/4 for trumpet solos. Perhaps the idea of a studio 'jam session' is an artificial one, but the results here , cleanly recorded with a pleasing immediacy and punch, are so enjoyable that there can be few quibbles. Watch out also for the rest of the session on *Dinah Jams 2*, which must soon emerge on CD.

DINAH WASHINGTON SINGS THE BESSIE SMITH SONGBOOK

After You've Gone/Send Me To The 'Lectric Chair/Jailhouse Blues/Trombone Butter/ You've Been A Good Ole Wagon/Careless Love/Back Water Blues/If I Could Be With You One Hour Tonight/Me And My Gin/ Fine Fat Daddy
1, 3, 7-10 Dinah Washington (voc), Fortunatus Ricard (tp), Julian Priester (tb), Eddie Chamblee (ts), Charles Davis (bars), Jack Wilson (p), Robert Lee Wilson (b), James Slaughter (d), January 1958; 2, 4, 6 Clark Terry, Ricard (tp), Quentin Jackson (tb), Chamblee (ts), McKinley Easton (bars), James Craig (p), Robart Edmonson (b) Slaughter (d), December 1957.
EmArcy 826 663
AAD Running time: 36.05
Performance: ★ ★   Recording: ★ ★ ★

Columbia's first LP reissue of the work of Bessie Smith, along with Edward Albee's play *The Death Of Bessie Smith*, revived public interest in the great blues singer to such an extent that Dinah Washington was one of at least four artists to release an album of her songs in 1958; of the others, easily the best qualified was the great R&B singer LaVern Baker.

Dinah Sings Bessie Smith, as it was originally called, was handicapped by what Whitney Balliet described at the time as 'inept, ricky-tick accompaniment - an apparent attempt either to copy or make fun of the original, sometimes classic support given Bessie Smith'. This has not improved with the passage of time, although there can no longer be any so pedantic as to be actually offended by a group of 1950s musicians half-heartedly distorting their own styles to suggest the 1920s. It no longer seems very important, because Dinah Washington remains herself (no singer could do otherwise); some of the songs suit her, some do not. She is comfortable and effective on a steady-paced *After You've Gone*, building to a fine climax; *Careless Love* is played in corny style but with some verve, and is an ideal vehicle for Dinah, as is *If I Could Be With You One Hour Tonight*; and she puts over *Back Water Blues* as if it were one of her own, Chamblee's sax blowing away most of the old-timey flavour.

Other numbers, particularly the last two tracks, really are weak, and it has to be admitted that this makes an already-short LP relatively poor value on Compact Disc. Those new to Dinah Washington might be better off with the *Compact Jazz* collection (Polygram), which arrived too late for review.

GROVER WASHINGTON, JR

(b. Buffalo, New York State, 12 December 1943)

With a fluid, instantly recognisable tenor and soprano sax sound, Grover Washington was one of the pioneers of a new wave of mellow, accessible crossover music in the 1970s.

Washington received his first saxophone from his father, who was himself a tenor player, at the age of ten. In his teens, he played with R&B bands before leaving home to tour with a group of friends called The Four Clefs. This unit played mainly around Colombus, Ohio, until it disbanded in 1963. After this, Washington worked in various groups, notably with organist Keith McAllister. He was drafted into the army in 1965, but his two year term at Fort Dix allowed him to make gigs in Philadelphia. He settled there on his release from the service, working with organist Charles Earland.

It was with another organist that got his big break in 1970, when he appeared on Johnny 'Hammond' Smith's album *Breakout*; this brought him critical acclaim and the chance to make *Inner City Blues*, his first album under his own name, on Creed Taylor's Kudo label. Washington, who picked his sidemen 'for total attitude before technique', now established his own kind of easy-on-the-ear fusion.

AT HIS BEST
It Feels So Good/Mister Magic/Do Dat/
Summer Song/A Secret Place/Ain't No
Sunshine/Masterpiece
Grover Washington, Jr (ts, ss) with various
personnel including Bob James (p, el p),
Richard Tee (org), Eric Gale (g), Gary King,
Phil Upchurch (b), Harvey Mason (d),
orchestra arr and cond Bob James, 1972-8.
Motown ZD72366
AAD Running time 59.35
Performance: ★ ★ Recording: ★ ★ ★

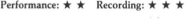

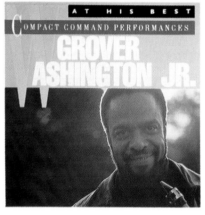

Motown have released a pair of two-albums-in-one Compact Discs, *Mister Magic/Feels So Good* (ZD72452) and *A Secret Place/All The King's Horses* (XD72494), but though these have respectively about eleven and seven minutes more playing time, *At His Best* does seem to offer just about the neatest cross-section of Washington's output on this label. Three out of the four title tracks are here anyway, with *It Feels So Good* representing Washington's archetypal funk groove, and *Mr Magic* providing fine solo work by guitarist Eric Gale. Probably the low spot of the disc is the corny girlie-chorus vocal 'sing that summer song . . .'; the singers are more effective on *Ain't No Sunshine*, the Bill Withers number, done here without the composer.

Finally, *Masterpiece*, actually taken from the Kudu double album *Soul Box*, offers almost the ultimate example of Creed Taylor's big production sound, opening with

faraway flutes and voices, then punchy, gutsy brass in the middle distance, scurrying strings like deer running before the storm, neatly-turned muted horns, all over a smoothly-flowing soft funk beat. There is a good bluesy solo from Gale and a pretty one from James, as well as typical Washington, the production, recording and overall sound quality of this track (particularly on CD) is superb; but in the end, appreciation of this track's almost tangible sonic delights gives way to a feeling of stasis, the realisation that in reality, nothing much has happened for the last few minutes. This the dilemma of all 'crossover' music; but then, with Washington, James, Creed Taylor and Rudy van Gelder involved, this disc does represent the very best of its kind.

WINELIGHT
Winelight/Let It Flow (For 'Dr J')/In The
Name Of Love/Take Me There/Just The
Two Of Us/Make Me A Memory (Sad
Samba)
Grover Washington, Jr (as, ts, ss), Eric Gale
(g), Ed Walsh (synth), Paul Griffin (clav 1, el
p 2, 4), Marcus Miller (b), Steve Gadd (d),
Ralph MacDonald (perc, synth d), Richard
Tee (el p except 2), Bill Eaton (synth 5),
Raymond Chew (clav 1), Robert Greenidge
(steel d), Bill Withers (voc 5), Hilda Harris,
Yvonne Lewis, Ullanda McCullough
(background voc), June/July 1980.
Electra 252 262
AAD Running time: 39.23
Performance: ★ ★ Recording: ★ ★ ★

Clear, sharp production helps *Winelight* grab attention immediately, as it opens with catchy, popping rhythms, a supple disco-based beat over which Washington floats a light and dreamy sax melody. But the standout track here has always been the Bill Withers vocal number, *Just The Two Of Us*, which also features immaculate work from the background singers, the exotic flavour of steel drums and a particularly warm tenor sound from Washington. Finishing the disc is the wistful *Make Me A Memory* on which Washington produces his purest, most enticing alto playing. Sound quality, it almost goes without saying, is exceptional in this flawlessly-crafted production.

WEATHER REPORT
(formed 1971)

Despite some turbulent changes of personnel in the rhythm section, Weather Report remained one of the most durable and influential fusion units through the 1970s. The group's coherence and continuity came from the combination of keyboard wizard Josef Zawinul and saxophone virtuoso Wayne Shorter, who had both played catalytic roles when they worked together in the melting pot of the Miles Davis group of the late 1960s.

In fact, they had met some years earlier in the Maynard Ferguson band, but both had impressive individual track records by the time they joined Davis; Zawinul, who had arrived from Austria in 1959, worked in the successful Cannonball Adderley band (for which he wrote numbers like *Mercy, Mercy, Mercy*), while Shorter made his mark in the early 1960s as an exceptional contributor to Art Blakey's Jazz Messengers.

With the brilliant Czech-born bassist Miroslav Vitous, Zawinul and Shorter formed Weather Report to develop the jazz/rock ideas they had started to work on while in the Davis group. For their first album, *Weather Report*, the line-up was completed by drummer Alphonse Mouzon and the percussionist Airto Moreira, but by the time they recorded *I Sing The Body Electric* Mouzon and Moreira had been replaced by Eric Gravatt and Dom Um Romao. Gravatt left, and was replaced by the subtler if generally quieter Ishmael Wilburn. The departure of Vitous 1973 was a serious setback, but a replacement was found in Alphonso Johnson; however, after this there were further changes of drummer.

Things stabilised again with the arrival of the virtuoso bassist Jaco Pastorius; he appeared on the 1977 album *Heavy Weather*, this including Zawinul's best-known composition, *Birdland*. In 1978, drummer Peter Erskine joined to complete the new rhythm section without (at first) the help of a percussionist.

In its latter days, Weather Report became more and more a vehicle for the keyboard explorations of Zawinul, and the early balance and intensity was lost. Although the band did survive into the 1980s, its importance in the end may be as a phenomenon of the previous decade; nonetheless, successful live appearances and recordings have continued in parallel with the main performers' other activities.

MYSTERIOUS TRAVELLER
Nubian Sundance/American Tango/ Cucumber Slumber/Mysterious Traveller/ Blackthorn Rose/Scarlet Woman/Jungle Book.
Wayne Shorter (ts, as), Josef Zawinul (key), Alphonso Johnson (b), Ishmael Wilburn (d), Dom Um Romao (perc), 1974.
Columbia CK 32494
AAD Running time: 48.26
Performance: ★ ★   Recording: ★

With considerable impact and coherence, *Mysterious Traveller* was the perhaps more throughtful follow-up to Weather Report's second album, *Sweetnighter*, which had been an enormous seller among the growing legions of jazz-rock enthusiasts.

Though subtler, *Mysterious Traveller* is full of energy from the start; *Nubian Sundance*, with the surging roar of a huge crowd and an ethereal chorus appearing around and behind the fast pulse of Wilburn and the flickering synthesiser sounds. *American Tango* is a pretty tune, laid down by Zawinul and taken up all too briefly by Shorter, while the straightforwardly funky *Cucumber Slumber* fades in with a lightly-bopping bass figure. Romao's congas help build up excitement, and while there are attractive solos from Johnson and Shorter, it is essentially the all-pervading and impressive collective power of the group that keeps up the pressure.

The title track is full of eerie space noises, 'mysterious' minor chords stabbing in the dark, the repeated theme (synth 'brass', bass and sax in unison), ending each time in a marvellous gong-like cymbal crash. *Blackthorn Rose*, with an uncluttered background provided by Zawinul, is a feature for Shorter, who displays a beautiful sound, with delicacy, tenderness and lizard-like agility. After a rumbling start, *Scarlet Woman* creates its effect with background winds sounds, wah-wah and sudden synth entries, while *Jungle Book*, opening with a long-held 'organ' chord, dispenses a carefully-blended *pot pourri* in which are mixed the whole range of familiar ingredients; more distant, fragmented and ethereal voices and 'spacy' tinkles.

Shorter and Zawinul's skilled production still effectively creates vast spaces, mood and atmosphere, but in absolute sound quality terms, the inherent electronic 'grunge' of the synthesiser (or perhaps the combined effect of all the complex electronics which tended to be used in an up-to-date 1970s studio) sometimes makes the sound a little hard; nonetheless, this is a disc that comes over quite impressively in CD form.

NIGHT PASSAGE
Night passage/Dream Clock/Port Of Entry/ Forlorn/Rockin' In Rhythm/Fast City/Three Views Of A Secret/Madagascar.
Wayne Shorter (ts, ss), Zawinul (key), Jaco Pastorius (b), Peter Erskine (d), Robert Thomas, Jr (perc), 1980.
Columbia CD 36793
AAD Running time: 48.08
Performance: ★ ★   Recording: ★ ★

A mobile, swinging kind of feeling pervades the title track, as Shorter sets out the clipped theme in the now-familiar perfect unison with Zawinul. Despite the bubbling embellishments of Pastorius and the prominent, precise and crisply urgent cymbals of Erskine, the effect is tight, lean and economical.

Weather Report's characteristic space sounds do appear, though, in *Dream Clock* (where Shorter's expansive, dreamy tenor and soprano hang in front of 'distant' harmonies. Bustling percussion and a wailing tenor characterise *Port Of Entry*, which features an urgent solo from the inimitable Pastorius; as a complete contrast comes *Forlorn*, Zawinul's subtly wavering and sliding high notes and Shorter's melancholy soprano sound hinting at the feeling of weightlessness, the strange sensation of leaving earth behind, as in a delirious floating nightmare.

Rockin' In Rhythm is the Ellington tune, taken fast, Zawinul playing the theme and sounding like a mad organist. The group leaves the changes behind with a frenetic middle section, then returns for a deliberately corny ending. *Madagascar*,

recorded live, has a loose, swinging beat and lopes along; there is fine playing from Shorter and fast but mellow, fat-sounding synth lines from Zawinul. Recording quality is fine, and though this fairly stylised album is, nonetheless, perhaps less consistent in terms of thematic links than some, *Night Passage* does very successfully represent the work of one of Weather Report's most effective line-ups.

SPORTIN' LIFE
Corner Pocket/Indiscretions/Hot Cargo/ Confians/Pearl On The Half Shell/What's Going On/Face On The Barroom Floor/Ice-Pick Willy.
Wayne Shorter (ts, ss), Zawinul (key), Victor Bailey (b), Omar Hakim (d), Mino Cinelu (perc), Bobby McFerrin, Carl Anderson, Dee Dee Bellson, Alfie Silas (voc).
Columbia CD 39908
AAD Running time: 39.14
Performance: ★ ★   Recording: ★ ★

Full of dynamic contrasts and dramatic flourishes, *Corner Pocket* (not, of course, the Freddie Green tune) uses speeded-up voices and horn/synthesiser ensemble effects to create intriguing textures; the quieter *Indiscretions* uses rich, plucked-string-like chords to set the mood, and support an attractive solo by Shorter before ending with a dreamily-repeating riff-like tune. *Hot Cargo* is an exotic concoction of talking-drum sounds, accordian-like lead, African-style horn ensemble and voices, while *Confians* is a number as far removed as you could imagine from the usual Weather Report idiom, opening with flute and folk-style guitar accompaniment in a gentle Latin vein, introducing an attractive vocal.

Pearl On The Half Shell is more or less back to normal, with a catchy, jagged theme fragmenting a supple dance rhythm. In *What's Going On*, casual voices are heard setting the street scene, though this seems to have turned out to be a welcoming, rather than a violent street. Shorter plays the evocative, melancholy theme of *Face On The Barroom Floor* against delicately-shaded banks of synthesiser cloud, before the street sounds (synth percussion fuelled by a rumbling undertow of a bass line) return in full vigour for the superbly-played *Ice Pick Willy*. Sound quality is good, though sometimes strangely lacking clarity, but with this album Zawinul (as he now prefers to be known) and Wayne Shorter show that they can still produce a programme of varied and exciting music.

EBERHARD WEBER

(b. Stuttgart, Germany, 1940)

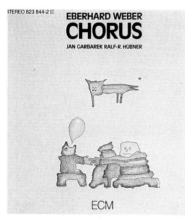

Outstanding among latter-day exponents of the bass is German-born Eberhard Weber.

A key figure in the music of the specialist German record company ECM, Eberhard Weber is a distinctive and melodic bass player and composer. He uses his own specially developed five-string electric bass, but his technique resembles that of an acoustic double-bass player.

As a child, Eberhard Weber learned the 'cello, only switching to bass at seventeen. He did not immediately become a professional musician, but worked for a time as a photographer and then as a film director; but in 1974 his distinctive bass sound was captured on his first album, *The Colours Of Chloe*. In 1975 he formed a new group, Colours, with Charlie Mariano on saxophones and keyboard player Rainer Bruninghaus.

In more recent years, Weber has continued to lead his own groups and has been a member of the German United Jazz Plus Rock Ensemble. He has also appeared on ECM albums under the studio leadership of Gary Burton, Pat Metheny, Ralph Towner and others, has worked with Keith Jarrett, and, outside the ECM 'family', has played with Joe Pass, Mal Waldron, Lucky Thompson and Jean Luc Ponty. Weber's own music continues to create the contemplative, space-filled moods now so clearly identified with ECM.

CHORUS
Part I/Part II/Part III, Part IV/Part V/Part VI/Part VII
Jan Garbarek (ts, ss), Eberhard Weber (el b, synth), Ralf-R Hubner (d), 1985
ECM 823 844
DDD Running time: 40.33
Performance: ★ ★   Recording: ★ ★ ★

STEREO 823 844-2 ⑤
EBERHARD WEBER
CHORUS
JAN GARBAREK RALF-R. HÜBNER

ECM

A spare, spacious album, *Chorus* starts with synth chords hanging like a cloud between the speakers; then Weber introduces a full-bodied, springy bass sound, out of tempo at first until Hubner ventures (as if timidly) a

simple drum beat. As Garbarek enters lyrically, Weber adds synth lines over and around his lead. The duet continues until, in the last section of *Part I*, the mood shifts with the introduction of an unhurried, almost plonking two-note pattern on fat-toned synth and bass; over this Garbarek re-enters climatically with a trilling, repeated upward-reaching high-register cry, echoed by trills from Weber's synthesiser.

Part II opens with a sort of puffing sound from Hubner's drums, Garbarek plays a mournful theme, this time in unison with Weber's synth. *Part III* has a hypnotically liturgical theme, which is repeated by tenor sax and synth while on another track, Garbarek spirals upward with a keening sound, here with an almost Barbieri-like tearing edge to it; *Part IV* returns to the two-note bass pattern, and Garbarek, always a master of such changes, softens his tone on tenor.

The next two sections are tempoless, eerie, with sounds again hanging in space in the manner that only ECM seem able to achieve. In *Part VII*, Weber repeats an almost rippling keyboard figure, then lunges up from below with his bass, Garbarek joining in a stately theme, then ending, as you might guess, in a sort of suspension. Recording and CD manufacturing quality are both up to the usual, exceptional standard of the label.

BEN WEBSTER

(b. Kansas City, Missouri, 27 March 1909; d. Amsterdam, Holland, 20 September 1973)

Identifiable by its sumptuous, breathy vibrato, Ben Webster's tenor on ballads seems to represent the ultimately romantic approach. Yet on faster tempos (and in earlier years) Webster's muscular tone and attack, based on Coleman Hawkins' but with a virile strength of its own, had earned him the nickname 'The Brute'.

Webster studied piano as a child and later played the accompaniment in a silent movie house. He got some saxophone tuition from Budd Johnson, then joined the travelling band of W. H. Young (Lester's father). He joined Benny Moten in 1931, went to Andy Kirk in 1933 and Fletcher Henderson in 1934, was then with Benny Carter, Willie Bryant, very briefly with Duke Ellington, and for nearly a year with Cab Calloway, returning to Henderson in 1937.

He worked with Stuff Smith and Roy Eldridge in 1938, and spent most of 1939 in Teddy Wilson's short-lived big band. He left in January 1940 to become one of the Ellington orchestra's unequalled galaxy of solo stars, his most rousing feature number being *Cottontail*. Webster left Ellington in August 1943, working again in the New York clubs with small groups that now contained 'modern' players like Al Haig, Argonne Thornton and Idrees Sulieman.

After another spell with Ellington, from November 1948 to September 1949, Webster returned to Kansas City and worked with Jay McShann, then toured with 'Jazz At The Philharmonic'. He settled in California, doing studio work and freelancing, but during the 1950s he recorded with strings, and collaborated memorably with Art Tatum and with Roy Eldridge, Budd Johnson and Coleman Hawkins. In 1962 he returned to New York but in 1964 left the USA for good, settling in Europe with Amsterdam as his base. In the last years of his life he toured Europe, playing with local musicians or other American ex-patriates when available. Though the CD selection is rather limited, it does offer a sampling of Webster as the supreme ballad artist.

BEN WEBSTER MEETS OSCAR PETERSON

The Touch Of Your Lips/When Your Lover Has Gone/Bye Bye Blackbird/How Deep Is The Ocean/In The Wee Small Hours Of The Morning/Sunday/This Can't Be Love.
Ben Webster (ts), Oscar Peterson (p), Ray Brown (b), Ed Thigpen (d), November 1959.
Verve 829 167
AAD Running time: 36.41
Performance: ★ ★ ★   Recording: ★ ★ ★

By the time of this recording, Webster had already recorded several series of ballad performances for Verve, some with strings, and he had also played on some of the label's recordings of the pianist Art Tatum.

Here, with supple, unobtrusive and always swinging support from Oscar Peterson's trio, he demonstrates the final refinement of his style; his phrasing is economical, yet the fewer notes he plays, the more lush the effect. *The Touch Of Your Lips* and *How Deep Is The Ocean* are taken at a moderate tempo, only *In The Wee Small Hours Of The Morning* coming down to the slowest ballad tempo. *This Can't Be Love* is taken quite steadily, with (inevitably) a careful measure of blues feeling injected by Peterson; but on the uptempo *Sunday*, a favourite tune of Webster's, the tenorist is relaxed, urbane and swinging, shifting subtly to a throaty tone in mid-flight.

BEN WEBSTER MEETS DON BYAS

Blues For Dottie Mae/Lullaby To Dottie Mae/Sunday/Perdido/When Ash Meets Henry/Caravan.
1-4, 6 Ben Webster, Don Byas (ts), Tete Montoliu (p), Peter Trunk (b), Albert Heath (d), 5 Webster (ts), Trunk (b), February 1968.
MPS 827 920
AAD Running time: 37.25
Performance: ★   Recording: ★ ★ ★

Expatriates both, Webster and Byas played together for the first time in many years at a Berlin jazz festival in 1965. Byas had come to Europe in the late 1940s with Don Redman and decided to stay, living first in France, then in Holland, where he married and settled down. By the time of this 1968 session, the big sound Byas had always been famous for had taken on something of a rasp, but this disc seldom becomes a tenor 'duel'; instead, Webster provides the foil to Byas by using his softer, buttery sound, only occasionally letting fly with his harder-edged cries, as on the two-tenor chase at the end of that favourite Webster vehicle *Sunday*; Webster also shines on what was once one of his features with Ellington, *Caravan*, where Byas, with an unexpectedly delicate touch, provides the exotic flavouring.

It has to be said that Webster's playing offers infinitely more subtlety, shading and variety than does that of the Byas at this late date, although in his last years, understandably enough, he did develop the art of playing no more notes than he had to. Webster's ballad solo *When Ash Meets Henry* (based on *My Romance* and accompanied only by the highly competent Trunk) proves his absolute mastery in this sphere. Characteristically, you can still hear the vibrato-producing puffs of air coming through his horn for several seconds after the last note has died away. With drummer Al 'Tootie' Heath (younger brother of bassist Percy and saxophonist Jimmy), top German bassist Trunk and experienced Catalan-born pianist Tete Montoliu, the rhythm team on this date was one of the best in Europe.

FOR THE GUV'NOR

I Got It Bad And That Ain't Good/Drop Me Off In Harlem/One For The Guv'nor/Prelude To A Kiss/In A Sentimental Mood/Rockin' In Rhythm/John Brown's Body/Worksong/The Preacher/Straight No Chaser 1-6, Ben Webster (ts), with Cees Slinger (p), Jacques Schols (b), John Engels (d), May 1969 (Holland); 7-10 Kenny Drew, Franz Wieringa (p), Neils Henning Orsted Pederson (b), Donald McKyre (d), October 1969.
Affinity CD CHARLY 15
AAD Running time: 69.12
Performance: ★ ★   Recording: ★ ★

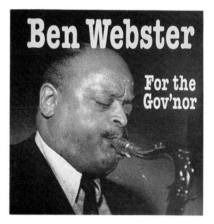

The Guv'nor is of course Ellington, composer or part-composer of five of the first six tunes here. He wrote *I Got It Bad* with Webster, who here gives hints and asides rather than a statement of the familiar theme. Balance-wise, the bass sounds a little too thunky and the piano a little tinkly alongside a soft-toned Webster here, but things start to bustle with *Drop Me Off*. The uptempo title track, on *Rhythm* changes, reveals the other side of Webster, his superbly controlled shouting tenor sound. *Prelude to a Kiss*, has vintage 'romantic' Webster, his long-perfected concision diluted slightly by a wandering piano solo; Slinger is better on *Sentimental Mood*. Finally, *Rockin'* really does rock, with obvious rapport and enjoyment from the quartet.

For the October session, Webster was joined by a couple of fellow expatriates, and immediately settled into a comfortable groove. Recording quality is excellent, though the second, softly-heard pianist makes for an odd balance. Predictably, perhaps, the two trade call-and-response phrases on *Worksong*, which bounces along happily enough.

In the end, there isn't quite as much substance here as you might think from the generous playing time. The sidemen offer able support but only Drew and Pedersen maintain much solo excitement. Webster plays no more than he needs too, but with this late, pared-down edition of his style he really could make every note count. Some of his playing here is truly exquisite, and this disc improves with listening.

LESTER YOUNG
(b. Woodville, Mississippi, 27 August 1909; d. New York City, 15 March 1959)

Just when Coleman Hawkins seemed to have done everything on the tenor saxophone, Lester Young arrived with a completely fresh approach to the instrument. His lighter tone, endless rhythmic subtlety and different view of harmony made him the first modern saxophonist, or, as Dexter Gordon said, 'the first one really to tell a story on the horn.'

Brought up playing drums in the touring family band led by his father, Young also learned trumpet and violin as well as sax. He left in his teens and in 1928 joined Art Bronson's Bostonians, but by late 1930 was gigging around Minneapolis with various local bands. In 1932 he joined the Original Blue Devils, but in 1933, along with other members of the band, he left to join Bennie Moten's band in Kansas City, and briefly worked with King Oliver. While playing in Little Rock, Arkanas, with the short-lived ex-Moten breakaway band led by Count Basie in 1934, he got an offer from Fletcher Henderson, who wanted him to replace Coleman Hawkins. But Young's sound did not go down well with Henderson's men, and he left after only three months, working with Andy Kirk and Boyd Atkins before rejoining Basie in 1936.

Young's first record date was in October 1936, a small group session with the Basie rhythm section under the name 'Jones-Smith Incorporated'. *Shoe Shine Boy, Boogie Woogie* and above all *Lady Be Good* reveal Young's mature style, his solos self contained and perfectly realised. Though Billie Holiday, who joined Basie in 1937, was contractually unable to record with the band and left with some acrimony after less than a year, her musical partnership with Young blossomed magically in the small-group sessions organised by Teddy Wilson, which continued until 1940. Meanwhile, with Basie's Kansas City Seven in 1939, Young produced *Lester Leaps In*, an improvisation on *I Got Rhythm* changes which provided material for innumerable Young copyists in later years.

Leaving Basie in December 1940, he briefly formed his own group in New York, then worked on the West Coast with his drummer brother Lee's band, and in July 1942 recorded a trio date with Nat 'King' Cole. After a spell with Al Sears, he rejoined Basie in December 1943, but the most notable recordings from this period are the 'unofficial' small-group recordings on Signature, Keynote and Commodore. In mid 1944, Young featured in Gjon Mili's film *Jamming' the Blues*, but by October that year he was in the army. Court martialed for possession of marijuana, he remained in detention barracks until summer 1945.

Much has been written about the traumatic effect of Young's maltreatment in the army and, misleadingly (as Dave Gelly points out), about its damaging effect on his music. In fact, Young made many superb recordings after the war, notably with Nat 'King' Cole in 1946, with his own groups led by trumpeter Jesse Drakes, with Oscar Peterson in 1952, and even with Teddy Wilson in 1956. On some occasions, though, he did sound casual, self-pitying and sloppy. Signing for Norman Granz made him financially secure, but he found the JATP concert format distasteful and so performed poorly; some recording dates were failures because of unsympathetic personnel. He was surrounded by imitators of his own style, and found this difficult to cope with.

After a nervous breakdown in 1955, his health deteriorated and he appeared to have little will to live. The end came in 1959 when he fell ill with internal bleeding and had to fly home, halfway through a two-month Paris season. He died within 24 hours of reaching New York. Today, Young's work is at last fairly well represented in LP form, but he is still unjustly ignored by the programmers of the silver disc.

THE SAVOY RECORDINGS
Circus In Rhythm/Poor Little Plaything/
Tush/These Foolish Things/Exercise In
Swing/Salute To Fats/Basie English/Blue
Lester/I Don't Stand A Ghost Of A Chance/
Indiana/Jump Lester Jump/Crazy Over J-Z/
Ding Dong/Blues 'n' Bells/June Bug
1–3 Joe Newman, Ed Lewis, Al Killian,
Harry Edison (tp), Eli Robinson, Dickie
Wells, Ted Donelly, Lou Taylor (tb), Earl
Warren (as, voc), Jimmy Powell (as), Lester
Young, Buddy Tate (ts), Rudy Rutherford
(bars), Clyde Hart (p), Freddie Green (g),
Rodney Richardson (b), Jo Jones (d), April
1944; 4–7 Billy Butterfield (tp), Hank
D'Amico (cl), Young (ts), Johnny Guarnieri
(p), Dexter Hall (g), Billy Taylor (b), Cozy
Cole (d), April 1944; 8–11 Young (ts), Count
Basie (p), Green (g), Richardson (b), Shadow
Wilson (d), May 1944; 12–15 Jesse Drakes
(tp), Jerry Elliot (tb), Young (ts), Junior
Mance (p), Leroy Jackson (b), Roy Haynes
(d), June 1949.
Savoy ZD70819
AAD Running time: 44.58
Performance: ★ ★ ★ Recording: ★ ★

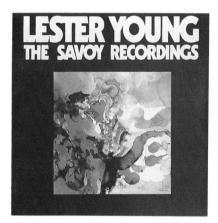

THE JAZZ GIANTS
I Guess I'll Have To Change My Plan/I
Didn't Know What Time It Was/Gigantic
Blues/This Year's Kisses/You Can Depend
On Me
Roy Eldridge (tp), Vic Dickenson (tb), Lester
Young (ts), Teddy Wilson (p), Freddie Green
(g), Gene Ramey (b), Jo Jones (d), January
1956.
Verve 875 672-2
AAD Running time: 42.33
Performance: ★ ★ ★ Recording: ★ ★ ★

Each of Lester Young's four record dates
with Savoy presented him in a different
setting. On the first, April 18 1944, he
appeared as a member of what was really
Basie's orchestra under the leadership of
Earle Warren. Eight bars of Young is barely
compensation for Warren's lugubrious vocal
on the torchy *Poor Little Plaything*, but he is
heard to good effect in his breaks on the
uptempo *Tush* (a variant of Basie's *Jive at
Five*). In the next session, which took place
on the same day with a pick-up group led by
Johnny Guarnieri, Young starts *These
Foolish Things* in magnificent form, but the
other soloists, bathetically, offer mere
competence, and it is the same story on the
next three numbers.

After Guarnieri's imitation in *Basie
English*, the Count and his rhythm section
provide the real thing on the recordings
made the following month. *Blue Lester*
makes expressive use of a favourite Basie
minor-key vamp, while a bright-tempoed
Indiana and *Jump* (a fast blues) are excellent.
So slow as to be sluggish, *Ghost Of A
Chance* is less successful.

Young's last Savoy recordings were made
five years later with the group of energetic
young be-boppers he called his 'kiddies', and
the results are quite remarkable. Young's
style had subtly changed, but he makes it
seem that the new rhythmic freedoms of be-
bop were something he had had in mind all

along. 'The kiddies' had their limitations, but
they provided him with a more comfortable
setting than he found in most of his post war
recordings.

Compared with the vinyl versions, the
recordings seem to have gained intimacy,
detail and excitement at the expense of a
slight hardness. This disc comes without the
numerous alternate takes which filled out
The Complete Savoy Recordings double
album, but in reality this just makes an
absolutely essential set of recordings all the
more listenable.

The members of this septet had their roots
firmly in the swing era, and in contrast to so
many all-star groups, things really came
together well in studio. Eldridge is superb on
all the tunes, while Dickenson offers his
usual blend of swing, sentiment and humour
(the liner note is incorrect in stating that he
had not previously recorded with Young;
they appeared together on the Philo/Aladdin
sessions of 1945-6).

Young is more outgoing here than on some
1950s sessions, but his tone still sounds a
little bloated on the opening ballad, and
rather quavering on *This Year's Kisses*; on
the fast *Gigantic Blues* (where the band
really roars) Young is effective, but lacks the
flying exuberance he showed on similar
numbers in the 1940s. The other two ballads
are good, and is a fair memento of the later
Young, but what makes this superbly-
recorded (mono) disc a memorable one is the
array of excellent performances from
Eldridge, Wilson and the others.

At the time of writing, the only other
Compact Disc listed under Young's name is
Prez and Teddy, recorded in January 1956
by Young, Wilson, Ramey and Jones.
Whatever the merits of these late
performances, it is a shame that Compact
Disc listeners coming to Young for the first
time have no chance of hearing the vigorous
earlier recordings when he was indeed the
'President' of the tenor saxophone.

INDEX